ACT Purple Reading

Version 2.0

Printed in the United States of America.

C2
education

C2
education

ACT Purple Reading
Table of Contents

rP1: INTRODUCTION TO ACT READING

TOPIC OVERVIEW

The ACT Reading Test will assess your reading comprehension skills. You will be tested on your vocabulary and critical thinking, but as with all standardized tests, familiarizing yourself with the question types and format of the test can be just as helpful as studying the material itself. This lesson will describe the structure and format of the test, the reading skills you will be asked to perform, and specific strategies to help you read the passages in a way that will maximize your score.

TEST STRUCTURE AND FORMAT

The test consists of four passages with ten questions each, for a total of 40 questions. The topics of the passages will always include prose fiction, humanities, social science, and natural science. A typical passage is between 700 and 800 words in length. On each test, one passage will be a paired passage made up of two shorter, related passages. You will have 35 minutes to read the passages and answer the questions.

The questions on the ACT Reading Test are multiple-choice. The letters of the answer choices will alternate between A, B, C, and D for odd questions and F, G, H, and J for even questions. The questions will require you to use your abilities to find facts, draw conclusions, find main ideas, and use context clues. All of these skills will be discussed in later sections. In this book, we'll use A, B, C, and for all questions.

READING PASSAGES ON THE ACT

The ACT Reading Test differs from other standardized reading tests in the following ways:

- Speed is key. The ACT asks you to answer a large number of questions in a short amount of time. Ideally, you should spend 90 seconds reading each passage and 30 seconds answering each question.
- The majority of the questions (about 60%) do not include references to line or paragraph numbers.
- The questions are based entirely on evidence found within the passage.
- Correct answers to the questions often involve a single fact from the passage.
- Writing on the test is permitted and will improve your ability to answer questions correctly.

Because of this, your best strategy is to actively read the entire passage once before answering the questions. Active reading involves hunting for and marking important information and creating a map of the passage that will help you find and recall the facts that you need. Active reading allows you to find a large amount of useful information in the passage in a short amount of time.

ACT ACTIVE READING STRATEGIES

Three strategies will help you to actively read the passages on the ACT:

1. breaking up the passages into portions
2. underlining key facts
3. summarizing each portion

Breaking up the passage into portions involves dividing a long, difficult passage into easily manageable pieces. Think of the passage in thirds or fourths to give your brain the break it needs to digest so much new information.

Underlining key facts involves considering the information that you read and marking any items that stand out. Make note of recurring phrases and topics that seem important. This will help you to recall needed information when you answer the questions.

Summarizing involves pausing briefly after reading a portion of the passage to consider the meaning and purpose of what you have just read. Pause briefly at the end of each portion of the passage or at the end of a paragraph to jot a short summary (three to five words) in the margin of your test. This may seem like it takes too much time, but understanding the passage as well as possible during your first read-through will save you lots of time later.

If you follow these three strategies, you will build a map of the passage that will allow you to correctly answer most of the questions without looking back at the passage. You will also be able to quickly find the information that you need for the questions that require you to look back in the passage.

As you read, avoid falling into the following traps:

- ☹ Quickly skimming through the passage without actively reading and taking note of specific points
- ☹ Reading the questions first and hunting through the passage for the answers without *also* reading through the entire passage.
- ☹ Reading and rereading the passage because you missed something important the first time

Read this passage carefully and then answer the questions that follow.

Prose Fiction: The following passage was adapted from *The Courage of Marge O'Doone* by James Oliver Curwood.

David held in his hands a photograph—the picture of a girl. He bent closer into the lampglow, and stared. The girl was standing on a flat slab of rock close to the edge of a pool. Behind her was a carpet of white sand, and beyond that a rock-cluttered gorge and the side of a mountain. She was barefooted. Her feet were white against the dark rock. Her arms were bare to the elbows, and shone with that same whiteness. He took these things in one by one, as if it were impossible for the picture to impress itself upon him all at once. She stood leaning a little forward on the rock slab, her dress only a little below her knees, and as she leaned thus, her eyes flashing and her lips parted, the wind had flung a wonderful disarray of curls over her shoulder. Against the savage background of mountain and gorge she stood out clear-cut as a cameo, slender as a reed, wild, beautiful. She was more than a picture. She was life. She was there—with David in his room—as surely as the woman had been with him in the coach.

For a time he stared blankly at the log of his room. Then he leaned over again and held the photograph a second time. The first strange spell of the picture was broken, and he looked at it more coolly, more critically, a little disgusted with himself for having allowed his imagination to play a trick on him. He turned it over in his hands, and on the back of the cardboard mount he saw there had been writing. He examined it closely and made out faintly the words, "Firepan Creek, Stikine River, August...." and the date was gone. There was no name, no word that might give him a clue as to the identity of the mysterious woman in the photograph.

Once more he tried to find some solution to the mystery in the picture of the girl herself, and as he looked, question after question pounded through his head. What had startled her? Who had frightened her? What had brought that hunted look—that half-defiance—into her poise and eyes? He made no effort to answer, but accepted the visual facts as they came to him. She was young, the girl in the picture; almost a child as he regarded childhood. Perhaps seventeen, or a month or two older; he was curiously precise in adding that month or two. He saw, now, that she had been wading in the pool, for she had dropped a stocking on the white sand, and near it lay an object that was a shoe or a moccasin. It was while she had been wading—alone—that the interruption had come; she had turned; she had sprung to the flat rock, her hands a little clenched, her eyes flashing; it was in this moment, as she stood ready to fight—or fly—that the camera had caught her.

Now, as he scanned this picture, as it lived before his eyes, a faint smile played over his lips, a smile in which there was a little humour and much irony. Tragedy! A woman in distress! Surely there was no tragedy or mystery in her poise on that rock. She had been bathing, alone, hidden away as she thought; someone had crept up, had disturbed her, and the camera had clicked at the psychological moment of her bird-like poise when she was not yet decided whether to turn in flight or remain and punish the intruder with her anger. It was quite clear to him. Any girl caught in the same way might have betrayed the same emotions.

His fingers tightened upon the photograph, ready to tear it into bits. The cardboard ripped an inch—and he stopped suddenly his impulse to destroy. The girl was looking at him again from out of the picture—looking at him with clear, wide eyes, surprised at his weakness, startled by the fierceness of his assault upon her, wondering, amazed, questioning him! His fingers relaxed. He smoothed down the torn edge of the cardboard, as if it had been a wound in his own flesh. After all, this inanimate thing was very much like himself. It was lost, a thing out of place, and out of home; a wanderer from now on depending largely, like himself, on the charity of fate. Almost gently he returned it to its newspaper wrapping. Deep within him there was a sentiment that made him cherish little things that had belonged to the past—a baby's shoe, a faded ribbon, a withered flower; and memories—memories that he might better have let droop and die.

1. All of the following things are true about the mysterious girl in the picture EXCEPT:

(A) She is barefooted.
(B) She is slender.
(C) Her hair is curled.
(D) The hem of her dress falls above her knees.

2. When the narrator says, "She was more than a picture. She was life," (lines 18-19) he is implying that:

(A) The girl has significance to David beyond the superficial picture.
(B) David had shared a coach with the girl in the past.
(C) The picture is remarkably vivid.
(D) Everything important to David centers around this girl.

3. What belongings of the mysterious girl in the picture does David see on the sand?

I. a dress
II. a stocking
III. a shoe or moccasin

(A) II only
(B) III only
(C) II and III only
(D) I, II, and III

4. In line 79, *inanimate* most nearly means:

(A) Cherished.
(B) Lifeless.
(C) Fragile.
(D) Transient.

5. As it is portrayed in the passage, David's attitude could best be described as:

(A) Fawning.
(B) Apathetic.
(C) Wistful.
(D) Juvenile.

6. What is the main idea of the third paragraph?

(A) David tries to determine what had happened when the picture was taken.
(B) David worries that the girl had been threatened when the picture was taken.
(C) David's second impression of the picture is not as positive as his first.
(D) The girl in the picture was feisty and youthful.

7. It can be reasonably inferred that David views the mysterious girl in the picture with a combination of:

(A) Fascination and disgust.
(B) Disinterest and exasperation.
(C) Worriment and sentimentality.
(D) Infatuation and curiosity.

8. Which of the following statements about the picture of the mysterious girl would David most likely agree with?

(A) It would be simple to determine the identity of the girl in the picture.
(B) There was a tragedy that caused the frightened look on the mysterious girl's face.
(C) While it is nominally worthless and of no use to anyone, it is nevertheless worth preserving.
(D) David should have gone with his first instincts about the picture rather than looking at it more critically.

9. In the last paragraph, David ultimately views the picture as:

(A) Wayward and dependent on the kindness of fate, much like himself.
(B) As worthless as a faded ribbon or discarded baby shoe.
(C) An interesting memento to ponder.
(D) Nothing more than a picture hidden in a newspaper.

10. It can be reasonably inferred from David's description of the mysterious girl as "almost a child as he regarded childhood" (lines 44-45) that:

(A) He perceives the girl as juvenile-looking.
(B) David is significantly older than seventeen.
(C) The frightened look on the girl's face made her seem somewhat childish.
(D) David was not good with children.

Read this passage carefully and then answer the questions that follow.

Humanities: This passage has been adapted from Franz von Reber's *History of Ancient Art*, originally published in 1882.

It is a curious chance that the most ancient monuments of human civilization should stand upon a land which is one of the youngest geological formations of our earth. The scene of that artistic activity made known to us by the oldest architectural remains of Africa and of the world was not Upper Egypt, where steep primeval cliffs narrow the valley of the Nile, but the alluvion of the river's delta. It would be difficult to decide whether the impulse of monumental creativeness were here first felt, or whether the mere fact of the preservation of these Egyptian works, secured by the indestructibility of their construction as well as by the unchangeableness of Egyptian art, be sufficient to explain this priority to other nations of antiquity—notably to Mesopotamia. The perishable materials of the buildings which stood in the plains of the Euphrates and Tigris, generally sun-dried bricks with asphalt cement, were not calculated to insure long duration, or to prevent their overthrow and obliteration by the continual changes in the course of these rivers, through the silting and swamping of their valleys. Yet, though tradition would incline us to assume that Chaldæan civilization and art were the more ancient, the oldest monuments known exist upon the banks of the Nile.

The changeless blue of the Egyptian sky, the strictly regular return of all the natural phenomena connected with the Nile, that wonderful stream of the land's life, are entirely in accord with the fixedness of Egyptian civilization in all its branches. Though the high state of advance which we first find in Egyptian art, three thousand years before the Christian era, must necessarily have been preceded by less perfected degrees, it is wholly impossible to perceive such stages of development in any of the monuments known. After Egypt had attained a certain height of civilization, its history, during the thousands of years known to us, shows none of those phases of advance or decline, of development in short, to be observed in Europe during every century, if not during every decade.

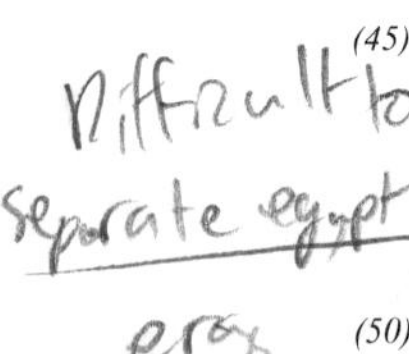

The Egyptian completed buildings and statues begun by his remote ancestors without the slightest striving for individual peculiarity. He commenced new works in the same spirit, leaving them for similar execution by his great-grandchildren. Numberless generations thus dragged on without bequeathing a trace of any peculiar character and ability. It is only by the cartouches of the kings in the hieroglyphic inscriptions that it is possible to separate the dynasties, and to group into periods of a thousand years or more, works of art which seem from their style to belong to one and the same age.

The fundamental motive of the pyramid is the funeral mound. A small upheaval above the natural level of the ground results of itself from the earth displaced by the bulk of the buried body. Increased dimensions elevate the mound to an independent monument. Many nations, some of a high degree of civilization, have contented themselves with such imposing hills of earth over the grave,—tumuli, which, from the manner of their construction, assumed a conical form. Others placed the mound upon a low cylinder, thus better marking its distinction from accidental natural elevations. The Egyptians and the Mesopotamians rejected the cone entirely, and formed, with plane surfaces upon a square plan, the highly monumental pyramid. Peculiar to the former people are the inclined sides which give to the pyramid its absolute geometrical form, as opposed to the terraced structures of Chaldæa. The sand of the desert ebbed and flowed fifty centuries ago as constantly as in our time, when the sphinx, after being uncovered to its base, has been quickly hidden again to the neck. Rulers, unwilling that their gigantic tombs should be thus submerged, were obliged to secure to them great height, with inclined and unbroken sides, upon which the sand could not lodge.

Egyptian sculptures and wall-paintings often represent the interiors of well-to-do private houses and of palaces; they show the plans of dwellings and adjoining vegetable-gardens so well that the very products of the latter can be distinguished; but, though these plans designate the separate rooms and their entrances, it is still impossible to comprehend the general arrangement of a normal house, or its exterior appearance. The views of the interiors, with their slim columns and narrow entablatures, with a system of perspective which shows things above one another instead of behind one another, with their evident misrepresentations and constructive impossibilities, must have stood in very much the same relation to the Egyptian reality as the fictitious architecture of the Pompeian wall-decorations does to the buildings of the Greeks and Romans. The architectural details introduced by the painter served only as a frame for the figures or for the contents of the store-rooms which he represented.

11. The author views Egyptian art as:

(A) Changeless and dull.
(B) Rich and diversified through the years.
(C) Fixed and consistent.
(D) Unique to each generation of Egyptians.

12. As used in line 32, *fixedness* most closely means:

(A) Functionality.
(B) Practicality.
(C) Inflexibility.
(D) Richness.

13. Which of the following is NOT described by the author as a quality of Egyptian art?

(A) Monumental height as a demonstration of governmental power
(B) An inclination towards geometric forms
(C) A lack of individual peculiarity across generations of Egyptian art
(D) A relatively changeless style between separate dynasties

14. It can be inferred from the passage that by "less perfected degrees" (line 36) the author means:

(A) Stages of development that were not as advanced.
(B) First drafts that were likely destroyed.
(C) Practice versions of artwork.
(D) Pieces that were completed by amateur artists.

15. It can reasonably be concluded that *execution* (line 48) means:

(A) The infliction of capital punishment.
(B) The style of performance.
(C) The motive.
(D) The purpose.

16. Based on the information given in paragraph 4, the pyramid's structure can best be described as:

(A) A result of the belief that a structure's size must match the importance of the person it is purposed for.
(B) A rigid adherence to absolute geometric forms for the purpose of aesthetics.
(C) The desire of Egyptian rulers to have the most impressive of monuments.
(D) A response to the shifting, sandy environment it is built upon.

17. Each of the following is discussed in the passage EXCEPT:

(A) Mesopotamia.
(B) Chaldaea.
(C) Pompeii.
(D) Athens.

18. The author would most likely agree with which one of the following statements?

(A) Egyptian rulers would prefer the pyramid over the structure of the sphinx for a burial monument due to the former not being able to be submerged in sand.
(B) Egyptian rulers would prefer the more elaborately detailed funeral monuments over lesser detailed structures.
(C) Every piece of Egyptian art can be traced back to its date in history by examining the style in which it was produced.
(D) Funeral monuments are the only known pieces of Egyptian art that exist today.

19. The primary function of the last paragraph is to:

(A) Explore the types of art found within Egyptian houses and palaces.
(B) Discuss the types of materials used to furnish Egyptian home interiors.
(C) Explain how artistic renderings of buildings were impossible to use as a realistic diagram.
(D) Review the various kinds of artistic designs that Egyptian artists used to construct buildings.

20. What is the main point of the passage?

(A) To discuss the history of Egyptian burial practices
(B) To examine particular qualities found within a variety Egyptian art
(C) To give a thorough comparison between Egyptian art with the art from other civilizations
(D) To offer a detailed description of the exterior and interior of Egyptian pyramids

Read this passage carefully and then answer the questions that follow.

Social Science: This passage discusses a decision that had an important impact on American history.

The year 2003 marks the bicentennial of the 1803 Treaty of France, by which the United States of America acquired the Louisiana Territory, an area of more than 828,000 square miles. Upon this brilliant acquisition, known as the Louisiana Purchase, the territory of the United States doubled. Historians consider the Louisiana Purchase to be a landmark event in American history.

President Thomas Jefferson faced an important decision during the summer of 1803. Napoleon, the emperor of France, had offered to sell the territory of Louisiana to the United States for $15 million. This vast territory extended westward from the Mississippi River to the Rocky Mountains and southward from the Canadian border to the Gulf of Mexico and the Spanish lands of what is now Texas and New Mexico.

Jefferson had offered to buy for $2 million only the region around the mouth of the Mississippi River, which included the port and city of New Orleans. The President wanted to protect the interests of farmers in the Ohio River Valley, who depended on access to the Delta. They sent crops down the Mississippi River to New Orleans, from which ships took the products to cities along the Atlantic coast of the United States. Americans feared that the French might interfere with by imposing high tariffs on products and ships moving through New Orleans. Even worse, the French might close the port to Americans.

To negotiate with the French, Jefferson sent James Monroe. President Jefferson was astonished by Napoleon's offer to sell not only the region around New Orleans, but also the entire Louisiana Territory. Although the total purchase price seemed high, it was not beyond the means of the United States to pay it.

The reasons for France's sale of the land were complex. France had owned the Louisiana area from 1699 to 1762, at which point it gave the territory to its ally, Spain. Under the reign of Napoleon, however, France took the territory back. Napoleon had grand schemes for an empire in North America. However, a slave revolt in Haiti, loss of money from damaged Caribbean sugar crops, as well as war with Britain on the European continent soon cooled Napoleon's ambitions for another continent, and he decided to sell the territory to those who wanted it most – and he could use the money to fund his war close to home.

Jefferson wanted to buy Louisiana, but he was reluctant to stretch too far what he believed to be the constitutional powers of the federal government. Jefferson believed that the powers of the federal government should be limited precisely to those explicitly granted in the Constitution. According to his strict constructionist interpretation of the Constitution, the President could not buy Louisiana because no part of the supreme law, the Constitution, granted this power to the government. Despite his reservations about the constitutionality of purchasing Louisiana, Jefferson decided to do it. The Senate ratified the decision, and Congress appropriated the money to carry it out. The President justified his decision with these words: "Is it not better that the opposite land of the Mississippi should be settled by our own brethren and children than by strangers of another family?"

The Louisiana Purchase was a groundbreaking event in American history. Because of it, the United States nearly doubled its land mass and became one of the world's largest countries. Eventually, the following 13 states were at least partially formed from the Louisiana Territory: Arkansas, Colorado, Iowa, Kansas, Louisiana, Minnesota, Missouri, Montana, Nebraska, North Dakota, Oklahoma, South Dakota, and Wyoming. Later on, Americans learned that the territory included vast tracts of fertile soil and other natural resources. Louisiana turned out to be a richer prize than anyone had imagined at the time of its purchase.

In 1828, the United States Supreme Court affirmed the constitutionality of Jefferson's decision to purchase Louisiana. In American Insurance Company vs. Canter, the Court ruled that the federal government could acquire new territory under the treaty-making clause of the Constitution.

The decision to purchase Louisiana was one of Thomas Jefferson's most important decisions as President. He added greatly to the size and wealth of the United States, and courageously established the precedent that the Constitution may be interpreted broadly when necessary to serve the public good.

21. It can be inferred from the third paragraph that:

(A) An economic competition existed between France and the United States.
(B) The French possessed a general disdain for American merchants.
(C) Americans were in continuous fear of a French invasion.
(D) Farmers in the Ohio River Valley relied on New Orleans for all of their profits.

22. In line 5 the word *acquisition* most nearly means:

(A) Accolade.
(B) Conquest.
(C) Attainment.
(D) Compensation.

23. Based on the information given in paragraph 5, all of the following were reasons for France's sale of the land EXCEPT:

(A) A slave revolt in Haiti.
(B) Great plans for an empire in North America.
(C) War with Britain on the European continent.
(D) Loss of money from damaged Caribbean sugar crops.

24. According to the passage, Thomas Jefferson believed:

(A) A broad interpretation of the Constitution would cause a hostile response from Congress.
(B) The Constitution did not provide the president with the right of land acquisition.
(C) The president had the right to obtain his own interpretation of the government.
(D) The French would eventually revoke their generous bargain.

25. In line 80, *richer* most nearly means:

(A) More costly.
(B) More fertile.
(C) More admirable.
(D) More advantageous.

26. At the time, the Louisiana Purchase was a landmark event in American history because:

I. It included 13 new states for the United States.
II. It included vast tracts of fertile soil.
III. It nearly doubled the size of the territory for the United States.

(A) I and III
(B) II and III
(C) III only
(D) I, II, and III

27. According to the passage, purchasing Louisiana was one of Jefferson's most important decisions for all of the following reasons EXCEPT:

(A) It contributed to the practice that the Constitution may be interpreted broadly.
(B) The purchase added greatly to the size of the United States.
(C) It greatly increased the wealth of the United States.
(D) It established a new application of the treaty-making clause of the Constitution.

28. The primary function of the eighth paragraph is:

(A) To explain the process of the United States Supreme Court.
(B) To provide supplemental information concerning the benefits of the Louisiana Purchase.
(C) To offer an examination of the treaty-making clause of the Constitution.
(D) To demonstrate that the legality of Jefferson's actions was later upheld.

29. The author of the passage would most likely agree with the statement that:

(A) Sometimes a liberal interpretation of the Constitution is beneficial for the American people.
(B) Seeking ways to undermine previously established political norms can have its benefits for all.
(C) The Constitution is fraught with inaccuracies concerning land acquisition.
(D) Napoleon's schemes for world denomination were destined for failure.

30. The primary purpose of this passage is:

(A) To provide a brief history of an important decision in American history.
(B) To explain how Louisiana became a part of the United States.
(C) To inform the reader about how states are acquired by treaties.
(D) To explain the reasons for Napoleon's offer of the Louisiana Purchase.

Read this passage carefully and then answer the questions that follow.

Natural Science: This passage discusses the development of the American and Soviet space programs.

The Soviets had watched the emergence of the US space shuttle program with discomfort, not merely because the shuttle seemed to be focused on American military dominance in space, but because it also seemed to be evidence that the Americans were getting ahead of the USSR again. In June 1974, the word came down from the Kremlin to the NPO Energia space-systems development organization to build a Soviet shuttle -- the "Reusable Space System" or "MKS" in its Russian acronym -- as soon as possible. The project was driven heavily by the Soviet military, which wanted a heavy-lift vehicle to launch large military space assets.

Various options were considered, with the minimum solution a spaceplane launched by a Proton booster, the maximum solution a lifting body twice the size of the US shuttle, and the middle-of-road solution a design based on the US shuttle. The middle-of-the-road solution was chosen in early 1976.

However, the result was by no means a flat copy of the NASA shuttle. Although the MKS used an orbiter named "Buran (Snowstorm)" that was based on and easily confused with the NASA shuttle orbiter, there were fundamental differences in design philosophy. The most important was that while Buran had an orbital propulsion system, designated the "ODS," comparable to that of the NASA shuttle orbiter's OMS, the Soviet orbiter did not have main engines. Buran was to be launched in a piggyback fashion on a large expendable booster, which would be named "Energia" after the design bureau very late in the development program.

The Energia booster featured a large core stage and four liquid-fuel strap-on boosters. The expendable booster configuration was chosen because Valentin Glushko, the boss of NPO Energia, believed that his bureau could develop an expendable engine that approximated the capabilities of the NASA shuttle's SSME within the given schedule, but building a reusable engine with such capabilities was not possible. Since the engines were not reusable, that meant that there was no reason to put the engines in the Buran orbiter and no great reason to try to recover the external booster. Liquid-fuel strap-ons were to be used since the USSR lagged the US in large solid rocket engines, while Soviet rocket designers felt perfectly comfortable with liquid-fuel rockets and were very experienced with their design.

The Soviet MKS would be much less reusable than the American shuttle, though given the history of the NASA shuttle a case might be made that the Soviets came out ahead with the less ambitious route. However, the MKS would have a greater payload capability, up to 30 tonnes (33 tons), and as an unambiguous plus, the Energia booster could also be launched with an expendable payload module in place of the Buran orbiter. This would give the Soviet Union both a shuttle and a heavy-lift booster, matching the American shuttle while making up for the unhappy N-1 program.

The Energia booster was to be designed in a modular fashion, allowing it to be used to launch lighter payloads if only fitted with two strap-ons and heavier payloads if fitted with six. Some of the subsystems on the Buran orbiter, such as the docking adapter, airlock, and robot arm were also to be designed in a modular fashion for re-use on other space projects.

The Soviets also modified two Tupolev Tu-154 jetliners to evaluate Buran flight systems and to help train Buran crews, providing an equivalent to the NASA Gulfstream II STA shuttle trainers. A new spacesuit, named "Strizh (Arrow)", was developed as well, being a "rescue suit" along the lines of the shuttle ACES suit. All in all, there was just too much to do, and by January 1986 the schedule had fallen so far behind that it was coming down to a choice between getting really serious or giving up. The decision was made to get serious, and the program was put on highest priority.

The chant of "the Reds are ahead" made a resurgence in the USA after a lapse of about two decades. Berk Breathed's popular Reagan-era comic strip “Bloom County” expressed the frustration of American space enthusiasts when one of the strip's characters, boy genius Oliver Wendell Jones, fumed: "The indignity of being beaten in space ... by a country that can't build a decent ... TRANSISTOR RADIO!"

The sense of being behind didn't last long. Within a year, the Soviet Union was falling apart. Buran and Energia never flew again; the orbiter was destroyed when its hangar collapsed in 2002. A nonflying test article of the orbiter survives as an attraction at Gorky Park in Moscow.

31. The passage states that the Soviet foray into space was driven by:

(A) Discovery.
(B) Compassion.
(C) Competition.
(D) Collaboration.

32. According to the passage, a fundamental difference between the U.S. space shuttle and the MKS was that one:

(A) Had the ability to launch itself from the ground.
(B) Had a lower altitude or orbit.
(C) Had a separate purpose.
(D) Had an orbital propulsion system.

33. The passage suggests that the primary factor that led the Soviets to use liquid fuel rockets was:

(A) Economic viability.
(B) Experience with designing such engines.
(C) The inability to build an expendable engine so quickly.
(D) The lack of resources devoted to more efficient alternatives.

34. The passage implies that the U.S. space shuttle:

(A) Was not as efficient as originally planned.
(B) Was superior in all ways to the MKS.
(C) Had more payload capacity than the MKS.
(D) Was envied by the Soviets.

35. The N-1 program (line 63) is most likely:

(A) A closed facility.
(B) A disastrous event.
(C) A potential boon.
(D) A failed program.

36. As used in line 32, the word *expendable* most nearly means:

(A) Easily spent.
(B) Easily accomplished.
(C) Easily replaced.
(D) Easily grown.

37. The passage suggests that the MKS' booster rockets were used in a "modular fashion" (line 65) in order to:

(A) Conform to existing subsystems.
(B) Prevent accidents.
(C) Hold more payload.
(D) Be recycled.

38. After reading paragraph 7, it can be reasonably inferred that:

(A) The space program in the United States had a head start on the one in the Soviet Union.
(B) January, 1986, was an auspicious time for space exploration.
(C) The safety of cosmonauts was not important for the Soviet Union until January, 1986.
(D) Prior the January, 1986, the Soviet Union had employed inefficient scientists to work in its space program.

39. The example from the comic strip "Bloom County" is a use of:

(A) Apathy.
(B) Irony.
(C) Ambiguity.
(D) Coercion.

40. The audience of this passage is mostly likely:

(A) Engineers of upcoming space programs.
(B) Space enthusiasts.
(C) General readership of a national newspaper.
(D) Political scientists.

Read this passage carefully and then answer the questions that follow.

Natural Science: This passages discusses an important milestone in space exploration.

The centuries-old quest for other worlds like our Earth has been rejuvenated by the intense excitement and popular interest surrounding the discovery of hundreds of planets orbiting other stars. There is now clear evidence for substantial numbers of three types of exoplanets: gas giants, hot-super-Earths in short period orbits, and ice giants. The challenge now is to find terrestrial planets (i.e., those one half to twice the size of the Earth), especially those in the habitable zone of their stars where liquid water might exist on the surface of the planet.

The Kepler Mission is specifically designed to survey our region of the Milky Way galaxy to discover hundreds of Earth-size and smaller planets in or near the habitable zone and determine the fraction of the hundreds of billions of stars in our galaxy that might have such planets.

When a planet passes in front of a star as viewed from Earth, the event is called a "transit." On Earth, we can observe an occasional Venus or Mercury transit. These events are seen as a small black dot creeping across the Sun—Venus or Mercury blocks sunlight as the planet moves between the Sun and us. Kepler finds planets by looking for tiny dips in the brightness of a star when a planet crosses in front of it—we say the planet "transits the star."

Once detected, the planet's orbital size can be calculated from the period (how long it takes the planet to orbit once around the star) and the mass of the star using Kepler's Third Law of planetary motion. The size of the planet is found from the depth of the transit (how much the brightness of the star drops) and the size of the star. From the orbital size and the temperature of the star, the planet's characteristic temperature can be calculated. From this the question of whether or not the planet is habitable (not necessarily inhabited) can be answered.

The Kepler instrument is a specially designed 0.95-meter diameter telescope called a photometer, or light meter. It has a very large field of view for an astronomical telescope — 105 square degrees, which is comparable to the area of your hand held at arm's length. It needs that large a field in order to observe the necessarily large number of stars. It stares at the same star field for the entire mission and continuously and simultaneously monitors the brightnesses of more than 100,000 stars for the life of the mission—3.5 or more years.

The photometer must be spacebased to obtain the photometric precision needed to reliably see an Earth-like transit and to avoid interruptions caused by day-night cycles, seasonal cycles and atmospheric perturbations associated with ground-based observing.

For a planet to transit, as seen from our solar system, the orbit must be lined up edgewise to us. The probability for an orbit to be properly aligned is equal to the diameter of the star divided by the diameter of the orbit. This is 0.5% for a planet in an Earth-like orbit about a Sun-like star. (For the giant planets discovered in four-day orbits, the alignment probability is more like 10%.) In order to detect many planets, one cannot just look at a few stars—or even a few hundred— for transits. One must look at thousands of stars, even if Earth-like planets are common. If they are rare, then one needs to look at many thousands to find even a few. Kepler looks at more than 100,000 stars so that if Earths are rare, a null or near null result would still be significant. If Earth-size planets are common, then Kepler should detect hundreds of them.

Considering that we want to find planets in the habitable zone of stars like the Sun, the time between transits is about one year. To reliably detect a sequence, one needs four transits. Hence, the mission duration needs to be at least three and one half years. If the Kepler Mission continues for longer, it will be able to detect smaller and more distant planets as well as a larger number of true Earth analogs.

Results from the Kepler mission will allow us to place our solar system within the context of planetary systems in the galaxy.

41. The passage implies that scientists:

(A) Are more concerned with finding planets outside our galaxy rather than ones within it.
(B) Don't know for certain whether Earth-like planets are common or uncommon.
(C) Are unable to monitor the brightnesses of more than approximately 100,000 stars.
(D) Are unable to find evidence of the existence of Earth-size planets within the Milky Way.

42. The main objective of the Kepler Mission is to:

 (A) Record the temperatures and sizes of solar systems outside our galaxy.
 (B) Measure the orbits of exoplanets around their stars.
 (C) Classify planets within the Milky Way as either gas giants, ice giants, or super-hot Earths.
 (D) Find planets within the Milky Way that might be inhabitable.

43. As it used in line 83, *analogs* most nearly means:

 (A) Compounds.
 (B) Likenesses.
 (C) Signals.
 (D) Displays.

44. According to the passage, the Kepler photometer must be spacebased for all of the following reasons EXCEPT:

 (A) To avoid interruption from Earth's day-night cycles.
 (B) To avoid atmospheric disturbances.
 (C) To avoid seasonal cycles.
 (D) To avoid human interference with the photometer's sensitive equipment.

45. The Kepler Mission is especially interested in planets with one-year intervals between transits because:

 (A) These planets are most likely to be located in an Earth-like "habitable zone."
 (B) Planets that transit in intervals greater than one year cannot be observed by the photometer.
 (C) These planets are the only type that will provide Kepler with four transits in the mission's 3.5 year span.
 (D) Planets that transit once per year are the most likely to indicate that an Earth analog is nearby.

46. According to the passage, Kepler has a higher chance of being able to view the transits of:

 (A) Planets one half to twice the size of Earth.
 (B) Planets outside the Milky Way.
 (C) Giant planets with four-day orbits.
 (D) Planets with Earth-like orbits around Earth-like stars.

47. According to the passage, the Kepler photometer needs to observe a huge number of stars because:

 (A) It is impossible to predict which planets will transit over which stars, so increasing the number of observed stars increases the chance of witnessing a transit.
 (B) The chance of being able to view a planet meeting the mission's criteria is actually quite small.
 (C) The mission intends to record every star in the galaxy.
 (D) Recording a large number of stars increases the chance of observing new types of giant planets.

48. The author's main purpose is to:

 (A) Drum up support for the Kepler Mission's objectives.
 (B) Highlight the importance of locating and classifying exoplanets.
 (C) Describe the difficulties of locating Earth analogs.
 (D) Explain the goals and methods of the Kepler Mission.

49. The passage states that the Kepler photometer detects transits by:

 (A) Detecting dips in the brightnesses of stars.
 (B) Photographing distant planets in relation to their nearest stars.
 (C) Measuring the distances between exoplanets and the stars their orbit.
 (D) Detecting changes in extra-solar light that makes its way to Earth's surface.

50. As it is used in line 48, the word *stares* most nearly means:

 (A) Glances at.
 (B) Intimidates.
 (C) Observes.
 (D) Analyzes.

rP2: PREDICTING ANSWERS AND ELIMINATION

TOPIC OVERVIEW

The ACT is a standardized test, which means that most aspects of the exam are consistent from test to test. Here are a few things that you can expect to be true when you take the Reading Test:

Almost every answer comes down to two things: **facts in the passage** (and only in the passage) and **logical conclusions** based on these facts.

These facts, and the logical conclusions you can draw from them, will be the key to eliminating answer choices that cannot possibly be the correct answer.

This section will describe strategies that will help you to use those facts to correctly answer questions and to eliminate answer choices that cannot be correct.

ACT READING QUESTIONS

The questions on the ACT Reading Test come in specific forms. The majority of the questions are "complete the sentence," which look like this:

- Information in the second paragraph (lines 5-15) suggests that the narrator is skeptical because:
- It can reasonably be inferred from the passage that after the invention of steam power, industry was:
- Lines 20-27 indicate that John has decided to relocate because:

Another common question type is the "which of the following" type, which looks like this:

- It can be inferred from the passage that which of the following is the most efficient method of analyzing climate data?
- Which of the following quotations best expresses the main idea of the passage?
- Which of the following is an example of the "mysterious process" mentioned in line 50?

These two basic forms can be changed by adding a negative word like LEAST, NOT, or EXCEPT. In addition, the "which of the following" questions may require you to choose one or more of several different options numbered from I to III or IV.

PREDICTING ANSWERS

The best way to approach answering a question is first to read the question and then to predict the answer before you even look at the answer choices. Reading the answers before you predict can be dangerous—you can be tempted by answer choices that "sound right" but are not supported by evidence from the passage.

If the question refers to a specific portion of the passage, briefly look back at that part of the passage and the lines around it. Pay attention to the notes you made and the key words you underlined.

The next step is to predict the correct answer. Without looking at the answers, write down a brief answer to the question in your own words. Do not just make a prediction in your head; putting your prediction into words will force you to be more specific and thus give you a better chance of making a prediction that matches the correct answer choice. If you took good notes and underlined key words and phrases, you should be able to do this without re-reading the passage. You may not be able to come up with a specific prediction for every question, but you should always try to predict as much as you can.

ELIMINATING ANSWER CHOICES

Here are five of the most common incorrect answer types and how to recognize them:

- **No Evidence**: the statement given cannot be supported exclusively by information in the passage. Don't assume anything that isn't stated in the passage.
- **Proven Wrong**: the statement given is mentioned somewhere in the passage, but is proven wrong by surrounding evidence.
- **Too General**: the statement given makes a broad statement that may contain some aspect of the correct answer, but generalizes too much. Look out for extreme words like *all/none/every* or answers that make a generalization about an entire group.
- **Too Specific**: the statement given may contain some aspect of the correct answer, but provides more detail than the question is asking for.
- **Wrong Section**: statement given is technically true according to the passage, but does not actually answer the question asked.

Read this passage carefully and then answer the questions that follow.

Prose Fiction: The following passage was adapted from *Crome Yellow* by Aldous Huxley.

The terrace in front of the house was a long narrow strip of turf, bounded along its outer edge by a graceful stone balustrade. Two little summer houses of brick stood at either end. Below the house the ground sloped very steeply away, and the terrace was a remarkably high one; from the balusters to the sloping lawn beneath was a drop of thirty feet. Seen from below, the high unbroken terrace wall, built like the house itself of brick, had the almost menacing aspect of a fortification—a castle bastion, from whose parapet one looked out across airy depths to distances level with the eye. Below, in the foreground, hedged in by solid masses of sculptured yew trees, lay the stone-brimmed swimming pool. Beyond it stretched the park, with its massive elms, its green expanses of grass, and, at the bottom of the valley, the gleam of the narrow river.

The tea table had been planted in the shade of one of the little summer houses, and the rest of the party was already assembled about it when Denis and Priscilla made their appearance. Henry Wimbush had begun to pour out the tea. He was one of those ageless, unchanging men on the farther side of fifty, who might be thirty, who might be anything. Denis had known him almost as long as he could remember. In all those years his pale, rather handsome face had never grown any older; it was like the pale grey bowler hat, which he always wore, winter and summer—unageing, calm, serenely without expression.

Next to him, but separated from him and from the rest of the world by the almost impenetrable barriers of her deafness, sat Jenny Mullion. She was perhaps thirty, had a tilted nose and a pink-and-white complexion, and wore her brown hair plaited and coiled in two lateral buns over her ears. In the secret tower of her deafness she sat apart, looking down at the world through sharply piercing eyes. What did she think of men and women and things? That was something that Denis had never been able to discover. In her enigmatic remoteness Jenny was a little disquieting. Even now some interior joke seemed to be amusing her, for she was smiling to herself, and her brown eyes were like very bright round marbles.

On his other side the serious, moonlike innocence of Mary Bracegirdle's face shone pink and childish. She was nearly twenty-three, but one wouldn't have guessed it. Her short hair, clipped like a page's, hung in a bell of elastic gold about her cheeks. She had large blue china eyes, whose expression was one of ingenuous and often puzzled earnestness.

Next to Mary a small gaunt man was sitting, rigid and erect in his chair. In appearance Mr. Scogan was like one of those extinct bird-lizards of the Tertiary. His nose was beaked; his dark eye had the shining quickness of a robin's. But there was nothing soft or gracious or feathery about him. The skin of his wrinkled brown face had a dry and scaly look; his hands were the hands of a crocodile. His movements were marked by the lizard's disconcertingly abrupt clockwork speed; his speech was thin, fluty, and dry. Henry Wimbush's schoolmate and exact contemporary, Mr. Scogan looked far older and, at the same time, far more youthfully alive than did that gentle aristocrat with the face like a grey bowler.

Mr. Scogan might look like an extinct reptile, but Gombauld was altogether and essentially human. In the old-fashioned natural histories of the 'thirties he might have figured in a steel engraving as a type of Homo Sapiens—an honour which at that time commonly fell to Lord Byron. Indeed, with more hair and less collar, Gombauld would have been completely Byronic—more than Byronic, even, for Gombauld was of Provencal descent, a black-haired young corsair of thirty, with flashing teeth and luminous large dark eyes. Denis looked at him enviously. He was jealous of his talent: if only he wrote verse as well as Gombauld painted pictures! Still more, at the moment, he envied Gombauld his looks, his vitality, his easy confidence of manner. Was it surprising that Anne should like him? Like him? —it might even be something worse, Denis reflected bitterly, as he walked at Priscilla's side down the long grass terrace.

1. According to the first paragraph, the house has all of the following EXCEPT:

   (A) A terrace wall.
   (B) A swimming pool.
   (C) A wooded park.
   (D) Massive pine trees.

2. To which of the following does Denis compare Henry Wimbush's appearance?

   (A) Wimbush's grey hat
   (B) The winter and summer seasons
   (C) An extinct bird-lizard of the Tertiary
   (D) Gombauld's painted pictures

3. As it is used in line 42, *enigmatic* most nearly means:

(A) Discernible.
(B) Enchanting.
(C) Mysterious.
(D) Indefinite.

4. Denis' comparison of Mr. Scogan and Gombauld is based on:

(A) Their appearances.
(B) Their professions.
(C) Their personalities.
(D) Their intellects.

5. Based on Denis' description in the fourth paragraph, Mary Bracegirdle's appearance can best be described as:

(A) Ordinary.
(B) Youthful.
(C) Eccentric.
(D) Sophisticated.

6. What does Denis most likely mean when he describes Mr. Scogan's hands as "the hands of a crocodile" (line 62)?

(A) Mr. Scogan had a reptilian demeanor.
(B) Denis does not want to shake hands with Mr. Scogan.
(C) The skin on Scogan's hands was cracked and dry.
(D) Mr. Scogan's fingernails were short and dull.

7. It can be inferred from the passage that Denis' profession is most likely in the field of:

(A) Zoology.
(B) Business.
(C) Painting.
(D) Poetry.

8. According to the passage, which two people attended school together?

(A) Henry Wimbush and Mr. Scogan
(B) Gombauld and Denis
(C) Jenny Mullion and Priscilla
(D) Mary Bracegirdle and Anne

9. As he is portrayed in the passage, Denis would be best described as which of the following?

I. Jealous
II. Confident
III. Observant

(A) I only
(B) II only
(C) I and III only
(D) I, II, and III

10. It can be most reasonably inferred from the final paragraph that:

(A) Priscilla is Denis's wife.
(B) Gombould and Anne are carrying on a secret affair.
(C) Denis feels inferior to Gombauld for many reasons.
(D) Priscilla is Denis's sister.

Read this passage carefully and then answer the questions that follow.

Humanities: This passage discusses the beginnings of an influential musical genre.

Little is known about the exact origin of the music we know as the blues. The blues has deep roots in American history, particularly African American history. Borrowing from the call-and-response format common to African music, the slave work songs of the plantations, and the spirituals sung at camp meetings and revivals in the 19th century, blues music reflects the struggles African Americans faced during the 19th and early 20th centuries.

The first appearance of music that approaches the modern conception of the blues appeared sometime between 1870 and 1900, a period that coincides with the emancipation of the slaves and the transition from slavery to sharecropping. Unfortunately, most of these early blues songs have been lost. For many years, blues was recorded only by memory and relayed only in live performances. These early blues musicians also tended to be wanderers, leaving little record of the music they played or where it came from. The early history of the blues also suffered a lack of documentation due to class and racial divides. Because blues music was associated with poor African Americans of the South, the middle- and upper-class white musicians who would have been more likely to leave a written record considered the music to be unfit for documentation.

The blues owes its introduction to mainstream culture to the simultaneous development of ragtime music, another popular musical genre with African American roots. Ragtime descended from the jigs played by black bands in the latter half of the 19th century. By 1900, ragtime became widely popular throughout the U.S. among both blacks and whites. Soon ragtime began to borrow from its less popular cousin, the blues. By 1910, several popular ragtime songs included the 12-bar scheme common to the blues.

The fusion of blues and ragtime helped to propel the blues onto the national stage, aided in no small part by the work of African American composer W.C. Handy. Handy was first introduced to the blues on a train traveling through Mississippi in 1903. At the time, Handy regarded this music as rather primitive and monotonous. Handy's music, which was a fusion of blues with ragtime and jazz, helped to popularize the blues; in fact, Handy billed himself as the "Father of the Blues." Although his music was not strictly blues music, Handy is responsible for the growth of the blues if only because he allowed the blues to reach a white audience for the first time.

As the blues spread in popularity, moving from the farm to the cities, the genre began to take on a regional flair, giving way to the St. Louis blues, the Memphis blues, and so on. By the 1920s, record companies across the country had begun to publish blues records, which led blues artists to expand their repertoires as they borrowed from different blues styles.

As the blues continued to develop in the first half of the twentieth century, it picked up bits and pieces from other musical genres and movements. During the 1930s and 1940s, boogie-woogie became popular and was incorporated into blues music. The big band music of the 1940s also influenced the blues, resulting in the jump blues style popularized by musicians such as T-Bone Walker, who dominated the blues-jazz scene of Los Angeles during the 1940s.

Around this same time, recording companies stopped labeling blues albums as "race records" and began marketing them under the heading Rhythm and Blues. This new classification helped the blues to become even more popular among a variety of American subcultures and encouraged further evolution of blues music. Following World War II, the electrification of the blues reached its pinnacle, personified by the lasting success of Muddy Waters, who recorded his first success, "I Can't Be Satisfied," in 1948.

Blues music was largely eclipsed by rock and roll during and after the 1950s, but if it wasn't for the growth of the blues, rock and roll never would have existed. In fact, many of the first rock and roll musicians, including Chuck Berry and Bo Diddley, were strongly influenced by the blues. Their early music could arguably be termed "the blues without the melancholy," for their musical style was drawn straight from the electric blues. As rock and roll took over the American music scene, blues artists like Muddy Waters found a new following in England. Sadly, by 1960, the blues wave had ended, but the blues never died: We see it to this day in such blues-rock artists as The Black Keys.

11. It can be reasonably inferred from the first paragraph that:

(A) Blues music is an integral part of American history.
(B) The blues has roots in African American ordeals.
(C) African Americans liked to sing while they worked.
(D) The 19th and 20th centuries were a difficult time for Americans.

12. The earliest blues music suffered a lack of documentation for all of the following reasons EXCEPT:

    (A) Class and racial divides.
    (B) It was recorded only by memory.
    (C) It appeared between 1870 and 1900.
    (D) Early blues musicians were wanderers.

13. Blues was able to reach a white audience because:

    (A) Popular ragtime songs began including the 12-bar scheme common to blues music.
    (B) Handy was introduced to the blues on a train in 1903.
    (C) Black bands began playing in the latter half of the 19th century.
    (D) Handy's fusion of blues with ragtime and jazz popularized the blues.

14. According to the passage, all of the following are true about W.C. Handy EXCEPT:

    (A) He declared himself "Father of the Blues."
    (B) He first considered the blues primitive and monotonous .
    (C) He helped propel the blues onto the national stage.
    (D) He introduced the blues on a train through Mississippi.

15. The passage indicates that the early popularization of the blues was influenced by:

    (A) The blues-jazz scene of Los Angeles.
    (B) Big band music of the 1940's.
    (C) The movement from farms to cities.
    (D) The simultaneous development of ragtime.

10/10

16. As used in line 56, *flair* most closely means:

    (A) Beauty.
    (B) Style.
    (C) Elegance.
    (D) Talent.

17. What encouraged further popularization of blues music?

    (A) Recording companies' new classification under the heading Rhythm and Blues
    (B) World War II promoted the electrification of the blues
    (C) The lasting success of Muddy Waters
    (D) The song "I Can't Be Satisfied," recorded in 1948

18. According to the passage, blues music began to decline:

    (A) With the emergence of Chuck Berry and Bo Diddley.
    (B) When blues artists found new followings in England.
    (C) When rock and roll took over the American music scene.
    (D) Following World War II.

19. The author would most likely agree with which one of the following statements:

    (A) Blues music began as a very regional genre of music.
    (B) Ragtime was a more developed genre of music than blues.
    (C) W.C. Handy was a minor character in the popularization of blues music.
    (D) Blues music made a considerable contribution to the formation of rock and roll.

20. The primary purpose of the passage is to:

    (A) Provide a general historical account of blues music within American society.
    (B) Discuss particular musical qualities found within blues music.
    (C) Elaborate on famous blues artists and their impact on blues music.
    (D) Examine the ways in which social attitudes concerning race played a part in the conception of blues music.

Read this passage carefully and then answer the questions that follow.

Social Science: This passage discusses the history of an early submarine vessel.

The concept of a boat that would sail under water goes back at least as far as the 16th century. In 1573, an Englishman named William Bourne published a design for a submersible boat that featured a mast that could operate as a snorkel. It doesn't appear that Bourne ever actually built the vessel, but his ideas influenced others. In 1620, a Dutchman living in England named Cornelius van Drebbel built several wooden submarines that could sink just under the surface of the water. They were propelled by oars and obtained air through tubes to the surface. Details of van Drebbel's submarines are sketchy since he was an extremely secretive man, but reports indicate that he made a number of submarine trips up and down the Thames.

In the following century and a half, many people made boats that could sink and, sometimes, come back up again. These experiments were often the nautical equivalent of tying on wings and jumping off towers in attempts to fly. However, by 1727 at least 14 patents had been issued for submarine designs in England alone. These were generally just submersible rowboats, but a few useful features were developed. In 1747, an Englishman named Nathaniel Symons, working from an idea suggested decades earlier, developed a vessel that could sink by letting water into leather bags, and then rise again by twisting the water out of the bags. This was the first known use of the concept of a "ballast tank."

The first attempt to build a submarine that actually seemed worthy of the name was the TURTLE, designed during the American Revolution by the genius David Bushnell, a student at Yale involved in resistance against the British. The precise details of Bushnell's design are not known since all he left behind was a written description. He was so innovative that the most common illustration of the TURTLE was drawn over a century later from that description, and the designers still couldn't figure out some of the features.

The TURTLE was a one-man craft, shaped like two bowls with tapered lips joined together, with a brass "conning tower" on top that provided portholes to allow the operator to see. The conning tower was capped by a hatch. The submarine was propelled by hand-driven horizontal and vertical propellers, and carried a 68 kilogram (150 pound) black powder charge. The charge was to be attached to a warship with a hand-driven screw, and detonated by a clockwork timing mechanism that released a spring-loaded hammer to strike a percussion cap.

The little submarine was kept upright by a lead weight in the bottom, which could be jettisoned in an emergency. The operator could make the craft sink by letting water into a tank, and rise again by pumping it out. He obtained air through pipes with valves that closed when the submarine bobbed completely under water. There was enough air to allow it to stay under for about half an hour. Back then, half an hour was an incomprehensible amount of time under water. The TURTLE was steered by a rudder, and had a compass and barometer for navigation. Handling the propellers, rudder, and all the other gear kept the operator extremely busy.

Bushnell proposed to use the TURTLE to attack British vessels that were blockading American ports. Although Bushnell himself wanted to pilot the craft and he was also an expert soldier, he fell ill, and substitutes were found. In August 1776, Sergeant Ezra Lee of the American Army took the TURTLE to sea. The little submarine was towed towards the British blockaders by two longboats, and then released to move forward on the tide. The tide swept him past his target, the warship HMS EAGLE, and Lee had to wait for the tide to reverse before he could make his way to his target. Lee failed to successfully attach the charge to the ship's hull, and was forced to give up the attack.

While he was struggling to return the TURTLE to shore, the British noticed the strange little vessel bobbing on the surface and sent out a boat to investigate. Lee released the charge, activating the clockwork timer. The charge exploded and the British decided to give up the chase. Lee escaped, but the TURTLE never managed to get close to another British warship. It was eventually found by the British and destroyed. Despite the failure of the TURTLE in combat, much later another submarine pioneer, John P. Holland, wrote that it was "the most perfect thing of its kind constructed before 1880." Considering the technology available, the little submarine was remarkably clever and well thought out.

21. Based on the passage, it can be inferred that the author would most likely agree with which of the following statements?

(A) Although a clever invention, the TURTLE failed to perform as a submarine.
(B) The TURTLE was one of the first truly functional submarines of its time.
(C) The concept of the submarine played a vital role during the American Revolution.
(D) There was no interest in designing a submarine until the invention of the TURTLE.

22. As used in line 13, *sketchy* most nearly means:

(A) Indiscernible.
(B) Incorrigible.
(C) Fascinating.
(D) Conditional.

23. What does the author mean when he states that early attempts at making boats sink were the "nautical equivalent of tying on wings and jumping off towers" (lines 19-20)?

(A) Early attempts at designing submarines were mostly conducted by thrill-seekers.
(B) Early attempts at designing submarines were dangerous and not worth the risk.
(C) Early attempts at designing submarines were foolish and socially discouraged.
(D) Early attempts at designing submarines were amateurish and risky.

24. Who was responsible for designing the first known vessel which made use of the concept of a ballast tank?

(A) Ezra Lee
(B) David Bushnell
(C) Cornelius van Drebbel
(D) Nathaniel Symons

25. Which one of the following is NOT necessary for the TURTLE to operate as a submarine?

(A) A lead weight
(B) Hand-driven propellers
(C) A percussion cap
(D) A rudder

26. The author indicates that most of the details about the TURTLE are derived from:

(A) Written descriptions accompanied by imperfect illustrations which were drawn over a century after the TURTLE was invented.
(B) Detailed drawings which depict the various parts of the TURTLE.
(C) Written description accompanied with illustrations drawn by a student at Yale during the American Revolution.
(D) Illustrations accompanied with precise details on the history of the inception of the TURTLE.

27. The author states that the function of the "conning tower" (line 45) is:

(A) To allow the operator to be jettisoned in an emergency.
(B) To provide portholes to allow the operator to see.
(C) To enable the operator to attach a black powder charge on to a warship.
(D) To provide enough air to allow the operator to stay under water for half an hour.

28. The author's tone can be described as:

(A) Vehement and opinionated.
(B) Scholarly and remote.
(C) Appreciative and academic.
(D) Critical and skeptical.

29. The primary purpose of the sixth paragraph is to:

(A) Discuss the technical flaws of the TURTLE.
(B) Inform the reader about how the TURTLE was first used.
(C) Provide criticism of the TURTLE for its failings during the American Revolution.
(D) Examine how the British blockade affected American ports.

30. What is the main point of the passage?

(A) To demonstrate how the concept of the submarine affected the American Revolution
(B) To offer a description on some of the technological shortcomings of the TURTLE
(C) To give a brief history of the development of the submarine
(D) To evaluate the uses of the modern submarine

Read this passage carefully and then answer the questions that follow.

Natural Science: This passage describes early developments in astronomy.

Humans have been observing the night sky since prehistory, but before the scientific revolution, all their observations were by "eyeball." The positions and movements of various objects in the sky could be tracked with mechanical aids, such as sticks or arrangements of stones -- the famous structure known as Stonehenge in southern England was laid out with an eye to tracking the sky and the seasons -- but nobody had any better idea of what the objects in the sky were than what could be seen with the naked eye.

Of course, the Moon appeared to be another world of its own, but the stars didn't seem to be anything more than points of light, any more than were the planets that wandered through the otherwise fixed patterns of the sky. Every now and then a fuzzy "comet" would pass through the sky on a completely unpredictable basis, often causing public consternation. In the West, in the 2nd century CE a scholar named Claudius Ptolemaeus (~100:170 CE), better known as "Ptolemy," published a description of the cosmos, in which the stars were simply lights or holes on a distant sphere, with the planets arranged on transparent spheres below. All the spheres were perfectly circular. Since the planets had irregular motions, sometimes reversing their course in the sky for short times, the planets actually moved on an "epicyclic" arrangement of spheres-on-spheres that became increasingly complicated.

The basic concept had been originally devised by Aristotle (384:322 BCE), the most influential ancient Greek scholar, and extended by the 2nd century BCE Greek astronomer Hipparchus (~190:120 BCE), one of the greatest of the "eyeball" astronomers. The Ptolemaic system did account for the movements of the planets, though it was cumbersome and not very elegant even on its own terms. The problem was that nobody thought the Earth orbited around the Sun; certainly that would have seemed like a bizarre idea, since the Sun could be seen cycling around the Earth on a highly predictable daily basis, and the Earth underfoot seemed entirely immobile.

The early astronomers did achieve some other successes with "eyeball" methods. About 240 BCE, the Greek geographer Eratosthenes (276:195 BCE) managed to determine the diameter of the Earth -- even in ancient times, educated people knew the Earth was round; it could be seen to be curved from the way ships would disappear over the horizon. Eratosthenes, who worked in Alexandria, Egypt, observed that the Sun was 7 degrees off the zenith (the line straight up into the sky) at noon on 21 June, the day of the summer solstice. He learned that the Sun was directly overhead at what is now Aswan, well to the south up the Nile, at the same time, and a little simple geometry gave him the size of the Earth.

Hipparchus later leveraged off this knowledge to obtain the distance from the Earth to the Moon, as well as the size of the Moon. In 129 BCE, there was a total eclipse of the Moon. As is true with all total eclipses, they only occur along a single track across the Earth, with areas outside of the track observing a partial eclipse. Knowledge of the locations of where the eclipse was total and where it was partial, by a given amount, allowed determination of the distance to the Moon by a little trigonometry. Of course, once the distance was known, its size was obvious as well.

Attempts to determine the distance from the Earth to the Sun and from the Earth to the planets didn't work out so well. Determining the distance to the stars was obviously impossible with the technology available. Still, astronomers continued to observe the heavens with "eyeball" methods. The tools they used could not provide magnification; they could only determine the celestial "longitude" and "latitude" of objects in the sky.

The "armillary" was one device used to measure celestial longitude. There were various forms, but a typical configuration involved a fixed ring mounted to parallel the Earth's equator. The ring was marked; the armillary included a second, movable ring or an arm to help pinpoint the position of a celestial object. The "quadrant" was one of the devices used to measure celestial latitudes. It consisted of a quarter of a circle, with markings along the rim, a plumbob to align the device to the vertical, and a moveable arm with sights that was used to target a celestial object. There were a number of variations on and combinations of these two schemes, but they were all functionally equivalent. It was also handy to have some sort of timepiece to match the celestial longitude of an object to a set time, but before the scientific revolution clocks were limited to sundials, water clocks, and primitive and inaccurate clockwork systems.

31. According to the passage, those who observed the night sky in ancient times used:

(A) Primitive telescopes.
(B) Epicyclic models.
(C) Mechanical aids.
(D) Powerful scientific aids.

32. The author begins the passage with a reference to Stonehenge primarily to:

    (A) Establish historical similarities.
    (B) Illustrate early methods of astronomy.
    (C) Show the crowning achievement of a Neolithic society.
    (D) Show how predecessors of Ptolemy advanced the techniques of stargazing.

33. Both paragraph 2 and paragraph 5 discuss:

    (A) The effect of the moon's gravitational pull.
    (B) Public terror of an event.
    (C) A mathematical justification of a theory.
    (D) An uncommon astrological phenomenon.

34. The third paragraph suggests that Aristotle:

    (A) Thought that the Earth revolved around the sun.
    (B) Was an unparalleled scientist.
    (C) Was a rival of Ptolemy.
    (D) Did not possess sophisticated instruments.

35. The primary difference between the fourth and fifth paragraphs is that:

    (A) The fourth paragraph shows an example, while the fifth paragraph says how that example was employed in future experiments.
    (B) The fourth paragraph suggests that the shape of the Earth was known, while the fifth paragraph doubts that assertion.
    (C) The fourth paragraph states that people thought the sun was the center of the solar system, while the fifth paragraph talks about discovering the size of the earth.
    (D) The fourth paragraph discusses using a solar eclipse, while the fifth paragraph discusses using a lunar eclipse.

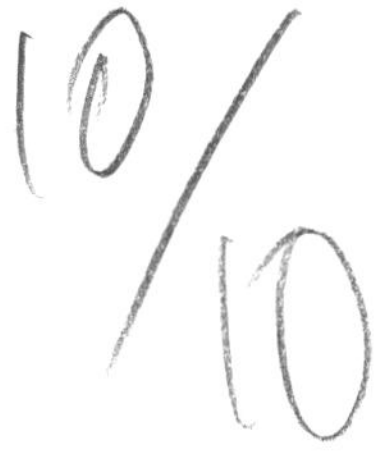

36. As used in the passage, the word *devised* (line 31) most nearly means:

    (A) Constructed.
    (B) Utilized.
    (C) Bequeathed.
    (D) Invented.

37. The fourth paragraph states that, when determining the size of the Earth, which of the following are correlated?

    (A) The viewer's angle to the sun and the height of the sun's zenith
    (B) The season and the angle from the viewer to the sun
    (C) The season and the degree of mathematical training
    (D) The bearing of Aswan to the sun and the season

38. The passage suggests that advanced technology was necessary to determine:

    (A) The distance of the Earth to the sun.
    (B) The size of the Earth.
    (C) The distance of the Earth to the moon.
    (D) The size of the moon.

39. The last paragraph suggests that the scientific revolution:

    (A) Produced more precise instruments for astronomers.
    (B) Made determining the distance from the Earth to the stars precise.
    (C) Integrated more advanced clocks with current designs.
    (D) Made "celestial longitude" an obsolete measurement.

40. The primary purpose of this passage is to:

    (A) Imply.
    (B) Argue.
    (C) Persuade.
    (D) Inform.

Read this passage carefully and then answer the questions that follow.

Natural Science: This passage discusses the implications of a meteorological phenomenon.

Researchers analyzing meteorite fragments that fell on a frozen lake in Canada have developed an explanation for the origin of life's handedness – why living things only use molecules with specific orientations. The work also gave the strongest evidence to date that liquid water inside an asteroid leads to a strong preference of left-handed over right-handed forms of some common protein amino acids in meteorites. The result makes the search for extraterrestrial life more challenging.

In January, 2000, a large meteoroid exploded in the atmosphere over northern British Columbia, Canada, and rained fragments across the frozen surface of Tagish Lake. Because many people witnessed the fireball, pieces were collected within days and kept preserved in their frozen state. This ensured that there was very little contamination from terrestrial life.

Proteins are the workhorse molecules of life, used in everything from structures like hair to enzymes, the catalysts that speed up or regulate chemical reactions. Just as the 26 letters of the alphabet are arranged in limitless combinations to make words, life uses 20 different amino acids in a huge variety of arrangements to build millions of different proteins. Amino acid molecules can be built in two ways that are mirror images of each other, like your hands. Although life based on right-handed amino acids would presumably work fine, they can't be mixed.

Since life can't function with a mix of left- and right-handed amino acids, researchers want to know how life – at least, life on Earth – got set up with the left-handed ones. "The handedness observed in biological molecules – left-handed amino acids and right-handed sugars – is a property important for molecular recognition processes and is thought to be a prerequisite for life," says Dr. Jason Dworkin, head laboratory where the analysis was performed.

The team ground up samples of the Tagish Lake meteorites, mixed them into a hot-water solution, then separated and identified the molecules in them using a liquid chromatograph mass spectrometer. "We discovered that the samples had about four times as many left-handed versions of aspartic acid as the opposite hand," says Glavin. Aspartic acid is an amino acid used in every enzyme in the human body. "Interestingly, the same meteorite sample showed only a slight left-hand excess (no more than eight percent) for alanine, another amino acid used by life."

"At first, this made no sense, because if these amino acids came from contamination by terrestrial life, both amino acids should have large left-handed excesses, because both are common in biology," says Glavin.

Isotopes are versions of an element with different masses; for example, carbon 13 is a heavier, and less common, variety of carbon. Since the chemistry of life prefers lighter isotopes, amino acids enriched in the heavier carbon 13 were likely created in space.

"We found that the aspartic acid and alanine in our Tagish Lake samples were highly enriched in carbon 13, indicating they were probably created by non-biological processes in the parent asteroid," said Dr. Jamie Elsila of NASA Goddard, a co-author on the paper who performed the isotopic analysis. This is the first time that carbon isotope measurements have been reported for these amino acids in Tagish Lake. The carbon 13 enrichment, combined with the large left-hand excess in aspartic acid but not in alanine, provides very strong evidence that some left-handed proteinogenic amino acids – ones used by life to make proteins – can be produced in excess in asteroids, according to the team.

Some have argued that left-handed amino acid excesses in meteorites were formed by exposure to polarized radiation in the solar nebula – the cloud of gas and dust from which asteroids, and eventually the Solar System, were formed. However, in this case, the left-hand aspartic acid excesses are so large that they cannot be explained by polarized radiation alone. The team believes that another process is required.

Additionally, the large left-hand excess in aspartic acid but not in alanine gave the team a critical clue as to how these amino acids could have been made inside the asteroid, and therefore how a large left-hand excess could arise before life originated on Earth.

"One thing that jumped out at me was that alanine and aspartic acid can crystallize differently when you have mixtures of both left-handed and right-handed molecules," said Dr. Aaron Burton. "This led us to find several studies where researchers have exploited the crystallization behavior of molecules like aspartic acid to get left-handed or right-handed excesses. Because alanine forms different kinds of crystals, these same processes would produce equal amounts of left- and right-handed alanine. We need to do some more experiments, but this explanation has the potential to explain what we see in the Tagish Lake meteorite and other meteorites."

41. The passage implies that the introduction of terrestrial life to a meteoroid specimen would:

 (A) Enhance experiments performed on the meteroid.
 (B) Compromise experiments performed on the meteoroid.
 (C) Accurately determine whether terrestrial life could survive on the meteoroid.
 (D) Accurately determine whether terrestrial life would change orientations when introduced to the meteoroid.

42. As it is used in line 19, the word *workhorse* most nearly means:

 (A) Farm animal.
 (B) Machine.
 (C) Hard-working.
 (D) Most essential.

43. In the author's comparison of amino acids to letters of the alphabet (line 22), proteins would be most comparable to which of the following?

 (A) Sentences
 (B) Words
 (C) Strokes of a pen
 (D) New fonts

44. According to the passage, left-handed amino acids and right-handed sugars:

 (A) Compose of biological life.
 (B) Were found on the Tagish Lake meteroid.
 (C) Cannot work together due to their different orientations.
 (D) Are found on terrestrial plants but not animals.

45. According to the passage, why were researchers initially puzzled by the fact that not all the amino acids on the meteroid were predominantly left-handed?

 (A) Because most terrestrial amino acids, like those that could have contaminated the meteoroid, are predominantly left-handed
 (B) Because most amino acids from extraterrestrial sources are predominantly left-handed
 (C) Because right-handed amino acids were thought to be extinct
 (D) Because a predominance of left-handed amino acids usually indicates biological life

46. The passage states that the research team analyzing the meteroid has found strong evidence that:

 (A) Carbon 13 is strongly associated with producing right-handed amino acids.
 (B) Carbon 13 is an unreliable indicator of whether a protein was formed on Earth or in space.
 (C) Left-handed amino acids are more likely to survive impact from space to earth.
 (D) Some left-handed amino acids can be produced in large quantities in asteroids.

47. The author suggests that an excess of left-handed amino acids could have arisen:

 (A) Only in asteroids with large quantities of carbon 13.
 (B) Even before life on Earth.
 (C) In response to an overabundance of right-handed sugars.
 (D) Only after life began to form.

48. Information in the last paragraph suggests that:

 (A) Amino acids will only form crystals when manipulated in a laboratory.
 (B) The Tagish Lake meteoroid remains a scientific enigma.
 (C) Scientists are capable of manipulating some amino acids into producing left- or right-handed excesses.
 (D) Aspartic acid is a particularly facile amino to work with.

49. According to the passage, radiation from the solar nebula:

 (A) Cannot account for the large quantities of left-handed acids on the Tagish Lake meteroid.
 (B) Contains toxic levels of gasses and dust.
 (C) Explains the unusual makeup of the Tagish Lake meteroid.
 (D) Promotes the development of right-handed amino acids.

50. The author's main point is to:

 (A) Provide the latest update in humanity's search for extraterrestrial life.
 (B) Explain one aspect of the origins of life on Earth.
 (C) Argue against the "solar nebula radiation" theory.
 (D) Explain the findings and implications of a set of research.

rP3: PROSE FICTION PASSAGES

TOPIC OVERVIEW

There will be one Prose Fiction passage in the Reading section of every ACT. While most of the other passages tend to be well-organized non-fiction essays with a thesis and specific supporting arguments, the Prose Fiction passage will be an excerpt from a short story or novel and will be driven by characters and their interactions. Prose Fiction passages will also contain more figurative language and old-style English.

READING PROSE FICTION PASSAGES

If you enjoy reading prose passages, be careful not to read through the passage too quickly or to read it only for entertainment. You must read all the passages on the ACT critically and actively. If you see a prose passage you have read before, don't assume you know everything about it, even if you have discussed it in class. There is always a wide variety of aspects you can analyze and discuss in a piece of fiction.

Although Prose Fiction passages probably won't have an explicit thesis, remember to look out for main ideas and important points of the passage. These may be trickier to spot in prose passages, but once you have read the entire passage, you should have a good idea of the main points in it. Look for both what is happening on the surface of the story and for the subtext, or the underlying meaning of the passage. Pay attention to the tone and style of the passage as a whole. Also make sure you can identify the time, place, and situation of the passage.

Figure out who the main character is and how he or she relates to the other characters in the passage. Seemingly small gestures, thoughts, and comments can actually show you a lot about a character if you pay close attention.

As you read, try to determine the narrator of the story. The narrator may be a nameless, all-knowing observer, or he or she may be one of the characters.

FIGURATIVE LANGUAGE

Pay special attention to figurative language, as you may be asked to interpret the meaning of a metaphor or simile. Notice the context of similes and metaphors and try to figure out what they mean.

A **simile** will compare two things using the words "like" or "as":

> Lola gave Thomas a blanket as scratchy and uncomfortable as the conversation that ended the night and went upstairs to sleep.

In this simile, a blanket is compared to a conversation because they were both uncomfortable and "scratchy."

A **metaphor** will not use "like" or "as;" instead, it will say that two seemingly different things are the same. A metaphor might be longer, more complex, or harder to interpret than a simile. Here's one example of a metaphor:

> The rain clouds that had formed in Joshua's mind that morning had roiled into a dangerous storm by lunch time.

In this metaphor, rain and storm clouds stand in for Joshua's presumably dark mood. When dealing with metaphors and similes, ask yourself which features of the two subjects the author is comparing and what effect the comparison produces.

OLD-STYLE ENGLISH

The ACT often uses old-style English in the Prose Fiction passage, but you shouldn't let this overwhelm you. Don't read a paragraph or section over and over again trying to understand it. This will take up too much time, and you may only need to understand one sentence from the paragraph to answer the questions. Passages written many years ago may contain words or phrases that have fallen out of fashion. See if you can derive their meanings from context clues, but don't waste too much time trying to puzzle them out unless a question asks you to.

Read this passage carefully and then answer the questions that follow.

Prose Fiction: The following passage was adapted from *The Alchemist's Secret* by Isabel Cecilia Williams.

Once more, the June sunshine is flooding the land and the air is heavy with the odor of June blossoms. In a small town in the south of France, a young woman, gowned in deepest mourning, sits by her own casement and gazes gloomily, despairingly, out into the gathering twilight. On a table at her side is a small pile of money, which she has counted over and over again in the vain hope that she may have made a mistake and that, perhaps, after all, the amount is not quite so small as she has made it out to be. That little pile of money represents her entire worldly wealth, and when it is gone what is to become of her? Work? She glances at the soft, delicate hands resting idly in her lap. Their whiteness is dazzling as compared with the black of her gown, and she smiles rather bitterly. They are beautiful certainly, but useless, absolutely useless, just as she herself is useless. There is not one thing by which she can earn her daily bread, and earn it she must or starve. To what a pass has she come; she, who at one time had wealth at her command and the world at her feet.

As she sits there, broken in spirit, broken in health, a middle-aged woman in appearance, while in years not much beyond her first youth, she recalls those triumphs of her past. Her success had been marvelous, though short-lived. Her mind wanders back to the days when she was the pet and idol of musical Europe. The mere announcement that she was to sing would pack the largest opera house to the very doors. Ah! Those days of triumph, when she had passed from one success to another, when the mighty ones of the earth were pleased to do her honor, when the incense of praise and flattery was burned day and night upon the shrine of her greatness. Her mother was with her then, the beautiful, fairylike little mother for whom her love had been almost worship. Her voice had been with her, too, that voice at which two continents had marveled. Both are gone now, the beautiful mother, the wonderful voice; gone, gone forever, and she is alone in the world, alone and poor and friendless.

She recalls the first and only time when she appeared in public in America, her native land. She did not want to sing that night, for her mother, who had been slightly ailing for some time, seemed very much worse. She had decided not to appear at all, but had finally yielded to the mother's entreaties and driven to the opera house. What an ovation she had received that night! She could see it all again: the lights, the flowers, the music, the vast audience simply frantic with delight at her performance. At the close she had been recalled again and again, and those enthusiastic plaudits still rang in her ears. How little she had dreamed as she smiled and bowed her thanks, and how little those who watched her had dreamed that never again was that wonderful voice to be heard by mortal ears, that voice which had stirred millions of hearts and made its owner one of the foremost singers of her day.

She had driven home from that scene of triumph to find that her mother's condition had become alarmingly worse in the few hours of her absence, and before morning she had stood beside a deathbed the recollection of which makes her shudder even now. The poor, pretty butterfly, her short summer over, fought frantically but vainly against the annihilation which was coming upon her. The memory of her early training at Saint Zita's, the memory too of that other death-scene she had witnessed when her father had passed away so calmly, so peacefully, came to the girl, and she had begged to be allowed to send for a priest. Her mother had never professed any belief, but it seemed terrible to the woman to have her mother die without even a prayer to help her in that last awful moment. Entreaties were of no avail. The idea of a priest, of religion, of even a final prayer, was laughed to scorn. Besides, she was not dying. She was young yet and was going to have many more years of sunshine and pleasure before sinking into the oblivion of the cold, dark grave. No, no, let them not speak of death, that fearsome, awful spectre. She was going to live. Take it away, take it away, that dreadful thing standing there beside her, laying its icy hand upon her forehead. Its touch was turning her to stone. She was cold, and it was growing so dark she could see nothing.

1. The author describes the woman's "soft, delicate hands" (line 14) in order to indicate that the woman:

   (A) Is a member of the upper class.
   (B) Has classically feminine features.
   (C) Is poorly suited for manual labor.
   (D) Has lived too lavishly in the past.

2. In the first paragraph, the woman reflects on:

   (A) The mistakes she has made in managing her money.
   (B) The recent and unexpected death of her mother.
   (C) How she will support herself financially.
   (D) The loss of her youthful beauty.

3. The tone of the woman as she describes the "triumphs of her past" (line 26) is primarily one of:

(A) Condescension.
(B) Nostalgia.
(C) Haughtiness.
(D) Self-pity.

4. The reader can infer that at the height of her career, the woman considered her greatest assets to be:

(A) Her voice and her mother.
(B) Her warmth and her modesty.
(C) Her American fans and her European fans.
(D) Her fame and her fortune.

5. After what event was the woman's voice "never again…heard by mortal ears" (lines 58-59)?

(A) Her unfavorable reception at the American opera house
(B) The death of her mother
(C) The death of her father
(D) The loss of her fortune

6. As it is used in line 75, the word *professed* most nearly means:

(A) Taught.
(B) Possessed.
(C) Lectured.
(D) Claimed.

7. In what way does the mother reveal her disinclination toward religion?

(A) She professes her opposition to it.
(B) She refuses to believe she is dying.
(C) She laughs at her daughter's suggestion that a priest be summoned.
(D) She regrets having sent her daughter to Saint Zita's.

8. When the woman mentions the "poor, pretty butterfly" in line 67, she is most likely referring to:

(A) Her mother.
(B) Herself.
(C) Her fleeting fame.
(D) Her singing voice.

9. The overall structure of the passage can be described as:

(A) A claim made by a character followed by supporting examples.
(B) A scene of a character's present life followed by flashbacks.
(C) A reflection given by a character at the end of her life.
(D) An assessment of a particular singer's career.

10. Based on the last two sentences in the passage, the reader can most reasonably assume that:

(A) The woman will return to Saint Zita's.
(B) The woman has begun singing again.
(C) The mother is terrified of priests.
(D) The mother has died.

Read this passage carefully and then answer the questions that follow.

Prose Fiction: The following passage was adapted from *The Count of Monte Cristo* by Alexandre Dumas.

The sun had nearly reached the meridian, and his scorching rays fell full on the rocks, which seemed themselves sensitive to the heat. Thousands of grasshoppers, hidden in the bushes, chirped with a monotonous and dull note; the leaves of the myrtle and olive trees waved and rustled in the wind. At every step that Edmond took, he disturbed the lizards glittering with the hues of the emerald; afar off he saw the wild goats bounding from crag to crag. Despite this, Edmond felt himself alone. He felt an indescribable sensation somewhat akin to dread—that dread of the daylight that even in the desert makes us fear we are watched and observed. This feeling was so strong that at the moment when Edmond was about to begin his labor, he stopped, laid down his pickaxe, seized his gun, mounted to the summit of the highest rock, and from thence gazed round in every direction.

But it was not upon Corsica, the very houses of which he could distinguish; or on Sardinia; or on the Island of Elba, with its historical associations; or upon the almost imperceptible line that to the experienced eye of a sailor alone revealed the coast of Genoa the proud, and Leghorn the commercial, that he gazed. It was at the brigantine that had left in the morning, and the tartan that had just set sail, that Edmond fixed his eyes. The first was just disappearing in the straits of Bonifacio; the other, following an opposite direction, was about to round the Island of Corsica. This sight reassured him. He then looked at the objects near him. He saw that he was on the highest point of the island, a statue on this vast pedestal of granite, nothing human appearing in sight, while the blue ocean beat against the base of the island, and covered it with a fringe of foam. Then he descended with cautious and slow steps, for he dreaded lest an accident similar to that which he had so adroitly feigned should happen in reality.

Dantes had traced the marks along the rocks, and he had noticed that they led to a small creek, which was hidden like the bath of some ancient nymph. This creek was sufficiently wide at its mouth, and deep in the centre, to admit the entrance of a small vessel of the lugger class, which would be perfectly concealed from observation.

The idea came upon Edmond that the Cardinal Spada, anxious not to be watched, had entered the creek, concealed his little boat, followed the line marked by the notches in the rock, and at the end of it had buried his treasure. One thing only perplexed Edmond, and destroyed his theory. How could this rock, which weighed several tons, have been lifted to this spot, without the aid of many men? Suddenly an idea flashed across his mind. Instead of raising it, thought he, they have lowered it. And he sprang from the rock in order to inspect the base on which it had formerly stood. He soon perceived that a slope had been formed, and the rock had slid along this until it stopped at the spot it now occupied. A large stone had served as a wedge; flints and pebbles had been inserted around it, so as to conceal the orifice; this species of masonry had been covered with earth, and grass and weeds had grown there, moss had clung to the stones, myrtle-bushes had taken root, and the old rock seemed fixed to the earth.

Dantes dug away the earth carefully, and detected, or fancied he detected, the ingenious artifice. He attacked this wall, cemented by the hand of time, with his pickaxe. After ten minutes' labor the wall gave way, and a hole large enough to insert the arm was opened. Dantes went and cut the strongest olive-tree he could find, stripped off its branches, inserted it in the hole, and used it as a lever. But the rock was too heavy and too firmly wedged to be moved by any one man, were he Hercules himself. Dantes saw that he must attack the wedge. But how? He cast his eyes around, and saw the horn full of powder that his friend Jacopo had given him. He smiled; the infernal invention would serve him for this purpose.

11. The author most likely mentions grasshoppers, lizards, and wild goats to indicate that:

(A) The island is not entirely uninhabited.
(B) The climate of the island is hospitable.
(C) Edmond is in danger of attack.
(D) The island likely has potable water.

12. What prompts Edmond to pick up his gun and climb to "the summit of the highest rock" (line 17)?

(A) The heat of the sun had become extreme.
(B) He saw a ship coming in.
(C) He felt a sensation of being watched.
(D) He realized that he was not alone.

13. Which of the following can the reader infer from Edmond's dread that "an accident similar to that which he had so adroitly feigned should happen in reality" (lines 37-39)?

(A) At a point in the past, Edmond suffered a fall.
(B) Edmond is a deceptive character.
(C) Edmond is particularly afraid of heights.
(D) At a point in the past, Edmond pretended to have had an accident.

14. Based on the context, a *brigantine* (line 25) is most likely a kind of:

(A) Ship.
(B) Island.
(C) Wave.
(D) Marine animal.

15. All of the following are features of the "small creek" (line 41) Dantes finds EXCEPT:

(A) It is hidden.
(B) Its middle is relatively deep.
(C) Its mouth is wide enough to allow a boat to pass.
(D) The stones in the water are marked.

16. In the fourth paragraph, the author reveals that Edmond Dantes' primary goal on the island is to:

(A) Learn more about Cardinal Spada.
(B) Map the island's water and land features.
(C) Replicate Cardinal Spada's methods.
(D) Locate hidden treasure.

17. What evidence does Edmond find that proves the rock had been lowered into place?

(A) The rock is covered with moss.
(B) There are flints and pebbles nearby.
(C) A slope had been formed.
(D) The rock has unique markings.

18. Dantes most likely smiles in the last sentence of the passage because:

(A) He has discovered a way to access the treasure.
(B) He is eager to become wealthy.
(C) He is thinking fondly of his friend Jacopo.
(D) He has successfully used the olive-tree branch as a lever.

19. The author indicates that which of the following characters had been on the island before the time at which the passage takes place?

I. Cardinal Spada
II. Jacopo
III. Dantes

(A) I only
(B) I and II only
(C) I and III only
(D) I, II, and III

20. Which of the following would serve as the best title for this passage?

(A) "Travels in the Mediterranean"
(B) "Improvised Excavation Techniques"
(C) "In Search of Treasure"
(D) "Navigation at Sea and on Land"

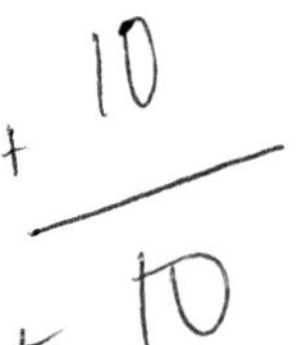

Read this passage carefully and then answer the questions that follow.

Prose Fiction: The following passage was adapted from *Grit A-Plenty* by Dillon Wallace.

There is no regret in life so bitter as regret for indiscretions that have ruined a career and ended life's hopes and ambitions. The world is a desolate place indeed for a man to live in when he has no ambition and no goal of attainment. He is simply existing—a clog in the moving throng of doers. The man who does not go forward must of necessity go backward. There is no possibility in the hustle and bustle and jostle along the trail of life for one to stand still.

Now, as Doctor Joe paced the beach, he was thinking of these things and looking in retrospection upon his own life. What a wreck he had made of it! Once he had all but gained his life's ambition, and a noble ambition it was. Through years of toil and tireless effort he had ascended the ladder of attainment. He had reached a high place in the world. In those days he was strong and able and self-reliant. The top rung of the high ladder, which he had climbed so tediously, was within his grasp. Then came a day when he lost his balance and slipped and fell to the very bottom. In an hour all that he had worked for and hoped for and won was lost, and with it his courage and ambition.

Doctor Joe, contemplating his past and reviewing the train of circumstances that had ended his career, showered upon himself bitter denunciation and condemnation. He had indulged in appetites which had seemed innocent and harmless enough at first, but which had gradually and insidiously wormed their way into his soul until they had gained possession of him and had become his master. Then they had mercilessly ruined him and wrecked his life. Even the little fortune he had accumulated was lost. If he had only clung to that, at least, he would now be able to meet the expense of Jamie's surgical operation.

What could Doctor Joe do? He was so indifferent a trapper that his earnings barely served to supply him with the ordinary comforts and necessities of life. The journey to New York would be expensive, and there appeared no other way by which Jamie's eyesight could be saved.

Through the mist of departed years, Doctor Joe turned his thoughts to his own boyhood home. He saw his father's house, where he had grown to young manhood, and had planned the great things he was to do in the world. That was when life and the world with all their possibilities lay before him. Now they were behind him. There were no hopes or prospects for the future beyond a hand-to-mouth living from day to day, with a gray shadow upon the past.

He saw the path leading up from the village street to the door of his father's cottage, and the green, well-kept lawn on either side, and his mother's flower beds which she loved so well and nurtured with her own dear hands. He was there again in fancy. An odor of roses and sweet peas and honeysuckles came to his nostrils. He could see the fat, saucy robins hopping about upon the grass. And there was his mother at the door! How gentle and loving she always was. How she used to tuck him into bed and kiss him good night, when he was little. What plans she built for him, and how she always told him that he must be a generous and noble man when he grew up.

And then he passed on to the years when he helped his father, after school hours, in the little store around the corner, and the terrible day when his father died quickly, to be soon followed by his mother. How desolate the world seemed then! What a lonely struggle lay before him!

And when his father's estate was settled, and the store and the home were sold, and he left the village, he had barely enough money in his pocket to meet his first year's expenses at college. But he had vowed to make his way, as his mother had wished, and also to be her ideal of a man.

The years that followed were years of struggle, for it was not easy with bare hands to finish his education. But in those days he had brains and hope and courage, and the basic tenacity that will not surrender. And he was inspired in those early years by a profound belief that his mother was near him. He could not see her, but her spirit walked with him and watched over him. It gave him courage to feel her near him, and kept him straight when he was tempted to do wrong.

21. Based on the first paragraph, with which of the following statements would the author most likely agree?

(A) Moving forward is essentially the same as moving backward.
(B) It is better for a man to stagnate than to move backward.
(C) Stagnation does not exist in reality.
(D) Only a man with no ambition ever moves backward.

22. The function of the second paragraph in telling the story of Doctor Joe's life is:

(A) To outline the rise and sudden fall of his career.
(B) To demonstrate his extraordinary ambition.
(C) To illustrate the state of ruination in which he now finds himself.
(D) To cause the reader to question Doctor Joe's integrity.

23. The word *meet* as it is used in line 36 most nearly means:

(A) Encounter.
(B) Afford.
(C) Overcome.
(D) Undergo.

24. According to the fourth paragraph, which of the following is located in New York?

(A) Opportunities for Doctor Joe to regain his fortune
(B) A surgeon who can save Jamie's eyesight
(C) Doctor Joe's father's house
(D) The "comforts and necessities of life"

25. Doctor Joe's attitude as a child can best be described as:

(A) Ambitious.
(B) Doleful.
(C) Prestigious.
(D) Prolific.

26. Doctor Joe recalls about his mother all of the following EXCEPT:

(A) She was a skilled gardener.
(B) She was affectionate.
(C) She had high expectations of his character.
(D) She hoped he would become a doctor.

27. Where did Doctor Joe's father work?

(A) In a store near their home
(B) In a surgeon's office
(C) In a nearby college
(D) In the community garden

28. The author reveals that Doctor Joe's primary motivation to succeed was:

(A) A desire to become wealthy.
(B) A fear of disappointing his father.
(C) A longing to make his mother proud.
(D) A passion for medicine.

29. In context, the phrase "in fancy" (line 59) most nearly means:

(A) In his imagination.
(B) With a flourish.
(C) Shortly afterward.
(D) In formal attire.

30. For the duration of the passage, the character is physically located:

(A) In New York.
(B) On a beach.
(C) In a garden.
(D) In the house in which he had grown up.

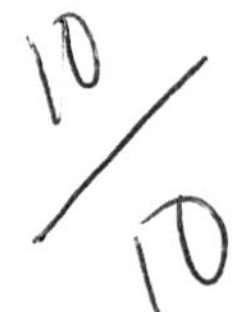

Read this passage carefully and then answer the questions that follow.

Prose Fiction: The following passage was adapted from *The Adventure of Princess Sylvia* by C.N and A.M. Williamson.

Twilight fell late in the tiny Rhaetian village of Heiligengelt. So high on the mountain-side were set the few brown chalets, the simple inn, and the church with its Oriental spire, that they caught the last red rays of sunlight, to hold them flashing on burnished copper tiles and small bright window-panes long after the valley below slept in the shadows of night.

One September evening a carriage toiled up the steep winding road that led to the highest hamlet of the Rhaetian Alps, and a girl walking by the side of the driver (minded, as he was, to save the tired horses) looked up to see Heiligengelt glittering like a necklace of jewels on the brown throat of the mountain. Each window was a separate ruby set in gold; the copper bulb that topped the church steeple was a burning carbuncle, while above the flashing band of gems towered the rocky face of the mountain, its steadfast features carved in stone, its brow capped with snow that caught the glow of sunset, or lay in blue-white seams along the wrinkles of its forehead.

The driver had assured the young English lady that she might remain in the carriage; her weight would be as nothing to the horses, who were used to carrying far heavier loads than this of today up the mountain road to Heiligengelt in the summer season, when many tourists came. But she had insisted on walking and the fellow with the green hat and curly cock-feather liked her the better for her persistence. She was plainly dressed, and not half as grand in her appearance as some of the ladies who went up with him in July or August to visit little Heiligengelt; but, apart from her beauty (which his eye was not slow to see), there was something else that captured both his admiration and respect. Perhaps, for one thing, her knowledge of Rhaetian—counted by other countries a difficult language, though bearing to German a cousinship closer than that which Romance bears to Italian—did much to warm the Rhaetian's heart. At all events, without stopping to analyze his feeling, or grope for its cause, the driver of the carriage found himself bestowing voluble confidences upon the charming foreigner.

The carriage driver told her of his life: how he had not always lived in the valley and driven horses for a living. Before he took a wife, and had had a young family to rear, and he had made his home in Heiligengelt, which was his native village. There his old mother, Frau Johann, still lived and kept the inn. He was glad that the lady meant to stop with her for a few days; after the season was over, and the strangers had all been driven away by the cold and early flurries of snow, the poor mother grew weary of idleness and longed for the sight of new faces. There were not many neighbors in Heiligengelt. She would be pleased to see the English lady, and would do her best to make her comfortable, though it was not often that strangers came so late in the year. The mother would be surprised as well as rejoiced at the sight of the woman, since it seemed that she had not written in advance.

Still, the English woman need not fear that her surprise would interfere with her welfare. Those who knew Frau Johann knew that her floors ever shone like wax, that her cupboard was never empty, that her linen was aired and scented like the new-mown hay. It was true for the driver to say this, although she was his mother. And besides, she had need always to be in readiness for distinguished guests, because—but the eloquent tongue of the driver was suddenly silenced like the clapper of a bell, which the ringer has ceased to pull, and his sunburned face grew sheepish.

31. Which of the following "caught the last red rays of sunlight" (lines 4-5)?

(A) The copper tiles and window-panes
(B) The church's Oriental spire
(C) The valley below the mountain
(D) The village of Heiligengelt

32. The word *toiled* as it is used in line 9 most nearly means:

(A) Attempted.
(B) Exhausted.
(C) Clambered.
(D) Twisted.

33. In the second paragraph, the author likens the buildings to gems and metals in order to:

(A) Illustrate the treacherousness of the carriages' path.
(B) Describe the glowing effect created by the light.
(C) Inform the reader of the village's affluence.
(D) Detail the features that make the buildings unique.

34. The driver admires all of the following in the English woman EXCEPT:

(A) Her beauty.
(B) Her persistence.
(C) Her knowledge of Rhaetian.
(D) Her elegant dress.

35. As it is used in line 38, the word *counted* most nearly means:

(A) Considered.
(B) Enumerated.
(C) Symbolized.
(D) Figured.

36. The author indicates that tourists leave Heiligengelt when:

(A) They long to meet new people.
(B) They are no longer welcome at Frau Johann's.
(C) The weather becomes inhospitable.
(D) The inn and chalets have no vacancies.

37. Frau Johann's growing "weary of idleness" (line 56) reveals that she:

(A) Is incapable of staying in one place.
(B) Longs to be occupied.
(C) Is becoming tired in her old age.
(D) Is fatigued by the guests who stay at her inn.

38. Why would Frau Johann most likely be surprised at the arrival of the English lady?

(A) The English lady had not informed Frau Johann of her visit prior to arriving.
(B) Frau Johann believed the mountain passes were closed due to the weather.
(C) Heiligengelt did not often have English tourists.
(D) Frau Johann was not prepared to receive guests so late in the year.

39. The author uses the statement that the driver spoke truthfully about Frau Johann "although she was his mother" (lines 70-71) to imply that:

(A) The driver has an unrealistically high opinion of his mother.
(B) A person's description of his own parents can be unreliable.
(C) Frau Johann is not actually hospitable.
(D) The driver is being modest about his mother.

40. It can be inferred that the driver stopped speaking because:

(A) He heard the bell cease its ringing.
(B) He realized that the English lady was not paying attention to his words.
(C) He didn't want to say something revealing about his mother's guests.
(D) The carriage has reached its destination.

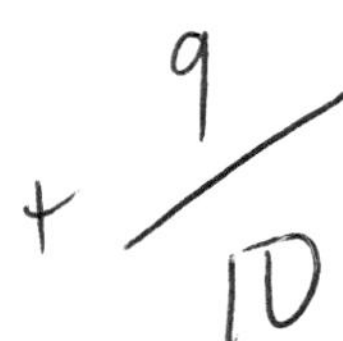

Read this passage carefully and then answer the questions that follow.

Prose Fiction: The following passage was adapted from *The Age of Innocence* by Edith Wharton.

Poor Medora, repeatedly widowed, was always coming home to settle down (each time in a less expensive house), and bringing with her a new husband or an adopted child; but after a few months she invariably parted from her husband or quarreled with her ward, and, having got rid of her house at a loss, set out again on her wanderings. As her mother had been a Rushworth, and her last unhappy marriage had linked her to one of the crazy Chiverses, New York looked indulgently on her eccentricities; but when she returned with her little orphaned niece, whose parents had been popular in spite of their regrettable taste for travel, people thought it a pity that the pretty child should be in such hands.

Everyone was disposed to be kind to little Ellen Mingott, though her dusky red cheeks and tight curls gave her an air of gaiety that seemed unsuitable in a child who should still have been in black for her parents. It was one of the misguided Medora's many peculiarities to flout the unalterable rules that regulated American mourning, and when Medora stepped from the ship her family was scandalized to see that the crepe veil she wore for her own brother was seven inches shorter than those of her sisters-in-law, while little Ellen was in crimson merino and amber beads.

But New York had so long resigned itself to Medora that only a few old ladies shook their heads over Ellen's gaudy clothes, while her other relations fell under the charm of her high color and high spirits. She was a fearless and familiar little thing, who asked disconcerting questions, made precocious comments, and possessed outlandish arts, such as dancing a Spanish shawl dance and singing Neapolitan love-songs to a guitar. Under the direction of her aunt (whose real name was Mrs. Thorley Chivers, but who, having received a Papal title, had resumed her first husband's patronymic, and called herself the Marchioness Manson, because in Italy she could turn it into Manzoni) the little girl received an expensive but incoherent education, which included "drawing from the model," a thing never dreamed of before, and playing the piano in quintets with professional musicians.

Of course no good could come of this; and when, a few years later, poor Mr. Chivers finally died in a madhouse, his widow (draped in strange weeds) again pulled up stakes and departed with Ellen, who had grown into a tall bony girl with conspicuous eyes. For some time no more was heard of them; then news came of Ellen's marriage to an immensely rich Polish nobleman of legendary fame, whom she had met at a ball at the Tuileries, and who was said to have princely establishments in Paris, Nice and Florence, a yacht at Cowes, and many square miles of shooting in Transylvania. She disappeared in a kind of sulphurous apotheosis, and when a few years later Medora again came back to New York, subdued, impoverished, mourning a third husband, and in quest of a still smaller house, people wondered that her rich niece had not been able to do something for her. Then came the news that Ellen's own marriage had ended in disaster, and that she was herself returning home to seek rest and oblivion among her kinsfolk.

These things passed through Newland Archer's mind a week later as he watched the Countess Olenska enter the van der Luyden drawing room on the evening of the momentous dinner. The occasion was a solemn one, and he wondered a little nervously how the Countess would carry it off. She came rather late, one hand still ungloved, and fastening a bracelet about her wrist; yet she entered without any appearance of haste or embarrassment the drawing-room in which New York's most chosen company was somewhat awfully assembled.

41. The passage suggests that Medora most recently married into which family?

(A) Mingott
(B) Rushworth
(C) Chivers
(D) Van der Luyden

42. The author implies that most people consider Medora to be:

(A) Excessively fond of travel.
(B) An insufferable companion.
(C) Not an ideal guardian for Ellen.
(D) Too romantic.

43. When Medora's disembarked from the ship, her family "was scandalized" (line 24) by which of the following?

(A) Medora's attire was inappropriate for a period of mourning.
(B) Medora's niece had unexpectedly accompanied her.
(C) Medora had again gotten a divorce from her husband.
(D) Ellen seemed indifference to her father's death.

44. Ellen is characterized in all of the following ways EXCEPT:

(A) She is high-spirited.
(B) She is inquisitive.
(C) She enjoys eccentric arts.
(D) She is an avid reader.

45. The author indicates that Ellen's education was:

(A) More effective than academics.
(B) Highly varied and unorthodox.
(C) Unusual but thorough.
(D) Worth the high cost.

46. Newland Archer's attitude towards Countess Olenska can best be characterized as:

(A) Indifferent.
(B) Sympathetic.
(C) Disdainful.
(D) Intrigued.

47. The passage indicates that Ellen met her husband:

(A) In Paris.
(B) At a ball at the Tuileries.
(C) In Transylvania.
(D) On a yacht at Cowes.

48. According to the passage, why did Ellen not help her financially ruined aunt?

(A) Medora had too much pride to ask Ellen for money.
(B) Ellen held strong feelings of resentment towards her aunt for the way she was brought up.
(C) Ellen's own marriage to a rich nobleman had ended.
(D) Ellen had already spent her husband's fortune.

49. The word *oblivion* (line 67) most nearly means:

(A) Obscurity.
(B) Destruction.
(C) Concern.
(D) Retirement.

50. Which of the following best describes Countess Olenska's demeanor as she enters the drawing room?

(A) Unimpressed
(B) Vexed
(C) Composed
(D) Harried

rP4: HUMANITIES PASSAGES

TOPIC OVERVIEW

Humanities Passages on the ACT are about the fine arts. This can cover a vast spectrum of topics: painting (fine art), sculpture, music, movies, dance, and literature are some of the more common topics you can expect to see. Passages can focus on a particular author, style, piece, or movement.

HOW TO READ HUMANITIES PASSAGES

When reading a humanities passage, it is important to remember that each passage will sufficiently explain its topic; it's not necessary to be familiar with the topic beforehand. If, on the other hand, you are fairly knowledgeable on this subject, try to keep in mind that any correct answers for the following questions will require evidence from the passage. **Do not rely on your existing knowledge** of the topic.

A Humanities passage may or may not be easy for you to get through, depending on the topic. A passage about opera or sculpture may not be thrilling for you to read, but remember that passages can always be broken up into manageable portions.

OBJECTIVE AND SUBJECTIVE PERSPECTIVES

It is important to note whether the author of the passage is being *objective* or *subjective*. Is the author presenting neutral facts and information, or does he or she have a definite opinion about what is being discussed?

Questions referencing the author's opinion are common, so pay attention!

A **subjective** passage is concerned with more than just facts; it also contains some element of the author's opinion. With subjective passages, discerning the author's opinion and tone will help you determine how to approach the material. You will probably see much more use of the first person (*I*, *me*, *we*) in subjective passages; often the subjective passage will speak of how the author is affected by the art discussed, though not all subjective passages include the first person. When the passage is subjective, you can expect to find some questions about the author's *attitude* and the *tone*.

An **objective** passage is concerned with facts. Most of the questions will ask you for logical conclusions based on evidence given in the passage. An objective passage might be a quick bio of a famous artistic movement or person. This type of passage can also compare two people or movements. The passage will usually explain why this subject is so famous or important.

Humanities and Prose Fiction passages will tend to be more *subjective* than objective; Social Science and Natural Science passages will generally be more *objective*.

FOLLOWING THE MAIN IDEA

As you are actively reading a passage, try to determine the passage's thesis, or main argument. The following are examples of possible theses of Humanity's passages:

- During World War II, the subjects of Pablo Picasso's paintings grew increasingly political, alienating segments of his fan-base.
- Without Ralph Waldo Emerson's endorsement, the poetry of Walt Whitman might never have gained popularity.
- Choreographer Jerome Robbins created beautiful numbers that integrated ballet with musical theater.

Theses will probably combine facts with the author's opinion. It is also possible that the passage will not make a subjective argument, however, and will focus mostly on facts (such as an artist's biography or an overview of an artistic movement).

Read this passage carefully and then answer the questions that follow.

Humanities: This passage describes the life and career of a famous actress.

Ask any American or European who doesn't live under a rock to name a famous actor, and he or she will probably be able to name at least a dozen off the top of his or her head. (Contemporary celebrity culture has made it difficult to remain ignorant of the exploits of the rich and famous.) Go back a hundred years, however, and only one name would come to the mind of your average 1910s theatergoer. The woman who played Lady Phedre, Lady Macbeth, Queen Elizabeth, and countless other roles in the French theater before touring all over Europe and then America: the "Divine Sarah" herself, Sarah Bernhardt.

It's difficult today to imagine just one person taking up the spotlight, but that was exactly what Bernhardt did. She began her career in France, and having taken that country by storm, she began touring in Britain and other parts of Europe, later expanding her tour to the Americas. By the end of her life in 1923, she was known worldwide. She played dozens of roles – male and female – over the almost sixty years that she performed. Her first performance as Hamlet – yes, the title role of the Shakespeare play – was one of her most controversial; afterwards, she played many male roles with less opprobrium.

A completely accurate story of her life is difficult to create because Bernhardt was given to exaggeration and distortion of the facts; Alexandre Dumas said of her that she was a notorious liar. Her life was truly a study in theatricality, and perhaps she treated her public persona as she did her characters on the stage. One famous tale about Sarah tells of her unconventional sleeping arrangements: she not only slept in a bed, but also spent some nights in a coffin. She did this, she said, "to understand the tragedy of my characters." Surely she knew the value of such a story to her legend – heightening her mystique and mystery.

Sarah started from humble beginnings; she was the illegitimate child of a courtesan and an anonymous father. Though she had Jewish heritage, she was raised for the first years of her life in a Catholic convent. When she entered her teenage years, her mother's current lover – a duke – decided that Sarah should take up acting. She was enrolled at the Conservatoire de Musique et Declamation in Paris, and was soon working at the Comedie-Francaise, one of the most prestigious theaters in France at the time. After a rocky start (she was fired, at first, for slapping another actress during Moliere's birthday party), she began to gain acclaim after spending some years acting at the Odeon, eventually being re-engaged by the Comedie-Francaise for a number of long-running roles. Her appeal lay not just in her looks – which were striking – but with her voice, which invited comparisons to a sweet flowing river or a ringing bell. To her, vocal training was one of the most vital aspects of acting – she even dedicated a large portion of her autobiography to speak about its importance.

In her personal life, Sarah had several discreet affairs – with Victor Hugo, the Prince of Wales, and the Greek actor Aristides Damala, among others – but never had any strong attachment to a man other than her son, Maurice, who managed her career in later years and was devoted to his mother. (He was the product of an affair with the Prince du Ligne, whose family disapproved of the Prince consorting with an actress; Sarah raised the child herself.) Even after Maurice had a family of his own, his mother was the center of his life. However, he was not incredibly successful as her manager, and often was dependent on her for his income.

In her later years, "The Divine Sarah" suffered some pitfalls: after she injured her leg in 1905, gangrene eventually took the limb and she had to have it amputated in 1915. From then on, she took mostly roles that didn't draw notice to her injury, roles with minimal mobility required of the actor. Though a disaster such as this may have set many people back, Sarah characteristically did not give up. She even became involved in the rise of a new medium – film – with ten silent films under her belt by the end of her career. With the help of her son, she ran the Sarah Bernhardt Theater until her death. Maurice ran the theater after her passing, but when the Germans took over during WWII, it was renamed the Theatre de la Cite, as Bernhardt had Jewish ancestry.

1. What is the main purpose of this passage?

(A) To argue that the Theatre de la Cite should have its name changed back to the Sarah Bernhardt
(B) To provide a brief biographical sketch of one of the world's earliest celebrities
(C) To compare celebrity culture from the modern day to its equivalent from one hundred years ago
(D) To provide a history of late 19th and early 20th century theatre

2. By using the phrase "…who doesn't live under a rock," (lines 1-2) the author implies which of the following?

(A) Most Americans and Europeans live in relatively comfortable homes
(B) Celebrity culture is more complex in the modern era than it was one hundred years ago
(C) Most Americans and Europeans have heard of Sarah Bernhardt
(D) Modern celebrity culture is difficult to avoid

3. As she is portrayed in the passage, Sarah Bernhardt can best be characterized as:

(A) Saintly.
(B) Conceited.
(C) Capricious.
(D) Mysterious.

4. As it is used in line 26, the word *opprobrium* most nearly means:

(A) Difficulty.
(B) Celebrity.
(C) Trouble.
(D) Disapproval.

5. According to the passage, Sarah Bernhardt was romantically linked with all of the following EXCEPT:

(A) Victor Hugo.
(B) Aristides Damala.
(C) Alexandre Dumas.
(D) The Prince du Ligne.

6. It can be inferred from the second paragraph that:

(A) By the end of her life, Sarah Bernhardt had performed at every major theater in the world.
(B) Many women had performed male roles in the theater before Bernhardt.
(C) Sarah Bernhardt performed in South America.
(D) Bernhardt began performing in 1883.

7. According to the passage, which of the following was a direct result of Bernhardt's injury in 1905?

(A) The Sarah Bernhardt Theater was renamed Theatre de la Cite.
(B) Bernhardt took many roles that required her to remain still.
(C) Bernhardt experimented more with other mediums, such as film.
(D) Bernhardt's closer relationship with her son after the incident

8. The author mentions Bernhardt's coffin most likely in order to:

(A) Emphasize the dramatic nature of Bernhardt's personality.
(B) Raise questions about Bernhardt's sanity.
(C) Make a statement on the eccentricity of actors.
(D) Imply Bernhardt's interest in the occult.

9. Which of the following conclusions could be drawn about Maurice Bernhardt?

(A) Maurice started to manage his mother's career after her accident.
(B) Maurice and his father were not close.
(C) Maurice's difficulty with money was due to a poor upbringing.
(D) Maurice had failed as an actor himself, so he supported his actress mother.

10. According to the passage, Bernhardt's felt the most important feature of her acting was her:

(A) Beautiful voice.
(B) Emotional range.
(C) Varied roles.
(D) Elegant carriage.

Read this passage carefully and then answer the questions that follow.

Humanities: This passage describes the role of a particular writer in changing popular notions of the novel.

It is well known that in the early days of the novel, a work was only proper if it had been written by a man. Women were notoriously sentimental creatures, and could not produce a great work of art such as a man could. Any novel penned by a woman was far too sentimental and romantic. In a culture such as this, many female authors took 'nom de plumes' – fake names – to avoid this pre-judgment. Among these women were the Bronte sisters (authors of such works as *Jane Eyre*, *Wuthering Heights*, and *Villette*) and the French novelist George Sand – who was born Amandine Lucile Aurora Dupin. (Those who say this stigma against female authors is entirely gone should recall that the best-selling author of the 21st century went by the fairly androgynous "J.K." before her books drew international attention.) It was difficult for a woman to be noticed, or to be taken seriously, as a writer – but George Eliot was one who grappled with her times, faced the issues of the day, and is remembered as one of the finest female authors of the 19th century.

George Eliot's true name was Mary Ann Evans. As a child, she grew up in a reasonably well-off family in Warwickshire; as she was not considered conventionally attractive, her father invested in her education instead – sending her to a prestigious academy. (If she couldn't marry a rich man, she could be educated and provide for herself.) A voracious reader, even as a child, she eventually joined a literary review at the age of 31, where she did a great deal of the editing. It was during this time she met the man who would be the love of her life: the philosopher and art critic George Henry Lewes. Throughout their twenty-six years together, Lewes was married to another woman, and for complicated reasons couldn't divorce her. It was a source of some scandal that the two of them were so open about their relationship.

Eliot wrote during a time of great literary upheaval. The Romantic era of literature was coming to an end, and the era of realism was beginning. For decades, since the days of Percy Bysshe Shelley, Lord Byron, and Sir Walter Scott, the ideals of the Romantics had held sway in England and across the continent. (French and German romanticism were especially lively – one needs only look at the adventures of Dumas's musketeers or the emotional growth of Goethe's Young Werther to see the ideals of Romanticism clearly delineated.) While the Romantic writers celebrated emotion, nature, and the liberty of the individual, they were often criticized for their over-the-top style, unbelievable stories, and artificial plotting.

From these criticisms – and worsening conditions for the lower class across the continent – came the idea of realism. Why focus only on spooky fairy tales or love stories when the world has gone through so much? Especially after the failed revolutions of 1848, many reactionary young writers were repulsed by the 'prettiness' of romanticism. Realism focused on, ostensibly, real people and their real struggles. Realist writers attempted to paint a fuller picture of the life of everyday people. Instead of following knights, lords, and other landed gentry, realist novels featured people from all walks of life, from the low to the high.

One of the reasons Evans took the name George Eliot (other than to honor her lover) was to make sure that she wasn't recognized as a female writer. She did not want her books linked to the romantic tradition. Her complicated romantic history may have prejudiced her against the traditional moral ending – that a fictional young man and woman will not be happy until wed in a church before God and witnesses, and should they deviate from this course they will be lost souls. There are few contrived 'happy endings' to a novel by Eliot; instead, events play out to their logical conclusion. In one work, *Middlemarch*, a young doctor marries unwisely and stays with a woman he despises until his death. Most of her novels are set in bucolic settings: small pre-industrial towns with a variety of characters, from farm-working peasants to stuffy bankers.

However, one must not think Eliot toothless in addressing that injustice towards her fellow female writers; she empathizes with them in the introduction to *Middlemarch*: "With dim lights and tangled circumstance they tried to shape their thought and deed in noble agreement; but after all, to common eyes their struggles seemed mere inconsistency and formlessness; for these [women] were helped by no coherent social faith and order which could perform the function of knowledge for the ardently willing soul." It would be a long time yet until women writers were treated with the respect they deserved, but the work performed by George Eliot took them a step closer to that goal.

11. The primary purpose of the passage's opening lines, "It is well known… too sentimental and romantic" (lines 1-6) is:

(A) To reconfirm an accepted fact.
(B) To illustrate the prevalent biases of the time.
(C) To share the author's opinion on the skill of female writers.
(D) To contrast George Eliot with the Romantic female writers.

12. It can be reasonably inferred from the first paragraph that:

(A) George Sand disliked her real name for its length.
(B) The Bronte sisters wrote in the Romantic tradition.
(C) The best-selling author of the 21st century is female.
(D) It is wise to use a nom de plume if you are a female writer.

13. What is the primary purpose of the third paragraph?

(A) To provide a brief historical overview of the literary movement directly preceding realism
(B) To criticize the Romantic movement for its foolish idealism
(C) To introduce the reader to several authors who fit the definition of "Romantic"
(D) To foreshadow the rise of the Realist movement

14. In which ways do George Eliot's books reflect the tenets of realist literature?

I. They depict people from all economic and social levels
II. They have predominantly unhappy endings.
III. They argued for the rights for women

(A) I only
(B) II only
(C) III only
(D) I and III

15. As used in line 68, the phrase *landed gentry* most nearly means:

(A) Aristocracy.
(B) Warriors.
(C) Peasantry.
(D) Intelligentsia.

16. All of the following authors can be classified as Romantic EXCEPT:

(A) Alexandre Dumas.
(B) Walter Scott.
(C) George Henry Lewes.
(D) Lord Byron.

17. The passage states that Eliot took her *nom de plume* in order to:

(A) Honor George Sand.
(B) Avoid comparisons with the Bronte sisters.
(C) Avoid the scandal around her lover's name.
(D) Be taken seriously as a Realist writer.

18. The difference between Romanticism and Realism can best be compared to the difference between:

(A) A pop song and a romantic slow ballad.
(B) An entertaining page-turner and a serious literary work.
(C) A romantic comedy and a gritty war film.
(D) Watching football on TV and playing football in the yard.

19. It can be reasonably inferred from the passage that:

(A) Because they focused on what was exciting and emotionally stirring, Romantics completely ignored the problems of the world.
(B) George Eliot accepted that George Henry Lewes was married to another woman.
(C) *Middlemarch* is George Eliot's greatest work.
(D) The revolutions of 1848 failed due to the efforts of the Romantics.

20. The main idea of the lines quoted from the introduction to *Middlemarch* (lines 92-99) is that:

    (A) Women are inconsistent creatures that cannot achieve their goals.
    (B) It is difficult for women to succeed in a world that does not support their dreams or goals.
    (C) An "ardently willing soul" is no guarantee of success.
    (D) Literary criticism is generally more partial to strong, forceful male writers than to more introspective female writers.

Read this passage carefully and then answer the questions that follow.

Humanities: This passage describes the history and impact of an influential film.

Citizen Kane – the very name itself was imposing. Most movie critics unanimously hail Orson Welles's 1941 film as the greatest movie of all time. So it was with some trepidation that I stepped into the movie theater, which was screening a series of classics movies over the course of the month – this one was, of course, the first. And then, after the movie, how did I feel?

Surprisingly, I was disappointed. It certainly wasn't a BAD movie. Welles himself was excellent as Charles Foster Kane, the eponymous newspaper magnate who slowly loses touch with other people and eventually dies alone in his massive, sprawling mansion Xanadu. I was intrigued by his mysterious last word, "Rosebud," the explanation for which a detective spends the entire movie trying to discover. (The answer comes at the very end, and is quite the clever twist – for the purpose of my readers, I won't reveal the mystery.) And the story – spanning the entire life of a larger-than-life man, from childhood to death of old age – was well-told, mostly through flashbacks. It was a good movie – maybe even a great one – but the best movie of all time? When it has competition like *The Godfather*, *Pulp Fiction*, and the films of Alfred Hitchcock? I just couldn't see it.

Curious about the film's reputation, I began to research information about the production of the film – and the more I learned about the movie, the more I respected it. Welles did some truly daring things with this movie. Film was still a young medium when *Citizen Kane* was made, but this movie pushed it forward years. It is possibly the most innovative movie ever made. Where to start? Welles used the camera as no one had ever used it before; he created such techniques as filming from a low angle (to make the actors in the shot seem taller or more intimidating) and deep focus – the camera's ability to switch its focus from the foreground to the background, acting almost as an eye might, focusing on the important parts of the shot. Another innovation that Welles pioneered was the effective use of makeup; as Kane aged from young to old, Welles's makeup aged him as well.

The story itself – as I have mentioned before – was told entirely in flashbacks. The detective who is trying to discover the secret of the word "Rosebud" must get his information from various sources – old friends, associates, and lovers of Kane's from throughout his life. Each narrator tells a different part of Kane's life, and the bias of each storyteller colors what we know about Kane. While other movies had employed flashbacks, this was the first movie to be composed almost entirely of them – and this innovation opened up new varieties of story structures for filmmakers to experiment with.

While these may not seem incredible to anyone who has seen a movie in the last twenty years, one must remember that *Citizen Kane* was the *first* movie to do all of these. A large portion of what we know about the storytelling art of cinema originated from *Citizen Kane.*

Welles was daring not only in his composition of the film, but also in its subject matter– for he wrote the script as well. The story of Charles Foster Kane is not-so-secretly the story of William Randolph Hearst, a decidedly non-fictional titan of the newspaper industry. Rumors of the movie's story had been circulating around Hollywood for months before the film's release, and Hearst was incensed at what he saw as a parody of his legend. The story is truly critical of Kane's choices – he chooses the pursuit of success over everything else, and at the end of his life he has nothing left to show for it, except a large, deserted mansion. Though Hearst's name was never mentioned in the script, Hearst furiously tried to prevent the film's release, suing Welles for libel. He banned any of his newspapers from writing a single word about the film – and, in fact, from writing anything about any movie from RKO Studios. Several theaters decided not to show the film, fearful of Hearst's wrath. As a result, *Citizen Kane* was not a blockbuster – it didn't have half the success that the filmmakers and studio had hoped – but Welles' refusal to censor his creation ensured that the film, while not a commercial success, was a critical success that was celebrated for decades afterwards.

21. The author of the passage can best be described as:

(A) A film critic re-evaluating his opinion of a classic film.
(B) A student of cinema encountering a famous movie for the first time.
(C) An average filmgoer finding out what the fuss is all about.
(D) A historian evaluating the importance of the movie to the 1940s Hollywood scene.

22. As it is used in line 4, the word *trepidation* most nearly means:

(A) Terror.
(B) Curiosity.
(C) Anxiety.
(D) Cowardice.

23. From the passage, one can reasonably infer that one of the major themes of *Citizen Kane* is:

(A) William Randolph Hearst's life was full of interesting events and is a story well worth exploring.
(B) If one works hard and has ambition, he or she can go far and achieve much.
(C) Hard-headed pursuit of success can sometimes have negative effects on one's personal life.
(D) Great people such as Charles Foster Kane or William Randolph Hearst have secrets that may never be discovered.

24. How does the phrase "Where to start?" (line 35) function in the third paragraph?

(A) It implies the large quantity of Welles's innovations.
(B) It shows that the author has some problems with Welles's creative decisions.
(C) It communicates the author's confusion about the choices Welles made.
(D) It begins the author's discussion of *Citizen Kane*'s sometimes-confusing plot.

25. Over the course of the passage, the author's attitude towards *Citizen Kane* changes from:

(A) Intimidation to confusion to disappointment.
(B) Awe to disappointment to respect.
(C) Indifference to excitement to reverence.
(D) Excitement to deep thought to dismissal.

26. As stated in the passage, Welles performed all of the following jobs on the set of *Citizen Kane* EXCEPT:

(A) Director.
(B) Actor.
(C) Screenwriter.
(D) Editor.

27. According to the passage, Hearst's efforts regarding the film resulted in which of the following?

(A) Orson Welles was convicted of libel.
(B) *Citizen Kane* became known as the greatest film of all time.
(C) The film's box office receipts were decreased.
(D) Orson Welles decided to create a film based on Hearst's life and career.

28. One can reasonably infer from the 6th paragraph that:

(A) W. R. Hearst valued success over all other human values.
(B) Orson Welles worked with RKO Studios.
(C) W. R. Hearst often paid very close attention to rumors circulating around Hollywood.
(D) Theater owners were overly cautious when dealing with W.R. Hearst.

29. Hearst's reaction to the rumors of *Citizen Kane's* plot can best be characterized as:

(A) Enraged.
(B) Humiliated.
(C) Indifferent.
(D) Proud.

30. The author's main argument would be most weakened if:

(A) Earlier movies had used extensive flashbacks and experimented with filming techniques.
(B) Welles admitted he had based Kane on several different wealthy men, not just Hearst.
(C) Many critics argued that *The Godfather* is the best movie ever made.
(D) Welles had received a great amount of help from other screenwriters and directors in drafting and shooting *Citizen Kane.*

Read this passage carefully and then answer the questions that follow.

Humanities: This passage describes a well-known novel and its colorful writer.

There are few characters of 20th century literature more well-known than Ken Kesey's Randle Patrick McMurphy of *One Flew Over the Cuckoo's Nest*, a roughneck brawler who represented, for many readers, the rebellious spirit of the 60s. In the midst of several mental patients whose emotions had been repressed, he was a loud, brash, bold gambler that bore more than a little resemblance to the man who created him. Kesey was at once an intellectual, an outdoorsman, and a rebel against whatever structures there were. All these clashing character traits produced what many people consider to be his masterpiece, *Sometimes a Great Notion.*

The novel takes place in a milieu that Kesey often called home – the untamed Pacific Northwest, specifically Oregon. The story follows a huge, sprawling family – the Stamper clan – that plays a vital role in the booming lumber industry of Wakonda, Oregon. When many of the unionized loggers go on strike for higher pay, the Stampers continue working, making a tidy profit for breaking the strike and earning the anger of the union. The Stamper family's motto is "Never Give an Inch!", and it is clearly shown through the irascible Henry Stamper and his stolid son Hank. Seeing an opportunity for themselves, the Stampers move decisively to their advantage. Their roughness and refusal to bend to authority recall McMurphy in the reader's mind. Instead of just one roughneck brawler, there's an entire clan of them.

However, Kesey shows his intellectual side through the character of Henry's estranged son and Hank's estranged brother, Leland Stamper. Raised in the east by his mother, Leland returns to Wakonda, ostensibly to join them in their work, but bearing old resentments against his family. He is college-educated and sensitive, and is often mocked by the more virile men of the clan for being weak, a "pansy." Leland's struggle comes from proving himself to his brothers and cousins; he feels intimidated and uncertain around his family, and only finds a sympathetic ear from his brother Hank's wife, Viv Stamper. Throughout the novel, Leland struggles against the clannishness of his relatives, trying to fit in. A discerning reader can see both facets of Kesey's personality – the wild individualist and the cultured academic – in the family's quarrels. Tellingly, Leland does not have a civilizing effect on his brothers; instead, he becomes more like them.

One of the most salacious aspects of Kesey's character was his experimentation; his name is listed among others such as Allen Ginsberg and Timothy Leary as one of the most outspoken advocates of lysergic acid diethylamide, or LSD, which was having its heyday in 1960s California. As a younger man, Kesey had volunteered for government-sponsored tests into the nature of LSD; often he worked shifts at the local mental hospital while acting as a guinea pig for psychedelic drugs. (It was this time working at the hospital that led to his eventual breakout work, *One Flew Over the Cuckoo's Nest.*) In fact, after *Sometimes a Great Notion* was published, Kesey went on a trip across the country in a rainbow-painted bus with several other like-minded devotees of spreading the good word about LSD. Later, he got in trouble with the law, faked his death and fled to Mexico for a time, and eventually was arrested for possession of marijuana.

Just as Kesey felt no compunction to follow the rules of society, his writing feels no need to pander to the traditional rules of narrative. The book is filled with flashbacks, shifting points of view, and stream-of-consciousness narration, and many readers might find it difficult until they grasp how Kesey switches from Leland's point of view to Hank's to Viv's. In fact, the majority of the book is a flashback, told to a visitor by Viv after most of the events have passed. One can see the influences of authors like Virginia Woolf and William Faulkner in Kesey's style; those readers who put in the effort to explore the book will find themselves amply rewarded.

Many books are clearly the work of their authors and reflect the men and women who wrote them. One cannot think of Graham Greene's works without recalling his history in espionage and his Roman Catholicism. Hemingway's tough, reticent heroes often recall the man himself. In such a way, Kesey created a book that was not just a rousing tale of family rivalry in the last wilderness known to America, but was also a clear and complete portrait of the man himself.

31. What function does the mention of "Randle Patrick McMurphy" (line 3) in the first paragraph serve in the passage?

(A) To emphasize the similarity between Randle Patrick McMurphy and the Stamper clan
(B) To catch the reader's attention with a more familiar character than those about to be discussed
(C) To elaborate upon a comparison between Randle Patrick McMurphy and Kesey himself
(D) To argue for the importance of *One Flew Over the Cuckoo's Nest* in Kesey's career

32. As it is used in line 15 the word *milieu* most nearly means:

(A) Story.
(B) Idea.
(C) Location.
(D) Point-of-view.

33. What is the author's attitude towards *Sometimes a Great Notion*?

(A) Forthright admiration
(B) Fond nostalgia
(C) Intellectual interest
(D) Slight disappointment

34. The main purpose of paragraphs 2 and 3 is to:

(A) Provide a synopsis of *Sometimes a Great Notion*'s plot.
(B) Illustrate how the Stampers represented the two warring sides of Kesey's character.
(C) Inform the reader about the conditions that caused loggers to strike.
(D) Argue that the rebellious side of Kesey's character was his most prevalent character trait.

35. As it is used in line 45 the word *clannishness* most nearly means:

(A) Exclusion.
(B) Provinciality.
(C) Anger.
(D) Protection.

36. It can reasonably be inferred from the fourth paragraph that:

(A) Kesey had trouble with the law throughout life.
(B) Kesey drew inspiration from his experiences to write his novels.
(C) Kesey's experimentation with LSD led him to become an author.
(D) Kesey was taken advantage of by the United States government.

37. The author employs the examples of Hemingway and Greene in the final paragraph in order to:

(A) Illustrate how authors are often more famous than their works.
(B) Compare Kesey's fame with the fame of these two famous writers.
(C) Compare their styles with those of William Faulkner and Virginia Woolf.
(D) Show how a novel's themes can sometimes illustrate aspects of its writer's character.

38. According to the passage, Kesey uses all of the following literary devices EXCEPT:

(A) Flashbacks.
(B) Stream-of-Consciousness.
(C) Foreshadowing.
(D) Multiple narrators.

39. The "last wilderness" mentioned in line 93 most likely refers to:

(A) The wild forests of Oregon.
(B) The difficulty readers encounter in reading *Sometimes a Great Notion.*
(C) The attitudes of the Stamper clan.
(D) Kesey's defiant attitude.

40. The author's argument in the fifth paragraph would be most weakened if:

(A) Readers do not care to be challenged by what they read.
(B) Kesey admitted that he never read Faulkner.
(C) The story of the Stamper clan was taken from the story of a logging family from the 1920s.
(D) *Sometimes a Great Notion* was actually one of Kesey's least complicated novels.

Read this passage carefully and then answer the questions that follow.

History: This passage describes the life and work of an influential artist.

At the age of six I wanted to be a cook. At seven, I wanted to be Napoleon. And my ambition has been growing ever since. – Salvador Dali

When one thinks of odd and intriguing modern art, Salvador Dali is one of the first artists to come to mind. Known for his eccentricity, Dali was a brilliant figure who embraced the absurd and surreal side of life. His paintings, depicting melting clocks and deformed elephants with giraffe legs, startle and provoke the imagination. His works span the mediums of paint, photography, sculpture, and film.

Dali was born in Figueres, Spain, in 1904. He was named Salvador after his father, as his brother had been. (His brother, born in 1901, had died before Dali was born; later, his parents would tell the younger Salvador that he was his brother's reincarnation, a belief the young man took to heart.) He was interested in art from a young age, an interest that his father tolerated and his mother encouraged. He attended drawing school and soon had established a reputation for himself among the local towns.

After he enrolled in the Academia de San Fernando in Madrid, Dali was exposed to cubism through the works of Pablo Picasso. His work grew steadily more surreal and strange, and he drew the attention of Joan Miro, a friend of Picasso's; Miro arranged for a meeting between the two in Paris. Dali idolized Picasso, and after this meeting, his paintings began showing clear influence of both Picasso and Miro as he worked to develop his own style. By 1929, he had become a prodigious artist in his own right, inspiring a devoted following.

An interesting factor of Dali's work is that he combines realistic detail (as inspired by the Old Masters, such as Raphael, Vermeer, and Velázquez) and strange, dream-like images. Most of the subject matter of Dali's works was, he said, derived from his subconscious and his dreams. Others were inspired by his wife, Gala, and his paranoid fantasies.

Over the years, Dali grew to be a major voice of the surrealism movement. The rise of modern art was in many ways a rise against the conventional nature of the art that had come before. As Dali himself said, "Surrealism is destructive, but it destroys only what it considers to be shackles limiting our vision." However, his refusal to pick sides during the rise of fascism in Europe – especially Franco's repressive government in Spain, but Hitler's Germany and Mussolini's Italy as well – caused many surrealists to feel that he did not represent their views. Many surrealists had posited that surrealism was in opposition with fascism; Dali rejected that hypothesis, saying that politics and art were not inherently related, that surrealism could exist in an apolitical context. When the Surrealists held a fake 'trial' in 1934, they expelled him from the Surrealist group; to this, Dali responded, "I myself am surrealism!"

In 1929, Dali collaborated with the filmmaker Luis Bunuel to create his most famous film: *Un Chien Andalou*. The film is infamous for its graphic opening – an eye is slit open with a razor – and for its dreamlike quality. There is no overarching narrative to the 17-minute film, and seemingly random scene changes and misleading cues gave the viewer the same unreal feeling as a dream might – at least, that's what Bunuel and Dali were striving for.

Though Dali created a variety of impressive works, he was just as well known for his flagrant personality. He always dressed in an incredibly gaudy fashion, and lived an extravagantly opulent life. (He traced his love of excess to an obscure Arabian ancestry; he claimed he was descended from the Moors who used to rule Spain.) His trademark mustache was waxed to points that stood out from his face. He owned a pet ocelot named Babou. Perhaps the most telling anecdote about Dali's behavior occurred in 1936, when he showed up for a lecture at the London International Surrealist Exhibition in a full diving suit and helmet, carrying a billiard cue and leading two Russian wolfhounds. He had to have the helmet unscrewed before he suffocated. In explanation, he said that he wanted to show he was plunging deeply into the human mind.

Throughout his life, Dali was a transgressive personality. He said things others would not say, and did things others would not do. Certainly, he painted what others would not paint. As he said, "It is good taste, and good taste alone, that possesses the power to sterilize and is always the first handicap to any creative functioning." Dali never let any idea of "taste" get in the way of what he thought he could express; while his work may disgust or startle some, it is revelatory for others.

41. The main purpose of the opening quote along with the second paragraph of the passage is to:

(A) Introduce the most prominent traits of Dali's personality and artistic style.
(B) Introduce major historical facts about Dali's life.
(C) Introduce details that demonstrate the kind of art that Dali produced.
(D) Introduce the style that Dali used to produce his paintings.

42. All of the following are true about Dali's art EXCEPT that it:

(A) Provokes the imagination.
(B) Exhibited a strict practice of the conventions of classic art.
(C) Spans from painting and sculpture to photography and film.
(D) Embraces the absurd and surreal.

43. It can be reasonably inferred that Dali considered his first name important for all of the following reasons EXCEPT that:

(A) He was named after his father.
(B) It was a popular name in Figueres, Spain.
(C) It was his brother's name as well.
(D) He believed he was his brother's reincarnation.

44. Dali drew the attention of Joan Miro because:

(A) He was a friend of Picasso's.
(B) He idolized Picasso.
(C) His paintings began to show a clear influence of Miro's.
(D) His works grew more surreal and strange.

45. The passage indicates that Dali's work exhibits all of the following EXCEPT:

(A) Realistic detail combined with dream-like images.
(B) Instructions from other art masters such as Raphael and Vermeer.
(C) Inspiration from his wife.
(D) His subconscious and paranoid fantasies.

46. According to the passage, the rise of modern art and surrealism were:

(A) A rebellion against the conventions of past art.
(B) Shackling and limiting to artistic vision.
(C) An opposition to fascism.
(D) Destructive because they were apolitical.

47. The Surrealists held a fake trial in 1934 because:

(A) Dali considered only himself as true surrealism.
(B) Surrealism was destructive.
(C) Franco created a repressive government in Spain.
(D) Dali refused to pick sides during the rise of fascism.

48. As used in lines 81, the word *anecdote* most nearly means:

(A) Discovery.
(B) Concern.
(C) Story.
(D) Trait.

49. Based on the passage, the author would most likely agree with which of the following statements?

(A) Although impressive in his own right, Dali as an artist had less of an impact within the cannon of Modern Art than Picasso.
(B) Dali was a master of surrealist art and was received favorably by all of his peers within the art community.
(C) Dali was a master of surrealist art, despite generating a mixed reception by his peers within the art community.
(D) Although inspired by Picasso's cubist art, Dali surpasses Picasso in terms of artistic accomplishment.

50. The passage can best be described as:

(A) A study of a particular artist, with an emphasis on his personal history and artistic style.
(B) A study of a particular artist, with an emphasis on his critical reception and influence on later surrealist artists.
(C) A study of Modern Art, with an emphasis on Dali's contributions to later surrealist artists.
(D) A study of Modern Art, with an emphasis on Dali's stylistic techniques within his surrealist paintings.

rP5: SOCIAL SCIENCE PASSAGES

TOPIC OVERVIEW

In this lesson we'll take on the Social Science passages. There will be one Social Science passage on the ACT. Generally, this passage will be a non-fiction essay concerned with the areas of history, sociology, or psychology.

READING SOCIAL SCIENCE PASSAGES

The Social Science passage will focus on the study of humans: their history, how they interact with each other, and how they have created societies. Remember that even if the topic is familiar to you, you should not bring outside knowledge into your reading. Previous knowledge of the subject or field of study may cause you to pick answers that seem true but are not based on evidence from the passage.

There are two ways to approach Social Science passages:

1. Read for facts, and causes & effects
2. Search out the thesis or theses

We can group Social Science passages into two general types: passages that focus on History/Anthropology and passages that focus on Psychology/Sociology. History/Anthropology passages will focus on past events, people, and social developments and are generally more focused on facts and cause/effect.

Psychology/Sociology passages, on the other hand, are slightly more subjective and tend to argue a point or compare two points of view. In this case, it is beneficial to try and figure out what view the passage is trying to get across.

HISTORY/ANTHROPOLOGY – FACTS AND CAUSE & EFFECT

With a History/Anthropology passage, the main point of the passage will be to discuss a person, event, or movement. It will tend to focus on facts and causes and effects. The passage will usually discuss a specific aspect of a broader field (for example, class structure in ancient Greece or a certain battle in the Civil War). Some questions to ask yourself while reading this type of passage are:

- What connection is the author trying to draw between topics in the passage?
- Does the author seem to be challenging a traditional viewpoint about the topic?
- Is the author establishing a cause & effect relationship between two aspects of the topic?

Answering these questions will help you come to a better understanding of the passage—and that will help you answer the questions that follow.

PSYCHOLOGY/SOCIOLOGY – FOLLOWING THE THESIS

Compared to History/ Anthropology passages, Psychology/ Sociology passages tend to deal with more recent ideas or issues. These passages will discuss issues that are relevant to today's society, such as multiculturalism, child psychology, or age discrimination. Because the authors of these passages are more likely to be arguing a certain point, more of the questions may involve the author's perspective. For these types of passages, make sure you know exactly what the author is trying to prove (find a thesis, if you can), and pay attention to tone.

Read this passage carefully and then answer the questions that follow.

Social Science: This passage discusses the future role of the United States in the international community.

As the twentieth century draws to a close, more and more Americans are beginning to understand that a new, highly interdependent global marketplace of producers and consumers has emerged. Leaders in many professions now realize that fluency in a foreign language and multicultural sensitivity are essential in their fields if the United States is to participate effectively in this global community and if we expect to maintain our standard of living in the context of increasing global competition and cooperation.

Compared to other countries, such as Japan and the Western European nations, the United States is ill-equipped in certain basic respects to take an effective role in the international community. For example, after English, Chinese is the most common language spoken in business, followed by French and Arabic. However, Chinese is number seven and Arabic is number eight on the list of foreign languages studied in American colleges. Due to these types of deficiencies, we lack citizens in many professional fields who can communicate in these foreign languages and understand the cultures and value systems that are imperative to effectively conduct business internationally. For the most part, our schools do not incorporate global perspectives in their curricula. Most college students do not develop the expertise to understand even one foreign language and culture. Consequently, most American professionals, whether in business, government, medicine, law, or other fields, lack the basic skills needed to cultivate working relationships with colleagues in foreign countries and do not have easy access to new ideas and developments from abroad.

For these reasons, the U.S. needs to train many more professionals who can communicate effectively with foreigners and who are sensitive to cultural differences. Knowledge of common foreign languages in the business world and familiarity with those cultures are a key to securing our national well-being in the twenty-first century. This realization has acted as the impetus for reforms in many institutions of higher education and public schools throughout the U.S., including the introduction of global perspectives in both elementary and secondary school curricula. In colleges and universities, internationally focused courses have been created, and interdisciplinary programs of study requiring foreign language proficiency and cultural knowledge have been developed. The application of foreign language and cultural studies to the field of business has emerged as a prominent component in these recent reforms. International education is interdisciplinary by definition, requiring collaboration across traditional disciplinary lines within academia. It also requires cooperation among educational institutions, government agencies, and the private sector.

The growing awareness of the connection between national security and prosperity, on the one hand, and foreign language expertise and international competence, on the other hand, prompted federal agencies and private foundations to begin funding innovations in this area in the late 1970s. Many of the newly introduced interdisciplinary business and foreign language programs encourage students to spend some time acquiring practical experience by working for a company, either in the United States or abroad. Other institutions have created study abroad opportunities focused specifically on international business practices and foreign language use. Foreign locations offer the advantages of total immersion, direct contact with foreign business people in a variety of economic sectors, and personal observation of foreign business operations.

With references to foreign-based program components and to studies done in the U.S., site visits and work assignments at businesses, chambers of commerce, government agencies, schools, and other locations are a normal part of these new academic programs of study. Such experiences, requiring collaboration with the public and private sectors, are considered to be essential in laying a broad foundation of professional training and awareness for students who will represent U.S. professions in the world at large.

After more than a decade of intensive experimentation and development, the field of interdisciplinary language and business studies has been established in U.S. higher education. The consensus for globalizing business education at colleges and universities in combination with the liberal arts has reached broad proportions. Internationalization is also one of the most important issues in business education in public schools, with significant initiatives occurring in more than a dozen states. On the basis of these and other long-overdue educational reforms, the U.S. will be able to compete and cooperate much more effectively in the new global community.

1. The primary purpose of this passage is to:

   (A) Argue for foreign language instruction as a means of securing national defense.
   (B) Describe how interdisciplinary business and foreign language programs have made the United States more competitive in the global economy.
   (C) Give context for an educational need and describe the resulting trend in educational reform.
   (D) Tell how interdisciplinary language and business studies came about.

2. It can be reasonably inferred from lines 12-25 that Japan and countries in Western Europe:

   (A) Are major world economic powers.
   (B) Offer courses in Arabic in their universities.
   (C) Offer foreign exchange programs.
   (D) Have implemented effective foreign language instruction in their schools.

3. The main function of the second paragraph in relation to the passage as a whole is most likely to:

   (A) Explain how the American education system fails to teach skills necessary to compete in the international economy.
   (B) Compare the United States with other, more linguistically diverse nations.
   (C) Compare the educational system of the United States with those of other countries.
   (D) Promote the idea that foreign language instruction and cultural sensitivity are key to our survival as a nation.

4. As it is used in line 43, the word *impetus* means:

   (A) Basis.
   (B) Motivation .
   (C) Need.
   (D) Condition.

5. According to the passage, all of the following are examples of the benefits of linguistic and cultural competence EXCEPT:

   (A) Increased access to technical knowledge that originates in other countries.
   (B) The possibility of being a producer rather than a consumer in the global marketplace.
   (C) The ability to interpret cultural acts.
   (D) The ability to communicate effectively with potential business partners.

6. According to the fourth and fifth paragraphs, what is the major benefit for students participating in interdisciplinary study abroad programs?

   (A) Practical experience in the language and culture
   (B) Cooperation between private and public sectors
   (C) The possibility of working in a government position
   (D) The opportunity to share one's experiences with people of the host country

7. The author’s reference to "the connection between national security and … international competence" (lines 60-63), implies that:

   (A) National prosperity is at odds with language expertise and international competence.
   (B) The government had to choose whether to fund security programs or language programs.
   (C) The government made a deal with private foundations to fund language programs.
   (D) Foreign language expertise could have a positive impact on both national security and prosperity.

8. As it is used in line 38, the phrase *sensitive to* means:

   (A) Delicate about.
   (B) Irritable about.
   (C) Open to.
   (D) Understanding of.

9. According to details in the passage, it can be reasonably inferred that the author of the passage thinks that:

   (A) The American education system is often slow to react to global trends.
   (B) The United States is somewhat arrogant in its monolinguistic tendencies.
   (C) American education should have incorporated linguistic and cultural courses long ago.
   (D) The global community should adopt English as the international language of business.

10. The passage suggests that, for the author, "increasing global competition and cooperation" (lines 10-11):

(A) Will mutually benefit the global marketplace.
(B) Will oblige smaller nations to specialize in language and technology.
(C) Will eventually lead to increased cooperation.
(D) Will eventually lead to linguistic and cultural understanding between nations.

Read this passage carefully and then answer the questions that follow.

Passage Type: This passage describes the history of a long-lived nation.

Little is known of the earliest inhabitants of what is now Thailand, but 5,000-year-old archaeological sites in the northeastern part of the country are believed to contain the oldest evidence of rice cultivation and bronze casting in Asia and perhaps in the world. In early historical times, a succession of tribal groups controlled what is now Thailand. The Mon and Khmer peoples established powerful kingdoms that included large areas of the country. They absorbed from contact with South Asian peoples religious, social, political, and cultural ideas and institutions that later influenced the development of Thailand's culture and national identity.

The Tai, a people who originally lived in southwestern China, migrated into mainland Southeast Asia over a period of many centuries. The first mention of their existence in the region is a twelfth-century C.E. inscription at the Khmer temple complex of Angkor Wat in Cambodia, which refers to syam, or "dark brown" people (the origin of the term Siam), as vassals of the Khmer monarch. In 1238 a Tai chieftain declared his independence from the Khmer and established a kingdom at Sukhothai in the broad valley of the Mae Nam (river) Chao Phraya, at the center of modern Thailand. Sukhothai was succeeded in the fourteenth century by the kingdom of Ayutthaya. The Burmese invaded Ayutthaya and in 1767 destroyed the capital, but two national heroes, Taksin and Chakkri, soon expelled the invaders and reunified the country under the Chakkri Dynasty.

Over the centuries Thai national identity evolved around a common language and religion and the institution of the monarchy. Although the inhabitants of Thailand are a mixture of Tai, Mon, Khmer, and other ethnic groups, most speak a language of the Tai family. A Tai language alphabet, based on Indian and Khmer scripts, developed early in the fourteenth century. Later in the century a famous monarch, Ramathibodi, made Theravada Buddhism the official religion of his kingdom, and Buddhism continued into the twentieth century as a dominant factor in the nation's social, cultural, and political life. Finally, the monarchy, buttressed ideologically by Hindu and Buddhist mythology, was a focus for popular loyalties for more than seven centuries. In the late twentieth century the monarchy remained central to national unity.

During the nineteenth century, European expansionism, rather than Thailand's traditional enemies, posed the greatest threat to the kingdom's survival. Thai success in preserving the country's independence (it was the only Southeast Asian country to do so) was in part a result of the desire of Britain and France for a stable buffer state separating their dominions in Burma, Malaya, and Indochina. More important, however, was the willingness of Thailand's monarchs, Mongkut (Rama IV, 1851-68) and Chulalongkorn (Rama V, 1868-1910), to negotiate openly with the European powers and to adopt European-style reforms that modernized the country and won it sovereign status among the world's nations. Thailand (then known as Siam) paid a high price for its independence, however: loss of suzerainty over Cambodia and Laos to France and cession of the northern states of the Malay Peninsula to Britain. By 1910 the area under Thai control was a fraction of what it had been a century earlier.

In the early decades of the twentieth century, Thailand's political system, armed forces, schools, and economy underwent drastic changes. Many Thai studied overseas, and a small, Western-educated elite with less traditional ideas emerged. In 1932 a bloodless coup d'etat by military officers and civil servants ended the absolute monarchy and inaugurated Thailand's constitutional era. Progress toward a stable, democratic political system since that time, however, has been erratic. Politics has been dominated by rival military-bureaucratic cliques headed by powerful generals. These cliques have initiated repeated coups d'etat and have imposed prolonged periods of martial law. Parliamentary institutions, as defined by Thailand's fourteen constitutions between 1932 and 1987, and competition among civilian politicians have generally been facades for military governments.

11. As it is used in line 46, the word *buttressed* means:

(A) Bolstered.
(B) Suggested.
(C) Defended.
(D) Represented.

12. The passage can best be described as:

(A) A thesis followed by supporting evidence.
(B) An overview of the subject followed by focused paragraphs expounding the subject.
(C) Historical context that evolves into a discussion of the current state of the subject.
(D) An ethnic genealogy followed by a sociopolitical analysis.

13. According to the passage, the Mon and Khmer peoples:

(A) Sometimes went to war, but generally coexisted peacefully.
(B) Share common ancestry.
(C) Intermixed with the Tai to form the modern Thai people.
(D) Implemented strict class structures and vassalages according to kingdoms.

14. It can be reasonably inferred from the fourth paragraph that Thailand's monarchs:

(A) Recycled monarchic names in a fashion similar to European kingdoms.
(B) Lost a significant amount of land to European empires.
(C) Would not have been able to defeat France and Britain in open war.
(D) Would have sacrificed other freedoms to keep their sovereignty.

15. The inscription in a Cambodian temple that refers to the *syam* people proves that:

(A) By that time a Thai alphabet had been forming.
(B) The subjects of the Khmer empire differed in complexion from the monarchy.
(C) The Khmer empire extended into at least the lands of Thailand and Cambodia.
(D) The Buddhist religion had gained widespread acceptance in the Khmer empire.

16. Which of the following have been threats to Thailand's sovereignty?

I. Burmese invaders
II. Military coups
III. The Cambodian suzerainty

(A) I only
(B) II and III only
(C) I and III only
(D) none

17. The author suggests that France and Britain were willing to negotiate with Thailand because:

(A) They were looking to expand their territory in Southeast Asia.
(B) They felt that the modernization of Thailand would benefit them directly.
(C) Thailand could appease them with material wealth.
(D) They had vested interest in maintaining peace between their territories.

18. The author mentions Thailand's "fourteen constitutions" (line 87) to emphasize:

(A) The effect that the changing political climate has on the government's most fundamental ideals.
(B) The ability of Thailand's government to adapt to shifting public opinion.
(C) The unsuitability of constitutional democracy to a historically monarchic country.
(D) The instability of the political situation in Thailand.

19. According to the passage, the consolidation of the young Thai nation under one religion:

(A) Colluded with the monarchic system to establish a cohesive national identity.
(B) Led to feelings of exclusion by the Hindu minority.
(C) Established a theocratic nation in which the monarch presided over both political and religious concerns.
(D) Acted as a cultural bulwark against European expansionism.

20. It can be reasonably inferred that Cambodia, Laos, and the northern states of the Malay Peninsula:

(A) Surround Thailand.
(B) Were once part of Thailand.
(C) Are Buddhist states.
(D) Have also become constitutional democracies.

Read this passage carefully and then answer the questions that follow.

Passage Type: This passage describes an important aspect of human communication.

When I use a word," Humpty Dumpty said in a rather scornful tone, "it means just what I choose it to mean..."

"The question is," said Alice, "whether you can make words mean so many different things."

"The question is," said Humpty Dumpty, "which is to be master—that's all." (Lewis Carroll, Through the Looking Glass 1872).

The nature and origins of words have long held a fascination for interested scholars and lay public, not only to satisfy intellectual curiosities, but also because word knowledge has particular importance in literate societies. For the same reasons, scholarly interests have turned toward determining the nature of vocabulary development -- that is, how and to what extent speakers and writers of English become, like Humpty Dumpty, masters of our lexical stock.

The vocabulary, or lexicon, of language encompasses the stock of words of that language which is at the disposal of a speaker or writer. Contained within this lexical storehouse is a core vocabulary of the words used to name common and fundamental concepts and situations of a culture, as well as subsets of words that result from one's personal, social, and occupational experiences.

Probably the most important influence on one's speech is the simple circumstance of the language spoken in the country of one's birth. Each of us grows up interacting with and interpreting the world around us, to a large degree through the medium of language.

Languages are as vibrant and dynamic as the cultures of which they are a part, and the lexical stock of a language is a vivid example of this linguistic principle. Words are, after all, no more than labels for concepts about the world around us, and as new concepts emerge or old ones change, the lexical stock changes accordingly. It is a linguistic paradox that change is a constant when applied to vocabulary. Many words in common use 200 years ago are now obsolete, just as many words in use today will be tomorrow's artifacts.

The English language is no exception, with a lexicon that reflects its many sources of origin and the effects of change over time. Besides the core stock of words rooted in Anglo-Saxon beginnings, English contains additional thousands of words borrowed from language communities with whom we have come in contact. Both of these sources have provided yet more words -- those that have been derived from earlier word forms by addition of prefixes and suffixes or those that have been shifted to new grammatical functions.

Still more words have emerged by the process of compounding, in which existing words are joined to form new combining parts of words (such as the portmanteau "smog" formed from the words "smoke" and "fog"), or simply by creating new words out of "whole cloth." The ingredients of our lexical stock are indeed rich and varied.

We do not learn most of our words by looking them up in a dictionary. Rather, we learn them in the context of our experiences with listening, speaking, reading, and writing. Many studies have been undertaken to determine the nature and extent of children's vocabulary development. These studies demonstrate the truly prodigious linguistic accomplishments that children attain by the time they reach school age. While estimates vary, by age six most children have active vocabularies numbering in the several thousands of words.

There is, however, an important difference between knowing words and understanding their broad range of uses and referents, for vocabulary development is first and foremost a matter of concept development. For this reason considerable attention has been turned in recent years to children's semantic development; that is, to the development of word meaning. These studies illustrate that how words are used, not their length or frequency of use, indicates children's lexical maturity and, commonly, their intellectual maturity as well.

The linguist W. N. Francis once commented that "many people...go through life with a vocabulary adequate only to their daily needs...but never indulging in curiosity and speculation about words. Others are word lovers -- collectors and connoisseurs. But even those who aspire no further than to the writing of good clear expository prose must become at least amateur connoisseurs of words. Only this way -- not by formal exercises or courses in vocabulary building -- will they learn to make the best possible use of the vast and remarkable lexicon of English."

21. As it is used in line 21, the phrase *at the disposal of* means:

(A) Available to.
(B) Organized.
(C) Used and discarded.
(D) Rejected.

22. The author suggests that mastery of one's lexical storehouse is:

(A) Being able to know the meanings of words without using the dictionary.
(B) Being able to create new words.
(C) Being able to use words correctly in context.
(D) Knowing many words from one's personal, social, and occupational spaces.

23. The author asserts that English vocabulary comes from all of the following EXCEPT:

(A) Words from other languages.
(B) The work of a body of linguists and scholars.
(C) The combination of existing words.
(D) Entirely new words that are created as necessary.

24. The author uses the quote at the beginning of the passage to make the point that:

(A) The meanings of words are dictated by those who use them.
(B) Vocabulary acquisition is a concern that spans the realms of linguistics and literature.
(C) The meanings of words change over time.
(D) To be a functioning part of a literate society is to know the meanings of the words in that society.

25. The author's attitude toward the shifting lexical stock in the fourth paragraph is:

(A) Subjugated.
(B) Resigned.
(C) Neutral.
(D) Excited.

26. When the author says that "there is...an important difference between knowing words and understanding their broad range of uses and referents" (lines 73-75) s/he is most likely referring to:

(A) The difference between identifying a word and knowing its meaning.
(B) The difference between recognizing a word and knowing its definition.
(C) The difference between knowing a word and where it comes from.
(D) The difference between comprehending a word's definition and its manifold uses.

27. It can be inferred from the quote that W.N. Francis would agree with which of the following statements?

(A) The skills of curiosity and speculation should be taught in schools.
(B) Vocabulary instruction does not make us better users of English.
(C) It's a shame that expository prose does not make full use of the remarkable lexicon of English.
(D) English instruction sorely lacks skills of vocabulary acquisition.

28. The primary purpose of this passage is to:

(A) Discuss the origins of the English lexicon.
(B) Comment on the nature of English's shifting vocabulary.
(C) Suggest ways to preserve and expand the rich and varied English lexicon.
(D) Discuss English vocabulary development and use.

29. The main function of the eighth paragraph (lines 73-84) in relation to the passage as a whole is most likely to:

(A) Clarify the difference between two ideas that can be mistakenly conflated.
(B) Introduce a scientific concept into a mostly theoretical discussion.
(C) Link the seemingly disparate concepts of vocabulary use and maturity.
(D) Qualify an assertion in the previous paragraph.

30. Which of the following would W.N. Francis consider to be an "amateur connoisseur" (line 92)?

(A) The "lay public" who know little about the vast nature of the English lexicon
(B) Someone who wants to write for practical purposes only
(C) Someone who has an interest in learning more about the English language
(D) Someone who is the "master" of his or her "lexical stock"

Read this passage carefully and then answer the questions that follow.

Social Science: This passage describes a potential path for a nation.

The preliminary work of empire-building has been accomplished—territory has been conquered, peoples have been subjected, and a ruling class organized. The United States has developed a plutocracy—a property holding class, that is, to all intents and purposes, the imperialist class—controlling and directing public policy. This plutocratic class, having developed a high degree of class consciousness, and led by its bankers, is taking the fat of the land. The plutocrats are at the present moment busy disposing of their surplus in foreign countries. As they build their industrial empires, they broaden and deepen their power.

Now it remains for the rulers of America to accept the implications of imperialism—to thrill with the will to power; to recognize and strengthen imperial purpose; to sell imperialism to the American people—in other words to follow the call of manifest destiny and conquer the earth.

However, the plain people of the United States have no will to power at the present time. They know only the necessities of self-defense. They are only asking to be let alone, in order that they may go their several ways in peace. It is in the ambitions of the leisure classes that the demands of conquest have their origin. It is among them that men dream of world empire. Therefore it becomes necessary to surround imperial action with such an atmosphere as will convince the man on the street that the acts are necessary or else that they are inevitable.

The first step in the campaign to advertise and justify imperialism is the teaching of a blind my-country-right-or-wrong patriotism. The object of this teaching is to instill in the minds of the people, and particularly of the young, the principles of "America first." As twenty million children in the public schools of the United States pledge allegiance to the flag, they receive daily lessons in this first principle of popular support for imperial policy.

Having taken this first step and made the state supreme over the individual will and conscience, the imperial class makes its next move—for "national defense." The country is made to appear in constant danger from attack. Men are urged to protect their homes and their families. They are persuaded that the white dove of peace cannot rest securely on anything less than a great navy and army large enough to hold off aggressors. The same forces that are most eager to preach patriotism are the most anxious about national preparedness.

Meanwhile the plain people are taught to regard themselves and their civilization as superior to anything else on earth. Those who have a different language or a different color are referred to as "inferior peoples." The people of Panama cannot dig a canal, the people of Cuba cannot drive out yellow fever, the people of the Philippines cannot run a successful educational system, but the people of the United States can do all of these things—therefore they are justified in interfering in the internal affairs of Panama, Cuba and the Philippines.

One more step must be taken, and the process of imperializing public opinion is complete. The people are told that the imperialism to which they have been called is the work of "manifest destiny." This argument is employed by the strong as a blanket justification for acts of aggression against the weak. Each time that the United States has come face to face with the necessity of adding to its territory at the expense of some weak neighbor, the advocates of expansion have plied this argument with vigor and with uniform success.

Before the United States lies the open road of imperialism. Manifest destiny points the way in gestures that cannot be mistaken. Surplus is to be invested; investments are to be protected, American authority is to be respected. Therefore the American nation, under the urge of economic necessity; guided half-intelligently, half-instinctively by the plutocracy, is moving along the imperial highroad, and woe to the man that steps across the path that leads to their fulfillment. He who seeks to thwart imperial destiny will be branded as traitor to his country and as blasphemer against God.

31. The tone of the author can best be described as:

(A) Triumphant.
(B) Indignant.
(C) Infuriated.
(D) Informative.

32. When the author asserts that the "plutocratic class...is taking the fat of the land" (lines 8-10), he most likely means that:

(A) It is exploiting the natural resources of the United States.
(B) It is reaping the benefits of slave labor.
(C) It is profiting from the obesity in America.
(D) It is taking the property of Americans through violence.

33. As it is used in line 11, the phrase *disposing of* means:

(A) Dumping.
(B) Throwing away.
(C) Investing.
(D) Buying.

34. In the first paragraph, the author suggests that the American people:

(A) Are ruthless in their pursuit of power.
(B) Are ignorant about their role in the building of an empire.
(C) Are pleased that the promise of manifest destiny has come true.
(D) Are outraged by the acts of the United States.

35. The main problem for the "rulers of America" (line 14) is:

(A) Protecting their investments abroad.
(B) Conquering the nations of Panama, Cuba, and the Philippines.
(C) Keeping the peace by any means necessary.
(D) Convincing the American people that conquering the world is right.

36. Why don't the American people have a "will to power" (line 21)?

(A) They are only concerned with national defense.
(B) They are not part of the leisure class that demands conquest.
(C) They prefer to be isolationist in matters of foreign policy.
(D) They demand world peace rather than conquest.

37. What is ironic about the author's assertion that "the white dove of peace cannot rest securely on anything less than a great navy and army large enough to hold off aggressors" (lines 47-49)?

(A) The image of a white dove on a navy ship is comical.
(B) The navy and army of the United States will never be large enough to hold off aggressors.
(C) Aggressors to the United States do not want peace.
(D) The idea of peace is used to justify the building of armies and the conquering of peoples.

38. According to the passage, all of the following are strategies that the ruling class uses to justify imperialism to the American people EXCEPT:

(A) Empowering Americans to recognize their duty to help the people of nearby countries.
(B) Using public schools to teach that the nation is more important than the individual.
(C) Using fear to influence public opinion on issues of national defense.
(D) Convincing the American people that they are culturally better than others.

39. The author says, "He who seeks to thwart imperial destiny will be branded as traitor to his country and as blasphemer against God" (lines 84-86) to:

(A) Reinforce the idea that imperialism is a historical inevitability.
(B) Advise the reader on religious grounds not to act against manifest destiny.
(C) Suggest how complete the imperialist class' control is over public opinion.
(D) Urge the reader to act.

40. The passage can be best described as:

(A) A rally cry for the American people to exercise the will of manifest destiny.
(B) A catalog of wrongs that Americans have perpetrated against the world.
(C) A justification for the expansion of territorial control by the United States.
(D) A warning to the American people about the intentions of a small class of people.

Read this passage carefully and then answer the questions that follow.

Social Science: This passage contains a letter of historical importance.

TO DAVID HARTLEY, MEMBER OF PARLIAMENT.

Passy, October 14th, 1777.

Dear Sir,

Happy should I have been, if the honest warnings I gave, of the fatal separation of interests as well as of affections, had been attended to, and the horrid mischief of this abominable war been thereby prevented. I should still be happy in any successful endeavors for restoring peace, consistent with the liberties, the safety, and the honor of America. As to our submitting to the government of Great Britain, it is vain to think of it. She has given us, by her numberless barbarities, in the prosecution of the war, and in the treatment of the prisoners, so deep an impression of her depravity, that we never again can trust her in the management of our affairs and interests.

It is now impossible to persuade our people that the war was merely ministerial, and that the nation bore still a good will to us. The infinite number of addresses printed in your gazettes, all approving the conduct of your government towards us, and encouraging our destruction by every possible means, the great majority in Parliament constantly manifesting the same sentiments, together with the recommendations of the same measures by even your celebrated moralists, all join in convincing us, that you are no longer the magnanimous enlightened nation we once esteemed you, and that you are unfit and unworthy to govern us.

But, as I have said, I should be nevertheless happy in seeing peace restored. This wish of mine, ineffective as it may be, induces me to mention to you, that between nations long exasperated against each other in war, some act of generosity and kindness towards prisoners on one side has softened resentment, and abated animosity on the other, so as to bring on an accommodation. You in England, if you wish for peace, have at present the opportunity of trying this means with regard to the prisoners now in your jails. They complain of very severe treatment. They are far from their friends and families, and winter is coming on, in which they must suffer extremely, if continued in their present situation; fed scantily on bad provisions, without warm lodging, clothes, or fire, and not suffered to invite or receive visits from their friends, or even from the humane and charitable of their enemies.

I can assure you, from my own certain knowledge, that your people, prisoners in America, have been treated with great kindness; they have been served with the same rations of wholesome provisions with our own troops, comfortable lodgings have been provided for them, and they have been allowed large bounds of villages in the healthy air, to walk and amuse themselves with on their parole.

Some considerable act of kindness towards our people would take off the reproach of inhumanity from the nation, and leave it where it ought with more certainty to lay, on the conductors of your war in America. This I hint to you, out of some remaining good will to a nation I once loved sincerely. But as things are, I shall content myself with proposing, that your government would allow us to send or employ a commissary to take some care of those unfortunate people. Perhaps on your representations this might speedily be obtained in England, though it was refused most inhumanly at New York.

If you cannot obtain for us permission to send a commissary, possibly you may find a trusty, humane, discreet person at Plymouth, and another at Portsmouth, who would undertake to communicate what relief we may be able to afford those unfortunate men, martyrs to the cause of liberty. Your king will not reward you for taking this trouble, but God will. I shall not mention the gratitude of America; you will have what is better, the applause of your own good conscience.

In revising what I have written, I found too much warmth in it, and was about to strike out some parts. Yet I let them go, as they will afford you this one reflection; "If a man naturally cool is so warmed by our treatment of his country, how much must those people in general be exasperated against us? And why are we making inveterate enemies by our barbarity, not only of the present inhabitants of a great country, but of their infinitely more numerous posterity; who will in future ages detest the name of Englishman, as much as the children in Holland now do those of Alva and Spaniard." This will certainly happen, unless your conduct is speedily changed, and the national resentment falls, where it ought to fall heavily, on your ministry, or perhaps rather on the king, whose will they only execute.

With the greatest esteem and affection, and best wishes for your prosperity,

B. FRANKLIN.

41. In the first paragraph, the author asserts all of the following EXCEPT:

(A) He is willing to work for peace as long as the United States' independence is not questioned.
(B) He is surprised and saddened by the war between Great Britain and the United States.
(C) Great Britain has proven to be a depraved country.
(D) The war has led to a dissolution of both practical and friendly relations.

42. As it is used in line 16, the word *prosecution* means:

(A) Executing legal action.
(B) Oppressing or harassing.
(C) Carrying out something begun.
(D) Inciting.

43. All of the following are reasons for which Great Britain cannot be trusted in the governance of the United States EXCEPT:

(A) Great Britain's celebrated moralists approving of the conduct of the government.
(B) Great Britain's treatment of prisoners of war.
(C) Newspapers and pubic media condemning the destruction of the United States.
(D) Members of Parliament calling for the demolition of the United States.

44. The main purpose of paragraphs 3-5 is to:

(A) Compare and contrast the treatment of prisoners of war in the United States and Great Britain.
(B) Claim that the United States has the higher ground in requesting a particular course of action.
(C) Point out that Great Britain has refused the United States' petition on one occasion, and that this has increased anti-British sentiments.
(D) Make a general comment about actions of good will between nations and then suggest a particular course of action.

45. Why will Franklin "not mention the gratitude of America" (lines 82-84)?

(A) Hartley should take for granted that Americans will be thankful to him.
(B) Americans will never know what deal was made between the two men.
(C) The topic of gratitude is not at issue in the letter.
(D) Americans will not thank Hartley for what he has done.

46. As it is used in line 79 the word *afford* means:

(A) Have the means to buy.
(B) Provide.
(C) Manage to spare.
(D) Give the benefit of.

47. In the last paragraph, "resentment...ought to fall heavily...on your ministry, or perhaps rather on the king, whose will they only execute" (lines 99- 101) is an expression of belief that:

(A) Government officials in a monarchy may not always agree with the king they serve.
(B) Americans should resent only the ruling authority rather than any of its subjects.
(C) The king of Great Britain will eventually murder those who disagree with him.
(D) One should not hold a grudge against the messenger who brings bad news.

48. The main function of the last paragraph in relation to the passage as a whole is most likely to:

(A) Attempt to soften the writer's harsh rhetoric.
(B) Compare America's plight with that of Holland.
(C) Warn the receiver of the letter of what will happen if he does not heed the writer.
(D) Condemn the king of England.

49. The author's tone in this letter can be best described as:

(A) Gracious but firm.
(B) Aggressive but diplomatic.
(C) Dreamy but intellectual.
(D) Pleading but insistent.

50. When Franklin says, "If a man naturally cool is so warmed by our treatment of his country, how much must those people in general be exasperated by us?" (lines 88-91) he is referring to the idea that:

(A) Hartley should be warmed emotionally by Franklin's honesty and friendliness.
(B) Hartley should be annoyed by the treatment of the United States by Great Britain.
(C) Franklin is warmed emotionally by the opportunity to speak openly with Hartley.
(D) Franklin has been incensed by Great Britain's actions against the United States.

rP6: NATURAL SCIENCE PASSAGES

TOPIC OVERVIEW

The fourth passage on the ACT Reading Test is the Natural Science passage. The Natural Science passages share many characteristics with the other passages:

- The mixture of fact finding, main idea, conclusion, and literary analysis questions is balanced.
- Usually, slightly less than half of the questions will contain line or paragraph references.
- No background knowledge of the subject matter is required to answer the questions.

The Natural Science passages also differ from the other passages in a few important ways:

- The passage will often describe either the viewpoint of one scientist or multiple conflicting viewpoints. It may also provide a general overview of a certain topic.
- Compared to questions of other passage types, the questions are more likely to require you to match specific viewpoints to specific people.

Because of this, while reading the Natural Science passage you should pay special attention to the author's specific topic and discover how the research or opinion of each scientist mentioned relates to that topic. To focus on these topics, underline names of researchers and the researchers' opinions and discoveries. You may also find it helpful to include names of scientists in your margin summaries. Also, be sure to read the introduction to the passage, as it will often contain helpful information.

Frequently, the author of Natural Science passages will have a neutral tone and deal mostly in facts rather than presenting his or her own opinions. Most often, the author doesn't hold a certain opinion, but may present the opinions of other scientists (usually referenced by name in the passage). The author's job is usually to frame the discussion and provide facts and context.

NATURAL SCIENCE PASSAGE STRUCTURE

The purpose of a Natural Science passage is to communicate an idea related to the sciences (biology, astronomy, chemistry, physics, etc.). The author will either try to describe the idea in a clear manner or show that scientists disagree about the idea.

Because most Natural Science passages are written to achieve one of these two goals, the passages can only be written in a small number of structures. The two most common structures are the Idea/Explanation structure and the Point/Counterpoint structure.

An **Idea/Explanation** passage describes one concept, phenomenon, or body of research in great detail. An Idea/Explanation passage will often only describe one or two researchers; if it mentions additional scientists, their work will support the main idea of the passage. In Idea/Explanation passages it is more important to focus on general concepts than on names.

A **Point/Counterpoint** passage describes the debate over one concept, phenomenon, or body of research. It will begin with the point of view of one scientist or group and then offer the opinions of disagreeing scientists or groups. Point/Counterpoint passages often contain a large number of names, and it is important to take note of which name belongs with each point. Many Point/Counterpoint passages deal with astronomy, physics, and similar topics.

The second or third paragraph can usually tell you which type of Natural Science passage you are reading. If these paragraphs seem to contain points contrary to points raised in the first paragraph, it is most likely a Point/Counterpoint passage. Otherwise, it is most likely an Idea/Explanation passage.

In summary, when reading a Natural Science passage you should:

- Learn the specific topic of the passage.
- Determine how each scientist or idea mentioned relates to the specific topic.
- Use the second or third paragraph to determine whether you are reading an Idea/Explanation passage (one idea with support) or a Point/Counterpoint passage (conflicting viewpoints).

Remember:

- If you are reading an Idea/Explanation passage, focus more on ideas than names.
- If you are reading a Point/Counterpoint passage, focus more on names.
- If you are reading an Other passage, focus more on the details of the passage.

Read this passage carefully and then answer the questions that follow.

Natural Science: This passage discusses a major astronomical event.

The only major impact of a celestial object on the Earth recorded in modern history occurred about a quarter after seven on the morning of June 30, 1908, when witnesses observed a huge fireball almost as bright as the Sun plunging across the Siberian sky, terminating in a huge explosion that registered on seismic stations all across Eurasia.

Surprisingly, there was little scientific curiosity about the impact at the time, and due to the subsequent occurrence of war, revolution, and civil war in Russia, it wasn't until the 1920s that anyone performed a serious investigation of what had happened in Siberia in 1908. In 1921, the Russian mineralogist Leonid Kulik visited the Podkamennay Tunguska River basin as part of a survey for the Soviet Academy of Sciences. Locals told him of the great blast, of huge stretches of forest being flattened, of people being blown over by the shock.

The reports were basically consistent with each other, and Kulik was able to persuade the Soviet government to fund an expedition to the Tunguska region. His group reached the "ground zero" of the "event" in 1927. Much to their surprise, there was no crater, just a great region of scorched trees about 50 kilometers across. The trees pointed away from the center of the event, with a few still bizarrely standing upright at ground zero, their branches and bark stripped off.

Expeditions sent to the area in the 1950s and 1960s did find microscopic glass spheres in siftings of the soil. Chemical analysis showed that the spheres contained high proportions of nickel and iridium, which are found in high concentrations in meteorites, indicating extraterrestrial origin. However, even this clue could not pin down the nature of the object precisely.

In 1930, the British astronomer F.J.W. Whipple suggested that the Tunguska event was the impact of a small comet, which vaporized itself in the explosion and left no obvious trace. Comets have traditionally been seen as "dirty snowballs" of ice and dust; modern examination by space probes has shown them to be more dust than ice, suggesting that the name "snowy dirtball" would be more appropriate, and also that they are low-density objects, full of voids, with one astronomer calling them "cosmic dust bunnies." A comet would be quickly destroyed by an impact with the Earth's atmosphere. The idea of a comet impact was reinforced by the fact that there were "skyglows" in the evenings across Europe for several days after the impact, obviously caused by dust dispersed through the upper atmosphere.

The comet idea remained popular for over 50 years, with some astronomers speculating that it might have been a piece of the short-period comet Encke. Materials from Encke apparently make up the stream of sky junk that create the "Beta Perseid" meteor shower, and the Tunguska event coincided with a peak in that shower. However, in 1983 an astronomer named Zdenek Sekanina, of the US National Aeronautics & Space Administration's Jet Propulsion Laboratory (NASA JPL), published an article that undermined the comet theory. Sekanina pointed out that eyewitness accounts and other evidence point only to one explosion, and that the object passed through the atmosphere at a shallow angle, remaining intact to an altitude of 8.5 kilometers. A dirty snowball of ice and gases would have not got that far in one piece.

Sekanina proposed that the object was a stony "chondritic" asteroid that rammed through the atmosphere until pressures and temperatures reached a point that caused it to abruptly disintegrate in a huge explosion, something like what would happen on a much smaller scale to an aspirin pill smashed with a hammer. The destruction was so complete that no remnants of substantial size survived. The material scattered into the upper atmosphere from the event would have caused the skyglows.

Sekanina's theory was appealing, but it was based on very limited information. Said one critic: "You can't make a sophisticated model from poor data." Sekanina admitted there was "a lot of handwaving" in his ideas. The comet theory still has its partisans, who point out that chemical analyses of the area have showed it to be enriched in cometary material, and suggest that the comet might have been extinct and had formed a tough "mantle" that allowed it to penetrate the atmosphere. In the absence of conclusive evidence the debate seems likely to continue, but at least nobody is seriously suggesting it was a UFO any more.

1. Which of the following does the author NOT suggest as a possible case of the Tunguska event?

   (A) A chondritic asteroid
   (B) A comet
   (C) A chemical reaction
   (D) A meteor

2. The phrase "ground zero" (line 23) is meant to denote:

(A) The point of impact.
(B) The center of the crater.
(C) The point with the most flattened trees.
(D) The point in time of the detonation.

3. Which of the following, if true, would most undermine the theory that the Tunguska area was hit by a chondritic asteroid?

(A) Scientists discover that a comet will likely hit the same area once every 225 years.
(B) Scientists realize that the trees that had been knocked down generally regenerate every 30 years.
(C) Scientists find that the atmospheric composition of the time had been unaltered by the event.
(D) Scientists discover a pattern along the edge of the valley consistent with a small crater.

4. According to the passage, the conclusion that the fireball was caused by a comet is based on:

(A) The lack of a crater.
(B) The chemical analysis of the surrounding soil.
(C) The lack of tremors following the event.
(D) The destruction of the trees at "ground zero."

5. Which of the following does the author suggest as a possible cause of the skyglow?

(A) The continued presence of unidentified flying objects
(B) The particular, longstanding elements in the local atmosphere
(C) Heat emanating from the site of the impact
(D) Comet dust in the atmosphere

6. Which of the following best describes the author's tone in this passage?

(A) Excited and accepting
(B) Skeptical and objective
(C) Cynical and personal
(D) Cathartic and heartfelt

7. The passage suggests that the Podkamennay Tunguska River basin is:

(A) Close to the North Pole.
(B) Moderately populated.
(C) A focal point for the Russian Revolution.
(D) Remote.

8. As used in line 27, the word *bizarrely* most nearly means:

(A) Eccentrically.
(B) Fantastically.
(C) Unexpectedly.
(D) Extravagantly.

9. The passage suggests that the event could not have been caused by a comet because of:

(A) F.J.W. Whipple's faulty scientific credentials.
(B) The fact that the surrounding soil contained too much nickel and iridium.
(C) The entry angle of the fireball.
(D) The lack of reproducible experiments.

10. The reader can infer that:

(A) Meteorites leave telltale signs when they impact the Earth.
(B) The number of seismic stations in Europe was minimal in 1908.
(C) Scientists had minimal financial backing from the post-revolutionary government in Russia.
(D) UFOs had been a plausible scientific explanation of the event in Siberia.

Read this passage carefully and then answer the questions that follow.

Natural Science: This passage presents a vision of scientific history.

The story of Robinson Crusoe is an allegory of human history. Man is a castaway upon a desert planet, isolated from other inhabited worlds—if there be any such—by millions of miles of untraversable space. He is absolutely dependent upon his own exertions, for this world of his, as Wells says, has no imports except meteorites and no exports of any kind. Man has no wrecked ship from a former civilization to draw upon for tools and weapons, but must utilize as best he may such raw materials as he can find. In this conquest of nature by man there are three stages distinguishable: The Appropriative Period, The Adaptive Period, and The Creative Period.

These eras overlap, and the human race, or rather its vanguard, civilized man, may be passing into the third stage in one field of human endeavor while still lingering in the second or first in some other respect. But in any particular line this sequence is followed. The primitive man picks up whatever he can find available for his use. His successor in the next stage of culture shapes and develops this crude instrument until it becomes more suitable for his purpose. But in the course of time man often finds that he can make something new which is better than anything in nature or naturally produced. The savage discovers. The barbarian improves. The civilized man invents. The first finds. The second fashions. The third fabricates.

The primitive man was a troglodyte. He sought shelter in any cave or crevice that he could find. Later he dug it out to make it more roomy and piled up stones at the entrance to keep out the wild beasts. This artificial barricade, this false façade, was gradually extended and solidified until finally man could build a cave for himself anywhere in the open field from stones he quarried out of the hill. But man was not content with such materials and now puts up a building which may be composed of steel, brick, terra cotta, glass, concrete and plaster, none of which materials are to be found in nature.

The first idol was doubtless a meteorite fallen from heaven or a fulgurite or concretion picked up from the sand, bearing some slight resemblance to a human being. Later man made gods in his own image, and so sculpture and painting grew until now the creations of futuristic art could be worshiped—if one wanted to—without violation of the second commandment, for they are not the likeness of anything that is in heaven above or that is in the earth beneath or that is in the water under the earth.

In the textile industry the same development is observable. The primitive man used the skins of animals he had slain to protect his own skin. In the course of time he—or more probably his wife, for it is to the women rather than to the men that we owe the early steps in the arts and sciences—fastened leaves together or pounded out bark to make garments. Later fibers were plucked from the sheepskin, the cocoon and the cotton-ball, twisted together and woven into cloth. Nowadays it is possible to make a complete suit of clothes, from hat to shoes, of any desirable texture, form and color, and not include any substance to be found in nature. The first metals available were those found free in nature such as gold and copper. In a later age it was found possible to extract iron from its ores and today we have artificial alloys made of multifarious combinations of rare metals. The medicine man dosed his patients with decoctions of such roots and herbs as had a bad taste or queer look. The pharmacist discovered how to extract from these their medicinal principle such as morphine, quinine and cocaine, and the creative chemist has discovered how to make innumerable drugs adapted to specific diseases and individual idiosyncrasies.

In the later or creative stages we enter the domain of chemistry, for it is the chemist alone who possesses the power of reducing a substance to its constituent atoms and from them producing substances entirely new. But the chemist has been slow to realize his unique power and the world has been still slower to utilize his invaluable services. Until recently indeed the leaders of chemical science expressly disclaimed what should have been their proudest boast. The French chemist Lavoisier in 1793 defined chemistry as "the science of analysis." The German chemist Gerhardt in 1844 said: "I have demonstrated that the chemist works in opposition to living nature, that he burns, destroys, analyzes, that the vital force alone operates by synthesis, that it reconstructs the edifice torn down by the chemical forces."

11. In this passage, the chemist represents:

(A) A textile manufacturer.
(B) A harbinger of the Appropriative Period.
(C) A false idol that replaces religion.
(D) Humanity’s attempt to subdue nature.

12. The author cites the textile industry to suggest:

    (A) That a retreat to the basics is called for.
    (B) A progression from primitive religion.
    (C) An example of three stages of human development.
    (D) That using metals is the next stage in developing clothing.

13. It can be reasonably inferred that Robinson Crusoe:

    (A) Is a peerless chemist.
    (B) Relies upon tools from a remote civilization to survive.
    (C) Is isolated from the rest of humanity.
    (D) Studies astronomy in a remote place.

14. According to the passage, the Adaptive Period marks:

    (A) A struggle.
    (B) A pinnacle.
    (C) Refinement.
    (D) Rudimentary existence.

15. According to the passage, humanity strives to:

    (A) Overcome the limits of nature.
    (B) Live in harmony with nature.
    (C) Make religion and nature exist in harmony.
    (D) Discover using deduction, not intuition.

16. How is the chemist like the civilized man?

    (A) Both seek to transcend current possibilities.
    (B) Both seek to ignore previous discoveries in searching for new knowledge.
    (C) Both rely on discovering raw materials for human use.
    (D) Both refine the discoveries of the past.

17. As it is used in the passage, the word *fashions* (line 29) most nearly means:

    (A) Edit.
    (B) Forms.
    (C) Conforms.
    (D) Tailors.

18. The second commandment (line 50) most likely involves:

    (A) The right to envision the divine in any way possible.
    (B) Ignoring cosmic influences in favor of the divine.
    (C) Choosing to worship multiple gods.
    (D) Creating idols representing natural, divine forces.

19. The pharmacist is to the chemist as the:

    (A) Bird is to the nest.
    (B) Idea is to the execution.
    (C) Hard drive is to the computer.
    (D) Architect is to the builder.

20. The author mostly likely views "nature" (line 12) as:

    (A) A limit that must be respected.
    (B) A boundary that must be surpassed.
    (C) An object of worship.
    (D) A blueprint for invention.

Read this passage carefully and then answer the questions that follow.

Natural Science: This passage discusses the range and effects of atomic weapons.

In nuclear explosions, about 90 percent of the energy is released in less than one millionth of a second. Most of this is in the form of the heat and shock waves which produce the damage. It is this immediate and direct explosive power which could devastate the urban centers in a major nuclear war.

Compared with the immediate colossal destruction suffered in target areas, the more subtle, longer term effects of the remaining 10 percent of the energy released by nuclear weapons might seem a matter of secondary concern. But the dimensions of the initial catastrophe should not overshadow the after-effects of a nuclear war. They would be global, affecting nations remote from the fighting for many years after the holocaust, because of the way nuclear explosions behave in the atmosphere and the radioactive products released by nuclear bursts.

When a weapon is detonated at the surface of the earth or at low altitudes, the heat pulse vaporizes the bomb material, target, nearby structures, and underlying soil and rock, all of which become entrained in an expanding, fast-rising fireball. As the fireball rises, it expands and cools, producing the distinctive mushroom cloud, signature of nuclear explosions.

The altitude reached by the cloud depends on the force of the explosion. When yields are in the low-kiloton range, the cloud will remain in the lower atmosphere and its effects will be entirely local. But as yields exceed 30 kilotons, part of the cloud will punch into the stratosphere, which begins about 7 miles up. With yields of 2-5 megatons or more, virtually all of the cloud of radioactive debris and fine dust will climb into the stratosphere. The heavier materials reaching the lower edge of the stratosphere will soon settle out, as did the Castle/Bravo fallout at Rongelap. But the lighter particles will penetrate high into the stratosphere, to altitudes of 12 miles and more, and remain there for months and even years. Stratospheric circulation and diffusion will spread this material around the world.

Both the local and worldwide fallout hazards of nuclear explosions depend on a variety of interacting factors: weapon design, explosive force, altitude and latitude of detonation, time of year, and local weather conditions.

All present nuclear weapon designs require the splitting of heavy elements like uranium and plutonium. The energy released in this fission process is many millions of times greater, pound for pound, than the most energetic chemical reactions. The smaller nuclear weapon, in the low-kiloton range, may rely solely on the energy released by the fission process, as did the first bombs which devastated Hiroshima and Nagasaki in 1945. The larger yield nuclear weapons derive a substantial part of their explosive force from the fusion of heavy forms of hydrogen--deuterium and tritium. Since there is virtually no limitation on the volume of fusion materials in a weapon, and the materials are less costly than fissionable materials, the fusion, "thermonuclear," or "hydrogen" bomb brought a radical increase in the explosive power of weapons. However, the fission process is still necessary to achieve the high temperatures and pressures needed to trigger the hydrogen fusion reactions. Thus, all nuclear detonations produce radioactive fragments of heavy elements fission, with the larger bursts producing an additional radiation component from the fusion process.

The nuclear fragments of heavy-element fission which are of greatest concern are those radioactive atoms (also called radionuclides) which decay by emitting energetic electrons or gamma particles. An important characteristic here is the rate of decay. This is measured in terms of "half-life"--the time required for one-half of the original substance to decay--which ranges from days to thousands of years for the bomb-produced radionuclides of principal interest. Another factor which is critical in determining the hazard of radionuclides is the chemistry of the atoms. This determines whether they will be taken up by the body through respiration or the food cycle and incorporated into tissue. If this occurs, the risk of damage from the destructive ionizing increases.

Three types of radiation damage may occur: bodily damage (mainly leukemia and cancers of the thyroid, lung, breast, bone, and gastrointestinal tract); genetic damage (birth defects and constitutional and degenerative diseases due to gonodal damage suffered by parents); and development and growth damage (primarily growth and mental retardation of unborn infants and young children). Since heavy radiation doses of about 20 roentgen or more are necessary to produce developmental defects, these effects would probably be confined to areas of heavy local fallout in the nuclear combatant nations and would not become a global problem.

21. Radiation affects:

(A) Child development around the world.
(B) Developing minds of unborn children.
(C) Only specific areas of the body.
(D) Primarily unborn babies.

22. The main idea of this passage is that:

    (A) Long-term effects of nuclear war pale in comparison to the short term disasters.
    (B) Heavy elements, combined with isotopes of hydrogen, make for more destructive nuclear weapons.
    (C) Nuclear fallout has far-reaching effects.
    (D) Long-term effects of nuclear war can be mitigated by intelligent construction of weapons.

23. The passage says that all nuclear weapons depend on:

    (A) A combination of fission and fusion.
    (B) Fusion of hydrogen atoms.
    (C) A component of deuterium and tritium.
    (D) Splitting heavy elements.

24. The passage indicates that heavy particles from a nuclear explosion are distributed across the world via:

    (A) The stratosphere.
    (B) Ocean currents.
    (C) The mushroom cloud.
    (D) The lower atmosphere.

25. The passage suggests that the devices most responsible for wide-ranging distribution of nuclear particles are:

    (A) Those that carry at least 5 kilotons of explosive power.
    (B) Those that use hydrogen as a explosive element.
    (C) Those that are localized.
    (D) Those that use only fusion to detonate.

26. The passage suggests that which of the following is true?

    (A) The long-term effects of a nuclear attack have greater impacts than do the short-term effects.
    (B) Hydrogen is the most destructive force known to humans.
    (C) Nations can minimize the aftereffects of a nuclear attack through intelligent deployment of resources.
    (D) All countries should be concerned about a nuclear attack, even those attacks that occur in remote locations.

27. As used in line 26, the word *signature* most nearly means:

    (A) Tremendous.
    (B) Signed.
    (C) Telltale.
    (D) Endorsed.

28. The author's claims in the first paragraph serve primarily to:

    (A) Note a cause of overwhelming destruction.
    (B) Inspire fear and action in the reader.
    (C) Set a dramatic tone.
    (D) Set up a counterpoint.

29. Which of the following is NOT listed as a cause of potential harm to humans after a nuclear attack?

    (A) The composition of specific nuclear particles
    (B) The level of radiation
    (C) The physiology of the victims of radiation
    (D) Atoms with specific half lives

30. The author suggests that which of the following is the cause of long-term danger following a nuclear explosion?

    (A) Exposure to heavy particles
    (B) Exposure to ionized hydrogen
    (C) A potential nuclear retaliation
    (D) An increased risk of global warming

Read this passage carefully and then answer the questions that follow.

Natural Science: This passage discusses challenges facing researchers in genetics.

Imagine you're in a car driving down the highway to visit an old friend who has just moved to Los Angeles. Your favorite tunes are playing on the radio, and you haven't a care in the world. You stop to check your maps and realize that all you have are interstate highway maps—not a single street map of the area. How will you ever find your friend's house? It's going to be difficult, but eventually, you may stumble across the right house.

This scenario is similar to the situation facing scientists searching for a specific gene somewhere within the vast human genome. They have available to them two broad categories of maps: genetic maps and physical maps. Both genetic and physical maps provide the likely order of items along a chromosome. However, a genetic map, like an interstate highway map, provides an indirect estimate of the distance between two items and is limited to ordering certain items. One could say that genetic maps serve to guide a scientist toward a gene, just like an interstate map guides a driver from city to city. On the other hand, physical maps mark an estimate of the true distance, in measurements called base pairs, between items of interest. To continue our analogy, physical maps would then be similar to street maps, where the distance between two sites of interest may be defined more precisely in terms of city blocks or street addresses. Physical maps, therefore, allow a scientist to more easily home in on the location of a gene. An appreciation of how each of these maps is constructed may be helpful in understanding how scientists use these maps to traverse that genetic highway commonly referred to as the "human genome."

Just like interstate maps have cities and towns that serve as landmarks, genetic maps have landmarks known as genetic markers, or "markers" for short. The term marker is used very broadly to describe any observable variation that results from an alteration, or mutation, at a single genetic locus. A marker may be used as one landmark on a map if, in most cases, that stretch of DNA is inherited from parent to child according to the standard rules of inheritance. Markers can be within genes that code for a noticeable physical characteristic such as eye color, or a not so noticeable trait such as a disease. DNA-based reagents can also serve as markers. These types of markers are found within the non-coding regions of genes and are used to detect unique regions on a chromosome. DNA markers are especially useful for generating genetic maps when there are occasional, predictable mutations that occur during meiosis—the formation of gametes such as egg and sperm—that, over many generations, lead to a high degree of variability in the DNA content of the marker from individual to individual.

Early geneticists recognized that genes are located on chromosomes and believed that each individual chromosome was inherited as an intact unit. They hypothesized that if two genes were located on the same chromosome, they were physically linked together and were inherited together. We now know that this is not always the case. Studies conducted around 1910 demonstrated that very few pairs of genes displayed complete linkage. Pairs of genes were either inherited independently or displayed partial linkage—that is, they were inherited together sometimes, but not always.

During meiosis—the process whereby gametes (eggs and sperm) are produced— two copies of each chromosome pair become physically close. The chromosome arms can then undergo breakage and exchange segments of DNA, a process referred to as recombination or crossing-over. If recombination occurs, each chromosome found in the gamete will consist of a "mixture" of material from both members of the chromosome pair. Thus, recombination events directly affect the inheritance pattern of those genes involved.

Because one cannot physically see crossover events, it is difficult to determine with any degree of certainty how many crossovers have actually occurred. But, using the phenomenon of co-segregation of alleles of nearby markers, researchers can reverse-engineer meiosis and identify markers that lie close to each other. Then, using a statistical technique called genetic linkage analysis, researchers can infer a likely crossover pattern, and from that an order of the markers involved. Researchers can also infer an estimate for the probability that a recombination occurs between each pair of markers.

31. As used in line 41, the word *locus* means:

(A) Heart.
(B) Axis.
(C) Capital.
(D) Nexus.

32. How does the passage compare genetic maps to interstate highway maps?

    (A) The author suggests that genetic maps mark precise distances.
    (B) The author suggests that genetic maps provide a general sense of location.
    (C) The author suggests that genetic maps are appropriate for uses within the human physiology.
    (D) The author suggests that genetic maps are easier to follow than physical maps.

33. Street maps function most like which of the following?

    (A) DNA-based reagents
    (B) Meiosis
    (C) Chromosomes
    (D) Genetic linkage analysis

34. How is the driver mentioned in the first paragraph similar to the researchers mentioned in the last paragraph?

    (A) Both use statistics to determine the relevance of their course.
    (B) Both use reason to reach a conclusion.
    (C) Both are enthusiastic about their tasks.
    (D) Both have imprecise directions.

35. Genetic markers:

    (A) Indicate unpredictable locations within the genome.
    (B) Indicate variation.
    (C) Add little to the map of the genome.
    (D) Always indicate a specific, observable trait.

36. The passage indicates that chromosomes:

    (A) Are located within genes.
    (B) Contain genetic markers that can be used to locate specific places within each chromosome.
    (C) Never contain any linkage to other chromosomes.
    (D) Are inherited as intact units.

37. The passage suggests that meiosis:

    (A) Plays a role in producing cells.
    (B) Keeps DNA sequences separate from one another.
    (C) Has no effect on pairing chromosomes.
    (D) Results in recombination.

38. The passage suggests that physical maps of the human genome are:

    (A) Inferred.
    (B) Identical.
    (C) Impossible.
    (D) Crude.

39. As used in line 31, the word *appreciation* most nearly means:

    (A) Catharsis.
    (B) Development.
    (C) Understanding.
    (D) Esteem.

40. The passage suggests that prior to 1910, researchers:

    (A) Believed that genes exhibited partial linkage.
    (B) Had no idea that the human genome could be mapped.
    (C) Had imprecise instruments with which to work.
    (D) Believed that pairs of genes within a chromosome were linked.

Read this passage carefully and then answer the questions that follow.

Natural Science: This passage discusses the composition of parts of the Earth.

Of what materials is the earth composed, and in what manner are these materials arranged? These are the first inquiries with which Geology is occupied, a science which derives its name from the Greek ge, the earth, and logos, a discourse. Previously we might have imagined that investigations of this kind would relate exclusively to the mineral kingdom, and to the various rocks, soils, and metals which occur upon the surface of the earth or at various depths beneath it. But, in pursuing such researches, we soon find ourselves led on to consider the successive changes which have taken place in the former state of the earth's surface and interior, and the causes which have given rise to these changes; and, what is still more singular and unexpected, we soon become engaged in researches into the history of the animate creation, or of the various tribes of animals and plants which have, at different periods of the past, inhabited the globe.

All are aware that the solid parts of the earth consist of distinct substances, such as clay, chalk, sand, limestone, coal, slate, granite, and the like; previous to observation it was commonly imagined that all these had remained from the first in the state in which we now see them— that they were created in their present form, and in their present position. The geologist soon comes to a different conclusion, discovering proof that the external parts of the earth were not all produced in the beginning of things in the state in which we now behold them, nor in an instant of time. On the contrary, he can show that they have acquired their actual configuration and condition gradually, under a great variety of circumstances, and at successive periods, during each of which distinct races of living beings have flourished on the land and in the waters, the remains of these creatures still lying buried in the crust of the earth.

The "earth's crust" refers to that small portion of the exterior of our planet which is accessible to human observation. It comprises not merely all of which the structure is laid open in mountain precipices, or in cliffs overhanging a river or the sea, or whatever the miner may reveal in artificial excavations, but the whole of that outer covering of the planet on which we are enabled to reason by observations made at or near the surface. These reasonings may extend to a depth of several miles, perhaps ten miles, and even then it may be said that such a thickness is no more than 1/400 part of the distance from the surface to the centre. The remark is just, but although the dimensions of such a crust are, in truth, insignificant when compared to the entire globe, yet they are vast, and of magnificent extent in relation to man, and to the organic beings which people our globe. Referring to this standard of magnitude, the geologist may admire the ample limits of his domain, and admit, at the same time, that not only the exterior of the planet, but the entire earth, is but an atom in the midst of the countless worlds surveyed by the astronomer.

The materials of this crust are not thrown together confusedly, but distinct mineral masses, called rocks, are found to occupy definite spaces, and to exhibit a certain order of arrangement. The term ROCK is applied indifferently by geologists to all these substances, whether they be soft or stony, for clay and sand are included in the term, and some have even brought peat under this denomination. Our old writers endeavoured to avoid offering such violence to our language, by speaking of the component materials of the earth as consisting of rocks and SOILS. But there is often so insensible a passage from a soft and incoherent state to that of stone, that geologists of all countries have found it indispensable to have one technical term to include both, and in this sense we find ROCHE applied in French, ROCCA in Italian, and FELSART in German. The beginner, however, must constantly bear in mind that the term rock by no means implies that a mineral mass is in an indurated or stony condition.

41. The most appropriate title for this passage would be:

(A) “Geology: A Blip on the Cosmic Radar”
(B) “The Crust’s Vast Scope”
(C) “Geology: The Evolving Composition”
(D) “Earth as a Singular Rock”

42. The passage includes the words *ROCHE*, *ROCCA*, and *FELSTART* in the final paragraph in order to:

(A) Suggest a collaborative approach to classification.
(B) Stress the differences of a term’s interpretation.
(C) Stress the universality of a term.
(D) Stress the most important element of a science.

43. In paragraph 1, the passage cites the Greek origin of the word *Geology* in order to:

    (A) Suggest a fundamental definition of the term.
    (B) Stress that the Greeks invented and perfected the art of discourse.
    (C) Pay homage to the civilization most central to the foundation of a science.
    (D) Note the varied species that occupy and occupied a country.

44. The passage suggests that the Earth's crust is:

    (A) Comparable in scope to the rest of the planet.
    (B) The most dynamic area in the world.
    (C) Less worthy of study than the work of the astronomer.
    (D) Cosmically small, but central to humanity.

45. The passage suggests that the Earth's configuration is:

    (A) Mutable.
    (B) Subjective.
    (C) Static.
    (D) Controversial.

46. As used in line 18, the word *animate* most nearly means:

    (A) Energetic.
    (B) Living.
    (C) Drawn.
    (D) Sprightly.

47. The passage suggests researchers minimize the distinction between *soil* and *rocks* because:

    (A) Precise language in geology is less important than common beliefs.
    (B) All rocks cannot be made of soil, but all soil consists of rocks.
    (C) The trouble in developing a coherent classification system is too arduous.
    (D) The world's substances are in a continual state of flux.

48. The passage writes about "animals and plants" (lines 18-19) in order to suggest that:

    (A) The makeup of the remains of animals and plants change in similar ways to the makeup of rocks throughout the ages.
    (B) Animals and plants have been responsible for some major geologic events.
    (C) Several sedimentary rocks consist of organic material.
    (D) The remains of animals and plants can be clues about the history of the Earth.

49. Which of the following is NOT suggested as a reason why geologists see the Earth's constituent elements as changing?

    (A) Experiments
    (B) Observations
    (C) Assertion
    (D) Historical data

50. According to the passage, geologists are most similar to:

    (A) Optimists.
    (B) Skeptics.
    (C) Detectives.
    (D) Philosophers.

rP7: FINDING FACTS

TOPIC OVERVIEW

This section will demonstrate the best way to identify and answer basic fact-finding questions.

Fact-finding questions are based entirely on direct evidence—they do not require you to draw conclusions, summarize, or compare viewpoints.

RECOGNIZING FACT-FINDING QUESTIONS

Here are a few examples of basic fact-finding questions. In boldface are key phrases that will help you identify fact-finding questions:

- **According to the passage**, compounds created in extraterrestrial environments tend to be:
- **The author indicates** that which of the following is Harley's main goal for the day?
- **According to the author**, early societies failed to produce written language because:
- **The passage states that** heavy metals are more likely to appear:

Always look for the key phrases *according to the author*, *according to the passage*, the *author indicates*, or *the passage states*. These phrases are the strongest indicators of a fact-finding question.

ANSWERING FACT-FINDING QUESTIONS

You should use general ACT Reading tactics to answer basic fact-finding questions. As you are eliminating wrong answers, you will have a small additional step: *you can safely eliminate any answers which are not stated directly in the passage*—the correct answer will not require you to draw a conclusion or use outside knowledge. In addition, look out particularly for **No Evidence**, **Proven Wrong**, and **Wrong Section** answer types in your elimination.

One of the more difficult aspects of fact-finding questions is that they don't always provide line reference numbers to guide your search. This means that your active reading will be especially important. Look to your notes to seek quickly the information you need. Look for key words in the question or answer choices (for example, "extraterrestrial locations," "main goal," "failed to produce"), and see if you can quickly scan the passage to find the locations that discuss these topics.

Keep in mind that **an answer choice can be true, but still incorrect**. An answer choice may be stated as fact in the passage, but that doesn't mean it accurately completes the question being asked.

LINE REFERENCES

Fact-finding questions will sometimes ask you to refer to a specific line within the passage. Here are some examples of fact-finding questions including line references. Notice that they usually retain the same indicator phrases as fact-finding questions without line references:

- **According to the passage**, the "common occupations" referred to in line 27 are mostly held by:
- **The author indicates** that "little mistakes" (line 30) often lead to:
- **According to the author**, "great social upheaval" (line 21) is responsible for what aspect of the modern break-dancing scene?

When a question includes a line reference, it's a good idea to return to that location in the passage to make sure you have a full idea of what the question is referring to.

Read this passage carefully and then answer the questions that follow.

Prose Fiction

The shop had an intentionally thrown-together, “ethnic” kind of look which, paradoxically, elevated its status to a high-end boutique in which you would pay exorbitant prices for clothing made in countries where there were no labor laws. Seemingly shoddily-built bamboo displays and shelves exhibited brightly colored blouses, skirts, and scarves. This was clothing that would have been made by my mother's hands in El Salvador thirty years ago. Clothing that my mother could never have bought on her salary. Back then, the finished product would leave the factory without a hint of its origins, but these days the preference is for a markedly foreign feel. Here, a pastiche of cultural dress: a mélange of Indian saris and Mexican folklorico dresses, like Fashion Week at the United Nations. Good luck wearing any of this next year when the style of another developing country is trending.

Martin asks me a question that I don't quite hear the first time. "I'm sorry, I didn't hear you," I say.

"No, how could you? You've only been staring through that shop window for ten minutes now."

"I'm sorry, I must have been thinking about something," I say. It strikes me as odd that I'm apologizing for thinking.

"There are some really nice dresses in there." He looks at me and pauses. "A little expensive, though."

I wondered for a second if he had asked me out because young women like me were in vogue these days. It was like being called "exotic" in college. Men thought they were flattering me, but I didn't want to be flattered in that way. Not based on a stereotype. More than one bad experience with men had to do with their skewed perceptions of women like me.

"Why don't we drink something and chat for a few minutes?"

The café was claustrophobically small and gloomily lit, but I relented a little when I noticed the number of couples sitting across from each other, smiling and ignoring the annoying lounge-renditions of pop hits that oozed from the cafe speakers. We sat with our drinks and assumed the posture of false comfort and familiarity.

"So what brings you to town?"

Not a good first question. "My father passed away last week."

His eyebrows darted upward slightly and a seemingly genuine shadow of remorse flashed across his face. "Oh, I'm sorry."

He was sorry that he asked. "Not to worry. I hadn't talked to him in years. He and my mom split up a long time ago."

I knew there was a reason I had given up dating. Even now I felt the impulse to prop up the conversation in order to buoy his ego. Every girl a damsel, making every prince feel important.

"Where did you grow up?"

"Actually, I grew up here in Old Town. Before these boutiques and cafés. My family lived in an apartment building down the road, but when the computer industry started to boom, rent got too high, so my mother and I moved even farther south."

"South, toward Huntington Street? Isn't that a dangerous part of town?"

"No, it's not. It's just us and a lot of Somalian and Central American families. Is there something dangerous about that?"

"No, I guess I didn't know anything about it." Of course he wouldn't know that my family left El Salvador to escape from violence, not find ourselves in it again. In that tiny country, gangs terrorized and robbed foreigners, Salvadoran business owners, and each other. They did it to show their dominance over the common people.

I could tell that he felt cornered, so I changed the subject.

"Where did you grow up?"

"Me? Well, nowhere near as exotic. West on the R line subway." I winced at his choice of words. West on the R line subway. Riverside, probably. With the Latin school and the university across the channel. A quick flicker of blue and red private school ties. He must have sensed what I was thinking, because he smiled.

"Yes, I am a Bosco prep school kid. I was on the debate team, and I played lacrosse." He shrugged.

"Lacrosse. You were the kids who..." I stopped. They were the kids who, ten years ago, had vandalized the outside of our gymnasium with a string of racial epithets. That same year, students from our school were harassed by the Bosco basketball team as their bus exited the parking lot after a humbling loss. It was as if they had to assert their dominance over us. A feeling of trepidation rose from my stomach and got trapped in my throat.

"What? Did we beat your team or something?"

I suddenly grew exhausted with the whole process and wanted to go home to the "dangerous" part of town.

1. Which of the following is an accurate description of the passage?

 (A) Two childhood classmates reunite after a long absence from their home town.
 (B) A couple's date is spoiled by the memory of racial tension between their two high schools.
 (C) Two people reveal details about their childhood and realize they have little in common.
 (D) A woman considers the cultural and gendered implications of a new relationship.

2. In the first paragraph, the word "paradoxically" (line 2) most nearly refers to:

 (A) How the mixture of clothing is incoherent.
 (B) How the type of clothing in the boutique is falsely "ethnic."
 (C) How the seemingly economical appearance of the boutique is actually an indication of worth.
 (D) How much someone would pay for cheaply produced clothing.

3. The narrator suggests that in the past, the fashion industry:

 (A) Capitalized on the clothing styles of common people in other countries.
 (B) Did not want its clothing to allude to the countries in which it was produced.
 (C) Sacrificed quality for quantity by having its clothes manufactured in developing countries.
 (D) Had little imagination for recognizing worldly fashions.

4. The narrator assumes a "posture of false comfort and familiarity" (line 47) most likely because:

 (A) She wants to make a good impression on her date.
 (B) She is consciously playing out a role in a social routine.
 (C) She is reluctant to trust Martin.
 (D) She and Martin have not seen each other in a long time.

5. It can most reasonably be inferred that as it is used in line 19, the term *trending* may refer not only to clothing but also to:

 (A) American men's tastes in women.
 (B) cultures from which to emulate fashions.
 (C) styles of clothing boutiques.
 (D) the technology industry.

6. Based on the characters' conversation, which of the following were part of the past, rather than the present, in their hometowns?

 I. A Latin school
 II. A computer industry
 III. Boutiques
 IV. A Central American population

 (A) I and II only
 (B) I, II, and III only
 (C) I, II and IV only
 (D) I and IV only

7. It can be inferred that the narrator winces in line 84 because:

 (A) She begins to comprehend the danger of their relationship.
 (B) She realizes where Martin has grown up.
 (C) She begins to realize the awkwardness of the situation they are in.
 (D) Martin uses a word that is connected to bad past experiences for her.

8. Which of the following statements best describes the way the eighteenth paragraph (lines 73-79) functions in the passage as a whole?

 (A) It reveals information about the narrator that explains her reluctance to meet new people.
 (B) It explains a model of behavior that will then be applied to another group of people later on.
 (C) It suggests that the narrator's family was safer before moving to the United States.
 (D) It illustrates the type of danger that is prevalent in countries where clothing is made.

9. The character of Martin can best be described as:

 (A) Likable but flawed.
 (B) Gentle but condescending.
 (C) Amiable but oblivious.
 (D) Good-natured but feeble.

10. It can reasonably be inferred that the narrator views the latter part of the conversation with a mixture of:

 (A) Compassion and anxiety.
 (B) Resentment and anger.
 (C) Rejection and loathing.
 (D) Deliberation and fear.

Read this passage carefully and then answer the questions that follow.

Humanities: The following passage was adapted from the introduction to *Adventures in the Arts* by Marsden Hartley.

The artist remains the artist precisely in so far as he rejects the simplifying and reducing process of the average man who at an early age puts life away into some snug conception of his mind. This one turns the key. He has released his will and love from the vast ceremonial of wonder, from the deep Poem of Being, into some particular detail of life wherein he hopes to achieve comfort or at least shun pain. Not so, the artist. In the moment when he elects to avoid by whatever makeshift the raw agony of life, he ceases to be fit to create. He must face experience forever freshly: reduce life each day anew to chaos and remold it into order.

The unresolved expectancy of the creator toward Life should also be his way toward criticism. He should hold it as part of his adventure. He should understand in it, particularly when it is impertinent, stupid and cruel, the ponderable weight of life itself, reacting upon his search for a fresh conquest over it. Though it persists unchanged in its role of purveying misinformation and absurdity to the public, he should know it for himself a blessed dispensation.

With his maturity, the creator's work goes out into the world. And in this act, he puts the world away. For the artist's work defines: and definition means apartness: and the average man is undefined in the social body. Here is a danger for the artist within the very essence of his artistic virtue. During the years of his apprenticeship, he has struggled to create for himself an essential world out of experience. Now he begins to succeed: and he lives too fully in his own selection: he lives too simply in the effects of his effort. The gross and fumbling impact of experience is eased. The grind of ordinary intercourse is dimmed. The rawness of family and business is refined or removed. But now once more the world comes in to him, in the form of the critic. Here again, in a sharp concentrated sense, the world moves on him: its complacency, its hysteria, its down-tending appetites and fond illusions, its pathetic worship of yesterdays and hatred of tomorrows, its fear-dogmas and its blood-avowals.

The artist shall leave the world only to find it, hate it only because he loves, attack it only if he serves. At that epoch of his life when the world's gross sources may grow dim, criticism brings them back. Wherefore, the function of the Critic is a blessing and a need.

The creator's reception of this newly direct, intense, mundane intrusion is not always passive. If the artist is an intelligent man, he may respond to the intervening world on its own plane. He may turn critic himself.

When the creator turns critic, we are in the presence of a consummation: we have a complete experience: we have a sort of sacrament. For to the intrusion of the world he interposes his own body. In his art, the creator's body would be itself intrusion. The artist is too humble and too sane to break the ecstatic flow of vision with his personal form. The true artist despises the personal as an end. He makes fluid, and distils his personal form. He channels it beyond himself to a unity which of course contains it. But criticism is nothing which is not the sheer projection of a body. The artist turns self into a universal form: but the critic reduces form to self. Criticism is to the artist the intrusion, in a form irreducible to art, of the body of the world. What can he do but interpose his own? This is the value of the creator's criticism. He gives to the world himself. And his self is a rich life.

When the creator turns critic, we are certain of a feast. We have a fare that needs no metaphysical sauce (such as must transform the product of the critic). Here is good food. Go to it and eat. The asides of a Baudelaire, a Goethe, a Da Vinci outweigh a thousand tomes of the professional critics.

11. In the first paragraph, the author suggests that the artist and the common man are different because:

(A) The artist understands love and will, but the common man does not.
(B) The common man is unfit to create because he lacks artistic talent, and the artist is unfit to create if he fails to use his talent.
(C) The common man avoids the pain of life whereas the artist embraces it.
(D) The artist is precise, but the common man is simplistic.

12. In the first two paragraphs, the author characterizes the artist as all of the following, EXCEPT:

(A) Someone who searches.
(B) A molder of chaos into order.
(C) One who writes poems of being.
(D) A creator.

13. The primary function of the third paragraph is to:

    (A) Show the major distinctions between an artist and a critic.
    (B) Criticize artists for being too willing to reject art in favor of family and business.
    (C) Underscore the cruel manner in which society treats artists.
    (D) Contend that critics play an important role in art.

14. As expressed in the passage, the author's view of the world might best be described as:

    (A) Pessimistic and indignant.
    (B) Hopeless and uncertain.
    (C) Loving and expectant.
    (D) Scornful and recalcitrant.

15. In the final line of the third paragraph, the phrase *fear-dogma* most likely refers to:

    (A) A deep terror of wolves, foxes, and other dog-like animals.
    (B) A religious or social doctrine that encourages people to be afraid.
    (C) The natural anxiety felt by the common man when he encounters great art.
    (D) Being "dogged-out" by enemies who have taken a blood vow to harm you.

16. From lines 56-59 ("When the creator…interposes his own body"), it may be most reasonably inferred that the author believes that an artist who becomes a critic:

    (A) Learns to use his body in his art.
    (B) Loses touch with the larger world.
    (C) Is a type of religious ritual.
    (D) Becomes an art consumer.

17. The tone of the passage can best be described as:

    (A) Exploratory and unkind.
    (B) Smooth yet skeptical.
    (C) Aloof but warm-hearted.
    (D) Intense and assured.

18. In the final paragraph, the author indicates that the work of an artist who becomes a critic:

    I. Can transform the product of the critic
    II. Needs no embellishment
    III. Is like a delicious meal

    (A) I only
    (B) II only
    (C) I and II only
    (D) II and III only

19. In the final sentence, the author suggests all of the following EXCEPT:

    (A) Baudelaire and Goethe were artists of some type.
    (B) A passing comment by a great artist is more valuable than the work of a professional critic.
    (C) A thousand tomes is roughly the weight of three men.
    (D) Great artists are uniquely qualified to serve as critics.

20. Based on the passage, the author is most likely to agree with which of the following statements:

    (A) Critics overestimate their importance to the art world.
    (B) To become truly great, an artist must spend time feasting with critics.
    (C) Artists can serve the art world by writing and speaking about art.
    (D) Many artists avoid the pain of life by becoming critics.

Read this passage carefully and then answer the questions that follow.

Humanities: The following passage was adapted from *We the Media* by Dan Gillmor.

We freeze some moments in time. Every culture has its frozen moments, events so important and personal that they transcend the normal flow of news.

Americans of a certain age, for example, know precisely where they were and what they were doing when they learned that President Franklin D. Roosevelt died. Another generation has absolute clarity of John F. Kennedy's assassination. And no one who was older than a baby on September 11, 2001, will ever forget hearing about, or seeing, airplanes exploding into skyscrapers.

In 1945, people gathered around radios for the immediate news, and stayed with the radio to hear more about their fallen leader and about the man who took his place. Newspapers printed extra editions and filled their columns with detail for days and weeks afterward. Magazines stepped back from the breaking news and offered perspective.

Something similar happened in 1963, but with a newer medium. The immediate news of Kennedy's death came for most via television; I'm old enough to remember that heartbreaking moment when Walter Cronkite put on his horn-rimmed glasses to glance at a message from Dallas and then, blinking back tears, told his viewers that their leader was gone. As in the earlier time, newspapers and magazines pulled out all the stops to add detail and context.

September 11, 2001, followed a similarly grim pattern. We watched—again and again—the awful events. Consumers of news learned the what about the attacks, thanks to the television networks that showed the horror so graphically. Then we learned some of the how and why as print publications and thoughtful broadcasters worked to bring depth to events that defied mere words. Journalists did some of their finest work and made me proud to be one of them.

But something else, something profound, was happening this time around: news was being produced by regular people who had something to say and show, and not solely by the "official" news organizations that had traditionally decided how the first draft of history would look. This time, the first draft of history was being written, in part, by the former audience. It was possible—it was inevitable—because of new publishing tools available on the Internet.

Another kind of reporting emerged during those appalling hours and days. Via emails, mailing lists, chat groups, personal web journals—all nonstandard news sources—we received valuable context that the major American media couldn't, or wouldn't, provide.

We were witnessing—and in many cases were part of—the future of news.

In the 20th century, making the news was almost entirely the province of journalists; the people we covered, or "news-makers"; and the legions of public relations and marketing people who manipulated everyone. The economics of publishing and broadcasting created large, arrogant institutions—call it Big Media, though even small-town newspapers and broadcasters exhibit some of the phenomenon's worst symptoms.

Big Media, in any event, treated the news as a lecture. We told you what the news was. You bought it, or you didn't. You might write us a letter; we might print it. (If we were television and you complained, we ignored you entirely unless the complaint arrived on a libel lawyer's letterhead.) Or you cancelled your subscription or stopped watching our shows. It was a world that bred complacency and arrogance on our part. It was a gravy train while it lasted, but it was unsustainable.

Tomorrow's news reporting and production will be more of a conversation, or a seminar. The lines will blur between producers and consumers, changing the role of both in ways we're only beginning to grasp now. The communication network itself will be a medium for everyone's voice, not just the few who can afford to buy multimillion-dollar printing presses, launch satellites, or win the government's permission to squat on the public's airwaves.

This evolution—from journalism as lecture to journalism as a conversation or seminar—will force the various communities of interest to adapt. Everyone, from journalists to the people we cover to our sources and the former audience, must change their ways. The alternative is just more of the same.

We can't afford more of the same. We can't afford to treat the news solely as a commodity, largely controlled by big institutions. We can't afford, as a society, to limit our choices. We can't even afford it financially, because Wall Street's demands on Big Media are dumbing down the product itself.

There are three major constituencies in a world where anyone can make the news. Once largely distinct, they're now blurring into each other.

21. The main purpose of the passage is to:

(A) Examine the manner in which advancements in technology have deformed the medium of news.
(B) Bring attention to an evolution in the coverage of news as a result in advancements in communication technology.
(C) Give a detailed exploration into the changes in technology that are changing the way people communicate information.
(D) Provide a grim prediction for the news industry as a result of emerging communication technologies.

22. The passage suggests that cultures "freeze" (line 1) moments in time because:

(A) The news largely publicizes these events.
(B) They are exclusively heartbreaking news.
(C) They are events that are important and personal to their identity.
(D) Consumers liked to be informed on the what of breaking news.

23. The author of this passage is:

(A) A student writing a report for a humanities class.
(B) A journalist recognizing the new mediums for the spread of news.
(C) A novelist writing a chapter for his next book.
(D) A news reporter denouncing the changes occurring in media.

24. The passage characterizes "Big Media" (line 64) as:

(A) Journalists.
(B) Arrogant institutions created by the economics of publishing.
(C) Newsmakers and marketing people.
(D) Emails, mailing lists, and web journals.

25. According to the passage, Big Media:

I. Ignored complaints unless they came from a lawyer
II. Lectured audiences telling them what news was
III. Was not concerned if you stopped watching its shows
IV. Was unsustainable

(A) I and II
(B) III and IV
(C) I, III, and IV
(D) I, II, and IV

26. As used in line 74, *bred* most closely means:

(A) Consumed.
(B) Prioritized.
(C) Propagated.
(D) Gestated.

27. According to the author, news reporting in the future will do all of the following EXCEPT:

(A) Be mainly a domain for multimillion-dollar institutions.
(B) Compel various communities of interest to adapt and change their ways.
(C) Transform from a lecture to a conversation or seminar.
(D) Be a medium for everyone's voice.

28. The author uses "more of the same" (lines 92-93) to refer to all of the following EXCEPT:

(A) Wall Street's demands diminishing the quality of the news.
(B) Big institutions demanding more from the news.
(C) News being treated as a commodity.
(D) Limiting choices as a society.

29. According to the passage, the major constituencies in a world where anyone can make news are:

I. Journalists and reporters, the producers of news.
II. Wealthy corporations, the funding behind Big Media.
III. Society as whole, the consumers of the news.

(A) I only
(B) II only
(C) II and III only
(D) I, II, and III

30. The author of the passage would likely agree with which of the following statements?

(A) Emerging technologies have weakened the dominance of "Big Media" within the news industry.
(B) Emerging technologies will inevitably terminate the various companies that make up "Big Media."
(C) Emerging technologies offer little benefit to society in respect to the communication of news.
(D) Emerging technologies have no negative effect to the coverage or communication of news.

Read this passage carefully and then answer the questions that follow.

Social Science: This passage discusses an important issue in education.

The escalating cost of higher education is causing many to question the value of continuing education beyond high school. Many wonder whether the high cost of tuition, the opportunity cost of choosing college over full-time employment, and the accumulation of thousands of dollars of debt is, in the long run, worth the significant investment. The risk is especially large for low-income families who have a difficult time making ends meet without the additional burden of college tuition and fees. In order to determine whether higher education is worth the investment, it is useful to examine what is known about the value of higher education and the rates of return on investment to both the individual and to society.

There is considerable support for the notion that the rate of return on investment in higher education is high enough to warrant the financial burden associated with pursuing a college degree. Though the earnings differential between college and high school graduates varies over time, college graduates, on average, earn more than high school graduates. Over an adult's working life, high school graduates earn an average of $1.2 million, associate's degree holders earn about $1.6 million, and bachelor's degree holders earn about $2.1 million. When you consider the fact that a full-time student at a public 4-year college pays an average of $15,605 per year and a full-time student in a public 2-year college pays an average of $7,925 per year for tuition, room and board, the sizeable differences in lifetime earnings put the costs of college in realistic perspective. These statistics support the contention that, though the cost of higher education is significant, given the earnings disparity that exists between those who earn a bachelor's degree and those who do not, the individual rate of return on investment in higher education is sufficiently high to warrant the cost.

College graduates also enjoy benefits beyond increased income. One study showed there are individual benefits that college graduates enjoy beyond pay, including higher levels of saving, increased personal/professional mobility, improved quality of life for their offspring, better consumer decision making, and more hobbies and leisure activities. Another study showed that other non-monetary individual benefits of higher education include the tendency for postsecondary students to become more open-minded, more cultured, more rational, more consistent and less authoritarian. These benefits are also passed along to succeeding generations. Additionally, college attendance has been shown to decrease prejudice, enhance knowledge of world affairs, and enhance social status, while increasing economic and job security for those who earn bachelor's degrees. On top of all of the benefits of higher education, college graduates appear to have a more optimistic view of their past and future personal progress.

Furthermore, recipients of higher education pass benefits on to their offspring as well. Research has consistently shown a positive correlation between completion of higher education and good health, not only for oneself, but also for one's children. In fact, parental schooling levels are positively correlated with the health status of their children. Also, a number of studies have shown a high correlation between higher education and cultural and family values. There is the tendency for more highly educated women to spend more time with their children. These women tend to use this time to better prepare their children for the future.

Not only does the individual benefit from a college education, but society does too. The public benefits of attending college include increased tax revenues, greater workplace productivity, increased consumption, increased workforce flexibility, and decreased reliance on government financial support. All of these factors help to strengthen the economy, businesses, and the government.

While it is clear that investment in a college degree, especially for those students in the lowest income brackets, is a financial burden, the long-term benefits to individuals as well as to society at large, appear to far outweigh the costs. Although most people might concentrate on the financial benefits that are provided by a college education, the individual benefits beyond monetary prosperity are invaluable to students in the lowest income brackets. A college education may be the key that will allow these students and their future generations to realize a future that is brighter than those of their ancestors.

31. The primary purpose of this passage is to:

(A) Explain the enrollment process for colleges in the United States.
(B) Give an extensive history of colleges in the United States.
(C) Provide a detailed assessment on the overall cost of college.
(D) Examine the benefits of a higher education.

32. The author considers all of the following factors when determining whether the investment in college is worth the costs EXCEPT:

(A) The benefits to society.
(B) The lifetime earnings of the graduate compared to the cost of college.
(C) The effect of a college degree on the offspring of the college graduate.
(D) The amount of investment in educational institutions by the government.

33. The risk for low income families of investing in college are large because:

(A) The families may already have trouble making ends meet before the financial burden of college.
(B) Low income students cannot get financial aid to go to college.
(C) Low income students are much less likely to be approved for loans to go to college.
(D) The families lose the income of the student who is going to college.

34. In line 18, *warrant* most nearly means:

(A) Authorize.
(B) Justify.
(C) License.
(D) Guarantee.

35. According to paragraph 3, the non-monetary benefits of higher education include:

I. Improved quality of life for offspring
II. Decrease in prejudice
III. Women spend more time with their children

(A) I only.
(B) III only.
(C) I and II only.
(D) I, II, and III only.

36. The author's attitude toward individuals receiving a college education is best characterized as one of:

(A) Reassurance.
(B) Fanaticism.
(C) Indifference.
(D) Vehemence.

37. One can reasonably infer from the author's reference to the positive correlation between parental schooling levels and the health status of their children (lines 61-78) that these children:

(A) Get sick more often than children of parents without college degrees.
(B) Like their doctors better than children of parents without college degree.
(C) Are healthier than children of parents without college degrees.
(D) Have more doctors' appointments than children of parents without college degrees.

38. According to paragraph 4, children of highly educated mothers are better prepared for their future because:

(A) Their mothers spend more time with them.
(B) Their mothers send them to better schools.
(C) They have better teachers.
(D) They prefer to spend more time learning than other children.

39. According to the passage, a person with a college education is:

(A) Less likely to be distracted by hobbies in the work place.
(B) Less likely to depend on government assistance.
(C) Less likely to have an optimistic worldview.
(D) Less likely to develop stress-related diseases.

40. The purpose of the second paragraph is:

(A) To compare the cost of a 2-year degree and 4-year degree.
(B) To illustrate how expensive college is for a student.
(C) To examine the costs and rewards of obtaining a college degree.
(D) To demonstrate how useless a college degree is compared to a high school diploma.

Read this passage carefully and then answer the questions that follow.

Natural Science: This passage describes the physics of sound.

A distinction is generally made in physics between sound and noise. Noise affects our tympanic membrane as an irregular succession of shocks and we are conscious of a jarring of the auditory apparatus; whereas a musical sound is smooth and pleasant because the tympanic membrane is thrown into successive periodic vibrations to which the auditory receptor (sense organ of hearing) has been attuned. To produce musical sounds, a body must vibrate with the regularity of a pendulum, but it must be capable of imparting sharper or quicker shocks to the air than the pendulum. All musical sounds, however they are produced and by whatever means they are propagated, may be distinguished by three different qualities: loudness, pitch, and quality.

Loudness depends upon the amount of energy expended in producing the sound. If I rub a tuning-fork with a well-rosined bow, I set it in vibration by the resistance offered to the rosined hair; and if while it is vibrating I again apply the bow, thus expending more energy, the note produced is louder. Repeating the action several times, the width of excursion of the prongs of the tuning-fork is increased. This I can demonstrate, not merely by the loudness of the sound which can be heard, but by sight; for if a small mirror be fixed on one of the prongs and a beam of light be cast upon the mirror, the light being again reflected on to the screen, you will see the spot of light dance up and down, and the more energetically the tuning-fork is bowed the greater is the amplitude of the oscillation of the spot of light. The duration of the time occupied is the same in traversing a longer as in traversing a shorter space, as is the case of the swinging pendulum. The vibrating prongs of the tuning-fork throw the air into vibrations which are conveyed to the ear and produce the sensation of sound. The duration of time occupied in the vibrations of the tuning-fork is therefore independent of the space passed over. The greater or less energy expended does not influence the duration of time occupied by the vibration; it only influences the amplitude of the vibration.

The second quality of musical sounds is the pitch, and the pitch depends upon the number of vibrations that a sounding body makes in each second of time. The most unmusical ear can distinguish a high note from a low one, even when the interval is not great. Low notes are characterized by a relatively small number of vibrations, and as the pitch rises so the number of vibrations increases. This can be proved in many ways. Take, for example, two tuning-forks of different size: the shorter produces a considerably higher pitched note than the longer one. If a mirror be attached to one of the prongs of each fork, and a beam of light be cast upon each mirror successively and then reflected in a revolving mirror, the oscillating spot of light is converted into a series of waves; and if the waves obtained by reflecting the light from the mirror of the smaller one be counted and compared with those reflected from the mirror attached to the larger fork, it will be found that the number of waves reflected from the smaller fork is proportionally to the difference in the pitch more numerous than the waves reflected from the larger. The air is thrown into corresponding periodic vibrations according to the rate of vibration of the sound-producing body.

Thirdly, the quality depends upon the overtones, in respect to which I could cite many experiments to prove that whenever a body vibrates, other bodies near it may be set in vibration, but only on condition that such bodies shall be capable themselves of producing the same note. A number of different forms of resonators can be used to illustrate this law; a law indeed which is of the greatest importance in connection with the mechanism of the human voice. Although notes are of the same loudness and pitch when played on different instruments or spoken or sung by different individuals, yet even a person with no ear for music can easily detect a difference in the quality of the sound and is able to recognise the nature of the instrument or the timbre of the voice. This difference in the timbre is due to harmonics or overtones. Could we but see the sonorous waves in the air during the transmission of the sound of a voice, we should see stamped on it the conditions of motion upon which its characteristic qualities depended; which is due to the fact that every vocal sound whose vibrations have a complex form can be decomposed into a series of simple notes all belonging to the harmonic series.

41. According to the passage, what distinguishes "noise" (line 2) from "sound" (line 5)?

(A) Volume
(B) Rhythm
(C) Pitch
(D) Quality

42. The passage uses the example of a mirror to demonstrate loudness (lines 27-33) in order to:

    (A) Assert that tuning forks operate in varied ways.
    (B) Appeal to a sense not associated with sound.
    (C) Suggest that sound involves a variety of wavelengths.
    (D) Demonstrate loudness using vibration.

43. As used in the passage, the word *amplitude* (line 32) most nearly means:

    (A) The extent of vibration.
    (B) The extent of dignity.
    (C) Great splendor.
    (D) Abundance.

44. According to the passage, *pitch* (line 46) is manifested by:

    (A) The clarity of a sound.
    (B) The energy producing a sound.
    (C) Concurrent sounds.
    (D) The depth of a sound.

45. The passage suggests that a singer who produces higher notes:

    (A) Produces vibrations in accordance with the surrounding air.
    (B) Produces fewer vibrations per second.
    (C) Produces more vibrations per second.
    (D) Produces identical vibrations to a singer producing lower notes.

46. The passage suggests that surrounding bodies can be made to vibrate if:

    (A) They are free-standing.
    (B) They can produce the same sound.
    (C) They are currently producing the same sound.
    (D) They resonate within the sounds capable of registering in the human ear.

47. According to the passage, if two different instruments have the same pitch and loudness, those instruments can be differentiated using:

    (A) Harmonics.
    (B) Vibrations per second.
    (C) The regularity of shocks to the tympanic membrane.
    (D) The energy produced by the vibrations.

48. The passage suggests that the tympanic membrane is:

    (A) The dividing line between pitch and loudness.
    (B) A means of registering sound.
    (C) A means of converting noise to sound.
    (D) The means to discover sound quality.

49. This audience of this passage is most likely:

    (A) Voice coaches.
    (B) Musicians.
    (C) The general public.
    (D) Physicists.

50. The purpose of this passage is most likely:

    (A) To define sound.
    (B) To distinguish sound from noise.
    (C) To discuss the wave properties of sound.
    (D) To outline what makes a sound pleasing.

rP8: CONCLUSIONS

TOPIC OVERVIEW

This section covers the process of answering questions that go beyond the information that is explicitly presented—specifically, questions that make generalizations, draw conclusions, ask you to make an inference, or describe cause & effect relationships.

RECOGNIZING BASIC CONCLUSION QUESTIONS

Here are several conclusion questions like the ones that you will see when you take the ACT. The parts in boldface mark key words and phrases common to conclusion questions:

- Mrs. Klaus would likely **describe** her step-daughter as:
- The nameless man's mysterious reaction to news of his father's death **suggests** that he:
- The main character in the passage **can best be characterized** as:
- Based on the passage, **it can be inferred** that the group most likely to oppose stem cell research is:
- **It can reasonably be concluded** from the passage that the brain's most fragile lobe is the:
- Francine would **most likely agree** that Harold's behavior was due to his:

Always look for key words or phrases like *describe*, *suggest*, *characterize*, *infer*, *conclude*, *most likely*, and *cause*. These words act as signals that you will need to make an inference or draw a conclusion in order to answer the question.

ANSWERING CONCLUSION QUESTIONS

Unlike the answers to fact-finding questions, the answers to basic conclusion questions are not directly stated in the passage. However, they are always **supported by evidence** found in the passage. You will need to use this supporting evidence, as well as your reasoning skills, to come up with a correct answer.

The supporting evidence for a basic conclusion question serves as proof that an answer is correct. There will only be one answer choice that can reasonably be supported.

Beware of question choices that appear in the passage but do not fit the question being asked. Just because an answer choice is supported by evidence in the passage does not mean it adequately answers or completes the question. In order to be correct, an answer choice must:

- **be supported by evidence** from the passage and
- **accurately answer** or complete the question.

For each conclusion question on the ACT, there will only be one answer choice that can reasonably be supported; the rest will be one of the types discussed in Lesson 2: **Proven Wrong**, **No Evidence**, **Too General** or **Too Specific**.

Using active reading strategies can be very helpful in locating supporting evidence for advanced conclusion questions. By underlining key facts and summarizing portions within a passage, you should be able to locate the supporting evidence.

Read this passage carefully and then answer the questions that follow.

Humanities: This passage describes a phenomenon in popular music.

The 27 Club: it's exclusive, it's elite, and some of the greatest performers in the history of popular music are members. But you wouldn't want to join. "The 27 Club" is the term used to refer to a group of famous rock and pop musicians who all died at the age of 27. The "club" includes influential electric guitarist Jimi Hendrix, "grunge rock" pioneer Kurt Cobain, and British soul singer Amy Winehouse.

Although a performer's age at the time of death is enough to qualify him or her for admission to the 27 Club (which is sometimes called the Forever 27 Club), it's also notable that most members died under tragic or mysterious circumstances. Brian Jones of The Rolling Stones drowned in his own swimming pool; Jim Morrison, leader of The Doors, died of unknown causes during a stay in Paris; singer Mia Zapata and rappers Fat Pat and Freaky Tah were all murdered; Cobain committed suicide. Drugs or alcohol figured in the deaths of Hendrix, Winehouse, singer Janis Joplin, Grateful Dead keyboardist Ron "Pigpen" McKernan, and Kristen Pfaff, bass guitarist for the rock band Hole (which, ironically, was led by Cobain's wife, Courtney Love).

Although the term "27 Club" seems to have been popularized following Cobain's death, 27-year-old musicians have been dying since the advent of the recording industry in the early 20th century. Robert Johnson, the legendary blues guitarist and singer widely considered the "founder" of the club, died after he was poisoned in 1938. Singer Jesse Belvin was killed in a car crash in 1960. Rudy Lewis, vocalist for The Drifters, a phenomenally popular doo-wop group, died of a drug overdose in 1964.

Regardless of when the club began, it has become a fixture in the rock music community and is often cited in music magazines and on news and entertainment websites. Several museums have held exhibitions about it; novels have been built around it; and at least one major motion picture has been made about it. Despite the hoopla, some researchers have concluded that the 27 Club is a matter of coincidence rather than fact. A study published in the British Medical Journal in 2011 found that even though musicians face an increased risk of death in their 20s and 30s, they do not face a higher mortality rate at age 27.

So if there really is no 27 Club, why does it persist in the public imagination? One possible reason is the power of circumstantial evidence. Much of the foundation for the 27 Club is built on a tragic coincidence: Brian Jones, Jimi Hendrix, Janis Joplin, and Jim Morrison all died between 1969 and 1971. In a matter of 3 short years, four of rock's reigning luminaries were gone. Some music journalists theorize that the 27 Club was a way for bereft music fans to explain this seemingly impossible circumstance. And although Cobain's death in 1994 came more than two decades later, it also played a significant role in undergirding the 27 Club legend.

Following the Nirvana singer's suicide, a newspaper carried an excerpt from a statement by Cobain's mother, Wendy Cobain O'Connor, in which she lamented that her son had "gone and joined that stupid club." The excerpt was widely repeated, bringing the 27 Club out of rock circles and into the wider culture. Ironically, some journalists have suggested that Wendy O'Connor wasn't referring to the 27 Club at all, but to three of Cobain's family members who also had committed suicide.

In the era of the internet, the fascination with the 27 Club has gone global. There are several websites devoted to the club, and following Amy Winehouse's death in 2011, blog writers and social media mavens were among the first to transmit the news worldwide, often focusing on the 27 Club connection. Still, for all the data-age fascination, one old-fashioned reality seems to undermine the 27 Club's presumptions about the mortality of young rock stars: most successful musicians live well beyond age 27. Just ask Mick Jagger and Keith Richards of the Rolling Stones. They're both approaching 70. Or talk to Cobain's widow, singer and guitarist Courtney Love. She's in her late 40s. Or consider the renowned R&B singer Etta James, who was a role model and inspiration for Janis Joplin. She won her fourth Grammy Award in 2005 - at the ripe young age of 68.

1. The primary purpose of the first paragraph is to:

   (A) Lament the passing of some important rock stars.
   (B) Introduce a report on an unusual cultural phenomenon.
   (C) Describe a famous nightclub frequented by big celebrities.
   (D) Celebrate the lives of Jimi Hendrix, Kurt Cobain, and Amy Winehouse.

2. According to the passage, most musicians who qualify for the "27 Club":

(A) Are 27 years old, world famous, and have at least one chart-topping hit.
(B) Have a history of bad behavior that leads to death at age 27.
(C) Die at age 27 under tragic or mysterious circumstances.
(D) Are suicidal, drug addicted, and die at age 27.

3. From Paragraph 3, it can be most reasonably inferred that "doo-wop" is:

(A) A type of music that was popularized by The Drifters.
(B) A style of pop music from the early 1960s.
(C) A dance style that was enjoyed by teenagers in the late 1950s.
(D) A nickname for Detroit, the city where the Drifters were performing the night Rudy Lewis died of a drug overdose.

4. As used in line 29, the word *advent* most likely means:

(A) Invention.
(B) Start.
(C) Collapse.
(D) Administration.

5. According to the passage, the legend of the 27 Club has continued because

I. Grieving music fans have kept it alive as a way to explain the deaths of their heroes.
II. Young rock stars are vulnerable and continue to die at age 27.
III. The media has made extensive use of the term "27 Club."

(A) I only
(B) III only
(C) I and III only
(D) I, II, and III

6. Paragraph 5 includes all of the following EXCEPT:

(A) Speculation by expert commentators.
(B) The year of Kurt Cobain's death.
(C) One reason why people believe in the 27 Club.
(D) The year of Jim Morrison's death.

7. It can be most reasonably inferred from the passage that:

(A) Fans of rock and pop music are often deeply affected by the deaths of musicians.
(B) Rappers are not rock or pop stars.
(C) The 27 Club phenomenon will never die.
(D) All the 27 Club members played a crucial role in the development of American popular music.

8. In the final line of the passage, the author most likely uses the term "ripe young age":

(A) Comparatively.
(B) Brilliantly.
(C) Sarcastically.
(D) Ironically.

9. The passage may best be described as:

(A) A journalistic exploration of an unusual cultural phenomenon.
(B) A detailed description of the lives and deaths of several important musicians.
(C) An earnest attempt to debunk a myth.
(D) A cautionary tale on the dangers of the rock star lifestyle.

10. The author's attitude toward the subject of the passage is best characterized as one of:

(A) Intense distaste.
(B) Suppressed indifference.
(C) Interested engagement.
(D) Passionate involvement.

Read this passage carefully and then answer the questions that follow.

Humanities: This passage discusses three individuals with a major impact on Western philosophy.

Socrates, Aristotle, and Plato – are there three greater names in Western thought? These men, connected by student-and-teacher relationships, are frequently cited as the fathers of modern thought. Among other such illustrious names such as Pythagoras, Diogenes, and Archimedes, these men stand above the others. Why? Because these men created our first methods of approaching the world and interpreting what we find.

First came Socrates. He lived from approximately 469 B.C.E. to 399 B.C.E. Our direct knowledge of Socrates is somewhat uncertain. Histories and direct records of his thoughts are rare; most of what modern historians know about Socrates came from the writing of his students - Plato, in particular, recorded many of Socrates' dialogues. (Some historians debate whether some of these dialogues were works of Socrates himself, or whether some of them may have been Plato projecting his own ideas onto his teacher.) Socrates was known for being a great orator, and even more, a great questioner. His now-famous "Socratic method" is perhaps his greatest legacy; it is also known as "elenchus." It is a style of instruction that is based around the instructor asking questions of the students. By making his students answer his questions, Socrates forced them to consider their opinions and attack problems from multiple angles. Any student who remembers sitting in a class, hoping the teacher will not call on them, has Socrates to thank. Yet his influence extends beyond the classroom – think, for example, of the scientific method. As Socrates did, scientists following the scientific method must come up with questions, prove which ones are right and which ones are wrong, and eliminate faulty courses of reasoning. (Socrates's pupil's pupil, Aristotle, would use this to a great degree.) This method was not without its drawbacks, however; his incessant questioning of everything, leaving nothing sacred, eventually angered authorities. Socrates was charged with "corruption of the youth" and was forced to commit suicide by drinking hemlock.

His most preeminent student had a much more welcoming reception from the authorities of Athens. Plato, who lived from 428 to 348 B.C.E., is perhaps better-known and more influential than either his teacher or his pupil. Rather than questioning everything, Plato sought to pursue truth directly. He believed that physical objects and physical events are only "shadows" of their ideal or perfect forms. Perhaps his most famous illustration of this concept was the "story of the cave." People, argues Plato, are like prisoners kept in a cave, facing a wall. Projected on these walls are shadows created by things passing in front of a fire behind them; as the prisoners know no better, they believe the shadows they see on the wall to be real things. A philosopher, in Plato's eyes, is like a prisoner who has escaped the cave and can see the actual "real" objects. In such a way, everything that we see or hear is just a reflection of its perfect form. Plato also had many ideas regarding an ideal government, enumerated in his work *The Republic*.

While Plato was prolific, he was nothing compared to his most famous pupil. Aristotle, the last in this line of great thinkers, was – among other things – tutor to Alexander the Great. There remains a great deal of Aristotle's writings, though it is estimated that perhaps two-thirds of his writings did not survive to the present. While his predecessor had focused on lofty, idealistic studies into the nature of the universe and truth, Aristotle was more concerned with the natural world. In natural study, he innovated in dozens of ways, creating new theories about optics, geology, and countless other fields. Using an elevated version of the Socratic method, Aristotle investigated everything he could, testing his hypotheses and discarding failed attempts. While some of his theories did not stand up in the modern world, his approach to logic and the study of natural science provided the basis of today's scientific inquiry. His inquiring mind had touched on nearly every subject known to man at the time, and he created several new fields of study during his lifetime.

Western civilization owes much to these three men. Yet another debt is often unacknowledged: those who kept these thoughts alive over the millennia, from the time of antiquity to the beginning of the modern era. In fact, much of Greek philosophical thought and study was kept alive in the minds and libraries of Islamic scholars; Alexander's excursions into Persia and Egypt left a lasting Greek influence in the area. Throughout the Arab world, the ideas of these three great Greek thinkers caused much debate for centuries. A great deal of these writings returned to the European world during the late medieval era, rekindling interest in ancient thought and causing a movement that we would know as the Renaissance.

11. The primary purpose of the first paragraph is to:

    (A) Discuss the author's motivations.
    (B) Introduce the three main names to be discussed In the passage.
    (C) Point out how some philosophers are connected to the fathers of thought.
    (D) Explain how philosophers influenced Western thought.

12. Modern historians' knowledge of Socrates:

    (A) Comes from direct histories and records of his thoughts.
    (B) Is still absolutely uncertain.
    (C) Comes mostly from his students' writings.
    (D) Was recorded only by Plato.

13. According to the passage, Socrates is known for all of the following EXCEPT:

    (A) Creating the teaching style "elenchus."
    (B) Pursuing the truth directly.
    (C) Writing several dialogues.
    (D) Being a great orator and questioner.

14. The passage indicates that which of the following is true about Socrates?

    I. He taught students to eliminate faulty courses of reasoning
    II. He utilized a technique similar to the scientific method
    III. He was charged with corrupting youth
    IV. He left a great legacy known as the Socratic method

    (A) I and II
    (B) III and IV
    (C) I, II, and IV
    (D) I, II, III, and IV

15. According to the passage, Plato believed the main difference between people and philosophers to be:

    (A) People are like prisoners while philosophers have escaped that prison.
    (B) Philosophers see and hear reflections of perfect form.
    (C) People were more interested in physical objects and physical events.
    (D) People believed the shadows created and rejected the philosopher's teachings.

16. As used in line 65, *prolific* most nearly means:

    (A) Productive.
    (B) Fertile.
    (C) Unsuccessful.
    (D) Yielding.

17. Aristotle was different from Plato in that:

    (A) He focused on lofty, idealistic studies into the nature of the universe.
    (B) He had a more welcoming reception from the authorities.
    (C) He was more concerned with the natural world.
    (D) He was better known and more influential than Plato.

18. The passage indicates that all of the following are true about Aristotle EXCEPT:

    (A) He created new theories in countless fields.
    (B) His methods of investigation elevated the Socratic method.
    (C) He provided the foundation for today's scientific inquiry.
    (D) He created several new fields of study.

19. As used in line 88, *debt* most nearly means:

    (A) To be responsible for the payment of.
    (B) To be forced to acknowledge the qualification of.
    (C) To attribute something or someone as the cause or source of.
    (D) To hold a liability over something or someone.

20. The author would most likely agree with which of the following statements?

    (A) Much of modern day practices of scientific inquiry are based on Aristotle's approach to logic.
    (B) The ideas of Socrates, Plato, and Aristotle are all of equal relevance and importance to modern day scientific inquiry.
    (C) What we know of Socrates is inaccurate because Plato projected his own ideas onto his recordings.
    (D) Socrates was more valuable for the advancement of the field of philosophy than either Plato or Aristotle.

Read this passage carefully and then answer the questions that follow.

Social Science: This passage describes a highly successful scam.

One of the most brilliant con artists who ever lived was Victor Lustig. Lustig was born in Bohemia and had gone west, demonstrating his talents even in his early twenties. He was a natural conman, glib and charming in multiple languages. He established himself by working scams on the ocean liners steaming between Paris and New York. Eventually, however, Lustig thought there was more money to be made in the city of Paris.

In 1925, France had recovered from the First World War and Paris was booming. Expatriates from all over the world went to Paris to witness the leading edge of the latest trends. It was flashy and fast moving, an excellent environment for a con artist. Lustig's master con began one spring day when he was reading a newspaper. An article discussed the problems the city was having maintaining the Eiffel Tower. Even keeping it painted was an expensive chore, and the tower was becoming somewhat run down. Lustig saw a story behind this article. Maybe the city would decide the Eiffel Tower wasn't worth saving any longer. What would happen then? Lustig outlined the possibilities in his head and realized they suggested a real opportunity.

With impressive precision, Lustig assumed the persona of a government official. He had a forger produce fake government stationery for him. Lustig then sent six scrap metal dealers an invitation to attend a confidential meeting at the Hotel Creon to discuss a possible business deal.

There, Lustig introduced himself as the deputy director-general of the Ministry of Posts and Telegraphs. He explained that the dealers had been selected on the basis of their good reputations as honest businessmen, and then dropped his bombshell: the upkeep on the Eiffel Tower was so outrageous that the city could not maintain it any longer and wanted to sell it for scrap. He told them that the matter was to be kept an absolute secret until all of the details were sketched out. Lustig said that he had been given the responsibility to select the dealer to carry out the task. The idea was not as implausible in 1925 as it would be today. The Eiffel Tower had been built for the 1889 Paris Exposition and had not been planned as a permanent fixture. City officials even planned to take it down in 1909 and move it someplace else. It didn't fit with the city's other great monuments like the gothic cathedrals or the Arc de Triomphe, and it was in very poor condition. However, they decided against such a big project during WWI.

Lustig took the men to the tower in a rented limousine to give them an inspection tour. The tower was made of 15,000 prefabricated parts, many of which were highly ornamental, and Lustig showed it off to the men. This encouraged their enthusiasm, and it also gave Lustig an idea who was the most enthusiastic and gullible. Back on the ground, Lustig asked for bids to be submitted the next day and reminded them that the matter was a state secret. In reality, Lustig already knew he would accept the bid from one dealer, Andre Poisson. Poisson was insecure and desired greatly to be a part of the inner circles of the Parisian business community. Furthermore, Poisson did not make a lot of money. Obtaining the Eiffel Tower deal would have been the best thing that ever happened to him. Lustig capitalized on Poisson's eagerness.

Although Poisson was gullible, his wife was not. In fact she was quite suspicious of the whole deal. She pestered her husband with questions, “Who is this official, why was everything so secret, and why was everything being done so quickly?” To appease her, Poisson eventually caved and discussed the matter with Lustig. To deal with the suspicious Poisson, Lustig arranged another meeting and then "confessed.” As a government minister, Lustig said, he did not make enough money to pursue the lifestyle he enjoyed, and needed to find ways to supplement his income. This meant that his dealings needed a certain discretion. Poisson understood immediately: he was dealing with another corrupt government official who wanted a bribe. That put Poisson's mind at rest since he was familiar with the type.

So Lustig not only received the funds for the Eiffel Tower, he also got a bribe on top of that. Lustig and his personal secretary, an American conman named Dan Collins, hastily took a train for Vienna with a suitcase full of cash. He knew the instant that Poisson called the government ministries to ask for further information the whole fraud would be revealed and the law would intervene. Nothing happened. Poisson was too humiliated to complain to the police.

Years later, Lustig finally emigrated to the US, and continued to conduct a number of scams. Eventually his dishonest ways caught up with him and he was arrested for counterfeiting and sent to Alcatraz Prison. He died in 1947.

21. As it is used in line 27, *persona* most nearly means:

    (A) Disposition.
    (B) Condition.
    (C) Appearance.
    (D) Ability.

22. The benefits for a con man living in Paris included:

    (A) The lack of intelligence of the citizens.
    (B) The information provided by the newspapers.
    (C) The rundown condition of the city.
    (D) The fast moving pace of the city.

23. According to paragraph three, Lustig was able to impersonate a government official by:

    (A) Having a forger produce fake government stationary.
    (B) Creating a fake identification card.
    (C) Convincing the scrap metal dealers that the matter was an absolute secret.
    (D) Disguising himself in the dress of a government official.

24. It can be inferred from the sixth paragraph that:

    (A) Poisson had never dealt with corrupt government officials before.
    (B) Many of France's government officials were corrupt.
    (C) Government officials had expensive lifestyles.
    (D) Mrs. Poisson was fine with her husband giving a bribe to Mr. Lustig.

25. The passage can be best described as:

    (A) The narrative of a successful con artist.
    (B) A description of an infamous con artist's biggest job.
    (C) A detailed summary of Andre Poisson's fall.
    (D) An informational piece on some of Paris's most famous con-artists.

26. According to the fifth paragraph, Lustig chose Andre Poisson for all the of following reasons EXCEPT:

    (A) Poisson wanted to be a part of the inner circles of the Parisian business community.
    (B) Poisson was a highly successful businessman.
    (C) Poisson was gullible enough to believe that the job was a state secret.
    (D) Lustig knew Poisson was insecure.

27. Based on the tone of the passage, the author would likely agree with the statement that:

    (A) Lustig's crimes deserved fierce punishments.
    (B) People should emulate Lustig's conduct.
    (C) Lustig's aptitudes were remarkable.
    (D) Poisson and Lustig should have received identical punishments.

28. According to the passage, all of the following are true about Lustig EXCEPT:

    (A) He was born in the West.
    (B) He was arrested for counterfeiting.
    (C) He died in 1947.
    (D) He could speak multiple languages.

29. Which of the following is true about the Eiffel Tower?

    (A) It was erected in 1909.
    (B) It was built for the Paris Exposition.
    (C) It worked well with the city's other monuments.
    (D) It was made of one solid piece of metal.

30. As it is used in line 38, *outrageous* most nearly means:

    (A) Contemptible.
    (B) Intense.
    (C) Brilliant.
    (D) Excessive.

Read this passage carefully and then answer the questions that follow.

Natural Science: This passage describes several forces underlying natural phenomena.

Oceanic currents are driven by several forces—some from space, some from the Earth's surface, and some from within the oceans themselves.

One of these forces is the rise and fall of the tides, which is driven by the gravitational attraction of the sun and moon on Earth's oceans. Tides create a current in the oceans, near the shore, and in bays and estuaries along the coast. These are called "tidal currents." Tidal currents are the only type of currents that change in a very regular pattern and can be predicted for future dates.

A second factor that drives ocean currents is wind. Winds drive currents that are at or near the ocean's surface. These currents are generally measured in meters per second or in knots (1 knot = 1.15 miles per hour or 1.85 kilometers per hour). Winds drive currents near coastal areas on a localized scale, and in the open ocean on a global scale.

In addition, ocean currents flow thousands of meters below the surface. These deep-ocean currents are driven by differences in the water's density, which is controlled by temperature (thermo) and salinity (haline). This process is known as thermohaline circulation.

In the Earth's polar regions ocean water gets very cold, forming sea ice. As a consequence, the surrounding seawater gets saltier, because when sea ice forms, the salt is left behind. As the seawater gets saltier, its density increases, and it starts to sink. Surface water is pulled in to replace the sinking water, which in turn eventually becomes cold and salty enough to sink.

This thermohaline circulation drives a global-scale system of currents called the "global conveyor belt." The conveyor belt begins on the surface of the ocean near the pole in the North Atlantic. Here, arctic temperatures chill the water and begin the process of salty water sinking and less-salty water rising.

This deep water moves south, between the continents, past the equator, and down to the ends of Africa and South America. The current travels around the edge of Antarctica, where the water cools and sinks again, as it does in the North Atlantic. Thus, the conveyor belt gets "recharged." As it moves around Antarctica, two sections split off the conveyor and turn northward. One section moves into the Indian Ocean, the other into the Pacific Ocean.

These two sections that split off warm up and become less dense as they travel northward toward the equator, so that they rise to the surface (upwelling). They then loop back southward and westward to the South Atlantic, eventually returning to the North Atlantic, where the cycle begins again.

The conveyor belt moves at much slower speeds (a few centimeters per second) than wind-driven or tidal currents (tens to hundreds of centimeters per second). It is estimated that any given cubic meter of water takes about 1,000 years to complete the journey along the global conveyor belt. In addition, the conveyor moves an immense volume of water—more than 100 times the flow of the Amazon River.

The conveyor belt is a vital component of the global ocean nutrient and carbon dioxide cycles. Warm surface waters are depleted of nutrients and carbon dioxide, but they are enriched again as they travel through the conveyor belt as deep or bottom layers. The base of the world's food chain depends on the cool, nutrient-rich waters that support the growth of algae and seaweed.

The global conveyor belt is a strong, but easily disrupted process. Research suggests that the conveyor belt may be affected by climate change. If global warming results in increased rainfall in the North Atlantic, and the melting of glaciers and sea ice, the influx of warm freshwater onto the sea surface could block the formation of sea ice, disrupting the sinking of cold, salty water. This sequence of events could slow or even stop the conveyor belt, which could result in potentially drastic temperature changes across the globe.

31. The main point of this passage is to:

(A) Convince readers that changes to ocean. temperatures will result in increased global climate change.
(B) Provide information about the process and route of the global conveyor belt.
(C) Explain the science behind thermohaline circulation.
(D) Differentiate between the several types of currents.

32. According to the passage, the global conveyor belt begins:

    (A) Near coasts and estuaries where tidal currents driven by the sun and moon grow stronger and stronger.
    (B) As water cools along the edge of Antarctica.
    (C) In the North Atlantic, where water freezes into sea ice.
    (D) Near the equator, where less-dense water rises in an upwelling.

33. Information in the passage suggests that one would probably find the most abundant growth of algae and seaweed in:

    (A) Warm surface waters
    (B) Water that has traveled through the conveyor belt as deep or bottom layers
    (C) The Amazon river
    (D) Recently melted freshwater from sea ice

34. According to the passage, which of the following affect ocean currents?

    I. Gravity
    II. Wind
    III. Salt
    IV. Sea life

    (A) I and II only
    (B) III only
    (C) I, II, and III
    (D) I, II, III, and IV

35. As it is used in line 72, the word *base* most nearly means:

    (A) Bottom.
    (B) Habitat.
    (C) Element.
    (D) Immoral.

36. According to the passage, which of the following would most likely disrupt the global conveyor belt?

    (A) The overgrowth of microorganisms in deep, nutrient-rich waters.
    (B) An influx of warm freshwater in the North Atlantic preventing ice from forming.
    (C) A sudden increase in the volume of water moving through the conveyor belt.
    (D) Tidal currents causing the conveyor belt to split into more than its two usual sections.

37. The passage suggests that sea ice:

    (A) Sinks.
    (B) Does not include salt.
    (C) Attracts nutrients that support sea life.
    (D) Travels to the North Atlantic or to the Antarctic.

38. The passage states that the global conveyor belt's thermohaline currents:

    (A) Have been slowed and occasionally stopped as a result of climate change.
    (B) Would cease to exist without activity from the tides and wind.
    (C) Gain nutrients as they move from the poles toward the equator.
    (D) Move more slowly than either tidal or wind currents.

39. According to the passage, all of the following could be potential results of disruptions in the global conveyor belt EXCEPT:

    (A) Temperature change around the globe.
    (B) Disruptions in the upwelling of nutrient-rich cool water to the ocean surface.
    (C) Dangerous changes in tidal activity.
    (D) The movement of immense volumes of water across the planet's oceans.

40. The passage's last 2 paragraphs differ from the rest of the passage in that they:

    (A) Are concerned with explaining the importance of the global conveyor belt rather than merely describing its natural processes.
    (B) Support a political rather than a scientific agenda.
    (C) Use more technical rather than vernacular language, indicating that they are intended for scientists rather than laymen.
    (D) Ask the reader to support an end to global warming, rather than conveying simple facts.

Read this passage carefully and then answer the questions that follow.

Natural Science: This passage describes a natural phenomenon with implications for agriculture and meteorology.

In July 2012, farmers in the U.S. Midwest and Plains regions watched crops wilt and die after a stretch of unusually low precipitation and high temperatures. Before a lack of rain and record-breaking heat signaled a problem, however, scientists observed another indication of drought from satellite data: plant stress.

Healthy vegetation requires a certain amount of water from the soil every day to stay alive, and when soil moisture falls below adequate levels, plants become stressed. Scientists with the U.S. Department of Agriculture's Agricultural Research Service (USDA-ARS) have developed a way to use satellite data to map that plant stress. The maps could soon aid in drought forecasts and prove useful for applications such as crop yield estimates or decisions about crop loss compensation.

"Crop drought monitoring is of high practical value, and any advance notice of drought conditions helps the farmer make practical decisions sooner," says Steve Anderson, an ecologist at University of Montana in Missoula.

A new animation of plant stress shows how drought evolved across the United States from January 2010 through September 2012. In spring 2010, satellites measured cool leaf temperatures, indicating healthy plants and wetter-than-average conditions, over many areas across the country. By summer 2011, satellites saw the warming of stressed vegetation, indicating significantly lower-than-usual water availability in many areas, most notably in Texas. Crops were either dead or would soon be dead.

The 2012 event is what experts call a flash drought, meaning that it evolved quickly and unexpectedly. Low soil moisture was further depleted by the heat wave that started in May, and drought abruptly followed. By about May 5, the core regions of drought began to appear on the plant stress map – earlier than the signs of drought appeared in other indicators, such as rainfall measurements.

"We think there's some early-warning potential with these plant stress maps, alerting us as the crops start to run out of water," Anderson says. Signals of plant stress may often appear first in satellite-derived maps of vegetation temperature before the crops have actually started to wilt and die. "The earlier we can learn things are turning south, presumably the more time we have to prepare for whatever actions might be taken."

For example, farmers may decide they need to buy supplemental feed from outside the drought-affected area to support their livestock, or they may need to adjust contract or insurance decisions.

The U.S. Drought Monitor already uses a combination of indices, such as rainfall, to describe drought conditions each week. The monitor currently does not include plant stress, but the potential is being explored. "Plant stress is one representation of drought impacts, and the drought monitoring community agrees that you can't do this with just one tool – you need a lot of different tools," Anderson says.

Plant stress information has the potential to improve the skill of existing forecasts that predict drought out to weeks or months. Also, because the plant stress information is derived from satellites, it can describe drought conditions in areas where rain gauge and radar networks are sparse -- and it can do so at the scale of individual fields.

To produce the maps of plant stress, scientists start with the Moderate Resolution Imaging Spectroradiometer (MODIS) on NASA's Terra and Aqua satellites. Images are processed to distinguish between land surfaces covered by soil and surfaces covered with vegetation.

Narrowing their focus to vegetated areas, scientists set out to measure moisture availability. Plants cool themselves by sweating water extracted from the soil by their roots. When access to water is limited, plants lessen their consumption and reduce evapotranspiration from leaf surfaces. As a result, leaves heat up and produce an elevated leaf or canopy temperature, which can be detected by thermal sensors on NOAA's geostationary weather satellites. Hotter plants imply limited water in the soil.

"This is not a drought forecast. It's a map of what's going on right now," Anderson says. "Is there more or less water than usual?"

What is "usual" or normal, however, can depend on the season or even the year. Scientists currently define normal by calculating and mapping plant stress averaged over periods of 1-3 months, from the start of MODIS data collection in 2000 to present. The mean of these historic maps is considered normal. Compare a current map with the longer-term "normal" map, and scientists get a picture of the magnitude by which current conditions deviate from normal.

"What was normal back in 1920 is not what's normal now, so the more years we have under the belt the better we can define normal," Anderson says. "But this year is so far out of line with respect to previous years, it is unusual regardless of the period of record used as the baseline."

41. The passage indicates that the first observable sign of drought is:

(A) Lack of rain.
(B) Record-breaking heat.
(C) Plant stress.
(D) Crop failure.

42. What is the "event" referred to in line 34?

(A) The advent of the use of satellite data to map plant stress
(B) The drought of 2012
(C) The beginning of the May heat wave
(D) The season's lack of rainfall

43. Which data are the most important for the creation of a drought-indicating plant stress map?

(A) Plant temperature
(B) Air temperature
(C) Inches of rainfall by region
(D) Number of plants experiencing failure to thrive

44. As it is used in line 63, the word *tool* most nearly means:

(A) Piece of farming equipment.
(B) Method.
(C) Utensil.
(D) Crony.

45. According to the passage, plant stress data can be collected from:

(A) Regions as remote as the poles.
(B) Crops that have already been harvested as well as those still in the ground.
(C) Heavily planted as well as seemingly fallow farms.
(D) Individual fields as well as entire regions of the country.

46. The passage states that, for plants, the process of excreting water through leaves:

(A) Cools the air surrounding the plant.
(B) Warms the air surrounding the plant.
(C) Has no effect on external air temperature.
(D) Is an indication of oncoming drought.

47. According to the passage, average plant temperatures are considered normal if they:

(A) Do not cause a loss of harvest for the year.
(B) Fit into averages set by data collected since 2000.
(C) Are neither much higher nor much lower than the average determined for the year 1920.
(D) Show no sign of causing stress in the plants.

48. The author's main point is that:

(A) Plant stress may be a helpful indicator of imminent growing conditions.
(B) Drought is a serious threat to crop production and should be monitored by all possible means.
(C) The drought of 2012 could have been better mediated if more data about plant stress had been available.
(D) Plant stress averages will be better established as we collect more data in upcoming years.

49. According to ecologist Steve Anderson, plant stress maps:

(A) Are the best indicator for future lack of rainfall and crop death.
(B) Require many more years of research before they can be considered useful.
(C) Are not forecasts for drought.
(D) Indicate past rather than current conditions.

50. The passage states that water travels:

(A) Up through plants' roots and out through their leaves.
(B) Up through plants' roots and out through their stems.
(C) In through plants' leaves and out through their roots.
(D) In through plants' leaves and out through their stems.

rP9: MAIN IDEA

TOPIC OVERVIEW

Several of the questions on the ACT Reading Test require you to find the main idea of an entire passage or a single paragraph. Sharpening your main idea skills will increase your ACT Reading score significantly. This section will improve your ability to identify main idea questions and answer them correctly.

RECOGNIZING MAIN IDEA QUESTIONS

Here are several main idea questions like the ones that you will see when you take the ACT. In boldface are the key phrases that identify them as main idea questions:

- One of the **author's main arguments** is that:
- Which of the following quotations best expresses the **main point** of the fifth paragraph?
- In terms of the **passage as a whole**, the most important piece of machinery in the earlier Industrial Revolution was:
- Which of the following descriptions most **accurately and completely represents** this passage?
- Which of the following would serve as the **best title for the passage**?

Always look for phrases about the *entire passage*, the *main claim*, the *whole paragraph*, the *best representation of the author's point*, and similar language. These words act as signals that you must find a main idea in order to answer the question.

ANSWERING MAIN IDEA QUESTIONS

Once you have identified a main idea question, you need to determine the topic, scope, and purpose of the passage or paragraph.

- The **topic** is the most general answer to the question, "What is this passage about?" The topic will be something like "mollusks" or "the linguistic development of children."
- The **scope** is the answer to the question, "What part of the topic does the author focus on?" If the topic is "mollusks," the scope might be "the features that differentiate mollusks from one another."
- The **purpose** is the answer to the question, "Why did the author write this?" If the topic is "mollusks," and the scope is "the features that differentiate mollusks from one another," the purpose might be "to suggest that scientists have been misidentifying mollusks for years."

Keep in mind that questions asking you to assess a single paragraph from the passage will probably have a different main idea than the passage as a whole. Each paragraph will have its own point that fits into the larger whole. Make sure you're paying attention to the paragraph in question and not conflating it with the passage as a whole.

Furthermore, remember that some passages will present multiple viewpoints. Unless the passage makes a case for one viewpoint over the other, a single viewpoint typically does not indicate the main idea of the passage as a whole.

FINDING THE BROADEST PERSPECTIVE

Because main idea questions are concerned with the passage's *broadest* theme, opinion, or topic, it is important to eliminate answer choices that are *part* of the passage, but not a proper summary of its *broadest* or most important point. The answer to a main idea question will never be a single opinion from within the passage; it will be a statement that sums up the entire passage.

This becomes especially important for "best title" questions, where many of the answer choices may seem possible. Choose the answer that most accurately represents the *entire* passage, and especially pay attention to **scope** and **purpose** while answering these questions.

Read this passage carefully and then answer the questions that follow.

Prose fiction

Andra frowned, gazing at the image displayed a foot or so in front of her. Those same blank, shiny eyes, she thought. The beautiful, childlike face, by now so familiar as to be utterly unremarkable—at times, even repellant. Andra had seen so many Daphnes by now that they no longer seized her attention, her heart in her throat, as they did for so many who weren't used to them. They certainly didn't look inhuman, but there was a confounding quality about each of them—something cat-like about the eyes, cow-like about expression, raw and bland but (what was it?) unfamiliar—that distinguished them from normal people.

"God, I'm tired of that look. As if they know so much. They don't know anything." Andra felt a swell of anger and revulsion in her stomach. She was tired of staring at these faces day after day, of having to pretend like she didn't hate all of them—or if not hate, at least resent. The entire world seemed to think they were so impressive, so ethereal and beautiful and talented, so adept at all which seemed impossible. Andra felt alone in the knowledge that these people, or beings, or whatever they were, were nearly nothing inside. There were no dramas or passions in those blank, clear minds; no poetry, or art, or feeling, or even boredom. There was only lack—a dull awareness of being alive, punctuated neither by pain nor by ecstasy. Like mollusks, Andra decided.

Willing the picture away, Andra blinked three times in succession and pronounced "pig, platypus, warlock, close all," signaling her ViaLenses to minimize all displays and close any open applications. While they were off, the lenses would store incoming data and organize it, ready to be presented to the wearer once they were activated again.

Though she was at work, Andra did herself the luxury of removing each slimy, circular lens from her eyes and popped them into two bioglass receptacles marked "L" and "R" respectively. Floating like jellyfish in their saline solution, the lenses glinted purple and blue. Without those blasted lenses constantly chirping with new messages and alerts for cases to be worked, Andra could Center herself.

Centering came easily to her. It was as simple as willing it. While some folks never got the hang of the mental and emotional process of it, Andra had been a model practitioner for as long as she could remember. In grade school, she remembered most of the boys and girls sitting, legs crossed, brows furrowed, toes wiggling impatiently, as their teacher directed them through a guided Centering practice. "Feel your heart open and your muscles relax," Mrs. Justine said. "Let your selfhood unwind and float away." Andra would watch this spectacle for a moment, then turn her gaze inward, breathe deeply, and be gone.

This is exactly what she did as an adult. As long as she had a moment to think about it, she could simply breathe and be gone. It was an important practice that everyone was meant to learn and an especially important talent for Communicators, whose job it was to relay instructions to these strange beings who suddenly, inexplicably, began to appear.

And instructions, it seemed, were all the Daphnes could understand. Presented with questions—about their origin, about their purpose, about the color of the sky or the number of objects set before them—the childlike creatures would send back mere white noise. They had nothing to say, no history to tell, no subjective reality to relate. Unlike the average human, practically bursting with information, the Daphnes were completely devoid of a relatable past, perceptions about the present, or expectations of the future. But instructions they understood, and for whatever reason, they were completely interested in receiving and fulfilling them. Their remarkable mechanical and computational aptitude and their total obedience made them an especially appealing addition to life in Earth. They were widely welcomed and thoroughly utilized.

Andra hadn't yet been born when the first Daphne had appeared, but she was among the first batch of children reared with a steady Communication curriculum from grade school onward. Her aptitude for the skills needed to reach the Daphnes—a natural talent for Centering, a calm and reliable disposition—marked her for a career in Communication from an early age. Perhaps it was the seeming inevitability of her destiny that galled her, the fact that these agentless creatures had been forced upon her before she'd known enough to say she'd rather not spend her life staring into the egoless abyss of their faces. But what could she do now?

1. According to the passage, Andra's attitude toward the Daphnes is one of:

(A) Disdain.
(B) Confusion.
(C) Fear.
(D) Ambivalence.

2. The description of the Daphnes given in the first paragraph suggests that the Daphnes are:

(A) Hideous.
(B) Perplexing.
(C) Arrogant.
(D) Unhappy.

3. Andra's comparison of the Daphnes to *mollusks* (line 29) suggests that she feels they are:

(A) Slow-moving.
(B) Unnatural.
(C) Disgusting.
(D) Simple.

4. What function does paragraph 4 serve in the passage?

(A) They introduce details of an advanced technology to imply the advanced status of Andra's society.
(B) They foreshadow upcoming contact lens technology that the author believes will exist soon.
(C) They shift the focus of the passage away from technologies to Andra's skill at Centering.
(D) They create a more positive tone for the remainder of the passage.

5. The process of "Centering" described in paragraph 5 is closest to:

(A) Running a marathon.
(B) Meditating.
(C) Brainstorming.
(D) Scheduling one's day.

6. As it is used in line 73, the phrase *mere white noise* most nearly means:

(A) Sarcastic remarks.
(B) An indecipherable code.
(C) Lacking useful data.
(D) Excessive information.

7. According to the passage, Daphnes differ from humans in that Daphnes:

(A) Do not age naturally.
(B) Lack a central nervous system.
(C) Seem to have no subjective experiences.
(D) Are reluctant to share their stories.

8. According to the passage, all of the following are true about Andra EXCEPT:

(A) She works as a Communicator.
(B) Her talents were apparent at an early age.
(C) She is particularly concerned with a single Daphne.
(D) She resents her work.

9. The passage suggests that the Daphnes are:

(A) A somewhat recent arrival to planet Earth.
(B) Planning something devious.
(C) Unable to receive information from any humans.
(D) Mostly interested in Andra.

10. According to information in the last paragraph, which of the following is true of Communication?

I. It requires knowledge of Centering.
II. It is taught to young children.
III. It is the method by which Daphnes speak to humans.

(A) I and II only
(B) I and III only
(C) II and III only
(D) I, II, and III

Read this passage carefully and then answer the questions that follow.

Humanities: This passage was adapted from *The Confessions of Jean Jacques Rousseau.*

I came into the world with so few signs of life, that they entertained but little hope of preserving me, with the seeds of a disorder that has gathered strength with years, and from which I am now relieved at intervals, only to suffer a different, though more intolerable evil. I owed my preservation to one of my father's sisters, an amiable and virtuous girl, who took the most tender care of me; she is yet living, nursing, at the age of eighty, a husband younger than herself, but worn out with excessive drinking. Dear aunt! I freely forgive your having preserved my life, and only lament that it is not in my power to bestow on the decline of your days the tender solicitude and care you lavished on the first dawn of mine. My nurse, Jaqueline, is likewise living: and in good health—the hands that opened my eyes to the light of this world may close them at my death. We suffer before we think; it is the common lot of humanity. I experienced more than my proportion of it. I have no knowledge of what passed prior to my fifth or sixth year; I recollect nothing of learning to read, I only remember what effect the first considerable exercise of it produced on my mind; and from that moment I date an uninterrupted knowledge of myself.

Every night, after supper, we read some part of a small collection of romances which had been my mother's. My father's design was only to improve me in reading, and he thought these entertaining works were calculated to give me a fondness for it; but we soon found ourselves so interested in the adventures they contained, that we alternately read whole nights together, and could not bear to give over until at the conclusion of a volume. I soon acquired, by this dangerous custom, not only an extreme facility in reading and comprehending, but, for my age, a too intimate acquaintance with the passions. An infinity of sensations were familiar to me, without possessing any precise idea of the objects to which they related— I had conceived nothing—I had felt the whole. This confused succession of emotions did not retard the future efforts of my reason, though they added an extravagant, romantic notion of human life, which experience and reflection have never been able to eradicate.

My romance reading concluded with the summer of 1719. My mother's library being quite exhausted, we had recourse to that part of her father's which had devolved to us; here we happily found some valuable books, which was by no means extraordinary, having been selected by a minister that truly deserved that title, in whom learning was but a secondary commendation, his taste and good sense being most conspicuous. The History of the Church and Empire by Le Sueur, Bossuett's Discourses on Universal History, Plutarch's Lives, the History of Venice by Nani, Ovid's Metamorphoses, La Bruyere, Fontenelle's World, his Dialogues of the Dead, and a few volumes of Moliere, were soon ranged in my father's closet, where, during the hours he was employed in his business, I daily read them, with an avidity and taste uncommon, perhaps unprecedented at my age.

Those hours that were not employed in reading or writing with my father, or walking with my governess, Jaqueline, I spent with my aunt. Whether seeing her embroider, or hearing her sing, I was ever happy. Her tenderness, unaffected enthusiasm, and the charms of her figure and countenance have left such indelible impressions on my mind that her manner, look, and attitude are still before my eyes. Though my taste, or rather passion, for music, did not show itself until a considerable time after, I am fully persuaded it is to her I am indebted for it. She knew a great number of songs, which she sung with great sweetness and melody. The serenity and cheerfulness which were conspicuous in this lovely girl, banished melancholy, and made all round her happy. The charms of her voice had such an effect on me, that not only several of her songs have ever since remained on my memory, but some I have not thought of from my infancy, as I grow old, return upon my mind with a charm altogether inexpressible.

11. The speaker's earliest years were:

    (A) Uncertain prior to his fifth or sixth year.
    (B) Full of suffering and evil.
    (C) Spent with his nurse Jaqueline.
    (D) Spent learning to read.

12. The speaker regrets:

    (A) The disorder that has gathered strength over the years.
    (B) His inability to overcome suffering and intolerable evil.
    (C) His inability to offer care for his aunt in her old age.
    (D) The fact that his nurse will be present at his death.

13. As used in line 19, *common lot* most nearly means:

(A) Numerous.
(B) Circumstance.
(C) Shared fate.
(D) Type.

14. As it is used in line 29, *design* most nearly means:

(A) Blueprint.
(B) Opinion.
(C) Hope.
(D) Intent.

15. The author states that reading his mother's romances:

(A) Was originally intended to develop a fondness of reading in the speaker.
(B) Was something he could not bear until the conclusion.
(C) Confused his emotions.
(D) Turned out to be a dangerous custom for his reading and comprehending.

16. The "dangerous custom" mentioned in line 36, resulted in all of the following EXCEPT:

(A) An intimate acquaintance with the passions.
(B) An extravagant and romantic notion of human life.
(C) A precise idea of the objects to which the sensations related.
(D) An infinity of sensations.

17. The speaker's grandfather is characterized as:

(A) A strict minister who deserved his title.
(B) A man whose good sense and taste were apparent.
(C) A man who put learning second.
(D) A minister who selected very religious books.

18. It can be inferred from the speaker's reference to "unaffected enthusiasm" and "charms of her figure and countenance" (lines 71-73) that the speaker's aunt:

(A) Was not easily affected by others.
(B) Was a sincere and beautiful young girl.
(C) Was enthusiastic about her charm.
(D) Was very charming but not enthusiastic.

19. The speaker credits having developed his passion for music to his aunt for each of the following EXCEPT:

(A) Exposing the speaker to a wide variety of songs.
(B) Introducing the complexities of forming music by voice.
(C) Banishing melancholy with her cheerfulness.
(D) Singing with a charming voice.

20. What is the main purpose of the passage?

(A) To give a narrative about a man's memory of his mother and father
(B) To offer a recollection of where a man's love of reading and music originated
(C) To tell a story about a man's developing taste for literature
(D) To investigate the progression of a man's artistic style

Read this passage carefully and then answer the questions that follow.

Social Science: This passage discusses the role of historically significant document in a social movement.

Different groups at different times have turned to founding documents of the United States to meet their needs and to declare their entitlement to the promises of the Revolution of 1776. At Seneca Falls, New York, in the summer of 1848, a group of American men and women met to discuss the legal limitations imposed on women during this period. Their consciousness of those limitations had been raised by their participation in the anti-slavery movement; eventually they used the language and structure of the Declaration of Independence to claim the rights they felt women were entitled to as American citizens.

America in the 1840s was in the throes of cultural and economic change. In the years since the Revolution and the Constitutional Convention, the nation's geographic boundaries and population had more than doubled, and many Americans' daily lives had drifted away from Jefferson's vision of a nation composed of independent farmers. Instead, farmers, artisans, and manufacturers existed in a world built around cash crops, manufactured goods, banks, and distant markets. Not all Americans welcomed these changes, which often left them feeling isolated and cut off from traditional sources of community and comfort.

In an effort to regain a sense of community and control over their nation's future, Americans, especially women, formed and joined reform societies. These groups attacked what they perceived as the various wrongs in their society, including the lack of free public school education for both boys and girls, the inhumane treatment of mentally ill patients and criminals, the evil of slavery, the widespread use of alcohol, and the "rights and wrongs" of American women's legal position. The Seneca Falls Convention is a part of this larger period of social reform movements.

What brought three hundred men and women to this small upstate New York town in July, 1848? Many women participated in reform organizations whose goals were to improve the lives of others and to fight for the rights of those who could not speak for themselves, such as schoolchildren and the mentally ill, so the air was ripe for a close examination of women's rights as well. A consciousness-raising experience, however, was necessary to turn these women's thoughts to their own condition.

The triggering incident was a direct result of participation in anti-slavery organizations by Elizabeth Cady Stanton and Lucretia Mott. In 1840 the World Anti-Slavery Convention met in London; some of the American groups elected women as their representatives to this meeting. Once in London, after a lengthy debate, the female representatives were denied their rightful seats and consigned to the balcony. It was at this meeting, while sitting in the balcony and walking through the streets of London, that Elizabeth Cady Stanton and Lucretia Mott met. Eight years later Stanton and Mott called a convention to discuss women's rights.

On July 14, 1848, the Seneca County Courier announced that on the following Wednesday and Thursday a "convention to discuss the social, civil, and religious condition and rights of women" would be held. The Convention issued a document titled the Declaration of Sentiments, a statement written by Stanton and modeled on the Declaration of Independence.

In adapting the Declaration of Independence, Stanton replaced "King George" with "all men" as the agent of women's oppressed condition and compiled a suitable list of grievances, just as the colonists did in the Declaration of Independence. These grievances reflected the severe limitations on women's legal rights in America at this time: women could not vote; they could not participate in the creation of laws that they had to obey; their property was taxed; and a married woman's property and wages legally belonged to her husband. Further, in the relatively unusual case of a divorce, custody of children was virtually automatically awarded to the father; access to the professions and higher education generally was closed to women; and most churches barred women from participating publicly in the ministry or other positions of authority.

Stanton's Declaration of Sentiments proclaimed that "all men and women were created equal" and that the undersigned would employ all methods at their disposal to right these wrongs. David Walker, in his efforts to gain recognition of the legal rights of Black Americans, similarly used the Declaration of Independence in his call to the American people on behalf of the oppressed Black population, both freed and enslaved. In the 1840s and even today, the language of Thomas Jefferson resonates through American life. Americans from every background believe that the ideals of the Revolution are alive and well, and applicable to life in the present, just as the women of the 1848 Seneca Falls Convention felt those ideals spoke to them.

21. The primary purpose of the first paragraph is to:

(A) Introduce the arguments that the author plans to convince the reader of.
(B) Provide a brief synopsis of the passage's main points.
(C) Point out the limitations placed on women in the 1840's.
(D) Explain how the Declaration of Independence made a difference in women's rights.

22. It can be reasonably inferred from the passage that the anti-slavery moment:

(A) Brought to light the limitations imposed on women.
(B) Encouraged slaves to fight for their freedom.
(C) Was the only time that women were allowed to participate in the government.
(D) Allowed women to read and re-interpret the Declaration of Independence.

23. According to the passage, women began to claim to their rights using:

(A) The Revolution of 1776.
(B) Seneca Falls, New York in 1848.
(C) The language and structure of the Declaration of Independence.
(D) The consciousness of their limitations.

24. According to the information in paragraph 2, all of the following are true about America in the 1840's EXCEPT:

(A) Some Americans felt cut off from traditional sources of community.
(B) America was becoming a nation of independent farmers as Jefferson had envisioned.
(C) The American boundaries and population had more than doubled.
(D) Farmers, artisans, and manufacturers lived around cash crops, manufactured goods, banks, and distant markets.

25. Which of the following were reasons for Americans joining reform societies?

I. They were an effort to regain a sense of community.
II. They attacked the rights and wrongs of women's legal position.
III. The fought for the rights of schoolchildren and the mentally ill.
IV. They advocated the inhumane treatment of criminals.

(A) I and IV only
(B) II and III only
(C) I, II, and III
(D) I, II, and IV

26. What does the author mean by "those who could not speak for themselves" (line 43-44)?

(A) Americans who are unable to speak
(B) Poverty-stricken citizens who are ignored by the government
(C) Americans who cannot represent themselves in government
(D) Slaves who are not allowed to represent themselves

27. It can be inferred from the passage that:

(A) Women joined reform societies explicitly to fight for their constitutional rights.
(B) Women's original goal was not an examination of women's rights.
(C) It took years for reform societies to achieve their goals.
(D) The mentally ill were mistreated and denied rights.

28. The author's reference to a "triggering incident" (line 50) implies:

(A) Choosing women as American representatives for the World Anti-Slavery Convention was a big step towards women's rights.
(B) The treatment of Stanton and Mott at the World Anti-Slavery Convention prompted the meeting at Seneca 8 years later.
(C) Stanton and Mott were infuriated when they were denied their rightful seats and left the Convention to walk the streets of London.
(D) Stanton and Mott become good friends because they were both elected as American representatives in the World Anti-Slavery Convention.

29. All of the following were grievances included in the Declaration of Sentiments EXCEPT:

(A) Churches only allowed women to hold menial positions in the ministry.
(B) Women could not participate in the creation of laws they had to follow.
(C) A married woman's property and wages legally belonged to her husband.
(D) Higher education was generally closed off to women.

30. This passage could best be described as which of the following?

(A) A diatribe against oppressive Americans in the 1840's
(B) A lighthearted retelling of one of America's reform rivalries
(C) An argument for the rightful treatment of those who cannot speak for themselves
(D) A historic account of how founding documents were used to improve American lives

Read this passage carefully and then answer the questions that follow.

Social Science: This passage discussed the contents and historical context of an important document.

By 1776, the Thirteen Colonies were embroiled in a battle with Great Britain to gain the rights the colonists felt they deserved as subjects of the British crown. Although they had been at war with Great Britain over a year, the Declaration of Independence made the official declaration that the American colonies were no longer part of the British Empire. The Declaration of Independence became the founding document of the United States of America.

The choice to proclaim independence from Great Britain was certainly riddled with problems. During June and July of 1776, the main question facing the Second Continental Congress at Philadelphia revolved around independence: should the American colonies represented at this Congress declare their separation and freedom from the United Kingdom of Great Britain? After intense debate, the delegates voted on July 2 in favor of Virginia Statesman Richard Henry Lee's resolution for independence. On July 4, the Congress discussed and approved, with a few changes, the formal Declaration of Independence written by Thomas Jefferson on behalf of a five-person committee appointed by Congress. Besides Thomas Jefferson, the five-person committee included Benjamin Franklin, Robert R. Livingston, Roger Sherman and John Adams. John Adams, who would later become the second President of the United States, was one of the chief proponents for declaring independence from Great Britain and the one who persuaded the committee to allow Thomas Jefferson to write the document. After the Declaration of Independence was formalized, it was signed by the fifty-six delegates of the Congress and sent to be published.

During July and August 1776, the Declaration of Independence was printed and distributed throughout the newly proclaimed United States of America. Americans recognized immediately that this document expressed widely held ideas about the proper purposes of government and the rights of individuals. Many years after writing the document, Jefferson acknowledged that the Declaration of Independence was "intended to be an expression of the American mind" and not an original or innovative statement. In fact, George Mason expressed the same ideas about government and rights in similar words in Articles I-III of the Virginia Declaration of Rights, which was drafted and approved a few weeks before the Declaration of Independence.

When reading the Declaration of Independence, it can be noted that it is divided into four main parts. The first part is an introduction that states the purpose of the document, which was to explain why the American people were declaring independence from the government of Great Britain. The second part is a theory of good government and individual rights generally accepted by Americans from the 1770s until today. In this theory, all individuals are equal in their possession of certain immutable rights. These rights include life, liberty, and the pursuit of happiness and should remain unaffected by the government's policies. They are inherent to human nature. Therefore, the first purpose of a good government is to secure or protect these rights. Further, a good government is based on the consent of the governed -- the people -- who are the sole source of the government's authority. If their government persistently violates this theory of good government, then the people have the right to overthrow it.

The third part of the document is a list of grievances against King George III, who was singled out to represent the actions of the British government. These grievances are examples of actions that violated the criteria for good government stated in the second part of the Declaration of Independence. These grievances, therefore, justify separation from the King's bad government and establishment of a good government to replace it. The fourth and final part of the document is an unqualified assertion of sovereignty by the United States of America. It proclaims the determination of Americans to defend and maintain their independence and rights.

The main ideas of the Declaration of Independence are essential to a good education for citizenship in the United States. These ideas are common cords of civic identity by which unity is forged and maintained among the diverse ethnic, religious, and racial groups within the United States. Beyond its influence in the United States, the Declaration of Independence has global significance because it set a standard for liberty and justice under law to which all people in the world may aspire.

31. The passage can best be characterized as:

(A) An editorial about the leadership style of King George III.
(B) A narrative written about the main historical figures in the Second Continental Congress.
(C) An exposé of the secret deals made before the Declaration of Independence was signed.
(D) A brief summary of the creation and composition of the Declaration of Independence.

32. As it is used in line 1, *embroiled* most nearly means:

(A) Entangled.
(B) Disbanded.
(C) Interwoven.
(D) Sacrificed.

33. When the passage states that the Declaration of Independence was "formalized" (line 34) it most likely means:

(A) Everyone agreed on the legitimacy of the Declaration.
(B) Thomas Jefferson was given the official job of writing the Declaration.
(C) The Declaration was completed with a definite structure.
(D) The Declaration had the consent of the people.

34. The author's attitude towards civic education is best expressed as one of:

(A) Advocacy.
(B) Provocation.
(C) Exasperation.
(D) Criticism.

35. Which of the following were included in the four sections of the Declaration of Independence?

I. A statement of the consequences for Great Britain if they failed to recognize the United States' demands for independence
II. A list of grievances against King George III
III. A theory of good government and individual rights

(A) II only
(B) I and III only
(C) II and III only
(D) I, II, and III

36. As a response to the grievances mentioned in paragraph 5, the Continental Congress decided to:

(A) Add a section on the Declaration that asserted the sovereignty of the United States.
(B) Create a government that established certain immutable rights.
(C) Declare war with Great Britain.
(D) Rouse the people to support the writing of the Declaration.

37. In line 63, *immutable* most nearly means:

(A) Desirable.
(B) Inarguable.
(C) Immovable.
(D) Established.

38. All of the following are true of the Declaration of Independence's definition of a good government EXCEPT:

(A) It protects the people's immutable rights.
(B) It is based on the consent of the governed.
(C) Its policies do not affect the immutable rights.
(D) It advocates democracy instead of a monarchy.

39. It can be inferred by the author's references to King George III that the colonists viewed King George III as:

(A) A figurehead with very limited power to control government decisions.
(B) A fair ruler who fought for their rights.
(C) An apathetic leader who made very few government decisions.
(D) An unjust monarch, who made most, if not all, decisions for the government.

40. The passage supports which of the following conclusions about Jefferson and the Declaration of Independence?

(A) He received widespread acclaim for his new and original ideas.
(B) The people felt represented by many of the ideas expressed in the document.
(C) He never expected the Congress to support his ideas.
(D) At first, John Adams regretted choosing Jefferson to write the document.

Read this passage carefully and then answer the questions that follow.

Natural Science: This passage discusses the characteristics of an aquatic animal.

Appearing as solitary forms in the fossil record more than 400 million years ago, corals are extremely ancient animals that evolved into modern reef-building forms over the last 25 million years. Coral reefs are the largest structures on earth of biological origin. Rivaling old growth forests in longevity of their ecological communities, well-developed reefs reflect thousands of years of history.

Colonies of reef-building corals exhibit a wide range of shapes, but most can be classified within ten general forms. Branching corals have branches that also have (secondary) branches. Digitate corals look like fingers or clumps of cigars and have no secondary branches. Table corals are table-like structures of fused branches. Elkhorn coral has large, flattened branches. Foliose corals have broad plate-like portions rising above the substrate. Encrusting corals grow as a thin layer against the substrate. Submassive corals have knobs, columns or wedges protruding from an encrusting base. Massive corals are ball-shaped or boulder-like corals which may be small as an egg or large as a house. Mushroom corals resemble the attached or unattached tops of mushrooms. Cup corals look like egg cups or cups that have been squashed, elongated or twisted. While the growth patterns of stony coral colonies are primarily species-specific, a colony's geographic location, environmental factors, and the density of surrounding corals may affect and/or alter the shape of the colony as it grows.

In addition to affecting the shape of a colony's growth, environmental factors influence the rates at which various species of corals grow. One of the most significant factors is sunlight. On sunny days, the calcification rates of corals can be twice as fast as on cloudy days. This is likely a function of the symbiotic zooxanthellae algae, which play a unique role in enhancing the corals' ability to synthesize calcium carbonate. Experiments have shown that rates of calcification slow significantly when zooxanthellae are removed from corals, or when corals are kept in shade or darkness.

Reef-building corals are restricted in their geographic distribution. This is because the symbiotic machinery of the coral needs a narrow and consistent band of environmental conditions to produce the copious quantities of limestone necessary for reef formation. The formation of highly consolidated reefs only occur where the temperature does not fall below 18°C for extended periods of time. This specific temperature restriction --18°C-- does not, however, apply to the corals themselves. In Japan, where this has been studied in detail, approximately half of all coral species occur where the sea temperature regularly falls to 14°C an approximately 25% occur where it falls to 11°C. Many grow optimally in water temperatures between 23° and 29°C, but some can tolerate temperatures as high as 40°C for limited periods of time. Most require very salty (saline) water ranging from 32 to 42 parts per thousand. The water must also be clear to permit high light penetration. The corals' requirement for high light also explains why most reef-building species are restricted to the euphotic (light penetration) zone.

The number of species of corals on a reef declines rapidly in deeper water. High levels of suspended sediments can smother coral colonies, clogging their mouths, which can impair feeding. Suspended sediments can also serve to decrease the depth to which light can penetrate. In colder regions or murkier waters, corals may still exist on hard substrates, but their capacity to secrete limestone is greatly reduced.

In light of such stringent environmental restrictions, reefs generally are confined to tropical and semitropical waters. The diversity of reef corals, i.e., the number of species, decreases in higher latitudes.

Another factor that seems to affect the diversity of reef-building corals is the ocean in which they are located. Over 650 reef-building species are known to exist in the waters of the Indo-Pacific region. In comparison, the Atlantic Ocean contains approximately 62 known species. The fossil record shows that many species once found across the Atlantic, Pacific and Indian Oceans gradually went extinct in the Atlantic, where the effects of ice ages had strong impacts on the Caribbean area wherein most of the Atlantic reefs reside. Following the closure of the seaway between the Caribbean and the Pacific, several species of corals became restricted to the Caribbean.

41. Which of the following is true about the relationship between sunlight, zooxanthellae, and the development of coral reefs?

(A) Sunlight encourages the growth of zooxanthellae, which increase corals' ability to produce the calcification characteristic of reefs.
(B) Sunlight discourages the growth of zooxanthellae, which increase corals' ability to produce the calcification characteristic of reefs.
(C) Sunlight encourages the growth of zooxanthellae, which decrease corals' ability to produce the calcification characteristic of reefs.
(D) Sunlight discourages the growth of zooxanthellae, which decrease corals' ability to produce the calcification characteristic of reefs.

42. The author's main point is to:

(A) Illustrate the differences between the most common types of reefs.
(B) Discuss the conditions of coral reef growth.
(C) Prove the importance of zooxanthellae in the development of coral reefs.
(D) Call for greater protection of tropical zones with the highest number of reef-building coral species.

43. As it is used in line 12, the word *branches* most nearly means:

(A) Tree boughs.
(B) Subspecies.
(C) Extensions.
(D) Diverges.

44. Corals differ from reefs in that:

(A) Corals thrive in dark, nutrient-rich waters while reefs can only form in the euphotic zone.
(B) Corals cannot support additional biological life, while reefs can.
(C) Corals can survive in temperatures below 18°C, while reefs typically cannot.
(D) Corals prefer highly saline waters, while reefs will not form under such conditions.

45. According to the passage, reef-forming corals:

(A) Typically take on one of five general forms.
(B) Can take on a variety of shapes depending on several conditions.
(C) Are analogous to the diverse species in old-growth forests.
(D) Are evolutionarily older than their solitary forms.

46. According to the passage, all of the following are conditions which affect the growth of coral reefs EXCEPT:

(A) Amount of sunlight.
(B) Geographic distribution.
(C) Density of surrounding corals.
(D) Migratory sea life populations.

47. The passage infers that reefs with the greatest biodiversity are located:

(A) Near the equator.
(B) Near the North Pole.
(C) Near the South Pole.
(D) Outside the euphotic zone.

48. All of the following are examples of the "narrow and consistent band of environmental conditions" (lines 47-48) necessary to support highly consolidated reefs EXCEPT:

(A) Temperatures that do not regularly fall below 18°C.
(B) Clear water allowing for the penetration of light.
(C) Nutrients from upwellings from the sea floor.
(D) Copious quantities of limestone.

49. According to the passage, the fossil record has been used to:

(A) Demonstrate the age and historical shift in locations of coral species.
(B) Prove that corals are the most ancient form of life on the planet.
(C) Suggest that current climate shifts follow a pattern linked to reef size.
(D) Forge a link between coral reefs and ancient forests.

50. The passage states that species of coral once prevalent in the Atlantic went extinct due to:

(A) Human introduction of polluted wastewater in the area.
(B) Changes in the Caribbean due to ice ages.
(C) Decreased salinization of the water as a result of global warming.
(D) Closure of the seaway between the Caribbean and the Pacific.

rP10: LITERARY ANALYSIS

TOPIC OVERVIEW

This section covers literary analysis questions. Questions of this type tend to focus on the author's or narrator's involvement in the passage and the relationship between the passage as a whole and the parts that make it up.

RECOGNIZING LITERARY ANALYSIS QUESTIONS

Here are several literary analysis questions like the ones that you will see when you take the ACT. In boldface are the key phrases that identify them as literary analysis questions:

- Which of the following describes the way the second paragraph (lines 20-30) **functions in the passage as a whole**?
- Which of the following statements describes how the third paragraph (lines 25-32) **functions in relation** to the first paragraph?
- The **author most likely intends** the description of the protagonist in lines 31-34 to be read:
- Which of the following statements best **characterizes the narrator's attitude** toward the electoral college?
- The passage is written from which of the following **points of view**:

Always look for key words or phrases like *function*, *author/narrator*, and *point of view*. These words act as signals that you will need to analyze the passage in order to answer the question.

ANSWERING LITERARY ANALYSIS QUESTIONS

Like the answers to conclusion questions, the answers to literary analysis questions are not directly stated in the passage. They are, however, always supported by evidence found in the passage. You will need to use this supporting evidence, as well as your skills of analysis, to come up with a correct answer.

Analysis is studying the fundamental parts that make up a whole. The fundamental parts of a passage that give it overall meaning include word choice, the ordering of ideas, and sentence structure, as well as the subtleties of imagery and ideas.

When approaching literary analysis questions, consider that you are being asked to handle parts of the passage as semi-independent pieces. Sometimes you will need to deal with two paragraphs in isolation and consider how they interact with one another from a rhetorical perspective.

Other times, you will need to consider the author or narrator as a being with certain intentions and methods. Answering these types of questions uses the skills of analysis you have probably learned while writing critical essays in your English class.

GENERAL PASSAGE STRUCTURE

As you have probably learned in school, short essays tend to follow a set structure:

Introduction
Body
Conclusion

ACT Social Science, Humanities, and Natural Science passages will often take a similar pattern. The introduction will likely discuss the passage's topic, the body paragraphs will discuss the topic and introduce any opposing viewpoints, and the conclusion will wrap up the "conversation" and possibly imply the topic's greater significance.

Literary analysis questions will often ask questions regarding this structure—that is, why an author presents certain information in a certain order—and thinking of the passage as any other short essay can help you see the progression of thought in a more familiar way.

Read this passage carefully and then answer the questions that follow.

Prose Fiction: The following passage was adapted from *Beatrice* by H. Rider Haggard.

Owen Davies tramped along the cliff with a light heart. The wild lashing of the rain and the roaring of the wind did not disturb him in the least. They were disagreeable, but he accepted them as he accepted existence and all its vanities, without remark or mental comment. There is a class of mind of which this is the prevailing attitude. Very early in their span of life, those endowed with such a mind come to the conclusion that the world is too much for them. They cannot understand it, so they abandon the attempt, and, as a consequence, in their own torpid way they are among the happiest and most contented of men. Problems, on which persons of keener intelligence and more aspiring soul fret and foam their lives away as rushing water round a rock, do not even break the placid surface of their days. Such men slip past them. They look out upon the stars and read of the mystery of the universe speeding on forever through the limitless wastes of space, and are not astonished. In their childhood they were taught that God made the sun and the stars to give light on the earth; that is enough for them. And so it is with everything. Poverty and suffering; war, pestilence, and the inequalities of fate; madness, life and death, and the spiritual wonders that hedge in our being, are things not to be inquired into but accepted. So they accept them as they do their dinner or a tradesman's circular.

In some cases this mental state has its root in deep and simple convictions, and in some it springs from a preponderance of healthful animal instincts over the higher but more troublesome spiritual parts. The ox chewing the cud in the fresh meadow does not muse upon the past and future, and the gull blown like a foam-flake out against the sunset, does not know the splendour of the sky and sea. He is not much troubled about the scheme of things. In the beginning he was "torn out of the reeds," and in the end he melts into the Unknown, and for the rest, there are beef and wives, and foes to conquer. But then oxen and gulls are not, so far as we know, troubled with any spiritual parts at all, and such things are not cultivated. They come with civilization.

But perhaps in the majority this condition, so necessary to the more placid forms of happiness, is born of a conjunction of physical and religious developments. So it was, at least, with the rich and fortunate man whom we have seen trudging along the wind-swept cliff. By nature and education he was of a strongly and simply believing mind, as he was in body powerful, placid, and healthy to an exasperating degree. It may be said that it is easy to be religious and placid on a high yearly income, but Owen Davies had not always enjoyed ten thousand a year and one of the most romantic and beautiful seats in Wales. From the time he was seventeen, when his mother's death left him an orphan, till he reached the age of thirty, some six years from the date of the opening of this history, he led about as hard a life as fate could find for any man. Some people may have heard of sugar drogers, or sailing brigs, which trade between this country and the West Indies, carrying coal outwards and sugar home.

On board one of these, Owen Davies worked in various capacities for thirteen long years. He did his drudgery well; but he made no friends, and always remained the same shy, silent, and pious man. Then suddenly a relation died without a will, and he found himself heir-in-law to Bryngelly Castle and all its revenues. Owen expressed no surprise, and to all appearance felt none. He had never seen his relation, and never dreamed of this romantic devolution of great estates upon himself. But he accepted the good fortune as he had accepted the ill, and said nothing. The only people who knew him were his shipmates, and they could scarcely be held to know him. They were acquainted with his appearance and the sound of his voice, and his method of doing his duty. But of his internal self they were in total ignorance. This did not, however, prevent them from prophesying that Davies was a "deep one," who, now that he had got the cash, would spend it in a way that would astonish them.

1. Which of the following descriptions most accurately and completely represents this passage?

   (A) A man's personal and religious philosophy allows him to overcome a major hardship in his life.
   (B) A man reflects on the events that have shaped his outlook on life.
   (C) A man is described through his personal philosophy and history.
   (D) A stoic philosophy is described and exemplified by one man.

2. The narrator describes "rushing water round a rock" (lines 15-16) to make the point that:

(A) Others wear themselves down by worry.
(B) Owen Davies' temperament is firm as a rock while earthly concerns slip past him.
(C) Problems can be a powerful but ultimately transient force.
(D) Those of "keener intelligence," by contrast, enjoy placid waters.

3. The discussion of God and belief (lines 20-29) serves mainly to describe Owen Davies':

(A) Childlike faith.
(B) Indifference to superfluous inquiry.
(C) Rationalization for his existence.
(D) Justification for the presence of evil in the world.

4. The comparison of "spiritual wonders" (line 26) to a "dinner" and a "tradesman's circular" (lines 28-29) serve to exemplify how Owen Davies:

(A) Lacks concern for either concept.
(B) Easily understands spiritual and earthly phenomena.
(C) Would as casually accept the existence of either.
(D) Equates poverty and fate with mundane daily experiences.

5. The narrator would characterize Owen Davies in which of the following ways?

I. Unsociable
II. Wealthy
III. Ignorant
IV. Healthy

(A) I and III only
(B) II and IV only
(C) I, II and IV only
(D) I, III, and IV only

6. As it is used in line 76, the word *devolution* means:

(A) Turn of fate.
(B) Transmission.
(C) Return.
(D) Profit.

7. Owen expressed no surprise at his inheritance because:

(A) It was his custom not to express emotion in front of his shipmates.
(B) He felt that he had paid his dues.
(C) He supposed the rest of his family members would pass away soon.
(D) He does not expect or reject anything that happens in life.

8. In evaluating Owen Davies' character, the shipmates may have operated under the assumption that:

(A) "Still waters run deep."
(B) "To each his own."
(C) "He who speaks the least has the most to say."
(D) "Every dog has his day."

9. Owen Davies would most likely agree that the "spiritual parts" (line 33-34):

(A) Differentiate humans from animals.
(B) Involve questioning and reasoning, which is often not conducive to happiness.
(C) Are more noble than animal instinct.
(D) Enable him to accept both blessings and misfortune as God's plan.

10. The author mentions Owen Davies' income and estate (lines 54-66) to suggest that:

(A) They, in addition to his health and religious beliefs, have given him a light heart.
(B) He is a hard-working man.
(C) His outlook on life is not influenced by his condition in society.
(D) Fate is kind to those who have positive attitudes.

Read this passage carefully and then answer the questions that follow.

Prose Fiction: The following passage is adapted from *Beside Still Waters* by Arthur Christopher Benson.

Hugh was the eldest child. Two other children, both sisters, were born into the household. Hugh in later days loved to trace in family papers the full and vivid life, which had surrounded his unconscious self. His mother had been married young, and was scarcely more than a girl when he was born; his father was already a man grave beyond his years, full of affairs and constantly occupied. But his melancholy moods, and they were many, had drawn him to value with a pathetic intentness the quiet family life. Hugh could trace in old diaries the days his father and mother had spent, the walks they had taken, the books they had read together. There seemed for him to brood over those days, in imagination, a sort of singular brightness. He always thought of the old life as going on somewhere, behind the pinewoods, if he could only find it. He could never feel of it as wholly past, but rather as possessing the living force of some romantic book, into the atmosphere of which it was possible to plunge at will.

And then his own life, how vivid and delicate the perceptions were! Looking back, it always seemed to be summer in those days. He could remember the grassy walks of the pleasant garden that wound among the shrubberies; the old-fashioned flowers, sweet-williams and Canterbury bells that filled the deep borders; the rose-garden. But there had been no thought of pathos to him in those years, as there came to be afterwards, in the fading of sweet things; it was all curious, delightful, strange. The impressions of sense were tyrannously strong, so that there was hardly room for reflection or imagination; the felling of a beloved tree was a mere delightful excitement, not a thing to be grieved over. The country was very wild all round, with tracts of heath and sand. The melodious buzzing of nightjars in hot mid-summer evenings, as they swept softly along the heather, lived constantly in his memory. In the moorland, half a mile away, stood some brick-kilns, strange plastered cones, with blackened tops, from which oozed a pungent smoke; those were too terrible to be visited alone; but as he walked past with his nurse, it was delightful and yet appalling to look into the door of the kiln, and see its fiery, glowing heart.

And then still more wonderingly, with a kind of interfusion of terror and mystery, did he love the woodlands of that forest country. To steal along the edge of the covert, with the trees knee-deep in fern, to hear the flies hum angrily within, to find the glade in spring carpeted with blue-bells—all these sights and sounds took hold of his childish heart with a deep passion that never left him.

All this life was, in memory, a series of vignettes and pictures; the little dramas of the nursery, the fire that glowed in the grate, the savour of the fresh-cut bread at meal-times, the games on wet afternoons, with a tent made out of shawls and chairs, or a fort built of bricks; these were the pictures that visited Hugh in after days, small concrete things and sensations; he could trace, he often thought, in later years, that his early life had been one more of perception than of anything else; sights and sounds and scents had filled his mind, to the exclusion of almost all beside. He could remember little of his relations with those about him; the figures of the family and servants were accepted as all part of the environment. The only very real figure was the old nurse, whose rare displeasure he had sorrowed over more than anything else in the world, and whose chance words, uttered to another servant and overheard by the child, that she was thinking of leaving them, had given him a deeper throb of emotion than anything he had before known, or was for many years to know.

But the time for the eager and romantic association with other people, which was to play so large a part in Hugh's life, was not yet come. People had to be taken as they came, and their value depended entirely upon their kindness or unkindness. There was no sense of gratitude as yet, or desire to win affection. If they were kind, they were unthinkingly and instinctively liked. If they thwarted or interfered with the child's little theory of existence, his chosen amusements, his hours of leisure, his loved pursuits, they were simply obstacles round which his tiny stream of life must find its way as it best could.

11. As it is used in line 14, the word *brood* most nearly means:

(A) Protect.
(B) Linger.
(C) Worry.
(D) Watch.

12. Hugh's father can most accurately be characterized as a man who is:

    (A) Gloomy but sometimes filled with irrepressible joy.
    (B) Industrious because he wants the best for his family.
    (C) Somber but grateful.
    (D) Successful but pathetic.

13. It can reasonably be inferred from the passage that the reason Hugh is so emotional about the news that his nurse may leave is because:

    (A) She had become linked with the strongest emotional experiences of his childhood.
    (B) He felt a romantic association to her as with all the people in his life.
    (C) Any change in his environment was infused with extreme sentiment.
    (D) She was a source of protection for him against frightening but exhilarating experiences.

14. According to details in the first paragraph, the author feels that the atmosphere of Hugh's childhood:

    (A) Is so full of vivacity that he is convinced it must live outside of his own mind.
    (B) Could be re-experienced by reading diaries and family papers like a novel.
    (C) Was the byproduct of his imagination in a mostly quiet home.
    (D) Was marred by the mental absence of his father.

15. Which of the following is NOT an accurate description of the passage?

    (A) A man reminisces about the general atmosphere of his childhood.
    (B) A man recalls particular moments that made impressions on his childhood mind.
    (C) A man yearns for the simplicity of his childhood.
    (D) A man explains how the events of his childhood have shaped his character.

16. According to the second paragraph, Hugh cannot feel *pathos* (line 29) because:

    (A) The overwhelming nature of his experiences does not leave room for reflection.
    (B) There were few things in his childhood that warranted sorrow.
    (C) He is not yet capable of feeling grief.
    (D) His emotions quickly transformed from terror to delight.

17. It can most reasonably be inferred that, as it is used in line 90, the word *obstacles* refers not only to people but also to:

    (A) Any hardships that Hugh encountered in his childhood.
    (B) Anything that stood in the way of Hugh's search for happiness.
    (C) Anything that antagonized his freedom.
    (D) Anything that was not gratifying to his senses.

18. It can reasonably be inferred that the Hugh views the "brick-kilns" (line 41) with a mixture of:

    (A) Disdain and interest.
    (B) Pleasure and fear.
    (C) Delight and disgust.
    (D) Enchantment and nausea.

19. Which of the following statements best describes the way the last paragraph (lines 79-91) functions in the passage as a whole?

    (A) It suggests that Hugh's childhood priorities would eventually change.
    (B) It extends Hugh's perspective on life to his interaction with people.
    (C) It concludes the passage using a metaphor to convey Hugh's self-absorbed nature.
    (D) It revisits themes introduced in the first paragraph.

20. Hugh's family can best be described as:

    (A) Newly rich.
    (B) Tightly-knit.
    (C) Wealthy.
    (D) Traditional.

Read this passage carefully and then answer the questions that follow.

Prose Fiction: This passage was adapted from *The Bright Shawl* by Joseph Hergesheimer.

When Howard Gage had gone, his mother's brother sat with his head bowed in frowning thought. The frown, however, was one of perplexity rather than disapproval: he was wholly unable to comprehend the younger man's attitude toward his experiences in the late war. The truth was, Charles Abbott acknowledged, that he understood nothing, nothing at all, about the present young. Indeed, if it hadn't been for the thoroughly absurd, the witless, things they constantly did, dispensing with their actual years he would have considered them the present aged. They were so—well, so gloomy.

Yet, in view of the jolliness of the current parties, it wasn't precisely gloom that enveloped them. Charles Abbott searched his mind for a definition, for light on a subject dark to a degree beyond any mere figure of speech. Yes, darkness particularly described Howard. The satirical bitterness of his references to the "glorious victory in France" was actually a little unbalanced. The impression Abbott had received was choked in mud. His nephew was amazingly clear, vivid and logical, in his memories and opinions; they couldn't, as he stated them in a kind of frozen fury, be easily controverted.

What, above everything else, appeared to dominate Howard Gage was a passion for reality, for truth—all the unequivocal facts—in opposition to a conventional or idealized statement. Particularly, he regarded the slightest sentiment with a suspicion that reached hatred. Abbott's thoughts centered about the word idealized; there, he told himself, a ray of perception might be cast into Howard's obscurity; since the most evident fact of all was that he cherished no ideals, no sustaining vision of an ultimate dignity behind men's lives.

The boy, for example, was without patriotism; at least, he hadn't a trace of the emotional loyalty that had fired the youth of Abbott's day. There was nothing sacrificial in Howard Gage's conception of life and duty, no allegiance outside his immediate need. Selfish, Charles Abbott decided. What upset him was the other's coldness: a young man had no business to be so literal! Youth was a time for generous transforming passions, for heroics. The qualities of absolute justice and consistency should come only with increasing age—the inconsiderable compensations for the other ability to be rapt in uncritical enthusiasms.

Charles Abbott sighed and raised his head. He was sitting in the formal narrow reception room of his city house. The street outside was narrow, too; it ran for only a square, an old thoroughfare with old brick houses, once no more than a service alley for the larger dwellings back of which it ran. Now, perfectly retaining its quietude, it had acquired a new dignity of residence: because of its favorable, its exclusive, situation, it was occupied by young married people of highly desirable connections. Abbott, well past sixty and single, was the only person there of his age and condition.

October was advanced and, though it was hardly past four in the afternoon, the golden sunlight falling the length of the street was already darkling with the faded day. A warm glow enveloped the brick façades and the window panes of aged, faintly iridescent glass; there was a remote sound of automobile horns, the illusive murmur of a city never, at its loudest, loud; and, through the walls, the notes of a piano, charming and melancholy.

After a little he could distinguish the air—it was Liszt's Spanish Rhapsody. The accent of its measure was at once perceptible and immaterial; and overwhelmingly, through its magic of suggestion, a blinding vision of his own youth—so different from Howard's—swept over Charles Abbott. It was exactly as though, again twenty-three, he were standing in the incandescent sunlight of Havana; in, to be precise, the Parque Isabel. This happened so suddenly, so surprisingly, that it oppressed his heart; he breathed with a sharpness that resembled a gasp; the actuality around him was blurred as though his eyes were slightly dazzled.

The playing continued intermittently, while its power to stir him grew in an overwhelming volume. He had had no idea that he was still capable of such profound feeling, such emotion spun, apparently, from the tunes only potent with the young. He was confused—even, alone, embarrassed—at the tightness of his throat, and made a decided effort to regain a reasonable mind. He turned again to the consideration of Howard Gage, of his lack of ideals; and, still in the flood of the re-created past, he saw, in the difference between Howard and the boy in Havana, what, for himself anyhow, was the trouble with the present.

21. As it is used in line 70, the word *illusive* means:

(A) Mysterious.
(B) Hidden.
(C) Difficult to define.
(D) Unreal.

22. Charles Abbott's interpretation of his nephew goes from:

    (A) Perplexed to pitying.
    (B) Uncertain to definite.
    (C) Abstract to concrete.
    (D) Distressed to melancholy.

23. According to Charles Abbot, all of the following are ways in which youth (represented by Howard Gage) differ from adults of his age EXCEPT:

    (A) Youth frequently do absurd things.
    (B) Youth are less idealistic than Abbot's generation was at their age.
    (C) Youth are usually married by the time they reach Gage's age.
    (D) Youth have no emotional loyalty to their country.

24. The contrast between Abbot's impression of Howard being "choked in mud" and Howard's "amazingly clear" nature (lines 21-22) represents:

    (A) Howard's unsuccessful attempt to make himself understood.
    (B) Abbot's tendency to separate two seemingly opposed ideas that are actually harmonious.
    (C) Howard's disturbing recollections of the war.
    (D) Abbot's initial difficulty in interpreting his nephew's attitude.

25. Abbott's main problem with his nephew can be summarized in which of the following statements?

    (A) "He cherished no ideals, no sustaining vision of an ultimate dignity behind men's lives." (lines 35-37)
    (B) "Selfish, Charles Abbott decided." (lines 43-44)
    (C) "The boy...was without patriotism." (lines 38-39)
    (D) "He regarded the slightest sentiment with a suspicion that reached hatred." (lines 30-31)

26. It can be reasonably inferred from the passage that Charles Abbott considers patriotism to be:

    (A) A figurative concept.
    (B) Something worth sacrificing for.
    (C) An example of an ideal that some people cherished.
    (D) Based on blind emotion.

27. Charles Abbott corrects his initial use of the word *gloomy* (line 12) because he eventually realizes:

    (A) That the word represents his initial reaction to something he finds regrettable.
    (B) That young people's participation in festivities disqualifies the his assessment.
    (C) That the word represents his own fumbling for a definition in the dark.
    (D) That his judgment is prematurely negative.

28. Charles Abbott attributes the *dignity* (line 59) of where he lives primarily to:

    (A) The tranquility of its space compared to the city.
    (B) The people who live there.
    (C) Its rising in importance from a back alley to a residential block.
    (D) Its charmingly antique nature.

29. The power of Abbott's vision of himself in Havana lies primarily in:

    (A) Its emotional connection to the piano air being played.
    (B) The clarity of detail that is evoked in Abbott's mind.
    (C) The brilliance of the sun that he envisions.
    (D) The immediacy of the emotion that he feels.

30. Which of the following is an accurate description of the passage?

    (A) A man's reflection on a young man of his day leads him to an emotional memory of his own adolescence.
    (B) A man is baffled by his nephew's cold logic and yearns for a more enthusiastic past.
    (C) A man ruminates on the changing nature of adolescence.
    (D) A man bemoans the loss of innocence in youth today.

Read this passage carefully and then answer the questions that follow.

Humanities: This passage discusses an influential figure in the world of art.

Jackson Pollock is certainly a divisive figure in the art world. Reactions to his works vary widely, with many considering Pollock's paintings to be sloppy messes and others regarding them as genius. A 1959 Reynolds News headline said of Pollock's work, "This is not art – it's a joke in bad taste." Art critic Robert Coates echoed this sentiment when he derided several of Pollock's paintings as "mere unorganized explosions of random energy, and therefore meaningless." Yet others regard Pollock's works as masterpieces, representative of modern art in every way, a defining moment in the art world that separated painting from conscious thought.

Regardless of one's opinions of Pollock's work, his impact on modern art and his fame as a cultural icon cannot be denied. To this day, Pollock's work remains highly valued; in fact, Pollock's famous No. 5 is currently the second highest valued painting in the world. A large part of Pollock's enduring legacy is the fact that his paintings forced people to consider the question: What is art? Many people felt that Pollock's work was not true art – any child could splatter paint on a canvas. Others hailed Pollock as the greatest artist in American history. Pollock is such a controversial figure that even among those who applaud his work there exist divergent schools of thought.

One such interpretation emphasizes the wild nature of Pollock's paintings, arguing that these paintings are not intended to be aesthetically pleasing and are instead intended to be expressions of Pollock's subconscious. From this point of view, we see a redefining of the meaning of art – art is not about beauty, but about self-expression. In fact, many critics referred to Pollock's drip painting method as action painting, which was considered to be a wild outpouring of self-expression. As critic Harold Rosenberg wrote, "The big moment came when it was decided to paint 'just to paint.' The gesture on the canvas was a gesture of liberation from value – political, aesthetic, moral." Pollock himself seemed to reinforce the idea that his paintings were not intended to represent anything more than his unconscious, saying, "When I am painting, I'm not aware of what I'm doing."

A second viewpoint takes a nearly opposite stance on Pollock's artwork, arguing that such abstract expressionist paintings as Pollock's were truly the epitome of aesthetic value. This view was supported by renowned critic Clement Greenberg, who argued that Pollock's work was the culmination of the evolution of painting stretching back to Monet. In this view, Pollock's paintings focused solely on the most essential part of painting: Markings on a flat surface. Pollock certainly paid great attention to his "markings," often pausing for hours to consider the canvas. His wife, Lee Krasner, once commented that Pollock's "control was amazing," indicating that even drip paintings required finesse and skill. Greenberg certainly recognized the skill that went into Pollock's masterpieces when he wrote of one of Pollock's paintings, "I took one look at it and I thought, 'Now that's great art,' and I knew Jackson was the greatest painter this country had produced."

Sadly, Pollock's famous drip paintings were produced for only a few years. For much of his career, Pollock's work was unremarkable. He did not achieve recognition until he was past thirty years old, when Peggy Guggenheim commissioned him to paint Mural, a twenty-foot-long abstract painting that was to grace Guggenheim's entryway. Even then, Pollock's distinctive drip technique did not come about until the mid-1940s, following his marriage to fellow painter Lee Krasner. At the peak of his fame, Pollock abandoned his distinctive technique out of fear of repeating himself. Beginning in 1950, Pollock explored different techniques, such as a collections painted in black on an unprimed canvas. During this time, Pollock's lifelong battle with alcoholism grew worse. In 1955, he produced his last two paintings, and in 1956, he died tragically in a single-car accident while driving under the influence of alcohol.

In many ways, Jackson Pollock redefined art. National Gallery of Art curator Harry Cooper says, "[Pollock] opened up a whole new way of thinking about what a painting could be, how you could make a painting, what it could do in an abstract way." More importantly, Pollock pioneered the idea that painting should reflect emotion rather than form, forging the way for generations of abstract artists.

31. Which of the following best summarizes the organization of the passage?

(A) A topic is examined through a series of general statements.
(B) A paradox is expressed and then undermined by clarifying paragraphs.
(C) A vague subject is discussed and then abandoned in favor of a clearer subject.
(D) Conflicting viewpoints are introduced and then explored in detail.

32. As used in line 12, the word *defining* most nearly means:

(A) Outlining.
(B) Meaningful.
(C) Decisive.
(D) Challenging.

33. In lines 15-16, the author most likely mentions that Pollock's "fame as a cultural icon cannot be denied" in order to:

(A) Present Pollock in a more appealing light.
(B) Challenge the notion that Pollock was unknown outside the art world.
(C) Show that Pollock's critics misunderstand his work.
(D) Suggests that Pollock's stature as a cultural symbol rivals his importance as an artist.

34. It may be most reasonably inferred from the second paragraph that the author believes that the controversy surrounding Pollock:

(A) Should have ended once the artist's paintings became valuable.
(B) Has served a useful purpose.
(C) Is rooted in jealousy and misunderstanding.
(D) Will never end because art critics enjoy debating each other.

35. The passage indicates that Pollock's work is all of the following EXCEPT:

(A) A gesture of liberation.
(B) The end result of an evolutionary period.
(C) A political, aesthetic, and moral statement.
(D) An outpouring of the artist's subconscious mind.

36. The primary purpose of Paragraphs 3 and 4 is to:

(A) Compare Pollock's inability to consciously apprehend his own art work with Lee Krasner's deep understanding of her husband's talent.
(B) Contrast two opposing viewpoints on the aesthetic value of Pollock's work.
(C) Discuss Pollock's unique method of applying paint to canvas.
(D) Examine the problems of modern artists.

37. It can be most reasonably inferred that Lee Krasner:

(A) Taught Pollock how to do abstract painting.
(B) Was a fellow artist who enjoyed much fame before meeting Pollock.
(C) Had always wanted to marry another artist.
(D) Played some role in helping Pollock develop his "drip" painting technique.

38. The author of the passage indirectly contrasts the viewpoints of:

I. Peggy Guggenheim and Lee Krasner
II. Harold Rosenberg and Clement Greenberg
III. Clement Greenberg and Robert Coates

(A) I only
(B) III only
(C) II and III only
(D) I, II, and III

39. According to the author, what was Pollock's most important contribution to art?

(A) He deemphasized form and focused on emotion.
(B) He proved that anybody could create great art by splattering paint on canvas.
(C) He served as a mentor to many abstract painters.
(D) He discovered a new way to present artistic forms.

40. Which of the following statements best describes the author's overall assessment of Pollock's life and work?

(A) Jackson Pollock was an extraordinary painter whose potential had not been fully realized at the time of his death.
(B) Although he produced some great paintings, Pollock's alcoholism kept his work from becoming true masterpieces.
(C) Jackson Pollock's ideas were the epitome of aesthetic value.
(D) Pollock created his most skilled and famous work before he was thirty years old.

Read this passage carefully and then answer the questions that follow.

Social Science: This passage discusses a trend in architecture.

It may be well to consider what is meant by the term "the evolution of the house." One hears much in these days about evolution in plans, plants, and animals. For present purposes, the following definition seems best suited: "Evolution is a process in which, by a series of continuous progressive changes, an arrangement, agency, or organism is developed from rude or simple beginnings as the evolution of civilization from savagery; the evolution of a chicken from an egg." The evolution of the house, then, means that progressive series of changes by which the modern house has developed or evolved from an earlier and simpler form.

What were some of these simpler forms? The modern house has a very definite meaning to most of us, but how little we know of its beginnings. Let us go back into that dim and murky past and find what it can tell us about the earlier human habitations.

It is so difficult to trace beginnings even of most important events and inventions. The origin of language, the origin of the family, the earliest home of the human race, are alike unknown; so we shall not hope to find the first human dwelling, but to find types of early human habitations, and in a study of these types to be enabled to see the evolution of the modern house.

However much the modern house may differ from the earliest dwelling place, since both were destined to serve the needs of human beings, we may assume that the earlier, as the later form, has been intended to meet some primal human need. Man today needs shelter from the summer's heat and the winter's cold, protection from the wind and the storm, defense from wild beasts; so it seems most probable that his brother man in the earlier ages of the world had these same human needs. Those who have studied most about early human habitations seem quite agreed that man found his first shelter under the spreading branches of a tree. In a warm climate and in the absence of wild beasts, a tree might meet his requirement for shelter from the sun's rays.

Among nomadic tribes whose place of habitation is dependent upon the water supply and the pasture, a movable dwelling is a necessity. A small amount of wood would serve as a frame work or support and skin for a covering, while its lightness and ease of transportation made the tent a most desirable dwelling. We read how Abraham sat at the door of his tent, and how the Israelites dwelt in booths at the time of one of their great festivals. "And ye shall take you on the first day the boughs of goodly trees, branches of palm trees and the boughs of thick trees and willows of the brook - ye shall dwell in booths seven days".

One other form of dwelling which Nature has provided for her children was that of the cave in the rock from which it was sometimes necessary to drive out the lower animals before it could be used by man. The cave finds its modern counterpart in the "dugout" of the west. The sod house or "dugouts" are neither as durable nor desirable as the log cabin which has served as a dwelling place for so many pioneers. The log cabin seems to be the most universal form of early dwelling. Types of it are found among primitive and modern races, in Russia, and in all parts of the United States.

In the primitive dwellings which we have considered the one requirement which they have all met has been that of protection or defense. As civilization advanced and man learned the use of tools, domesticated animals, learned the arts of weaving and of working in wood and metal, his dwelling came to mean something more than a place of shelter. Moreover, the character of the country, the climate, the kind of building material at hand, all had a part in determining the kind of dwelling that was built in any locality.

41. The passage can be best described as:

(A) A description of the evolution of houses over different times and geographical locations.
(B) A detailed depiction of the ways weather and temperature shape the houses being built.
(C) An in-depth analysis of the dwellings of different nomadic tribes.
(D) A study of how the physical attributes of houses have evolved depending on their distance to bodies of water.

42. The author implies in the third paragraph that the origins of human dwellings are unknown due to:

(A) A lack of evidence.
(B) A debate between historians about which type of dwelling was used first.
(C) The destruction of written records by warring tribes.
(D) The refusal of historians to determine the origins of human dwellings.

43. The most universally used early homes were:

(A) Caves.
(B) Dugouts.
(C) Tents.
(D) Log cabins.

44. According to the passage, homes provide humans with protection against all of the following EXCEPT:

(A) Summer heat.
(B) Wild beasts.
(C) Enemies.
(D) Storms.

45. The example of the "evolution of civilization from savagery" (line 9) in the definition of evolution is used to:

(A) Provide an example of an entity that moved from simple beginnings to complexity.
(B) Illustrate how human morality has grown to be more complex since ancient times.
(C) Point out how modern human beings are much more intelligent than their predecessors.
(D) Describe the evolution that houses have undergone since ancient times.

46. Why is a movable dwelling necessary for nomadic tribes?

(A) They were easily able to purchase movable dwellings.
(B) Movable dwellings are light and easy to transport.
(C) Movable dwellings are more stable than any other form of dwelling.
(D) They were able to create doors on movable dwellings.

47. According to paragraph 4, early man's first shelter was most likely:

(A) A cave in the rock.
(B) Movable dwellings.
(C) The spreading branches of a tree.
(D) A sod house.

48. In line 17, *murky* most nearly means:

(A) Imprecise.
(B) Suspect.
(C) Illuminated.
(D) Compelling.

49. The kind of dwelling that was built by man was based on:

I. The kind of building materials at hand
II. The local climate
III. The religious beliefs of the builder

(A) II only
(B) I and II only
(C) II and III only
(D) I, II, and III

50. The author of this passage can most reasonably be described as:

(A) A homemaker who is trying to convince her children that the modern home is much more advanced than early homes.
(B) A homebuilder writing about the benefits of buying a home.
(C) An historian who is writing to inform people about early human habitations.
(D) A critic hoping to expose the incorrect use of the term evolution to describe the changes in housing throughout history.

rP11: CONTEXT

TOPIC OVERVIEW

The ACT Reading Test will occasionally ask you to define a word or phrase based on how it is used in the passage. The questions are short and specific, so they can be answered quickly. That being said, you must read carefully because many words have several possible meanings and the test-makers are likely to include several answer choices that will seem correct out of context.

RECOGNIZING CONTEXT QUESTIONS

Context questions are the easiest questions to identify on the ACT Reading Test. They will refer to a particular word or phrase, and they will give you its specific location in the passage. The word or phrase selected will appear either italicized or in quotation marks. The question will ask you to choose a word or phrase from a list of options that most closely matches the intended meaning of the selection. Look at these example questions. In boldface are the words and phrases that signal that you are working with a context question:

- **As used in line** 22 the word *application* **most nearly means**:
- The "strange sensations" **mentioned in line** 72 **refer to**:

Phrases like *as it is used in line*, *most nearly means*, and *mentioned in line* signal that you are working with a context question.

ANSWERING CONTEXT QUESTIONS

When answering a context question, first read the sentences surrounding the word or phrase in question. As you assess the context, think of a replacement word or phrase (the simpler the better) that would not change the meaning of the sentence. After you have done this, look at the options given and find one that most nearly matches your replacement.

To check an answer (or if you can't think of a replacement), read the sentence back using the answer choice you selected. If the sentence makes sense and its intended meaning has not changed, then you should have a correct answer.

MULTIPLE MEANINGS

Many words have multiple meanings. The key to answering context questions about words (or phrases) that could have more than one meaning is to determine exactly how the author is using the word. For example, the word "color" might be either a noun ("The apple was a greenish color") or a verb ("The sun colored the sky"). It can denote an actual color like red or blue ("That is my favorite color"), or it can refer to the mood of a situation ("The conversation had a strange color to it"). Given that your answer choices will probably include some of the word's multiple correct meanings, it is crucial that you discover which meaning the author intends.

Accordingly, you should NEVER answer a context question without first referring back to the passage. It will be nearly impossible to determine the correct answer without understanding it in the original context.

Read this passage carefully and then answer the questions that follow.

Prose Fiction

The rules are simple: treat everyone with the respect and courtesy that you would expect for yourself. Don't cut in line at the coffee shop, don't talk about other people's mothers, ask how to pronounce someone's name before mangling it. It's basic courtesy, common sense. We all have to live with one another, so it's the least we can do. And it's not long after kids start forgetting to say "please" and "thank you" that they start flipping off other drivers on the interstate.

But some people just don't follow the rules. Sadly, these people are your friends, your neighbors, even your husbands and wives. You spend years cultivating a perfectly respectful friendship, but then it becomes clear that your friend is gunning for your promotion. Or your husband is always doing things like buying that boat that you told him not to buy or forgetting to tell you that he invited his friends over to watch the game and can you make those really delicious nachos?

Well, I'm a stickler for the rules, so I don't usually wait around for explanations when someone fouls up -- I walk away. Since bad habits rarely diminish with age, it's important to nip these problems in the bud. A dispassionate severance is sometimes best for both parties. This keeps my life relatively free of pain and frustration, because I remember that no one is entitled to my friendship. Guided by this philosophy, I have excommunicated more friends and acquaintances than the Church.

Admittedly, this practice of cutting out those who are ignorant of basic courtesy didn't leave me with many friends, and fewer boyfriends. But I didn't have a lot of time for boyfriends anyway – I had places to see, things to do, and goals to accomplish. Our blue-collar town didn't offer a lot of opportunity, so I had my sights set on Princeton, law school, and bigger and better places. I wasn't going to marry out of high school like my mother, bound by law to a man who would never rise above mediocrity.

My mother is devoutly Catholic, which explains why she remained stuck in her merry-go-round of a marriage with my father. Religion, you see, smoothes our rough edges like airbrushing removes the blemishes from supermodels' faces in Cosmo. Religion makes the imperfect perfect, blinding us to human fault in the belief that all that is meant to be will be. Doctrinally, we pass from wickedness to blamelessness in one cleansing act, a sequence of events that perfectly suited my father's personality. His routine acts of infidelity were met, not with rebuke, but with forgiveness. "We are called to forgiveness," my mother would say, as she prayed for hours on end. He never admitted guilt, but he was always atoning. His atonement did not take the form of the confessional, but of largesse and bribery. The refrigerator may have been empty, but he would bring home a television set, a peace offering. My older sister, Sandra, and I didn't just get dollhouses; we got dollhouses large enough for us to live in, a silent apology for the fights that never ended. We enjoyed a CD player before anyone else had one, and new furniture when the upholstery wore out. Dad bought new, never used. He liked new things – they were untainted, untarnished, and pure. Not like his marriage. Not like his life.

But he always said that the warranty was a salesperson's trick. Nothing is guaranteed.

Mom finally divorced Dad when I was ten. The merry-go-round was over. This was difficult for Sandra, who idolized our father. She moved out of the house a few years later. She would return from time to time, always certain of her welcome, even if that welcome was rarely warm. Finally, she left for good, calling Mom a Nazi for trying to control her life and keying Mom's car on her way down the driveway. (Sandra, like Dad, never formally apologized, but I think she meant "I'm sorry" when she repainted Mom's entire house). Sandra inflicted a lot of pain and struggle on herself for no other reason that I could discern but to hurt Mom. I grew up afraid of what Sandra might say or do, feeling like my father had never left the house and had simply inhabited Sandra instead.

By the time I grew up, I had seen enough television specials to recognize that my mother, father, and sister were participating in a cycle of abuse, like those made-for-TV movies where the battered wife wears sunglasses the next day to hide her bruises, and the husband comes home with flowers. Mom's bruises weren't on her face, weren't visible at all, but they were always there beneath the surface. I think all wives have bruises of some kind, somewhere.

Not me, though. Never me.

1. It can be inferred from the passage that the examples in the second paragraph are acts that the narrator:

(A) Would consider explicit "rules."
(B) Finds slightly amusing but frustrating.
(C) Would consider offenses that merit "excommunication."
(D) Attributes to increasingly relaxed standards of propriety.

2. The narrator would most likely agree with which of the following statements about basic courtesy?

(A) Its presence or absence in people will only be magnified with time.
(B) It is a precious commodity that few people recognize as important.
(C) It is the only factor that matters when choosing our partners in life.
(D) Its absence in society is a direct effect of bad parenting.

3. By the end of the passage, it can be inferred that the narrator's strict adherence to her standards of propriety is due to:

(A) Her reluctance to be the victim of impropriety herself.
(B) Her aversion to the religion of her mother.
(C) Her unwillingness to repeat the mistakes of her mother.
(D) Her desire to make amends for her involvement in her parents' divorce.

4. As it is used in line 58, the word *largesse* most nearly means:

(A) Reconciliation.
(B) Reparation.
(C) Generosity.
(D) Immensity.

5. The narrator suggests that her father's penchant for new things came from a desire to:

(A) Make up for his absence in his daughters' lives.
(B) Restore other aspects of his life.
(C) Pacify his wife's anger.
(D) Appease his own yearning for material goods.

6. The narrator's use of the word "merry-go-round" (lines 44-45) most directly refers to which of the following aspects of her parents' marriage?

I. Its abusive nature
II. Its amusement to the children
III. Its farcical nature
IV. Its cycle of forgiveness and relapse

(A) IV only
(B) III and IV only
(C) I and IV only
(D) I, II, and IV only

7. According to the narrator, the aspect of religion that facilitated her mother's commitment to her marriage was:

(A) Prayer.
(B) Love.
(C) Atonement.
(D) Forgiveness.

8. The first five paragraphs (lines 1-69) establish all of the following about the narrator EXCEPT:

(A) She is lonely.
(B) She is frank.
(C) She is ambitious.
(D) She is uncompromising.

9. The passage implies that, to the narrator, the idea of a "warranty" (as it is used in line 70) could refer not only to a guarantee that a product is reliable and refundable, but also to:

(A) The promise that marriage is for life.
(B) The assurance that everything will turn out fine.
(C) The guarantee that a person is reliable.
(D) The assertion that something can be replaced within a certain amount of time.

10. Which of the following statements best describes the way the second to last paragraph (lines 88-97) functions in the passage as a whole?

(A) It suggests that the narrator's experience of abuse is not uncommon.
(B) It implies that participants in abusive relationships should know better.
(C) It connects the specific details of the narrator's experience to a larger pattern of behavior.
(D) It suggests that few marriages are perfect.

Read this passage carefully and then answer the questions that follow.

Humanities: This passage discusses an influential musician.

"You can play a shoestring if you're sincere."
– John Coltrane

There are very few names that stand in the highest echelon of jazz history. Louis Armstrong, Miles Davis, Charles Mingus, Thelonius Monk – and, of course, John Coltrane. The saxophonist, known as "Trane" to his friends, lived only 40 years, but he organized and led 50 jazz recordings, several of which are considered untouchable classics – *Giant Steps, Blue Train*, and the sublime *A Love Supreme*.

John William Coltrane first delved into music in his early school years. This interest in music, and especially jazz, grew when he was in the Navy; he joined in 1945, once he met the age requirements, and though he didn't serve overseas (he spent most of his time in Hawaii) he did play with the Navy jazz band. Returning to civilian life in 1946, Coltrane moved to Philadelphia to study jazz theory. Meeting the jazz pianist Thelonius Monk forged a creative bond between the two that led to dozens of collaborations, and Monk introduced Coltrane to another famous horn-blower, Miles Davis. Working with Davis and a team of similarly talented musicians such as Paul Chambers and Philly Joe Jones, Coltrane contributed music to many of Davis's albums, such as *Cookin', Relaxin', Workin'*, and *Steamin' with Miles Davis*. It was during this time that Coltrane got to lead his first session in 1957, which resulted in the classic album *Blue Train*, several tracks from which have become classics.

Despite the fruits of his collaboration with Davis, which none could doubt was fruitful, Coltrane had friction with many within the group. Many of his fellow musicians were put off by Coltrane's stormy temperament. The reason for this was likely his heroin addiction, which made it difficult for other musicians to deal with him. Davis was somewhat understanding – he himself had gone through a dark time during his own addiction to heroin in the 1940s – but had to part ways with Coltrane for a time. In 1958, when Coltrane was clean again, they worked together again on many recordings – including what some call the quintessential jazz album of the era, *Kind of Blue*.

After working with Davis, Coltrane's own renown grew. He assembled a roster of young and talented jazz musicians and released many recordings. After sharpening his skills with some of the finest jazz musicians of the era, Coltrane had finally developed his own style, one known for quick tone variations and complicated and difficult chord progressions. His style was known for what were called 'Coltrane changes' – a harmonic progression chord variation that led to new and interesting variations on traditional song structures.

While many focus on Coltrane's musical accomplishments, he was also a remarkably spiritual man. He was raised in a strictly Methodist family, but he was dedicated to learning about all religions. His first wife, Juanita Naima Grubbs, was a Muslim convert; later in his life he explored Hinduism, Zen Buddhism, and the Kabbalah. After his recovery from his heroin addiction, Coltrane ascribed his remarkable turnaround to a religious experience: "I experienced, by the grace of God, a spiritual awakening which was to lead me to a richer, fuller, more productive life. At that time, in gratitude, I humbly asked the means and privilege to make others happy through music." His supreme achievement, *A Love Supreme*, is almost presented as a prayer, or devotion, to God – as there are no words beyond the repeated refrain "a love supreme," Coltrane's goal was to communicate a religious or spiritual idea through the music itself. Interestingly, some churches have incorporated Coltrane's divinely-inspired music into their services; in fact, the African Orthodox Church has canonized the jazz legend, making him Saint John William Coltrane.

Coltrane died in 1967 from liver cancer. Despite his young age, he left the jazz world completely different from when he started. His family continues the musical traditions; his son, Ravi Coltrane, is a saxophonist like his father, and his wife, Alice Coltrane, was a fairly famous jazz pianist. (She passed away in 2007.) A grandnephew, Stephen Ellison, records electronic music under the moniker of Flying Lotus. But perhaps the most lasting monument to John Coltrane is the vast number of recordings he has left behind – an inspiring and glorious collection that will inspire musicians well into the future and give music historians – and devoted jazz listeners and aficionados - a view into the revolution of sound that Coltrane and his compatriots created.

11. The function of the fifth paragraph is to:

(A) Illustrate where most of Coltrane's inspiration came from.
(B) Show a major turnaround in John Coltrane's life.
(C) Describe how Coltrane recovered from his drug addiction.
(D) Offer a side of Coltrane that is often left unmentioned by his fans.

12. According to the passage, the following facts are all true about John Coltrane EXCEPT:

(A) His recording *Giant Steps* is considered a classic.
(B) He began playing music as a young boy in the Methodist church.
(C) At one point in his life, he moved to Philadelphia to study jazz theory.
(D) He eventually developed his own style that was known for quick tone variations and difficult chord progressions.

13. The quote at the beginning of the passage suggests which of the following?

(A) Coltrane always considered himself a sincere person.
(B) Playing an instrument is not as complicated as people may think.
(C) Coltrane felt that musicians worry too much about the types of instruments they play.
(D) Coltrane believed musicians should possess certain personal qualities.

14. The primary function of paragraph 2 is to:

(A) Offer a detailed list of John Coltrane's collaborators and underscore how much Miles Davis and Thelonius Monk helped the saxophonist's career.
(B) Demonstrate how Coltrane's influences helped shape his style.
(C) Provide a brief biographical sketch identifying some early influences on an important instrumentalist.
(D) Debunk the myth that great jazz musicians avoid learning music theory.

15. As it is used in line 50, the word *renown* most nearly means:

(A) Infamy.
(B) Notoriety.
(C) Opprobrium.
(D) Rectitude.

16. It can be most reasonably inferred from lines 34-44 that:

(A) At that time, many jazz musicians spent some time addicted to drugs.
(B) Heroin was not the only reason for Coltrane's conflicts with other musicians.
(C) Davis was once fired from a band due to his drug use.
(D) The other musicians urged Davis to fire Coltrane.

17. It can be most reasonably inferred from the passage that:

(A) Coltrane is regarded as an influential figure by many different kinds of artists.
(B) Coltrane had a lasting impact on the genre of jazz.
(C) Coltrane is mostly remembered for his devout spiritual life.
(D) Coltrane had to overcome oppression and poverty before achieving success.

18. The word "fruits" (line 34) is used to describe:

(A) The new musical skills that Coltrane acquired while working with Miles Davis.
(B) The commercial success that Coltrane enjoyed after contributing to several of Miles Davis's albums.
(C) The roster of young and talented musicians that came to Coltrane after working with Miles Davis.
(D) The impact of Coltrane's innovation on musicians of future generations.

19. The tone of the passage can best be described as:

(A) Admiration and reverence.
(B) Praise and salutation.
(C) Eulogy and emulation.
(D) Ambition and accommodation.

20. According to the passage, the author believes that Coltrane's memory will be kept alive by which of the following:

    I. Coltrane's compatriots
    II. the music of Coltrane's wife, son, and grandnephew
    III. Coltrane's many recordings

    (A) I only
    (B) I and II only
    (C) II and III only
    (D) I, II and III

Read this passage carefully and then answer the questions that follow.

Humanities: This passage discusses a field of thought and its history.

Within the realm of philosophy there exists a branch known as normative ethics. Normative ethics examines the standards for moral action – precisely what makes an action right or wrong? Within the field of normative ethics there are many different theories. For example, philosophers who subscribe to deontological ethics believe that it is not the consequences of an action but the action itself that determines its moral worth. This contrasts greatly with those who subscribe to consequentialist viewpoint in which the morality of an action can be determined by examining the consequences of the action. Within the latter school of thought lie the utilitarians, a group of philosophers who believe that an action's morality can be determined by the amount of happiness or suffering that it produces.

Imagine that you are driving a bus full of people. There is a toddler in the street in front of you. You have two choices: You can either run over the toddler and save the dozens of people on the bus, or you can swerve to miss the toddler, but run off a cliff and kill everyone on your bus. A utilitarian would answer this moral quandary by telling you to run over the toddler. By running over the toddler, you cause suffering for the toddler and his parents and immediate family, but you cause happiness for the families of the dozens of people on board the bus. By saving the toddler, you would cause suffering for dozens more people and happiness for just a few. Thus by the standards of utilitarianism, the most moral course of action would be to save the bus passengers.

As a school of philosophical thought, utilitarianism did not appear until the late 18th century in the writings of Jeremy Bentham, but the ideas behind utilitarianism can be found in the writings of ancient philosophers such as Aristotle. Bentham conceived of utilitarianism as a code of governance, using his philosophy as a basis for many suggested social and political reforms. According to Bentham, a legislator's course of action ought to be determined by the "greatest happiness principle," which stated that the best course of action was that which produced the greatest aggregate happiness for all sentient beings.

Bentham's ideas made few waves in the political world, but his student, John Stuart Mill, made quite the splash. Mill expanded and revised Bentham's utilitarian ideas, refining the "greatest happiness principle" and casting a somewhat elitist point of view across Bentham's work.

One of Mill's biggest problems with Bentham's work was that the "greatest happiness principle" treated all happiness as the same. In Mill's writings, he created a hierarchy of pleasures, arguing that intellectual and moral pleasures deserve greater weight than simple or physical forms of pleasure. In other words, the pleasure that we get from helping another human being (moral pleasure) or from mastering a new skill (intellectual pleasure) is of greater value than the pleasure we get from a good night's sleep or a full stomach. This is in direct contrast with Bentham's ideas, which argued that it was the quantity and not the quality of happiness that mattered. Unlike Bentham, who argued that the people should get what makes them happy, Mill argued that the simple pleasures are generally preferred by those who have no experience of higher pleasures, and are therefore not in a proper position to judge.

This allows us an introduction into the more elitist flavorings of Mill's version of utilitarianism. In his writings, Mill suggests that the utility of an action should be judged not only by the happiness that it might produce, but also by how the action might lead to future happiness by helping man to develop and evolve to a higher mode of existence. In other words, Mill argues that the best course of action is one that produces the greatest happiness and encourages future happiness by turning our attention to developing higher forms of intellectual and moral pleasure. Mill acted on this belief when he supported legislation that would have granted extra voting power to university graduates, arguing that they were in a better position to judge what would be best for society, they having presumably experienced the higher pleasures that Mill so greatly valued.

Subtly shifting theories such as Bentham's and Mill's help to make the study of ethics more interesting and unique. Unlike other fields, which typically seek truth with at least some hope of discovering a finite answer, ethics seeks truth without ever expecting to arrive at a conclusion. Should happiness be a basis for moral action? If so, are there different types of happiness? These are the kinds of questions that ethics seeks to answer, but the answers will always shift depending on one's point of view.

21. The passage may best be described as

(A) An encyclopedic reflection on a philosophical trend.
(B) A detailed description of the work of several important philosophers.
(C) An attempt to find the truth about a misunderstood philosopher.
(D) An examination of conflicting philosophical viewpoints.

22. The primary purpose of the first paragraph is to:

(A) Discuss the ideas of Jeremy Bentham.
(B) Offer detailed descriptions of several branches of philosophy.
(C) Explain the disagreement between two 18th century philosophers.
(D) Provide background on a specific branch of philosophy.

23. According to the passage, the "utilitarians" (line 14) might also be described as:

(A) Consequentialists.
(B) Moralists.
(C) Deontologists.
(D) Optimists.

24. From Paragraph 3, it can be most reasonably inferred that:

(A) Philosophers often work with legislators to create social and political reforms.
(B) Jeremy Bentham wrote about utilitarianism in government.
(C) The ancient Greeks invented utilitarianism.
(D) Lawmakers are often influenced by philosophical ideas.

25. As used in line 72, the word *flavorings* most likely means:

(A) Underpinnings.
(B) Aspects.
(C) Preferences.
(D) Formations.

26. In Paragraphs 5 and 6, the author implies that Mill's ideas are elitist because:

I. They suggest that people who enjoy simple pleasures are unsophisticated.
II. They would lead to a society in which the poor could not vote.
III. They promote the idea that well-educated people should have more power in society.

(A) I only
(B) II and III only
(C) I and III only
(D) I, II, and III

27. According to the Passage, the philosophies of John Stewart Mill and Jeremy Bentham differ in all the following, EXCEPT:

(A) Mill's philosophy argues that there are degrees of happiness and Bentham's does not.
(B) Bentham's philosophy teaches that an outcome is acceptable if it results in happiness for most people while Mill's philosophy contends that an outcome that produces moral or intellectual happiness is superior to one that produces only physical pleasure.
(C) Under Bentham's philosophy, a person who enjoys a good night's sleep is better able to follow the "greatest happiness principle," but according to Mill's philosophy, a good night's sleep has little value.
(D) Mill's philosophy might be deemed "elitists" while Bentham's philosophy can be termed "utilitarian".

28. It can be most reasonably inferred from the passage that:

(A) The author believes that there are no easy answers to certain philosophical questions.
(B) Mill was a legislator who used his philosophies to influence the law.
(C) The author considers Bentham a better philosopher than Mill.
(D) Utilitarianism is no longer a branch of philosophy.

29. In the final paragraph, what is the likeliest reason the author includes the questions about "moral action" (line 95) and "types of happiness" (96)?

    (A) To remind readers of Mill's and Bentham's differing philosophies
    (B) To end the passage with some thought provoking queries
    (C) To give examples of difficult ethical questions
    (D) To force readers to think philosophically by giving them unanswerable questions

30. The author's approach to the subject of the passage is best characterized as one of:

    (A) Balanced inquiry.
    (B) Detached understanding.
    (C) Assertive inquisition.
    (D) Meandering logic.

Read this passage carefully and then answer the questions that follow.

Social Science: This passage investigates the context surrounding a social phenomenon.

There are two lines of thought regarding poverty in the United States. The first, and lamentably most common, line of thought suggests that people are poor because of personal failings. Those who adhere to this belief base their reasoning on the ideas of a meritocracy in which people are rewarded for hard work. The phrase "pull yourself up by your bootstraps" is an excellent summation of this world view. In the minds of the meritocrats, those who struggle with poverty do so due to laziness or other failings; after all, if those who work hard will succeed, then those who fail must not have worked hard.

But there is a logical fallacy at work here. First, one must recognize that although hard work would produce success in a more perfect world, in reality, hard work alone does not guarantee success. Second, one must recognize that outside forces directly influence a person's available opportunities for success.

Those who agree that the idea of a perfect meritocracy, while admirable, is unrealistic tend to also agree with the second line of thought regarding poverty in the U.S.: That poverty is perpetuated by societal failings.

Decades worth of studies have confirmed the reality of a cycle of poverty, the economic phenomenon wherein a family becomes trapped in poverty for at least three generations. The cycle of poverty includes a set of factors that perpetuate poverty unless there is outside intervention. These factors are myriad, but among the three most influential are family background, geographic and socioeconomic surroundings, and education opportunities.

While no child is necessarily doomed to a life of poverty from birth, children who are raised in certain family situations are more likely to live in poverty as adults. The number one factor – and the easiest to understand – is family income. Children who are raised in low-income households face many obstacles that children from well off families do not. These children are far less likely to be given education opportunities such as summer camps or extracurricular activities; they are less likely to have access to special education or gifted education; and they are more likely to live in neighborhoods with high crime rates. All of these factors place low-income children at risk for poverty in adulthood.

A child's parents' marital status also impacts future achievement. Children who come from single-parent households, for example, are statistically more likely to drop out of high school, be arrested by the age of 30, or have children early in life. There are many theories behind these statistics, but the most common one is that two-parent households provide increased stability, increased income, and increased oversight, meaning that children from two-parent households are more likely to have certain opportunities and more likely to have adequate parental supervision.

Like marital status, parental education also has a direct influence on children's future success. The more education a parent has, the more likely his or her child is to attain higher education. In one study, only 21% of students whose parents had a high school diploma or less enrolled in college after graduation, while 65% of students whose parents had a bachelor's degree or higher enrolled. Many factors are at play here, including parental involvement in a child's schooling, parental expectations for their children, and student role models. Regardless of the explanations, statistics clearly demonstrate that parental education achievement directly impacts student education achievement.

Furthermore, poor single parents are likely to live in poor neighborhoods with poor schools, thus creating a new problem for children in poverty: a complete lack of adequate education opportunities. Students attending poor schools often have the least experienced teachers, a lack of updated curriculum materials, a lack of extracurricular opportunities, and the distractions of poverty-stricken neighborhoods, including high crime rates and gang activity. These hefty obstacles, combined with factors outside of school, create an environment in which even the most brilliant and dedicated students would find it difficult to succeed.

Thus it becomes clear that low-income, single, and poorly educated parents are likely to produce low-income and poorly educated children. These children eventually become parents themselves, passing those same problems on to yet another generation. Such families are not poor because they want to be poor, nor are they poor because they are lazy. These families do not live in poverty because they don't want to pull themselves up by their bootstraps – they live in poverty because they don't have any bootstraps to pull on.

31. What is the main idea of the passage?

(A) The cycle of poverty remains a prolonged issue because of societal failings.
(B) Children who are raised in poverty are likely to live in poverty as adults.
(C) Most people believe that meritocracy is a valid explanation for why poverty exists.
(D) Family income is the main factor involved in the issue of poverty.

32. It can be reasonably inferred that a meritocrat:

(A) Would be generous to a family in need.
(B) Attributes a lack of success to a lack of effort.
(C) Believes most people are generally good.
(D) Thinks that some people are born with the ability to succeed.

33. According to the passage, success cannot be guaranteed because:

(A) Success is achieved only by those who work hard.
(B) Outside forces eliminate a person's ability to succeed.
(C) Success is perpetuated by societal failings.
(D) Only in a perfect world does hard work assure success.

34. According to the passage, the following is NOT a factor in the cycle of poverty:

(A) Work ethic.
(B) Education opportunities.
(C) Geographic location.
(D) Family background.

35. The passage indicates that children raised in low-income households:

I. Are less likely to have access to transportation
II. May not have access to special education
III. Are more likely to live in areas of high crime rates

(A) I only
(B) I and II
(C) II and III
(D) I, II, and III

36. As it is used in line 24, the word *perpetuated* most nearly means:

(A) Maintained.
(B) Decreased.
(C) Galvanized.
(D) Depreciated.

37. The primary purpose of the seventh paragraph is to:

(A) Show that children in high-income families achieve more.
(B) Give statistics showing the achievement gap between low-income and high-income families.
(C) Demonstrate how parental education level can directly impact a child's achievement.
(D) Explain how parental education is like marital status.

38. According to the passage, all of the following are true about children in poor neighborhoods EXCEPT:

(A) Schools lack updated curriculum materials.
(B) There is less opportunity for extracurricular activities.
(C) There is high crime and gang activity creating obstacles.
(D) Only the most brilliant and dedicated students are able to succeed.

39. It can be reasonably inferred from the final paragraph that families living in poverty:

(A) Often lack the means to better their condition for their children.
(B) Will always produce low-income and poorly educated children.
(C) Will pass the problems on to the next generation and be stuck in the cycle of poverty forever.
(D) Are lazy because they will not pull themselves up by their bootstraps.

40. The author's tone can best be described as one of:

(A) Scholarly detachment.
(B) Restrained criticism.
(C) Cultured understanding.
(D) Disgusted indifference.

Read this passage carefully and then answer the questions that follow.

Natural Science: This passage discusses an important technology.

High above the Earth, a constellation of satellites orbits our planet, transmitting radio signals that allow us to determine where we are on the Earth's surface. This Global Positioning System (GPS), when used according to specified procedures, can determine positional coordinates to centimeter-level accuracy anywhere on the surface of the Earth.

GPS has revolutionized surveying, providing latitude, longitude, and height information more quickly, inexpensively, and accurately than was possible by traditional surveying methods. Integrating GPS data into the National Spatial Reference System (NSRS) is enhancing the reliability of many systems that require positioning information.

There are three types of "traditional" surveys: triangulation, traverse, and leveling. Prior to the advent of GPS surveying in the early 1980s, these surveys provided the basis for information contained within the NSRS.

A triangulation survey determines the position of a point by measuring vertical and horizontal angles to control points using an instrument called a theodolite. Because this method required clear lines-of-sight, control points were generally placed at the greatest available elevations. In flat or obstructed areas, large towers, often 100-feet or more tall, were sometimes constructed to help assure line-of-sight. Also, distances were measured at intervals to provide scale to the survey. It often took days to acquire the observations and longer to process them.

A traverse survey determines the position of a point relative to an out-of-sight control point by creating a cumulative series of distance and angular measurements from the control point to the point to be positioned.

A clear line-of-sight is still required in traverse surveying, meaning that a high number of measurements are needed to complete a survey. Thus, the cost and complexity of the survey is often very large, and errors accumulate as more distances and angle measurements are necessary to connect to the new control point.

A leveling survey determines the heights of locations above or below a model of the Earth known as the "geoid." There are three different types of leveling surveys: differential, trigonometric, and barometric.

The most accurate method of leveling is differential leveling. In this method, the height of one location is measured relative to the known height of another location. Readings are made on graduated rods held in an upright position ahead of and behind a carefully leveled instrument. The difference between the readings is the difference in elevation between the points.

Trigonometric leveling involves measuring a vertical angle from a known distance with a theodolite and computing the elevation for the point using trigonometry. This method permits the surveyor to do both triangulation and leveling at the same time, which is efficient, but less accurate than differential leveling.

Barometric leveling involves measuring the differences in atmospheric pressure between points in the survey. While barometric leveling is the least accurate of the leveling techniques, it does rapidly provide relative heights.

Differential and trigonometric leveling require clear lines-of-sight, thus increasing the number of measurements needed and the cost and complexity of the survey.

Since 1983, GPS has revolutionized surveying. GPS offers an alternative to traditional surveying and can eliminate several of the limitations imposed by traditional surveys. Using GPS, it is now possible to perform surveys much more easily over long ranges and in areas where clear lines-of-sight between points are not available.

The use of GPS does have limitations. In environments where the view of the sky is limited, such as urban areas, the traditional survey techniques must still be used. This is because while GPS surveying does not require a line-of-sight between points within a survey, it does require unobstructed lines-of-sight to at least four satellites.

GPS observing sessions of only a few hours can yield three-dimensional positions with accuracies of a few centimeters. GPS antennae can be set up on tripods and connected to separate receivers, or antennae and receivers can even be carried in a backpack arrangement.

The diverse uses of GPS include post-mission static positioning, post-mission kinematic positioning (aircraft, boat, or land vehicle), crustal motion, meteorology, and space weather and sea level studies. Static positioning refers to missions in which the GPS receivers are stationary during data collection. Kinematic missions are those in which the receivers are moving while collecting data.

The evolution of surveying from chains, bars, tapes, theodolites, and levels through the EDMI of the 1950s to the GPS antennae and receivers of today has produced a dramatic increase in the speed and accuracy with which positioning can be accomplished.

41. The main point of this passage is to:

(A) Illustrate survey processes and the value of GPS.
(B) Indicate the need for better surveying systems.
(C) Argue against the maintenance of older forms of surveying.
(D) Enumerate and describe the various uses of GPS.

42. The main point made in paragraphs 3-11 (lines 17-74) is that:

(A) Leveling surveys are far more complex than triangulation or traverse surveys.
(B) Triangulation, traverse, and leveling surveys provided useful but sometimes slow or cost-ineffective positioning information before the advent of GPS.
(C) While older methods of surveying weren't as efficient as GPS, they nevertheless provided science with invaluable data that GPS has been unable to replicate.
(D) Without a clear line-of-sight, older methods of surveying were rendered useless.

43. As it used in line 22, the word *survey* most nearly means:

(A) Investigation.
(B) General view.
(C) Scientific questionnaire.
(D) Geographical record.

44. According to the passage, barometric leveling would be most useful in which of the following scenarios?

(A) A city-dweller needed to map the fastest route from her location to the nearest highway.
(B) A surveyor quickly needed to know the height of a mountain in relation to his position.
(C) A mapmaker found that his measurements were off by miles and needed more accurate data.
(D) A pilot wanted to find the height of a local mountain to the inch in order to map the best flight route through a mountain range.

45. The passage indicates that GPS would work best:

(A) In a heavily forested area that had been surveyed by traditional methods many times.
(B) In a crowded urban area where many local citizens held GPS devices.
(C) In an open area with an unobstructed view of the sky.
(D) In an area with signal from only one or two satellites.

46. The passage states that one distinct advantage of GPS over most older methods of surveying is that GPS:

(A) Does not require a clear line-of-sight between points within a survey.
(B) Can be used particularly effectively in urban areas.
(C) Includes other important data, like atmospheric pressure.
(D) Provides more accurate data due to its use of highly-elevated towers.

47. According to the passage, all of the following statements about theodolites are true EXCEPT:

(A) They measure vertical and horizontal angles to control points.
(B) They require clear lines of sight between the points being measured.
(C) They are only useful in situations where GPS cannot be used.
(D) They are used to provide data for triangulation and trigonometric surveys.

48. Paragraphs 14 and 15 suggest that:

(A) GPS can monitor mobile as well as stationary points.
(B) The use of GPS has been adopted by several government agencies.
(C) The GPS method is so effective as to be impossible to improve.
(D) Without the use of satellites, GPS would be only half as effective as it is now.

49. When the author refers to the "evolution of surveying," (line 104) he or she is referring to:

(A) The simplification of surveying over the years.
(B) Planetary changes that will require new methods of surveying.
(C) Technological advancements.
(D) Hopes for the future.

50. The passage states that, among leveling techniques, the most-to-least effective types of measurement are:

(A) Differential, trigonometric, and barometric.
(B) Trigonometric, barometric, and differential.
(C) Differential, barometric, and trigonometric.
(D) Barometric, trigonometric, and differential.

rP12: SPECIAL QUESTION TYPES

TOPIC OVERVIEW

Many of the questions on the ACT Reading Test may contain the words NOT or EXCEPT or contain a list of statements written with the Roman numerals I, II, and III. These questions test the same skills that you use on the rest of the test, but require slightly different tactics to answer them correctly.

Each one of these questions is actually three simpler problems put together. This makes the questions more time-consuming to answer, so NOT/EXCEPT and I/II/III questions should be saved until you have answered the passage's other questions.

In addition, the format of the questions will not allow you to predict the correct answer in the way that you have for other question types. You will have to read each choice thoroughly and assess its validity.

ANSWERING NOT/EXCEPT QUESTIONS

NOT/EXCEPT questions can involve fact-finding, drawing conclusions, literary analysis, or main ideas. In a NOT/EXCEPT question, three of the answer choices contain true statements and one contains a false statement. The false statement is the correct choice.

To answer these questions:

1. Decide what type of question is being asked (fact finding/conclusion/etc.).
2. Look at each answer choice, one at a time, ignoring the word NOT or EXCEPT. Using the tactics you have learned, decide if each is true.
3. If a choice is true (that is, if it cannot be a correct answer choice), place a checkmark next to it.
4. Choose the answer choice with no checkmark.

If more than one answer has no checkmark, make an educated guess from the choices available.

The ACT includes the words "NOT" and "EXCEPT" in all capital letters, so they are hard to miss, but be careful that you are sure to read the question carefully, even if you're hurrying. It would be a shame to miss the question because you hastily missed a "NOT" or an "EXCEPT"!

ANSWERING I/II/III QUESTIONS

I/II/III questions are likely to involve fact-finding but can also involve drawing conclusions or literary analysis. The question will list three statements with the Roman numerals I, II, and III in front of them. One or more of the statements will be true. The question will never have only false statements.

To answer a I/II/III question you should:

1. Decide what type of question is being asked.
2. Look at each statement, one at a time. Using the tactics you have learned, decide if each is true.
3. If a statement is false, cross it out.
4. Choose the answer choice that contains all of the remaining statements.

If there is no answer choice containing all of your remaining statements, you have made an error. Repeat steps 1-4.

I/II/III questions can appear daunting since they include more text to assess and ask you to group them in specific ways, but paring down the information by crossing out false statements makes these questions much more manageable.

Read this passage carefully and then answer the questions that follow.

Prose Fiction: The following passage was adapted from *The Metamorphosis* by Franz Kafka.

One morning, as Gregor Samsa was waking up from anxious dreams, he discovered that in his bed he had been changed into a monstrous verminous bug. He lay on his armor-hard back and saw, as he lifted his head up a little, his brown, arched abdomen divided up into rigid bow-like sections. From this height the blanket, just about ready to slide off completely, could hardly stay in place. His numerous legs, pitifully thin in comparison to the rest of his circumference, flickered helplessly before his eyes.

"What's happened to me," he thought. It was no dream. His room, a proper room for a human being, only somewhat too small, lay quietly between the four well-known walls. Above the table, on which an unpacked collection of sample cloth goods was spread out—Samsa was a travelling salesman—hung the picture which he had cut out of a magazine a little while ago and set in a pretty gilt frame. It was a picture of a woman with a fur hat and a fur boa. She sat erect there, lifting up in the direction of the viewer a solid fur muff into which her entire forearm had disappeared.

Gregor's glance then turned to the window. The dreary weather—the rain drops were falling audibly down on the metal window ledge—made him quite melancholy. "Why don't I keep sleeping for a little while longer and forget all this foolishness," he thought. But this was entirely impractical, for he was used to sleeping on his right side, but in his present state he could not get himself into this position. No matter how hard he threw himself onto his right side, he always rolled onto his back again. He must have tried it a hundred times, closing his eyes so that he would not have to see the wriggling legs, and gave up only when he began to feel a light, dull pain in his side which he had never felt before.

"Oh God," he thought, "what a demanding job I've chosen! Day in, day out, on the road. The stresses of selling are much greater than the work going on at the head office, and anyway, I still have to cope with the problems of travelling, the worries about train connections, bad food, temporary and constantly changing human relationships, which never come from the heart. To hell with it all!" He felt a slight itching on the top of his abdomen. He slowly pushed himself on his back closer to the bed post so that he could lift his head more easily, found the itchy part, which was entirely covered with small white spots—he did not know what to make of them and wanted to feel the place with a leg, but he retracted it immediately, for the contact felt like a cold shower all over him.

He slid back again into his earlier position. "This getting up early," he thought, "makes a man quite idiotic. A man must have his sleep. Other travelling salesmen live like harem women. For instance, when I come back to the inn during the morning to write up the necessary orders, these gentlemen are just sitting down to breakfast. If I were to try that with my boss, I'd be thrown out on the spot. Still, who knows if maybe that would even be the best thing for me. If I didn't hold back for my parents' sake, I would have quit ages ago. I would've gone to the boss and told him just what I think from the bottom of my heart. He would've fallen right off his desk! How weird it is to sit up at that desk and talk down to the employee from way up there. What's more, the boss has trouble hearing, so the employee has to step up quite close to him. Anyway, I haven't completely given up that hope yet. Once I've got together the money to pay off my parents' debt to him—that should take another five or six years—I'll do it for sure. Then I'll make the big break. In any case, right now I have to get up. My train leaves at five o'clock."

1. The passage's main conflict is between:

   (A) Gregor's condition and his boss' tyranny.
   (B) The source of Gregor's stress and the seriousness of Gregor's condition.
   (C) The stress of Gregor's job and the excellence of his work.
   (D) Gregor's conception of reality and reality itself.

2. The passage suggests that Gregor:

   (A) Seems mostly unconcerned that he has turned into a giant bug overnight.
   (B) Is more concerned with his current state than with his parents' debts.
   (C) Knows he is dreaming.
   (D) Is a hardworking and dedicated employee.

3. The picture on Gregor's wall (lines 18-23) serves which purpose in the narrative?

   (A) To suggest that Gregor has questionable tastes
   (B) To show the attempts Gregor made to beautify his dreary room
   (C) To reinforce the fact that Gregor makes a living selling things like furs
   (D) To suggest that Gregor works at a magazine specializing in discount clothing

4. According to information in the third paragraph, Gregor can't go back to sleep because:

   (A) He is too anxious about getting up to go to work.
   (B) He has been having bad dreams all night.
   (C) His new shape prevents him from getting into a comfortable position.
   (D) His mind is busy trying to figure out why he has transformed.

5. The author most likely uses the phrase "another five or six years" (line 74-75) in order to suggest that:

   (A) Gregor has reason to be optimistic.
   (B) Gregor has trapped himself in a stagnant life.
   (C) Gregor has no other prospects of employment.
   (D) Gregor believes he will be in this new shape for that amount of time.

6. Gregor compares "other traveling salesmen" to "harem women" (lines 57-58) to suggest that other traveling salesmen:

   (A) Are relics of the past.
   (B) Do not have to travel all day.
   (C) Make fewer sales than Gregor does.
   (D) Live easier lives than Gregor does.

7. As it is used in line 68, the expression "fallen right off his desk" most nearly means:

   (A) Been shocked.
   (B) Been terrified.
   (C) Acted clumsily.
   (D) Caused a panic.

8. Throughout the passage, Gregor is characterized mostly as

   (A) Panicked.
   (B) Dejected.
   (C) Irresponsible.
   (D) Confused.

9. Which of the following can be inferred from the passage?

   (A) Gregor's condition was caused by the stress of his job.
   (B) Gregor will soon be fired from his job.
   (C) Gregor's parents were responsible for his choice of job.
   (D) Gregor has woken up too late to catch his train.

10. The narrator's attitude toward Gregor is mostly:

    (A) Incredulous.
    (B) Sympathetic.
    (C) Mocking.
    (D) Impartial.

Read this passage carefully and then answer the questions that follow.

Humanities: This passage discusses an influential story.

Origin myths are myths that attempt to explain the creation of some feature of the natural or social world, be it the origin of man or the creation of the universe. Most major cultures have several origin myths that explain certain events from the past. For example, one common creation myth in China is the story of Pangu, the first living creature. According to this Chinese origin myth, the heavens and earth were mixed together in an egg, along with Pangu. Feeling suffocated, Pangu cracked the egg open, allowing heaven and earth to separate. When Pangu died, he was absorbed into the universe, giving us the sun and moon, stars, wind, rain, and other features of earth.

Although many origin myths are vastly different, one can find surprising correlations between myths from very different cultures. One such example is the connection between the Greek myth of Pandora's Box and the Biblical story of Eve's fall.

Interestingly, Greek mythology and the stories of the Old Testament are separated by both time and space. The Pandora myth first appears in the poem Theogony by Hesiod and later in Hesiod's Works and Days, both of which were written around 800, BCE. Tradition suggests that the Book of Genesis, which contains the story of Eve, was written by Moses during Biblical times; the book is in fact anonymous and archaeologists believe that it was written around 600, BCE. In other words, these two tales were written several hundred years apart and in very different parts of the world.

These origin myths differ in the creation of woman. In Greek mythology, woman's creation was a punishment for man after Prometheus gave man the gift of fire. Zeus, angry about Prometheus's actions, decided to give man a punishing gift in order to compensate for the boon that Prometheus had given. Zeus ordered Hephaestus, the god of craftsmanship, to create the first woman from clay. Other gods contributed to Pandora's creation, including Hermes, who gave her "a shameful mind and deceitful nature" and the gift of speech that allowed for Pandora's "lies and crafty words."

In the Book of Genesis, woman's creation was a blessing to man. According to this origin myth, God decides that "It is not good that the man should be alone; I will make him a companion fit for him." And so God put the first man, Adam, into a deep sleep, took his rib, and used the rib to form woman. Adam names this creation Woman "because she was taken out of Man."

In both stories, the first woman is tempted by her creator. In the case of Pandora, the gods gave Pandora to Prometheus's brother, Epimetheus. Zeus also gave the couple a jar (which later became a box due to mistranslation) with a warning to never open it. In the case of Eve, God placed Adam and Eve in the Garden of Eden, which was home to the tree of the knowledge of good and evil. God instructed Adam and Eve to never eat the fruit of this tree, but a serpent tempts Eve to eat the fruit.

Needless to say, both mythical women succumbed to their respective temptations. Pandora, who was endowed with curiosity in addition to her other god-given traits, opened her box. Eve, tempted by the serpent, ate some of the forbidden fruit and then gave some to her husband, who also ate it.

Although Pandora was created as a punishment and Eve as a blessing, both myths blame women for the suffering of man. When Pandora opened her box, she released all the evils known to man. Startled, she quickly slammed the box closed, trapping within it the one thing that had not escaped: Hope. This was the end of the Golden Age for mankind and the beginning of the Silver Age, which subjected man to illness and death and cursed woman with the travails of childbirth. When Eve partook of the forbidden fruit – and encouraged her husband to do the same – God subjected the couple to similarly severe punishment. God expelled Adam and Eve from the Garden of Eden, condemning mankind to illness, death, and toil, and dooming woman to create new life through painful childbirth.

Although historians believe that the tale of Pandora predates the tale of Eve, the similarities between the two stories likely came well after each tale was first told. Many of today's historians believe that in the centuries following the conquest of western Asia by Alexander the Great, both tales were retold to more closely resemble one another, perhaps explaining why two such well known origin myths share so many parallels.

11. The main purpose of the passage is to:

(A) Use two different myths to reveal how sexism of women is rooted in the mythologies of Western culture.
(B) Illustrate that there are many similarities between myths of different cultures.
(C) Examine the similarities and differences of two different myths.
(D) Compare the nuances of mythologies from two different civilizations.

12. The third paragraph's function is to:

(A) Refute any notion that the myths were written in the same time and place.
(B) Establish when the Pandora and Eve myths were written.
(C) Challenge the religious tradition that believes that Genesis was written by Moses in Biblical times.
(D) Reveal the obvious connections between the Pandora's box and Eve myths.

13. It can be inferred from the passage that:

(A) Some of the ways modern society discriminates against women is believed to have originated in ancient Greece.
(B) The Bible and Greek myths were inspired by similar geological events.
(C) Certain attributes from the Pandora myth were added to the Eve story after it was originally written.
(D) The Pandora myth and Eve story were likely not always so similar.

14. As used in line 38, *boon* most closely means:

(A) Asset.
(B) Gift.
(C) Punishment.
(D) Disobedience.

15. According to the passage, all of the following are true about the creation of woman in Greek mythology EXCEPT:

(A) Hermes gave her a deceitful nature.
(B) She had the gift of speech.
(C) She was meant to be a punishment for man.
(D) She was created from the rib of a man.

16. According to the passage, woman's creation in the Bible is different from her creation in Greek mythology because in the Bible:

(A) Woman is tempted by her creator.
(B) Woman is a blessing to man.
(C) Woman is made from clay.
(D) Woman can construct lies from crafty words.

17. The passage indicates that:

I. Both Eve and Pandora are tempted by a serpent
II. Pandora was given to Prometheus's brother
III. Eve eats the fruit from the tree of knowledge

(A) I only
(B) I and III only
(C) II and III only
(D) I, II, and III

18. Which of the following details would further the ideas presented in the passage?

(A) Algebra originated in Arabic countries and was introduced to the West during the Crusades.
(B) Before the Tang dynasty, China was a Taoist country, with each village having its own deity.
(C) The modern day Christian holiday Easter has a lot in common with a Germanic pagan solstice celebration.
(D) The nine planets are named after Roman gods by modern-day scientists.

19. The author's tone can best be described as:

(A) Scholarly and indifferent.
(B) Passionate and biased.
(C) Attentive and discerning.
(D) Interrogative and skeptical.

20. According to the passage, the myths' similarities:

(A) Are purely coincidental since the stories were written several hundred years apart.
(B) Were meant to explain the origin of man.
(C) Likely came later following the conquest of western Asia.
(D) Were crafted and retold to closely resemble one another.

Read this passage carefully and then answer the questions that follow.

Humanities: This passage discusses a profession and its relevance to society.

The translation profession has been in existence for a long time. Translators have enabled the works of great writers to be read by many people of different cultures and linguistic backgrounds. In school, students learn about scientific discoveries, great voyages, and different philosophies, thanks in part to the work of translators. Translation has also long played a role in the dissemination of scientific information. With increased contact between nations through the internet and other products of modern technology, it has become easier and faster to learn about what is happening in the rest of the world. The exchange of ideas and printed matter between different linguistic communities has necessitated an unprecedented amount of translation. Today, the majority of individuals working in the translation field deal more with technical and semi-technical works than with literary ones.

Translation involves the skill of working with written language, whereas interpretation involves working with spoken communication. A translator renders written materials in one language into written form in another language. Interpreters attempt to transpose statements given orally by speakers representing one culture into the spoken form that is characteristic of the culture of those listening to the interpretation.

Translators generally work either in-house for a business, translation agency, or other institution, or as freelancers. Most are freelancers who either find their own clients or translate for firms or translation bureaus, and who are paid depending on the length and difficulty of a translation. Salaried translators are part of the in-house staff of an agency, firm, or institution. For the vast majority of this type of translator, expertise in a specific subject matter, such as chemistry or economics, is necessary. They may need to be able to translate from several languages. Translator positions in the United States government, for example, require the ability to translate from at least two languages, and World Bank translators must be able to translate from three.

Translators must be capable of expressing, in the target language, ideas that someone else has formulated in the source language. They need to understand the language from which they are translating and be able to write well in the language into which they are translating. This requires understanding subject-specific terminology and having an awareness of style and grammar, regional language, and nuances and idiomatic expressions. Translators must understand the technical area in which they are working and are often expected to possess an in-depth knowledge of highly specialized subjects. Subject matter is becoming so important that the European Economic Community has recently changed its language-specific translation divisions into subject matter ones. Translators are required to stay up-to-date with respect to terminology and must be able to look at a text for meaning and not necessarily translate it literally. For learning technical vocabulary, translators should frequently consult subject-specific articles, have access to new glossaries, and have contacts in a given field. Freelance translators also need access to word processing equipment, a fax machine, and the internet.

In order to understand the languages and cultures of the nations with whom the United States does business, many companies have turned to translators to render advertisements into the language of the client. Translators may be called on to provide companies with information that will enable them to find out what their competitors are doing to improve their products; to facilitate communications with subsidiaries; and to translate company publications, such as employee manuals, safety regulations, and company policy. Information on research or marketing efforts within the company must be provided to foreign subsidiaries in order to promote the technological advancement of the firm as a whole, and countless letters and e-mails sent from one subsidiary to another must be translated.

Many scientific journals are now written in languages that have not received much attention in the United States, such as Japanese, Russian, Portuguese, and Chinese. Currently, one-fourth to one-half of all scientific scholarly production is in languages not handled by U.S. scientists, and only about 20 percent of the 10,000 technical journals published in Japan are translated into English. Translators are needed to keep up with the discoveries taking place in research throughout the world.

The demand for competent translators is at an all-time high. With the internationalization of science and the global market, materials are being produced in many languages, just as American products are being marketed in many countries. Because of the advanced state of science, subject-matter specialization is a must for a translator, as are highly developed writing skills.

21. The primary purpose of this passage is:

(A) To give a history of the translating profession.
(B) To explain why translators are increasing in demand.
(C) To explain the difference between translators and interpreters.
(D) To encourage translators to learn various languages.

22. According to the first paragraph, there is now an unprecedented amount of translation needed because:

(A) It is easier and faster to learn about what is happening in the rest of the world.
(B) Translators have enabled the works of great writers to be read by many people.
(C) The majority of individuals working in translation deal more with technical works.
(D) The exchange of ideas and printed matter between different linguistic communities makes translation necessary.

23. In line 9, *dissemination* most nearly means:

(A) Circulation.
(B) Production.
(C) Exhibition.
(D) Simulation.

24. According to the passage, the main difference between interpretation and translation is:

(A) Interpretation is spoken and translation is written.
(B) Translation involves more skill than interpretation.
(C) An interpreter renders written materials in one language into written form in another.
(D) Interpreters must understand the cultures they are interpreting for.

25. In lines 98-99 the author says, "The demand for competent translators is at an all-time high." Why does the author think this?

(A) There is an increasing demand for different nations to understand each other's cultures.
(B) Many scientific journals are writing articles in languages unfamiliar to American scientists.
(C) Fewer immigrants are obtaining positions in the scientific and political communities.
(D) Many companies are suffering from language barriers.

26. The passage establishes all of the following about freelance translators EXCEPT that they:

(A) May translate for firms or translation bureaus.
(B) Are paid depending on how long and/or difficult a translation is.
(C) Need to be able to translate from several languages.
(D) Often find their own clients.

27. The passage indicates that a translator must:

I. Know subject-specific terminology in several different languages
II. Express ideas in their target language that someone else formulated in the source language
III. Have an awareness of style, grammar, regional language, and nuances

(A) I and III
(B) II and III
(C) III only
(D) I, II, and III

28. The author states that it is important for translators to stay up-to-date with subject matter terminology because:

(A) Translators are often expected to possess an in-depth knowledge of highly specialized subjects.
(B) The European Economic Community will no longer hire those without specialized knowledge.
(C) Translators must write well in the language into which they are translating.
(D) Subject matter is more important than language-specific translation.

29. Many United States companies have turned to translators for all of the following reasons EXCEPT:

(A) To make communications with clients easier.
(B) To find out and provide information about what their competitors are doing.
(C) To provide information about research and marketing efforts from foreign competitors.
(D) To translate advertisements into the client's language.

30. It can be reasonably inferred from the passage that:

    (A) Freelance translators make more money than salaried translators.
    (B) Interpreters with cultural awareness of both their source and target languages are in high demand.
    (C) There is a high likelihood that a translator can get a job if he or she has a high knowledge of a specific subject matter in various languages.
    (D) Translators that are highly specialized in their subject matter are more likely to find a job than interpreters.

Read this passage carefully and then answer the questions that follow.

Natural Science: This passage discusses techniques used to measure a natural phenomenon.

Climate models use mathematical formulas run by computers to simulate the Earth's climate. Such tools allow scientists to manipulate and thus better understand the physical, chemical, and biological processes that influence climate.

Climate models are critical tools for improving our understanding and predictions of the behavior of the atmosphere, the oceans, and the climate system. Since we cannot recreate the Earth's atmosphere in a test tube in order to run experiments, scientists use computer-based simulations known as "general-circulation models" to study the chemical, biological, and physical processes that drive climate. These models rely on mathematical formulas to simulate the complexities of the atmosphere, oceans, and land. These complexities include things such as exchanges of heat and moisture, the effect of volcanic eruptions on temperature patterns, the effect of melting land ice on the ocean, and the reflection of sunlight off the Earth's surface (known as albedo).

Prior to development of climate models, our knowledge of oceanic and atmospheric circulations and how these circulations affect each other was based purely on theory and observation. Climate models provide the best available answers to important questions about whether the Earth's climate is changing and what may be causing the change. Models help us gain insight into climate patterns, changes, and events that occur as a result of natural variability or changes brought on by human activities, and the interplay of both. Models are also used for seasonal and long-term forecasting and for projecting high-impact features of climate such as seasonal hurricane activity and drought.

Observational climate data alone does not reveal much about cause and effect of climate change, but models allow us to determine the distinct influence of different climate features. Changes can be made to one feature in a climate model, such as warming or cooling ocean surface temperatures, to see how those changes impact climate. Today's complex climate models are used to investigate the extent to which observed climate changes may be due to natural causes or may be attributable to human activities. Models are an essential tool for estimating the effects of increasing greenhouse gases on future climate, on spatial scales from global to regional. For example, using various computer models, scientists estimate that the average global temperature will increase 2° to 6° F over the next century. For comparison, at the peak of the last ice age, the temperature was only 7° F cooler than it is today.

The computer used to develop and run the earliest climate prediction models was a Univac 1108 with half a megabyte of memory - not enough to store a song or a high-resolution picture today. Most watches, cell phones, MP3 players, and other electronic gadgets now have chips that process faster than the Univac 1108. It took 20 minutes to simulate one day for just the atmosphere. A modern supercomputer currently provides more than 100,000 times the computing power of that early computer. Pushing the limits of increasingly powerful supercomputers, efforts are underway to use climate models with high enough resolution to produce regional or local predictions, on timescales spanning hours to centuries.

Elements which are the building blocks of life, such as oxygen, carbon, and nitrogen, continually cycle through Earth's systems. Climate—temperature, precipitation and solar radiation—affects and, at the same time, is affected by, these cycles. The next generation of models—Earth system models— simulate the biological, geological, and chemical processes in which these elements are transported and stored. Earth system models will simulate global ecosystem dynamics and exchanges of water, energy, and carbon between plants, soil, and the atmosphere.

Scientists have already begun to incorporate biological and chemical processes to more realistically simulate the Earth's staggeringly complex climate system. Components of these models include temperature, humidity, wind direction and speed, and air pressure in the atmosphere; ocean surface temperature, salinity, and currents; land vegetation, soil type, soil moisture, and rivers; sea-ice concentration, thickness, and ice movement; and the interactions of a variety of biogeochemical processes within these components.

The ongoing development of Earth system models is just the latest chapter in the story of climate modeling that began a few decades ago. Continually fueled by increasing scientific knowledge, innovation, and computer power, each successive generation of climate models has evolved to be more comprehensive, more complex, and ultimately more capable of being applied to questions that are of great importance to society.

31. As it is used in line 10, the phrase *test tube* most nearly means:

(A) Scientific supplies.
(B) Small, controlled environment.
(C) Sterile location.
(D) Unnatural place.

32. According to the passage, which of the following are factors that can be accounted for in a computerized model of the Earth's climate?

I. Volcanic eruptions
II. Melting land ice
III. Albedo

(A) I only
(B) II and III only
(C) I, II, and III
(D) None

33. The passage implies that one of the most important uses for general-circulation models is:

(A) To assess the possible impact of human activity on global climate.
(B) To investigate what caused historical climatologic shifts.
(C) To learn how Earth's climate operates so that we may mold it to our needs.
(D) To determine which chemicals and elements are the most influential over global climate.

34. According to the passage, the major difference between general-circulation models and an Earth system model is that an Earth system model would:

(A) Focus more on plant and animal life and less on climate and atmosphere.
(B) Generate data 100,00 faster than current models.
(C) Accurately predict weather patterns.
(D) Include biological, chemical, and geological factors.

35. The passage suggests that one crucial aspect of generating better and faster general-circulation and Earth system models is:

(A) The accumulation of more accurate data on existing geological conditions.
(B) Increased computer power.
(C) Public interest in the topic of climate change.
(D) Increased dedication of manpower and funding to the projects.

36. The author includes the detail about the global temperature during the last ice age (line 52-54) in order to:

(A) Prove the global warming is a real and present danger.
(B) Suggest that any changes in Earth's current average temperatures are negligible compared with those necessary to cause a dramatic shift in the global climate.
(C) Demonstrate the tremendous impact that a few degrees of temperature change can have on the climate.
(D) Draw a comparison between the last Ice Age and the one awaiting us as a result of climate change.

37. The main point of the third paragraph is:

(A) To explain what is causing climate change and how we can reverse it.
(B) To name some of the important uses of climate models.
(C) To detail the future plans scientists have for climate modeling.
(D) To foreshadow the advent of Earth system modeling.

38. The passage suggests that climate modeling is:

(A) A relatively young science.
(B) Declining and being replaced by Earth system modeling.
(C) Limited by the small amount of available data concerning global warming.
(D) Relatively easy due to the predictability of weather patterns.

39. The author of the passage would most likely agree that:

(A) Biological and chemical factors have a greater impact on global climate than geological ones.
(B) Current generations of climate models are still woefully inadequate to model Earth's complex systems.
(C) The Univac 1108 was useless in predicting climatologic conditions.
(D) Global climate change will have a tremendous impact on life on Earth.

40. The author's main point is to:

    (A) Demonstrate the complexity and value of climate modeling.
    (B) Provide a brief history of the science of climatology.
    (C) Enumerate the several conditions that affect global climate.
    (D) Suggest that climatology deserves public attention and increased funding.

Read this passage carefully and then answer the questions that follow.

Natural Science: This passage discusses research concerning the phenomena surrounding a particular marine area.

Deep-sea hydrothermal vents and their associated biological communities were first discovered on the Galápagos Rift in 1977. The discovery of life thriving in the absence of sunlight and nourished by chemicals in the vent fluids profoundly and permanently changed our view of how and where life could exist. It fundamentally changed the biological and earth sciences and our view of the deep sea. It also opened the door for biologists, chemists and geologists to explore the fundamental properties and complex interactions between magmatic, hydrothermal, chemical and biological processes along the global mid-ocean ridge system.

The objectives of two recent expeditions to the rift included revisiting the historic low-temperature hydrothermal vents like Rose Garden and the Garden and Eden (discovered in 1977) and searching for high-temperature vents along the largely unexplored western portion of the eastern rift. The Autonomous Benthic Explorer (ABE) vehicle mapped meter-scale bathymetry, near-bottom magnetics and bottom water-properties and discovered three low-temperature hydrothermal vent fields and biological communities (including Calyfield, a large clam field and the shallowest known vent site on the Rift at 1690m). The iconic Rose Garden site was paved over with lava from a recent eruption, and a low-temperature vent field (named Rosebud) was found to host nascent developing communities on a fresh-looking sheet flow at a location approximately 200 meters northwest of the former Rose Garden area. Despite extensive exploration, no high-temperature hydrothermal black smokers were discovered.

In December 2005, the OE Galápagos Expedition (Galápagos Acoustical, Plumes, and Geobiological Surveys) explored a 400 nautical mile-long section of the western Galápagos Rift between 94.5°-89.5°W, which is near the mantle plume that created the Galápagos Islands. This led to the first discovery of active high-temperature black smoker venting on the Galápagos Rift. This brief encounter with these new vents sites revealed more than 30 black smoker vents, vent-endemic species, including giant tubeworms, clams and mussels inhabiting sites with names such as Iguanas, Penguinas, and Navidad vent fields.

Understanding the biology and microbiology of the Galápagos Rift has important implications for expanding our knowledge of the evolution, ecology, and biogeochemical impact of life at hydrothermal vents. For example, the hydrothermal vents of the neighboring East Pacific Rise host a rich group of more than 160 species of bivalves, worms, and crustaceans while vent habitats along the Galápagos Rift host less than 60 species, many of which are not found anywhere else on the global mid-ocean ridge system. For more than two decades, we have hypothesized that either the complete absence of high-temperature black smokers (found on every other deep-sea ridge system) or the physical presence of the Hess Deep and triple junction acts as a strong barrier to dispersal or migration and were responsible for the differences in species between the EPR and the Galápagos Rift. Upcoming expeditions with high-definition cameras and remote-controlled vehicles will allow us to address questions such as whether the composition, diversity and habitats of biological communities in the Galápagos high temperature fields are fundamentally different than those of the rest of the rift, indicating differences in the underlying geochemical processes.

The wide expanses of low-temperature hydrothermal venting, far from focused high temperature venting, also make the Galápagos Rift an exciting place to search for microbial life within the Earth's crust. It has been suggested that a large portion of the planet's total biomass exists as microbes inside the ocean floor, and regions of vast low-temperature venting can often produce the largest biogeochemical changes to the chemistry of the deep ocean. This expedition also provides an opportunity to identify some of the most promising sites for future detailed study. In addition to the Rift, there are other exciting habitats that will be explored during this expedition such as the unexplored Paramount Seamounts, off-axis sulfide mounds, and deep fracture zones that may host deep-water coral and vent ecosystems.

Although deep-sea hydrothermal vent research may have started with the discovery of venting along the Galápagos Rift, the work needed at this site is far from done. New technologies such as high-definition cameras and satellite video feeds enable us to address important emerging questions about hydrothermal vent ecology and evolution. This expedition takes us closer to understanding deep-sea life at the Galápagos Rift and throughout the world.

41. The passage implies that vents that have been recently covered with sheets of lava:

(A) Become uninhabitable.
(B) Can still support life.
(C) Are often host to the most diverse plant life.
(D) Are of particular interest to scientists due to their ability to mimic conditions present during Earth's infancy.

42. According to the passage, extensive exploration of the western portion of the eastern rift revealed:

(A) No high-temperature hydrothermal black smokers.
(B) Nascent biological communities on the site of the former Garden of Eden.
(C) A new species of tubeworm native only to the area.
(D) Some of the hottest temperatures on Earth.

43. The passage states that the East Pacific Rise, in comparison with the Galápagos Ridge, hosts:

(A) More than twice as many native species.
(B) Less than half as many native species.
(C) Deep-water coral and vent ecosystems.
(D) A more complex geochemical makeup.

44. According to the passage, future expeditions will attempt to determine:

(A) The exact ages of the deep-sea ridges in question.
(B) Whether species located near high-temperature vents can survive in lower-temperature environments.
(C) Whether biological communities at high-temperature fields are fundamentally different from those of other areas of the Galápagos Ridge.
(D) The primary geochemical differences between the Galápagos Ridge and the East Pacific Rise.

45. The passage states the Galápagos Ridge is especially interesting in terms of finding new microbial life due to its:

(A) Young communities of mollusks.
(B) Off-axis sulfide mounds.
(C) Areas of high-temperature-withstanding biological communities.
(D) Large expanses of low-temperature hydrothermal venting.

46. As it is used in line 69, the word *address* most nearly means:

(A) Locate.
(B) Respond to.
(C) Send to.
(D) Number.

47. The passage implies that ecosystems on deep-sea vents gain nutrients from:

(A) Chemicals.
(B) Water.
(C) Sunlight.
(D) Pollution.

48. According to the passage, all of the following are species present at deep-sea rifts EXCEPT:

(A) Clams.
(B) Worms.
(C) Crustaceans.
(D) Primitive fish.

49. The passage states that scientists hypothesize that the differences in species between the East Pacific Rise and the Galápagos Ridge is caused by either:

(A) The isolation of the Galápagos Ridge by ocean currents or the ferocity of species on the East Pacific Rise.
(B) The absence of high-temperature black smokers on Galápagos Ridge or the physical presence of the Hess Deep and triple junction.
(C) The extensive distance between the two areas or the vastly different geochemical makeup between the two.
(D) The presence of the Paramount Seamounts between them or disturbances in volcanic activity.

50. The author's main point is to:

(A) Discuss the current state of exploration of the Galápagos Ridge.
(B) Compare and contrast the Galápagos Ridge and the East Pacific Rise.
(C) Describe the benefits of gaining insight into seafloor ecosystems.
(D) List the goals of future exploration of the Galápagos Ridge.

rP13: ADVANCED PROSE FICTION PASSAGES

TOPIC OVERVIEW

In Lesson 3, you learned how to handle some of the features of Prose Fiction passages, including figurative language and old-style English. In this section, you'll learn strategies for handling some of the more complex questions likely to show up for Prose Fiction passages, including characterization and subtext.

CHARACTERIZATION

Many questions for Prose Fiction passages will ask you questions about the personalities of the characters in the narrative. Such questions might look like these:

- Mrs. Martin **would most likely agree** with which of the following statements?
- What is Claudia's **attitude** toward the young boy who knocks at her door?
- If given the opportunity, John **would most likely** inform the barrister that:

These types of questions aren't asking you to deal with a direct detail in the story; rather, they're trying to test your understanding of a character's overall personality. Your idea of this personality does, of course, come from details in the passage, but it's up to you to interpret them accurately.

While reading the passage, it helps to mark the introduction of new characters and to write a word or two describing his/her personality. This can include something of the character's mood (grouchy, enthusiastic, frightened) and something of their overall personality (greedy, unhelpful, generous). Make sure that whatever you write has basis in the story and isn't purely your knee-jerk opinion of the character.

SUBTEXT

When a piece of fiction seems confusing—when its characters seem to act in strange, unpredictable ways, or when there seems to be "more going on" than you can totally grasp—it is likely that there is an element of *subtext*, or underlying meaning, to the text. Prose Fiction passages are likely to have been written by accomplished authors who have probably put some effort and thought into each character they include. This means that characters will be presented with some subtlety to their personalities. If Evelyn is upset, she won't say "I am so upset." She will probably purse her lips, sigh heavily, or pace the floor. She might say something like "Mrs. Barnham must not have considered my opinion," or "Rick certainly has a way of coming by unannounced." Both of these statements have a subtext, or underlying meaning. The first indicates that Evelyn is upset because Mrs. Barnham acted without thinking of her. The second indicates that Evelyn is upset because Rick has surprised her with a visit, and does so often. In literature, the bald meaning of the words isn't always the only meaning.

Considering the subtext of what characters do and say will help you understand their actions and personalities, and will help you answer questions about them, too.

MINDING THE BLURB

Passages will typically include a "blurb" at the beginning that provides some context (author, title, year) to the passage. While you will not be tested on this information, it can help put the passage "in its place" in your mind. If you see that the passage was written many years ago, you'll be prepared for some out-dated language. If you see that it was written recently, you might be prepared for more recent language and/or topics. While you should never approach a passage using your outside knowledge to answer questions, reading a piece from an author you may be familiar with can only help your chances of ingesting and understanding what you read.

Don't spend much time with the blurb, but do be sure to read it.

Read this passage carefully and then answer the questions that follow.

Prose Fiction: The following passage was adapted from *Aladdin of London* by Max Pemberton.

Alban's garret lay within a stone's throw of the tenement occupied by the Boriskoffs; but, in truth, they knew very little of him. They called him "The Hunter," in the courts and alleys round about; and this was as much as to say that his habits were predatory. He loved to roam far in quest, not of material booty, but of mental sensation.

An imagination that was simply wonderful helped him upon his way. He had but to stand at the gate of a palace to become in an instant one of those who peopled it. He could create himself king, or prince, or bishop as the mood took him. If a holiday sent him to the theatre, he was the hero or villain at his choice. In church he would preach well-imagined sermons to spellbound listeners. The streets of the West End were his true world—the gate without the scene of his mental pleasures.

He had no friends among the youths and lads of Thrawl Street and its environment, nor did he seek them. Those who hung about him were soon repelled by his seemingly secretive manner and a diffidence that was, in actuality, little more than natural shyness. If he fell now and then into the speech of the alleys, constant association was responsible for the lapse. Sometimes, it is true, an acquaintance would defy the snub and thrust himself stubbornly upon the unwilling wanderer. Alban was never unkind to such as these. He pitied these folk from his very heart; but before them all, he pitied himself.

His favorite walk was to the precincts of Westminster School, where he had spent two short terms before his father died. The influence of this life had never quite passed away. Alban would steal across London by night and stand at the gate of Little Dean's Yard as though wondering still what justice or right of destiny had driven him forth. He would haunt St. Vincent's Square on Saturday afternoons, and, taking his stand among all the little ragged boys who watched the cricket or football, he would, in imagination, become a "pink" delighting the multitude by a century or kicking goals so many that the very Press was startled. In the intervals he revisited the Abbey and tried to remember the service as he had known it when a schoolboy.

The sonorous words of Tudor divines remained within his memory, but the heart of them had gone out. What had he to be thankful for now? Did he not earn his bitter bread by a task so laborious that the very poor might shun it? His father would have made an engineer of him if he had lived—so much had been quite decided. He could tell you the names of lads who had been at Westminster with him and were now at Oxford or Cambridge enjoying those young years that no subsequent fortune can recall. What had he done to the God who ruled the world that these were denied to him? Was he not born a gentleman, as the world understands the term? Had he not worn good clothes, adored a loving mother, been educated in his early days in those vain accomplishments which society demands from its children? And now he was an "East-ender," down at heel and half starved; and there were not three people in the entire city who would care a straw whether he lived or died.

This was the lad who went westward that night of the meeting in Union Street, and such were his frequent thoughts. None would have taken him for what he was; few who passed him by would have guessed what his earlier years had been. The old gray check suit, frayed at the edges, close buttoned and shabby, was just such a suit as any loafer out of Union Street might have worn. His hollow cheeks betrayed his poverty. He walked with his hands thrust deep into his pockets, his shoulders slightly bent, his eyes roving from face to face as he numbered the wayfarers and speculated upon their fortunes and their future. Two or three acquaintances who hailed him were answered by a quickening of his step and a curt nod of the handsome head.

1. The word *peopled* as it is used in line 11 most nearly means:

   (A) Reigned over.
   (B) Represented.
   (C) Populated.
   (D) Opposed.

2. According to the passage, Alban imagines himself as all of the following people EXCEPT:

   (A) A member of a royal family.
   (B) A member of the clergy.
   (C) An actor in a play.
   (D) A renowned hunter.

3. The author implies that Alban has few friends for which of the following reasons?

   (A) Alban's peers mistake his reticence for secretiveness.
   (B) Alban is rude to those who try to approach him.
   (C) Alban is too full of self-pity to care for others.
   (D) Alban is disinterested in people of his own age.

4. The author's reference to the "speech of the alleys" (line 24) most nearly means:

(A) Accent.
(B) Slang.
(C) Threats.
(D) Rudeness.

5. The passage indicates that Alban's life was most influenced by:

(A) The Boriskoffs.
(B) His father.
(C) His time at Westminster.
(D) His sole friend.

6. According to the passage, while watching cricket or football Alban would:

(A) Think about the death of his father.
(B) Reflect on the words of a sermon.
(C) Imagine himself as a famous athlete.
(D) Leave the game to stand in Little Dean's Yard.

7. The function of the fifth paragraph in relation to the passage as a whole is to:

(A) Illustrate that Alban is lonely as a result of his asocial character.
(B) Describe the events that caused Alban to lose his faith.
(C) Contrast Alban's dire present situation with his youthful expectations.
(D) Criticize Alban's failure to fulfill his father's plans for him.

8. Which of the following traits does the author indicate characterizes an "East-ender" (line 63)?

(A) Impoverished
(B) Well-educated
(C) Orphaned
(D) Religious

9. The author indicates that nobody would guess what Alban's "earlier years had been" (line 70) because

(A) He hid his face from passersby.
(B) He refused to speak of his childhood.
(C) He had a destitute appearance.
(D) He walked proudly despite his poverty.

10. The primary purpose of this passage is to:

(A) Describe the life of a character
(B) Serve as a cautionary tale
(C) Lay the scene for a dramatic event
(D) Demonstrate the effects of poverty

Read this passage carefully and then answer the questions that follow.

Prose Fiction: The following passage was adapted from *Aliens* by William McFee.

It was a week later, and we were sitting on the veranda looking out across Essex County towards Manhattan. To us, who some five years before had been shaken from our homestead in San Francisco and hurried penniless and almost naked across the continent, our location here in the Garden State, looking eastward towards the Western Ocean and our native isle, had always appeared as "almost home." We endeavored to impress this upon our friends in England, explaining that "we could be home in four or five days easily"; and what were four or five days? True, we have never gone so far as to book our passage; but there is undoubted comfort in the fact that in a week at the outside, we could walk down Piccadilly. Out on the Pacific Slope we were, both physically and spiritually, a world away.

It pleased us, too, to detect in the configuration of the district a certain identity with our own county of Essex, in England, where a cousin of Bill's had a cottage, and where, some day, we were to have a cottage too. Our home is called Wigboro House, after the cousin's, and we have settled it that, just as in England you catch a glimpse of Mersea Island from Wigborough, so we may catch the glint and glare of the lights of Manhattan, and, on stormy nights, feel on our lips the sharpness of the salt wind that blows across Staten Island from the Atlantic. It is an innocent conceit, and our only critic so far had been Miss Fraenkel, who had objected to the name, and advocated with American succinctness the advantage of a number. As Bill had remarked mournfully, "It wouldn't be so bad if it was number three or four, but Five hundred and Eighty-two Van Diemen's Avenue is horrible!" We had given in to Miss Fraenkel of course, save that none of us had the courage to disillusion Bill's cousin. We still received from him letters addressed in his sprawling painter's hand "Wigboro House, Netley Heights, N. J., U. S. A.," a mail or so late. We never told him of Van Diemen's Avenue, nor for that matter had we mentioned our neighbors. Curiously enough, it was he, that painter cousin of Bill's, thousands of miles away in that other Essex, who told us something that we were only too quick to appreciate, about our neighbors.

We were talking of him, I remember, that afternoon as we sat on the stoop, Bill saying he would be writing soon, and Mac raising the vexing question of the Fourth Chair. You see, we have four rocking chairs on our veranda, though there are but three of us, and Bill usually claims the hammock. It was no answer, I found, to suggest future friends as occupants for this chair. It grew to be a legend that some day I should bring home a bride and she should have it. I submitted to this badinage and even hinted that at first we should need but one chair.... I had heard ... nay seen, such things in San Francisco, before the earthquake. In the meantime I had vamped up a very pretty story of the painter-cousin getting a commission to paint a prima donna in New York and coming over to visit us in great state. He might be induced to sit awhile in the vacant chair. It seemed more probable than Bill's legend, for I knew Miss Fraenkel or anybody I married, say, would want the hammock. There was one drawback to my dream, and that was the humiliation of revealing to him Van Diemen's Avenue. He is a university man, and from his letters and Bill's description I should say he has a rather embarrassing laugh when he finds a person out in a deception like that. But so far he had not yet received a commission to paint a prima donna in New York, and he still pictures our Wigboro house standing alone on Netley Heights, looking out across rolling country to the sea. Of course the photos that we send do not show any other houses near, and the verandas make the place look bigger than it really is. He must be tremendously impressed, too, by Bill's “courageous declaration” that at the back the land is ours "as far as the eye can see." It is true, too, though the eye cannot see very far. There is a "dip," you know, common enough to Triassic regions; and as you stand at the back door and look westward the sky comes down and touches our cabbages, fifty yards away. It does, really!

11. The author implies that the speaker in the first paragraph considers his true home to be:

(A) San Francisco.
(B) the Garden State.
(C) England.
(D) Manhattan.

12. Which of the following comforts the narrator after his family moves across the continent?

(A) Being on the Pacific Slope allows him to be alone.
(B) The trip to England only takes several days.
(C) He has a second home in San Francisco.
(D) He has friends in England.

13. According to the passage, Miss Fraenkel wishes the name of the house in New York to include:

    (A) Some form of the name Wigboro House.
    (B) A street number.
    (C) A reference to England.
    (D) A reference to Van Diemen.

14. In the second paragraph, the narrator draws a parallel between which of the following places?

    (A) Wigboro House in England and Wigboro House in New Jersey
    (B) A house bearing a name and a house bearing a number
    (C) His English neighbors and his American neighbors
    (D) The view of Mersea Island and the view of Manhattan

15. In the last sentence of the second paragraph (line 43-46), the author implies that Bill's cousin:

    (A) Provided insight into the narrator's neighbors that the narrator had not noticed.
    (B) Was resentful of the narrator's neighbors and openly insulted them.
    (C) Preferred the Wigboro House in America to his own home in England.
    (D) Approved of the narrator's decision to give the home a numerical address.

16. The word *vexing* (line 49) in context most nearly means:

    (A) Disturbing.
    (B) Frustrating.
    (C) Annoying.
    (D) Critical.

17. The "deception" mentioned in line 72 refers to:

    (A) The narrator's assessment of Bill's cousin's character.
    (B) The narrator's belief that his bride will not be Miss Fraenkel.
    (C) Bill's cousin's receiving a fake invitation to paint a prima donna.
    (D) Bill's cousin's being told false information concerning the house in New Jersey.

18. According to Bill, the Fourth Chair will soon be occupied by:

    (A) The narrator's future wife.
    (B) His cousin.
    (C) Miss Fraenkel.
    (D) Some of the narrator's friends.

19. According to Bill's letter to his cousin, the American house has which of the following?

    (A) Close neighbors
    (B) An expansive backyard
    (C) A view of Staten Island
    (D) Private beach access

20. The author places the phrase "courageous declaration" (line 80) in quotes in the passage to indicate that:

    (A) Bill is bragging to his cousin.
    (B) Bill is quoting someone.
    (C) Bill's statement is intentionally misleading.
    (D) Bill will soon invite his cousin to see the house.

Read this passage carefully and then answer the questions that follow.

Prose Fiction: The following passage was adapted from *All Men are Ghosts* by L.P. Jacks.

Dr. Piecraft was reflecting on the hardness of his lot. Ten years had elapsed since he first mounted his brass plate, and he was still virtually without a practice. He earned just enough from casual patients to pay his rent and keep body and soul together. To be sure, his father had left him a hundred a year; but Piecraft had given the old man a promise "that he would look after Jim." Now Jim was a half-brother, many years younger than himself; and he was also the one being in the world whom Piecraft loved with an undivided heart. So the whole of his income from that source was earmarked for the boy's education; not for worlds would the doctor have spent a penny of it on himself. He even denied himself cigars, of which he was exceedingly fond, restricting himself to the cheapest of tobacco, in order that Jim might have plenty of pocket money; and whenever the question arose as to who was to have a new suit of clothes, Jim or the doctor, it was always Jim who went smart and the doctor who went shabby.

He was over forty years of age, and, in his own eyes, a failure. Yet no man could have done more to deserve success. His medical qualifications were of the widest and highest; diplomas of all sorts covered the walls of his consulting-room; a gold medal for cerebral pathology lay in a glass case on his writing-table. He was actively abreast of advancing medical science; he had run into debt that he might keep himself supplied with the best literature of his profession, and he was prepared at a moment's notice to treat a difficult case in the light of the latest discoveries at Paris, St Petersburg, or New York. Moreover, he had led a clean life, and was known among his friends as a man of irreproachable honor. But somehow the patients seemed to avoid him, and only once in two years had he been summoned to a consultation.

To account for Piecraft's failure as a medical man, several theories were in circulation, and it is probable that each of them contained an element of truth. Some persons would set it down to the shabbiness of his appearance, or to the brusqueness of his manners, or to the fact that his consulting-room often reeked with the fumes of cheap tobacco. Others would say that Piecraft was constitutionally unable to practice those "intelligent hesitations" so often needed in the application of medical principles. They would remind you of his fatal tendency to determine diagnosis on a sudden impulse, which Piecraft called "psychological intuition," and about this they would tell you a story: how once, when the vicar's wife had brought her petted daughter to be treated for hysteria, the fit happening to come on in the consulting-room, Piecraft had cured the young lady on the spot by soundly boxing her ears.

Concerning this incident, he had been taken severely to task by an intimate friend of his, an old practitioner of standing. "It will be time enough to adopt those methods of treatment," the friend had said to him, "when you are earning five thousand a year. At the present stage of your career it is almost fatal. Learn so to treat a patient that the story of the cure when subsequently related after dinner may have the characteristics of High Tragedy, or at all events may reflect some credit on the sufferer. Help him to create a drama, and see to it that he comes out ultimately as its hero. Don't you see that in the present instance you have spoilt a moving story, than which nothing gives greater offence, turning the whole situation into Low Comedy and making the patient a laughing-stock? People will never stand that, Piecraft. It is idle to insist that the cure was efficacious and permanent. So no doubt it was. A better remedy for that type of hysteria could not be devised. But reflect on the fact that you have deprived the vicar's family of a legitimate opportunity for dramatic expression and dethroned the vicar's daughter from her place as heroine. In short, you have committed an outrage on the artistic rights of medicine, and, mark my words, you will have to pay for it. Always remember, Piecraft, that in medicine, as in many other things, it is not the act alone which ensures success, but the gesture with which the act is accompanied."

21. The word *smart* (line 21) in context most nearly means:

(A) Well-dressed.
(B) Intelligent.
(C) Respected.
(D) Pompous.

22. According to the passage, what had Dr. Piecraft promised his father he would do?

(A) Not partake of indulgences such as fine cigars
(B) See to Jim's upkeep and education
(C) Always dress in a modest fashion
(D) Maintain his father's successful practice

23. The author indicates that there is an apparent contradiction between:

    (A) The medical techniques Dr. Piecraft uses and the ones he has learned.
    (B) Dr. Piecraft's education and the extent of his actual knowledge.
    (C) Dr. Piecraft's love of Jim and Jim's love of Dr. Piecraft.
    (D) The success Dr. Piecraft has had and the success he merits.

24. According to the second paragraph, Dr. Piecraft is most likely to purchase for himself which of the following?

    (A) A lab coat
    (B) A medical journal
    (C) A pocket watch
    (D) A stethoscope

25. Which of the following is implied about the theories concerning Dr. Piecraft's unpopularity?

    (A) They came as a result of his treatment of the vicar's daughter
    (B) Dr. Piecraft is unaware of the theories
    (C) A competitor originated the theories out of spite
    (D) No single theory is entirely false

26. All of the following are proposed reasons Dr. Piecraft has few patients EXCEPT:

    (A) His office is inconveniently located.
    (B) He looks unkempt.
    (C) He is tactless in his patient interactions.
    (D) He makes diagnoses impulsively.

27. For what purpose does the author refer to the story of the vicar's daughter's treatment?

    (A) To move the narrative forward
    (B) To defend Dr. Piecraft's skill
    (C) To serve as a counterargument
    (D) To illustrate a point stated previously

28. In context, "taken severely to task" (line 58-59) most nearly means:

    (A) Admonished.
    (B) Lauded.
    (C) Intimidated.
    (D) Venerated.

29. The word *related* (line 65) most nearly means:

    (A) Retold.
    (B) Connected.
    (C) Correlated.
    (D) Corresponded.

30. Which of the following statements most closely summarizes the advice of Dr. Piecraft's friend?

    (A) A doctor should emphasize his own role in the patient's care.
    (B) A doctor should allow the patient to be the hero of his own story.
    (C) A doctor should see as many patients as possible.
    (D) A doctor should prioritize art over science.

Read this passage carefully and then answer the questions that follow.

Prose Fiction: The following passage was adapted from *A Crystal Age* by W.H. Hudson.

I do not know how it happened, my recollection of the whole matter ebbing in a somewhat clouded condition. I fancy I had gone somewhere on a botanizing expedition, but whether at home or abroad I don't know. At all events, I remember that I had taken up the study of plants with a good deal of enthusiasm, and that while hunting for some variety in the mountains, I sat down to rest on the edge of a ravine. Perhaps it was on the ledge of an overhanging rock; anyhow, if I remember rightly, the ground gave way all about me, precipitating me below. The fall was a very considerable one—probably thirty or forty feet, or more, and I was rendered unconscious.

How long I lay there under the heap of earth and stones carried down in my fall it is impossible to say: perhaps a long time, but at last I came to myself and struggled up from the debris, like a mole coming to the surface of the earth to feel the genial sunshine on his dim eyeballs. I found myself standing (oddly enough, on all fours) in an immense pit created by the overthrow of a gigantic dead tree with a girth of about thirty or forty feet. The tree itself had rolled down to the bottom of the ravine; but the pit in which it had left the huge stumps of severed roots was, I found, situated in a gentle slope at the top of the bank! How, then, I could have fallen seemingly so far from no height at all, puzzled me greatly: it looked as if the solid earth had been indulging in some curious transformation pranks during those moments or minutes of insensibility.

Another singular circumstance was that I had a great mass of small fibrous rootlets tightly woven about my whole person, so that I was like a colossal basket-worm in its case, or a big man-shaped bottle covered with wickerwork. It appeared as if the roots had grown round me! Luckily they were quite sapless and brittle, and without bothering my brains too much about the matter, I set to work to rid myself of them. After stripping the woody covering off, I found that my tourist suit of rough Scotch homespun had not suffered much harm, although the cloth exuded a damp, moldy smell; also that my thick-soled climbing boots had assumed a cracked rusty appearance as if I had been engaged in some brick-field operations; while my felt hat was in such a discolored and battered condition that I felt almost ashamed to put it on my head. My watch was gone; perhaps I had not been wearing it, but my pocket book in which I had my money was safe in my breast pocket.

Glad and grateful at having escaped with unbroken bones from such a dangerous accident, I set out walking along the edge of the ravine, which soon broadened to a valley running between two steep hills; and then, seeing water at the bottom and feeling very dry, I ran down the slope to get a drink. Lying flat on my chest to slake my thirst animal-fashion, I was amazed at the reflection the water gave back of my face: it was, skin and hair, thickly encrusted with clay and rootlets! Having taken a long drink, I threw off my clothes to have a bath; and after splashing about for half an hour, I managed to rid my skin of its accumulations of dirt. While drying in the wind I shook the loose sand and clay from my garments, then, dressed and feeling greatly refreshed, proceeded on my walk.

For an hour or so I followed the valley in its many windings, but, failing to see any dwelling-place, I decided to ascend a hill to get a view of the surrounding country. The prospect that disclosed itself when I had gotten a couple of hundred feet above the surrounding level appeared unfamiliar. The hills among which I had been wandering were now behind me; before me spread a wide rolling country, beyond which rose a mountain range resembling in the distance blue banked-up clouds with summits and peaks of pearly whiteness. Looking on this scene, I could hardly refrain from shouting with joy, so glad did the sunlit expanse of earth, and the pure exhilarating mountain breeze, make me feel.

31. What had the narrator been doing immediately prior to falling?

(A) Searching for rare plants
(B) Resting on the edge of a ravine
(C) Climbing on a boulder
(D) Planning a botanizing expedition

32. The word *rendered* as it is used in line 14 most nearly means:

(A) Caused to become.
(B) Made into.
(C) Handed down.
(D) Depicted as.

33. The author indicates that the earth seemed to be "indulging in some curious…pranks" (lines 30-31) in order to emphasize:

    (A) That something supernatural is happening to the narrator.
    (B) The ongoing conflict between man and nature.
    (C) That the narrator is the victim of a hoax.
    (D) The narrator's sense of disorientation and confusion.

34. After the narrator breaks free of the roots, he notices all of the following EXCEPT:

    (A) His pocket watch is not on his person.
    (B) His hat appears battered.
    (C) His boots have become cracked.
    (D) His pocket book is missing.

35. The reader can infer that "homespun" (line 43) is a type of:

    (A) Fabric.
    (B) Watch.
    (C) Hat.
    (D) Root.

36. Which of the following statements about the narrator's journey can be inferred from the fourth paragraph?

    (A) The narrator expected to get dirty and disheveled.
    (B) Due to his experiences, the narrator has developed a fear of heights.
    (C) It is through an uninhabited area.
    (D) The narrator himself had few expectations for this journey.

37. The narrator's attitude can most closely be described as:

    (A) Capricious.
    (B) Genial.
    (C) Juvenile.
    (D) Agitated.

38. Based on the narrator's demeanor in the last paragraph, the reader can assume that he:

    (A) Is alone and in danger.
    (B) Has recovered from his earlier fall.
    (C) Is apprehensive about continuing his journey.
    (D) Is proud that he has accomplished his task.

39. For which of the following reasons did the narrator "ascend a hill" (line 71)?

    (A) To retrace his steps back home
    (B) To gather his bearings and survey the surrounding land
    (C) To take in the view of the blue sky and rolling hills
    (D) To feel the cool mountain breeze

40. The title that most closely describes this passage is:

    (A) "A Beginner's Guide to Botany"
    (B) "Earthquake Survival in the Wild"
    (C) "A Curious Excursion"
    (D) "The Joys of Hiking"

Read this passage carefully and then answer the questions that follow.

Prose Fiction: The following passage was adapted from *At the Villa Rose* by A.E.W. Mason

It was Mr. Ricardo's habit as soon as the second week of August came round to travel to Aix-les-Bains, in Savoy, where for five or six weeks he lived pleasantly. He pretended to take the waters in the morning, he went for a ride in his motorcar in the afternoon, he dined at the Cercle in the evening, and spent an hour or two afterwards in the baccarat-rooms at the Villa des Fleurs. An enviable, smooth life without a doubt, and it is certain that his acquaintances envied him. At the same time, however, they laughed at him and, alas with some justice, for he was an exaggerated person. He was to be construed in the comparative. Everything in his life was a trifle overdone, from the fastidious arrangement of his neckties to the feminine nicety of his little dinner-parties. In age Mr. Ricardo was approaching the fifties; in condition he was a widower—a state greatly to his liking, for he avoided at once the irksomeness of marriage and the reproaches justly leveled at the bachelor; finally, he was rich, having amassed a fortune in Mincing Lane, which he had invested in profitable securities.

Ten years of ease, however, had not altogether obliterated in him the business look. Though he lounged from January to December, he lounged with the air of a financier taking a holiday; and when he visited, as he frequently did, the studio of a painter, a stranger would have hesitated to decide whether he had been drawn thither by a love of art or by the possibility of an investment. His "acquaintances" have been mentioned, and the word is suitable. For while he mingled in many circles, he stood aloof from all. He affected the company of artists, by whom he was regarded as one ambitious to become a connoisseur; and amongst the younger businessmen, who had never dealt with him, he earned the disrespect reserved for the dilettante. If he had a grief, it was that he had discovered no great man who in return for practical favors would engrave his memory in brass. He was a Maecenas without a Horace, an Earl of Southampton without a Shakespeare. In a word, Aix-les-Bains in the season was the very place for him; and never for a moment did it occur to him that he was here to be dipped in agitations, and hurried from excitement to excitement. The beauty of the little town, the crowd of well-dressed and agreeable people, the rose-colored life of the place, all made their appeal to him. But it was the Villa des Fleurs that brought him to Aix. Not that he played for anything more than an occasional Louis; nor, on the other hand, was he merely a cold onlooker. He had a bank note or two in his pocket on most evenings at the service of the victims of the tables. But the pleasure to his curious and dilettante mind lay in the spectacle of the battle that was waged night after night between raw nature and good manners. It was extraordinary to him how constantly manners prevailed. There were, however, exceptions.

For instance: on the first evening of this particular visit he found the rooms hot, and sauntered out into the little semicircular garden at the back. He sat there for half an hour under a flawless sky of stars watching the people come and go in the light of the electric lamps, and appreciating the gowns and jewels of the women with the eye of a connoisseur; and then into this starlit quiet there came suddenly a flash of vivid life. A girl in a soft, clinging frock of white satin darted swiftly from the rooms and flung herself nervously upon a bench. She could not, to Ricardo's thinking, be more than twenty years of age. She was certainly quite young. The supple slenderness of her figure proved it, and he had moreover caught a glimpse, as she rushed out, of a fresh and very pretty face; but he had lost sight of it now. For the girl wore a big black satin hat with a broad brim, from which a couple of white ostrich feathers curved over at the back, and in the shadow of that hat her face was masked. All that he could see was a pair of long diamond eardrops, which sparkled and trembled as she moved her head—and that she did constantly. Now she stared moodily at the ground; now she flung herself back; then she twisted nervously to the right, and then a moment afterwards to the left; and then again she stared in front of her, swinging a satin slipper backwards and forwards against the pavement with the petulant bearing of a child. All her movements were spasmodic; she was on the verge of hysteria. Ricardo was expecting her to burst into tears, when she sprang up, and as swiftly as she had come, she hurried back into the rooms.

41. The author indicates that Mr. Ricardo enjoys his widowed status because it allows him to:

(A) Avoid the annoyances he associates with married life.
(B) Focus on making investments with the fortune he has amassed.
(C) Spend more time vacationing in Savoy.
(D) Play baccarat late into the night.

42. Which of the following best characterizes Mr. Ricardo as he is described in the second paragraph?

(A) Ruthless
(B) Shallow
(C) Flexible
(D) Handsome

43. The word *air* as it is used in line 27 most nearly means:

(A) Atmosphere.
(B) Demeanor.
(C) Illusion.
(D) Firmament.

44. The author suggests which of the following regarding Mr. Ricardo's social life?

(A) Mr. Ricardo associates with many people, but has no true friends.
(B) Mr. Ricardo has many friends, but has not stayed in contact with them.
(C) Mr. Ricardo's acquaintances suspect he is untrustworthy.
(D) Mr. Ricardo only befriends artists and businessmen.

45. The reader can infer that a "Louis" (line 52) is a type of:

(A) Prize.
(B) Casino.
(C) Currency.
(D) Game.

46. Which of the following activities does Mr. Ricardo partake in at the Villa del Fleurs?

I. Playing baccarat for high stakes
II. People-watching
III. Helping those who had lost at the tables

(A) I only
(B) II only
(C) I and III
(D) II and III

47. Which of the following pairs bears a relationship most similar to that between "raw nature" and "good manners" (line 58)?

(A) Loss and regret
(B) Vulgarity and gentility
(C) Iniquity and neutrality
(D) Perception and truth

48. The primary purpose of the last paragraph is to:

(A) Provide an example of Mr. Ricardo's good taste.
(B) Introduce a romantic interest for Mr. Ricardo.
(C) Prove that good manners always prevail.
(D) Illustrate a point made in the previous paragraph.

49. What confirms Mr. Ricardo's belief that the woman in the garden is young?

(A) Her slim figure
(B) Her elegant dress
(C) Her quick entrance into and exit from the garden
(D) Her hysterical attitude

50. The word *petulant* (line 89) most nearly means:

(A) Ungrateful.
(B) Soft-spoken.
(C) Fractious.
(D) Well-off.

rP14: ADVANCED HUMANITIES PASSAGES

TOPIC OVERVIEW

In Lesson 4, you became familiar with Humanities passages and learned how to identify subjective/objective perspectives. In this lesson, you'll extend your familiarity with these passages and their more difficult question types, such as the "accurately and completely" main idea question and "two-part answer" question.

"ACCURATELY AND COMPLETELY" QUESTIONS

Sometimes, one of the first questions for a Humanities passage (and sometimes other passages, too) will ask you:

Which of the following descriptions most accurately and completely represents this passage?

The answer choices will include some kind of descriptive phrase, one of which encapsulates the main idea of the passage. This is the correct answer. Here's an example of what an "accurately and completely" question might look like:

Which of the following descriptions most accurately and completely represents this passage?

- A plea to stop the destruction of the integrity of dance by the infusion of ballet with jazz and hip hop.
- A description of several modern dance pieces that incorporate various styles.
- A balanced presentation of the positive and negative aspects of blending dancing styles.
- A biased catalogue of the reactions of famous choreographers to the idea of "the integrity of dance."

The best way to approach these questions is to check descriptive words for *extremes* or *inaccuracies*. Humanities passages will rarely contain an extremely negative opinion, so answer choices involving strong (especially negative) emotions like "hate," "abhor," or "detest," are probably wrong. So are answer choices that give an inaccurate description of the main idea.

However, it is entirely possible that the passage contains an "enthusiastic," "impassioned," or "determined" tone. Ask yourself if each descriptor used in the answer matches with the tone and topic of the passage. Cross out any answer choices that contain inaccurate descriptors.

"TWO-PART ANSWER" QUESTIONS

Some Humanities passages will include questions that ask you to answer two questions in one. These contain some kind of figurative or interpretable language inside a quotation, then ask you to use the meaning of that quotation to answer another question. Here are some examples:

- The author's statement that Marissa Paland's dancing "infused the audience with life and vigor as the sunshine infuses winter soil" (line 23) foreshadows that Paland's dancing would eventually:
- The author's belief that "the local art scene was a stagnant cesspool producing nothing of note for nearly a decade" (line 11) contrasts with which of the following opinions?

As you can see, the questions not only ask you to interpret a piece of the text; they also ask you to apply your interpretation to a second question. For these types of questions, make a note of what you believe the quotation to mean. Then, use your note as the stand-in for answering the second part of the question. Here are some examples of how to interpret and apply this strategy using the questions given above:

- That author's statement that Marissa Paland's dancing **invigorated the audience** foreshadows that Paland's dancing would eventually:
- The author's belief that **the local art scene was dead for a decade** contrasts with which of the following opinions?

Read this passage carefully and then answer the questions that follow.

Humanities: This passage describes a popular and historically significant television program.

A wartime hospital camp hardly seems the place for laughter, but one of the most popular and influential shows of the 1970s and 80s took place in a medical camp during the Korean War. M*A*S*H, which ran from 1972-1983, followed the doctors of the 4077th Mobile Army Surgical Unit (the abbreviation of which gives the show its name) as they lived through the conflict and operated on wounded soldiers helicoptered in from the battlefield. One startling discrepancy is often mentioned affectionately by fans – that even though the Korean War lasted 3 years (1951-1954), the show ran for 11 years. The show was an adaptation of the 1970 movie, which was nominated for 5 Academy Awards (and won one, for its screenplay), and the movie was an adaptation of the book *MASH: A Novel about Three Army Doctors* by Richard Hooker.

The protagonist, Benjamin "Hawkeye" Pierce (Alan Alda) played a role made popular by Catch-22's John Yossarian: the reluctant soldier. Pierce disagrees with the war and often speaks out against it; after all, every day, he must operate on young men hurt or mutilated by warfare. (One can spot several soon-to-be stars as young soldiers that Hawkeye treats in the hospital, including a very young Patrick Swayze.) Pierce's rebellious attitude and crafty sense of humor caused some of his more punctilious colleagues to charge him with insubordination, but crafty Hawkeye almost always contrived a way out of his troubles. He was assisted by the company clerk, Walter "Radar" O'Reilly, and his colleagues "Trapper" John McIntyre and, later, B.J. Hunnicutt.

Against Hawkeye were arrayed his superiors: Major Frank Burns, Major Margaret Houlihan, and Colonel Henry Blake. While Blake and Pierce kept up a mostly friendly relationship, Blake often had to act as a disciplinarian with his rogue surgeon. Burns and Houlihan, on the other hand, were initially portrayed as foolish plotters against Hawkeye and the other free-spirited surgeons, though later seasons would humanize them and add depth to their characters.

The early years of M*A*S*H were broadly humorous; the later years, after the departure of actors McLean Stevenson (Henry Blake) and Larry Linville (Major Burns), tended to veer more towards the dramatic side of things. More and more was said about the uselessness of the conflict and the toll on human life. Alda, noted for his political leanings, sometimes took the helm behind the camera, and many of his were known for being 'political' episodes. In fact, even the movie itself wasn't entirely about the Korean War. Both the movie and the television show reflected not just the Korean War, but the ongoing war in Vietnam. Many of Hawkeye's statements about the futility and savagery of war echoed what many in America were feeling about the conflict in Vietnam.

In fact, M*A*S*H was one of the first sitcoms not to use a laugh track for all scenes. While the producers had argued for no laugh track at all ("Just like the Korean War," one producer said), the network insisted; how else would the audience know it was a comedy? However, the network and the producers ironed out a compromise: they decided not to have a laugh track during scenes in the operating room, as that would distract from the gravity of the situation. Later episodes would drop the laugh track completely, as the subject matter became more serious. Some critics say that M*A*S*H paved the way for short half-hour sitcoms to address important issues and dramatic subjects.

The show also experimented with form and presentation of episodes. Some episodes were filmed from the point-of-view of a soldier arriving at the military camp, or took place in real time. One famous episode was presented as a series of interviews with the characters by a documentary film crew. (From this episode may have come some of the inspiration for the popular 'mockumentary'-styled sitcoms, such as *The Office* or *Modern Family*.)

After eleven long years, the show finally wound to an end in 1983. The writers had run out of ideas (and the Korean War doctors who wrote to send in their stories often found that a similar story had already been told five or six years ago), and the cast was itching to move on to new projects. The final episode of M*A*S*H, "Goodbye, Farewell, and Amen," aired on February 28, 1983, and set historic records for viewership. While that record is no longer held (it was broken several Super Bowls ago), it is clear evidence that M*A*S*H was a cultural phenomenon that has had a lasting effect on American television.

1. Which of the following most clearly illustrates the passage's main idea?

   (A) M*A*S*H was a landmark program that addressed contemporary themes through humor.
   (B) Because of its controversial themes in later seasons, MASH lost viewership over the course of the series.
   (C) The television shows that came after M*A*S*H owe it a large creative debt.
   (D) M*A*S*H slowly became more dramatic over the course of its 11-year run.

2. As it is used in line 31, *contrived* most nearly means:

   (A) Fooled.
   (B) Engineered.
   (C) Assembled.
   (D) Fabricated.

3. The "discrepancy" mentioned in line 10 ("One startling discrepancy… 11 years") is most analogous with which of the following?

   (A) A newspaper article about an incident confuses the identities of those involved
   (B) A novel set during the Revolutionary War misidentifies certain key dates in the history of the American Revolution
   (C) A child character in a comic strip stays the same age over the course of 30 years
   (D) A theatrical performance runs over time, ending half an hour later than scheduled

4. It can be reasonably inferred from the fourth paragraph that:

   (A) The war in Korea was incredibly similar to the Vietnam War.
   (B) Many Americans had conflicting feelings about the Vietnam War.
   (C) Larry Linville left the show because he disagreed with its politics.
   (D) M*A*S*H explicitly condemned the war in Vietnam.

5. As it is used in line 39, *disciplinarian* most nearly means:

   (A) Taskmaster.
   (B) Teacher.
   (C) Bully.
   (D) Parent.

6. According to the passage, why did the producers of M*A*S*H fight the inclusion of a laugh track?

   (A) A laugh track would not be fitting for operating room scenes.
   (B) The subject matter of M*A*S*H was often too somber to require a laugh track.
   (C) Alan Alda wanted to direct more serious episodes during later seasons.
   (D) They wanted to present the show as a serious drama.

7. As he is portrayed in the passage, Colonel Blake could best be described as:

   (A) Foolish.
   (B) Friendly.
   (C) Punctilious.
   (D) Witty.

8. According to the passage, which of the following characters left the show?

   I. Margaret "Hot Lips" Houlihan
   II. Colonel Henry Blake
   III. Major Frank Burns

   (A) I only
   (B) III only
   (C) I and III
   (D) II and III

9. M*A*S*H innovated on the traditional sitcom format by doing all of the following EXCEPT:

   (A) Creating "interview" segments with the characters.
   (B) Reducing the use of the laugh track.
   (C) Using "up-and-coming" young actors in brief roles.
   (D) Introducing darker, more dramatic material.

10. The passage states that the show reached its end because:

   (A) The on-screen talent wanted to work on other shows or in the movies.
   (B) The show had become too dramatic to carry the humorous aspects.
   (C) Doctors had stopped sending in their wartime medical stories.
   (D) The Super Bowl threatened the show's ratings.

Read this passage carefully and then answer the questions that follow.

Humanities: This passage describes a major American cultural institution.

As any tourist will tell you, a trip to New York isn't complete without taking in a Broadway show. In fact, last year alone, more than 12 million people attended a Broadway play, making the Broadway theater district one of the biggest attractions in New York. It may seem as if Broadway is an integral part of New York City – a timeless treasure that is as much a part of Manhattan as the subway or the Statue of Liberty – but Broadway as we know it today is actually several decades younger than the subway and far younger than Lady Liberty.

Today's Broadway theater district is settled around Times Square, surrounded by the massive advertisements and flashing lights that have become a permanent part of the Broadway backdrop. But theater in New York originally began downtown in the Bowery, among middle and lower class neighborhoods. Beginning around 1850, the theater district gradually migrated uptown along Broadway. By 1870, the heart of Broadway centered on Union Square around 14th Street; by the end of the century, it had travelled up to Madison Square around 34th Street. It was not until the 1920s and 1930s, when several large theaters were constructed near Times Square near 42nd Street, that the heart of Broadway found its permanent home.

As the theater district began its uptown migration, entertainment was often divided along class lines: operas for the upper classes, melodramas and minstrel shows for the middle classes, and variety shows for the lower classes. The modern musical – complete with singing and dancing and songs that help to tell the story – did not come into existence until 1866 when *The Black Crook* premiered. *The Black Crook* is commonly considered to be the father of the modern musical, but it became a musical by accident. Originally, the play was intended to be a melodrama; when a fire at a nearby theater displaced a ballet troupe and its orchestra, *The Black Crook*'s producers decided to turn the play into a "musical spectacular." Despite its length – the musical was five and a half hours long – *The Black Crook* ran for over a year, completing a record-breaking 474 performances. Thus musical theater was born.

The plays of Broadway have greatly evolved in the intervening decades. Until the 1920s and 1930s, Broadway plays were typically musical comedies with little plot. The popular plays of the time featured lighthearted singing and dancing – often with a slight burlesque twist – but with little to tie the songs together. The transition from loosely-plotted variety shows to full musical plays was marked by the premier of *Show Boat* in 1927. Show Boat featured a fully integrated book and score; the music, dialogue, setting, and movement were woven together seamlessly to fully develop dramatic themes in a way that no musical had done before.

The Great Depression of the 1930s kept Broadway on a more serious wavelength with dramas and classical revivals being the fare of the day. Broadway changed its tune in the 1940s, particularly with the smash hit *Oklahoma*, Rodgers and Hammerstein's first show. The playwright duo went on to write some of the most beloved musicals in history, including *South Pacific*, *The King and I*, and *The Sound of Music*. Just a few years later, Rodgers and Hammerstein were joined by another great playwright duo, Lerner and Loewe, who created *Brigadoon*, *My Fair Lady*, and *Camelot*. To this day, the musicals of the 1940s and 1950s form the core of musical theater.

But Broadway's Golden Age dimmed significantly in the 1960s and 1970s. Beginning with the Great Depression, the area around Times Square had begun to worsen, growing poorer, seedier, and more dangerous. By the 1960s, though the rest of the country had largely recovered from the Depression, Times Square had gained a reputation as a dangerous neighborhood, which was off-putting to theater patrons. As a result, the number of new legitimate plays declined. Meanwhile, in response to the cultural upheaval of the 1960s, those few musicals that did make it to the stage departed rather dramatically from those of the 1950s. Musicals such as *Hair* featured counter-culture themes and rock-inspired songs, bringing Broadway into a more liberal era.

Today's Broadway is a bit more diverse. One Broadway trend is to convert existing films and books into musical productions, as evidenced by such Broadway hits as *Wicked* or *The Producers*. Another current trend is the revival of classic musicals, such as the upcoming revival of *Les Miserables*. But some of the most interesting Broadway plays of recent decades have come from off-Broadway, such as the classic and long-running *Rent*.

To the average tourist, the Broadway theater district seems timeless and classic, an original part of New York City. But the truth is that Broadway has evolved slowly over the course of a century and a half, both reflecting and shaping American culture.

11. The primary purpose of the first paragraph is to:

(A) Give a detailed background of Broadway theater before discussing its plays.
(B) Suggest a good place to visit in New York if you like theater.
(C) Describe why Broadway is as timeless as the Statue of Liberty.
(D) Briefly introduce Broadway theater as timeless before delving into its history.

12. The passage states that the theater district as we know it today began:

(A) Around Times Square.
(B) Downtown in the Bowery.
(C) At Madison Square around 34th Street.
(D) Near Union Square around 14th Street.

13. According to the third paragraph, all of the following are true of *The Black Crook* EXCEPT that it:

(A) Completed a record-breaking 474 performances.
(B) Was supposed to be a melodrama.
(C) Became a musical because of fire at a nearby theater.
(D) Was written to appeal primarily to the middle classes.

14. According to the passage, the premiere of *Showboat*:

(A) Marked the beginning of full musical plays.
(B) Offered lighthearted singing and dancing with a burlesque twist.
(C) Was the last of the loosely plotted variety shows.
(D) Had weak dramatic themes fully integrated with book and score.

15. The 5th paragraph indicates that:

I. Theater in Broadway dealt with more serious themes in the 1930's
II. The *Sound of Music* was written by Rodgers and Hammerstein when they were joined by Lerner and Loewe
III. The plays of the 1940's and 1950's still form the core of musical theater

(A) I only
(B) III only
(C) I and III only
(D) I, II, and III

16. As used in line 63, *fare* most nearly means:

(A) Price.
(B) Preparation.
(C) Offering .
(D) Charge.

17. It can be reasonably inferred from the sixth paragraph that:

(A) The end of the Great Depression greatly improved conditions around the Broadway Theater district.
(B) The new counter-culture musicals of the time were off-putting to theater patrons and resulted in Broadway's decline.
(C) Broadway's relocation to Times Square vastly improved conditions in that neighborhood.
(D) A successful theater district depends as much on the safety and atmosphere of its surrounding area as on the plays being performed.

18. The 7th paragraph establishes all of the following about modern Broadway EXCEPT:

(A) It is more diverse today than it was in the past.
(B) There is a trend to convert films and books into musical productions.
(C) Some of the most interesting recent plays have come from off-Broadway.
(D) Classical musicals are still very popular.

19. The passage can best be described as:

(A) A history of Broadway theater's development from its earliest beginnings to its modern day popularity.
(B) A description of the plays that have been popular on Broadway.
(C) An explanation of how Broadway has survived many difficult and changing times.
(D) A guide to Broadway's best shows and theaters for those visiting New York.

20. The author's attitude is best characterized as one of:

(A) Scholarly detachment.
(B) Restrained criticism.
(C) Informative interest.
(D) Passive indifference.

Read this passage carefully and then answer the questions that follow.

Humanities: This passage has been adapted from Arthur Johnstone's *Musical Criticisms*, originally published in 1905.

The "Symphonie Fantastique" offers a more complete picture of the composer's musical personality than any other single work. As a specimen of youthful precocity it also stands alone. It was written at the age of twenty-six, when Berlioz was still a student at the Conservatoire, being persistently snubbed by a group of dons, who all—with the possible exception of Cherubini, the Principal—were utterly his inferiors in every kind of musical power, knowledge, and skill. We have said that, as a work of precocious genius, the "Symphonie Fantastique" stands alone. No doubt other composers, such as Mozart and Schubert, had shown genius of a higher order at an even earlier age. But the "Symphonie Fantastique," as the work of a 'prentice-hand showing absolute mastery of the greatest and most complex resources, has no parallel.

The great fact that has always to be remembered in regard to Berlioz is that he devoted himself with all the energy of an enormous and highly original talent to one particular task in music. That task was the winning of new material for the musical medium, and what Berlioz accomplished in the world of tone was very like what Christopher Columbus accomplished in the world of land and sea. Berlioz too opened up a new hemisphere, and he did his work much more thoroughly than the great navigator. This mighty achievement secures for Berlioz a permanent place of the first importance in the musical hierarchy. But to be deterred by respect for his genius from admitting his faults is not the best way of using his magnificent legacy. Those faults are none the less monstrous for being inseparable from his individuality, and a thoroughly enlightened modern musician would probably find it very difficult to define the attitude of his mind towards the works of Berlioz's art. In a sense, everything in the best of those works is justified. When one finds an artist dealing with certain subjects with enormous power and resource, one must not condemn him because those subjects are unpleasant or even horrible in the extreme. Artistic power is associated with qualities of the highest and rarest that human nature produces, and it is always justified.

The favorite subjects of Berlioz may well prove a stumbling-block. In at least three different works of his we find a movement called by some such name, and, his appetite for horrors not being satisfied with the "Witches' Sabbath" in the first of those three works, he gives us another movement representing a procession to the guillotine of a young man condemned for murdering his sweetheart. In close association with this love of the lurid, spectral, and ghastly is the bitterly ironical spirit which conceived an "Amen" chorus in mock ecclesiastical style to be sung over a dead rat, the guying of the composer's own love-theme with a jig-like variation on a specially ugly instrument (the E flat clarinet) introduced into the orchestra for that purpose, and the use of the stern and majestic Plain Song theme of the "Dies Iræ" as a cantus firmus, to which the mocking laughter of witches rushing past through the air in a huge weltering broomstick cavalcade makes a kind of fantastic counterpoint.

For the "Symphonie Fantastique" the orchestra had to be considerably enlarged. In addition to all the usual instruments the score requires an E flat clarinet, two bells (G and C), a second harp, an extra kettledrum, and a second bass tuba. Everything had been rehearsed with infinite care, and in all five movements the rendering was a display of virtuosity such as only a very rare combination of favourable circumstances would allow one to hear. No other composer displays a very powerful and skillful orchestra to quite such immense advantage. As Mr. Edward Dannreuther has finely and truly remarked—"With Berlioz the equation between a particular phrase and a particular instrument is invariably perfect." His violently willful character manifests itself in the harmony. His fancies devour one another, like dragons of the prime, instead of progressing and developing in an orderly manner. But the marvelous beauty of the tone-colouring and aptness of the passage-work never fail.

21. The author characterizes Berlioz's "Symphonie Fantastique" as:

(A) Berlioz's greatest musical achievement.
(B) A unique musical work due to its composition with early mastery of complex resources.
(C) The cause of Berlioz being persistently snubbed by his inferiors.
(D) A picture of the composer's personality.

22. It can be inferred from the author's use of "precocious genius" (line 11) that Berlioz's composition demonstrates:

(A) Great skills developed by few.
(B) A child's work that surpasses adult talent.
(C) Talent that is great and beautiful .
(D) Incredible talent developed earlier than is expected.

23. It can be reasonably inferred from the passage that Berlioz's peers:

(A) Showed genius of a higher order than Berlioz.
(B) Possessed great musical knowledge and skill.
(C) Dismissed Berlioz's skill.
(D) Admired Cherubini as an equal.

24. As it is used in line 23, *winning* most nearly means:

(A) Conquering.
(B) Charming .
(C) Achieving.
(D) Mastering.

25. The author's comparison of Berlioz to Christopher Columbus suggests that:

(A) Berlioz was a more thorough navigator than Columbus.
(B) Berlioz discovered a new hemisphere in music.
(C) Berlioz searched for and explored new material for his compositions.
(D) Christopher Columbus and Berlioz were accomplished in the world of tone.

26. According to the passage, great artists dealing with certain subjects:

(A) Should be condemned for unpleasant or horrible subjects.
(B) Have monstrous faults due to their individuality.
(C) Are not enlightened like modern musicians.
(D) Possess rare qualities and are always justified even if their subject matter is not pleasing to the audience.

27. What is the purpose of the third paragraph?

(A) To give a description of Berlioz's use of ironic musical juxtaposition
(B) To discuss Berlioz's love of horrors
(C) To give specific examples of his popular inspirations
(D) To show the author's distaste for Berlioz's favorite subjects

28. Which of the following is NOT discussed in the passage as a great strength of Berlioz as a composer?

(A) His ability to progress and develop music in an orderly manner
(B) His highly original talent of winning new material for musical medium
(C) His ability to display a powerful and skillful orchestra
(D) The marvelous beauty and aptness of his passage-work

29. It can be inferred from the passage that the author would most likely agree with which one of the following statements?

(A) Art is considered great only when accepted techniques are used to produce it.
(B) Finding new artistic mediums is risky and rarely produces good results.
(C) It is not necessary to have favorable subject matter to produce masterful work
(D) Exploration of style will earn you a permanent place of importance in history.

30. What is the main purpose of the passage?

(A) To describe a great musical work
(B) To discuss a composer's skill and style
(C) To give a biography of a composer
(D) To highlight a composer's love of horror

Read this passage carefully and then answer the questions that follow.

Humanities: This passage discusses the life and legacy of an American writer.

Edgar Allan Poe is commonly considered to be the inventor of the detective fiction genre and one of the first American writers to practice short story writing. His literary legacy is well known – students everywhere study a myriad of Poe's poems and short stories – but his personal legacy is too often misunderstood.

Poe was born in 1809. Shortly after his birth, Poe's father abandoned the family; his mother died of consumption soon after. Left parentless, Poe was taken in by John Allan, a successful merchant in Richmond, Virginia. Although Poe lived with the Allan family for most of his youth, the Allans never adopted him, instead giving him the name Edgar Allan Poe.

Poe briefly attended the University of Virginia, but left after a falling out with his foster father over Poe's gambling debts. Unable to support himself, Poe spent time in the army before enrolling in West Point. Less than a year after entering West Point, Poe decided to leave by purposefully getting court martialed.

Upon leaving the army for good, Poe travelled to Baltimore to stay with his aunt, Maria Clemm, his cousin, Virginia Clemm, and his invalid grandmother. It was at this time that Poe began his writing career in earnest, but he chose a terrible time to attempt to become an author. A lack of international copyright law meant that it was cheaper for publishers to steal material from British authors than to pay American authors. Those publishers who did agree to pay American authors often failed to follow through or paid them far later than was originally promised. This led Poe to a financially difficult life that forced him to beg for money on more than one occasion.

For several years, Poe drifted between Baltimore, Philadelphia, and Richmond, taking on various posts with different publications. He also married his first-cousin, Virginia Clemm, in 1835. At the time, Poe was 26; Virginia was 13. After seven years of marriage, Virginia showed the first signs of consumption; this must have been a very difficult time for Poe, who had lost his mother to the disease while still in infancy. Under the stress of Virginia's illness, Poe began to drink more heavily. He continued to pursue his writing career, but began to alienate himself from other literati, in part by publically accusing Henry Wadsworth Longfellow of plagiarism. Despite brief success with "The Raven", which was published in 1845, Poe's career was largely financially and critically unstable, especially after the death of his wife in 1847.

Poe's death remains mysterious to this day. He left Richmond for New York on September 27, 1849. Nearly a week later, he was found wandering the streets of Baltimore, delirious and incoherent, and wearing someone else's clothes. Poe was taken to Washington College Hospital where he died several days later on October 7, 1849. We may never know what transpired between the time when Poe was found and the time he died. The only person to have had contact with Poe during that time was Dr. John Joseph Moran, whose testimony had a tendency to change dramatically the more often he told it. Moreover, all hospital records relating to Poe have been lost, including his death certificate. As a result, no one is quite certain of Poe's cause of death. Theories include everything from alcohol or drug abuse to syphilis to epilepsy.

Theories regarding alcohol and drug abuse remain quite popular, but are unlikely to be true. These theories have been propagated and perpetuated by an obituary and memoir penned by a fellow author, Rufus Wilmot Griswold. Griswold and Poe began as friends, but over the course of their acquaintance, became competitors and enemies. Griswold had attempted to assassinate Poe's character even before his death. After Poe's death, Griswold anonymously published an obituary that claimed that Poe routinely wandered the streets talking to himself. Griswold then managed to become Poe's literary executor, claiming that Poe himself had chosen Griswold for the job. While publishing a collection of Poe's work, Griswold included a "Memoir of the Author" in which he described Poe as a depraved, drunk, drug-addled madman.

Although many of Poe's contemporaries came forward to dispute Griswold's account, this memoir became the popular conception of Edgar Allan Poe. In fact, historians continued to base their own biographies about Poe on Griswold's account for nearly 100 years after Poe's death. By the time historians had managed to prove the inaccuracies in Griswold's account, the damage had been done – Poe would forever be known in the mind of the public as a deranged madman.

31. Which of the following sentences best summarizes Paragraphs 2-6:

(A) An objective biographical sketch is followed by a subjective argument.
(B) A brief biographical summary leads into a discussion of a controversy.
(C) A writer's life is discussed in great detail.
(D) A discussion of how Poe created the detective story is abandoned in favor of an examination of the tawdry circumstances surrounding his death.

32. As used in line 27, the expression *in earnest* most nearly means:

(A) In this life.
(B) In an unfortunate way.
(C) In a serious manner.
(D) With remarkable talent.

33. It may be most reasonably inferred from the fourth paragraph that the "lack of international copyright law" (line 29) was bad for foreign writers because:

(A) Publishers liked international copyright law and would not publish any writer who did not obey the law.
(B) Many American authors liked to steal work from foreign writers.
(C) International copyright law protected American writers but forced foreign writers to give their work to American publishers.
(D) In the absence of such a law, American publishers could sell books by foreign writers without paying the writers.

34. The passage indicates that at various times in his life, Poe held all of the following occupations EXCEPT:

(A) Writer.
(B) Merchant.
(C) Publishing house worker.
(D) Soldier.

35. From the passage, it is impossible to determine which of the following?

(A) The exact year of Poe's birth
(B) The exact year in which Poe married Virginia Clemm
(C) The exact year in which Poe's mother died
(D) The exact year in which a delirious and incoherent Poe was taken to Washington College Hospital

36. According to Paragraph 5, Poe's writing career was likely diminished by:

(A) His excessive drinking and his irresponsible treatment of his wife.
(B) His attack on Longfellow and his stress-induced excessive drinking.
(C) The death of his wife and the guilt he felt about the death of his mother.
(D) His gambling debts and the abuse of his publishers.

37. The fact that Poe's mother and wife both died from consumption most strongly suggests:

(A) That Poe might have had the disease and infected other people with it.
(B) That women contract the disease more often than do men.
(C) That consumption was a serious health threat in the 19th century.
(D) That the Poe family was not able to afford the best medical care.

38. Which of the following phrases best expresses the author's view of Rufus Wilmot Griswold?

(A) A self-serving liar who intentionally misrepresented Poe's life
(B) A reckless fool who tried to build his career at Poe's expense
(C) An incompetent author whose ridiculous work has done much to damage the reputation of a great American writer
(D) A misguided soul who believed that he would feel better about himself if he could convince other people to dislike Poe

39. In Paragraphs 6-8, what reasons does the author give for why "Poe's death remains mysterious to this day" (line 55)?

    (A) The loss of hospital records, the effort of a Poe enemy to distort the facts, and the failure of Poe's friends to find the truth
    (B) The loss of hospital records, the inevitable confusion that comes with the passing of time, and the inability of modern historians to get the facts
    (C) The ever-changing testimony of a hospital doctor, the effort of a Poe enemy to distort the facts, and the loss of hospital records
    (D) The inevitable confusion that comes with the passing of time, the failure of Poe's friends to find the truth, and the ever-changing testimony of a hospital doctor

40. As used in line 92, the word *popular* most likely means:

    (A) General.
    (B) Favored.
    (C) Unified.
    (D) Approved.

Read this passage carefully and then answer the questions that follow.

Humanities: This passage describes an unusual historical practice.

A few years ago I lighted on a book, first published in 1906, with the surprising title *The Criminal Prosecution and Capital Punishment of Animals* by E. P. Evans. The frontispiece showed an engraving of a pig, dressed up in a jacket and breeches, being strung up on a gallows in the market square of a town in Normandy in 1386; the pig had been formally tried and convicted of murder by the local court. When I borrowed the book from the Cambridge University Library, I showed this picture of the pig to the librarian. "Is it a joke?" she asked.

No, it was not a joke. All over Europe, throughout the Middle Ages and right on into the 19th century, animals were, as it turns out, tried for human crimes. Dogs, pigs, cows, rats and even flies and caterpillars were arraigned in court on charges ranging from murder to obscenity. The trials were conducted with full ceremony: evidence was heard on both sides, witnesses were called, and in many cases the accused animal was granted a form of legal aid — a lawyer being appointed at the tax-payer's expense to conduct the animal's defense.

In 1494, for example, near Clermont in France a young pig was arrested for having "strangled and defaced a child in its cradle." Several witnesses were examined who testified that "on the morning of Easter Day, the infant being left alone in its cradle, the said pig entered during the said time the said house and disfigured...the child ... which in consequence departed this life." Having weighed up the evidence and found no extenuating circumstances, the judge gave sentence:

"We, in detestation and horror of the said crime, and to the end that an example may be made and justice maintained, have said, judged, sentenced, pronounced and appointed that the said porker, now detained as a prisoner and confined in the said abbey, shall be by the master of high works hanged and strangled on a gibbet of wood."

Evans' book details more than two hundred such cases: sparrows being prosecuted for chattering in Church, a pig executed for stealing a communion wafer, a cock burnt at the stake for laying an egg. As I read my eyes grew wider and wider. Why did no one tell us this at school? Why were we taught so many dreary facts of history at school, and not taught these?

We all know how King Canute attempted to stay the tide at Lambeth; but who has heard, for example, of the solemn threats made against the tides of locusts which threatened to engulf the countryside of France and Italy? The Pied Piper, who charmed the rats from Hamelin, is a part of legend; but who has heard of Bartholomew Chassenée, a French jurist of the sixteenth century, who made his reputation at the bar as the defense counsel for some rats? The rats had been put on trial in the ecclesiastical court on the charge of having "feloniously eaten up and wantonly destroyed" the local barley. When the culprits did not in fact turn up in court on the appointed day, Chassenée made use of all his legal cunning to excuse them. They had, he urged in the first place, probably not received the summons since they moved from village to village; but even if they had received it they were probably too frightened to obey, since as everyone knew they were in danger of being set on by their mortal enemies, the cats. On this point, Chassenée addressed the court at some length, in order to show that if a person be cited to appear at a place to which he cannot come in safety, he may legally refuse. The judge, recognizing the justice of this claim, but being unable to persuade the villagers to keep their cats indoors, was obliged to let the matter drop.

For an animal found guilty, the penalty was dire. The Normandy pig, depicted in the frontispiece of the Evans book, was charged with having violently attacked a baby in its cradle. The pig was sentenced to be "mangled and maimed in the head forelegs," and then – dressed up in a jacket and breeches – to be hung from a gallows in the market square.

But, as we have seen with Chassenée's rats, the outcome of these trials was not inevitable. In doubtful cases, the courts appear in general to have been lenient, on the principle of "innocent until proved guilty beyond reasonable doubt." In 1587, a gang of weevils, accused of damaging a vineyard, were deemed to have been exercising their natural rights to eat – and, in compensation, were granted a vineyard of their own.

41. As used in line 1, the expression "lighted on" most nearly means:

(A) Heard about.
(B) Walked into.
(C) Came upon.
(D) Landed on.

42. Which of the following statements best summarizes the first two paragraphs?

    (A) The author finds an unusual book, questions a librarian about the book's meaning, and then concludes that the book is a hoax.
    (B) A librarian's surprising reaction to a book raises concern for a reader.
    (C) An interesting discovery leads to further research on an unusual topic.
    (D) A reader is disgusted to learn that a famous university library carries books about strange legal practices.

43. In lines 21-22, the author most likely mentions that "in many cases the accused animal was granted a form of legal aid" in order to:

    (A) Show how foolish people were in the Middle Ages.
    (B) Raise questions about the quality of early European courts and argue that the legal representation given to animals was superior to that received by people.
    (C) Suggest that people in Europe believe that even animals are entitled to a fair trial.
    (D) Demonstrate that at one time people in Europe took the prosecution of animals very seriously.

44. It may be most reasonably inferred from the fourth paragraph that the judge in the pig's murder trial most likely wanted to:

    (A) Assure the dead child's parents that justice has been done, and punish the owner of the pig for allowing the animal to run loose.
    (B) Execute a pig as a way of entertaining the public, and convince farmers to keep their livestock from committing crimes.
    (C) Poke fun at a foolish law, and send a message to "porkers" that the court will not tolerate pig-on-human violence.
    (D) Put farmers on notice that the court will prosecute all animals, and let the public know that no one - not even a pig - is above the law.

45. The passage indicates that all of the following animals have been accused of crimes EXCEPT:

    (A) A rooster.
    (B) A dog.
    (C) A horse.
    (D) A gang of weevils.

46. In lines 47-48, the author contrasts "dreary facts of history" with:

    (A) The story of a pig stealing communion wafers.
    (B) Two hundred cases of animals being accused of crimes.
    (C) All the evidence presented against animals.
    (D) The fun of library research.

47. It can be most reasonably assumed that King Canute is:

    (A) A historical figure who the author learned about in school.
    (B) A Western European monarch who convicted an animal of a crime.
    (C) A medieval ruler who tried to prevent a flood in Lambeth.
    (D) The head of a country that was overrun by locust.

48. The author of the passage contrasts:

    I. Chassenée's rats and the Normandy pig
    II. King Canute and people in Italy and France who faced a tide of locust
    III. the Pied Piper and a 16th century French jurist

    (A) I only
    (B) III only
    (C) II and III only
    (D) I, II, and III

49. The rats in Paragraph 6 are tried in court for:

    (A) Having eaten some barley.
    (B) Being a general nuisance.
    (C) Failing to show up for trial.
    (D) Escaping the Pied Piper.

50. In Paragraph 6, Chassenée's argument that the rats had good reason for not appearing in court would have been most weakened by:

    (A) A report showing that the court was willing to provide the rats with food and shelter for the duration of the trial.
    (B) Proof that the summons had been accepted by someone at the rats' home.
    (C) Evidence that the rats had nothing to fear from the village cats.
    (D) An admission by the villagers of a hatred for rats.

rP15: ADVANCED SOCIAL SCIENCE PASSAGES

TOPIC OVERVIEW

In Lesson 5, you learned how to search for facts and cause & effect, as well as how to follow a thesis in Social Science passages. In this lesson, you'll learn how to answer tricky "fact or opinion" questions, as well as how to separate various opinions present in the passage.

"FACT OR OPINION" QUESTIONS and VARIOUS OPINIONS

One tricky question type that may appear on a Social Science passage asks you to solve a series of problems in a single question. Here is an example:

> In the author's view, would the assertion that the early man was the first animal to use a form of written language be an expression of fact or opinion, and why?

This question asks you to determine three pieces of information:

1) The author's view
2) Whether the assertion is fact or opinion
3) Why the author would name the assertion as a fact or an opinion

In order to answer this question, you must be able to separate the author's opinion from any other opinions that may be present in the text. The author may present arguments from several scientists, authors, or contributors to the field, but he or she may support one perspective above the others. The author might also be presenting facts rather than arguing an opinion. You must first establish what you know the author believes, or presents as fact.

The passage's **conclusion paragraph** is the best place to look if you're not sure of the author's opinion. A passage will rarely end in the middle of a debate, and the conclusion will likely contain some clues as to which opinion (if any) the author supports.

Next, you must determine whether the piece of information given in the question fits into the author's facts, or whether the author would call that piece of information an opinion. Next to the question, write an "F" for fact or an "O" for opinion.

Finally, you must answer the question "why?". What information does the author give that establishes whether the information is fact or opinion? You must have evidence to support your answer.

When approaching "Fact or Opinion" questions, use the following strategy:

1) Establish the author's view (or the view of the person named in the question), as opposed to any other views possibly present in the passage.
2) Determine whether the information given is a fact or an opinion from that person's perspective. Write an "F" near the question for "fact" and an "O" for "opinion".
3) Determine why the author believes the information to be either fact or opinion. Look to the text to find support and evidence.
4) Choose the answer the best matches your determination.

Read this passage carefully and then answer the questions that follow.

Social Science: This passage was adapted from *Language: An Introduction to the Study of Speech* by Edward Sapir, published in 1921.

Speech is so familiar a feature of daily life that we rarely pause to define it. It seems as natural to man as walking, and only less so than breathing. Yet it needs but a moment's reflection to convince us that this naturalness of speech is but an illusory feeling. The process of acquiring speech is, in sober fact, an utterly different sort of thing from the process of learning to walk.

In the case of the latter function, culture, in other words the traditional body of social usage, is not seriously brought into play. The child is individually equipped, by the complex set of factors that we term biological heredity, to make all the needed muscular and nervous adjustments that result in walking. Indeed, the very conformation of these muscles and of the appropriate parts of the nervous system may be said to be primarily adapted to the movements made in walking and in similar activities. In a very real sense the normal human being is predestined to walk, not because his elders will assist him to learn the art, but because his organism is prepared from birth, or even from the moment of conception, to take on all those expenditures of nervous energy and all those muscular adaptations that result in walking. To put it concisely, walking is an inherent, biological function.

Not so with language. It is of course true that in a certain sense the individual is predestined to talk, but that is due entirely to the circumstance into which he is born. Eliminate society and there is every reason to believe that he will learn to walk, if, indeed, he survives at all. But it is just as certain that he will never learn to talk, that is, to communicate ideas according to the traditional system of a particular society. Or, again, remove the new-born individual from the social environment into which he has come and transplant him to an utterly alien one. He will develop the art of walking in his new environment very much as he would have developed it in the old. But his speech will be completely at variance with the speech of his native environment. Speech is a human activity that varies without assignable limit as we pass from social group to social group, because it is a purely historical heritage of the group, the product of long-continued social usage. It varies as all creative effort varies—not as consciously, perhaps, but none the less as truly as do the religions, the beliefs, the customs, and the arts of different peoples. Walking is an organic, an instinctive, function (not, of course, itself an instinct); speech is a non-instinctive, acquired, "cultural" function.

There is one fact that has frequently tended to prevent the recognition of language as a merely conventional system of sound symbols. This is the well-known observation that under the stress of emotion, say of a sudden twinge of pain or of unbridled joy, we do involuntarily give utterance to sounds that the hearer interprets as indicative of the emotion itself. But there is all the difference in the world between such involuntary expression of feeling and the normal type of communication of ideas that is speech. The former kind of utterance is indeed instinctive, but it is non-symbolic; in other words, the sound of pain or the sound of joy does not, as such, indicate the emotion, it does not stand aloof, as it were, and announce that such and such an emotion is being felt. What it does is to serve as a more or less automatic overflow of the emotional energy; in a sense, it is part and parcel of the emotion itself. Moreover, such instinctive cries hardly constitute communication in any strict sense. They are not addressed to any one, they are merely overheard, if heard at all, as the bark of a dog, the sound of approaching footsteps, or the rustling of the wind is heard. If they convey certain ideas to the hearer, it is only in the very general sense in which any and every sound or even any phenomenon in our environment may be said to convey an idea to the perceiving mind. If the involuntary cry of pain which is conventionally represented by "Oh!" be looked upon as a true speech symbol equivalent to some such idea as "I am in great pain," it is just as allowable to interpret the appearance of clouds as an equivalent symbol that carries the definite message "It is likely to rain." A definition of language, however, that is so extended as to cover every type of inference becomes utterly meaningless.

1. As it is used in line 5, the word *illusory* means:

   (A) Deceptive.
   (B) Momentary.
   (C) Incorrect.
   (D) Elusive.

2. The author asserts that that walking is a biological function because:

(A) It cannot be proven that walking is influenced by cultural idiosyncrasies.
(B) Genes that dictate physical characteristics are biologically inherited.
(C) The muscles and nervous system are appropriately configured for walking.
(D) No one is ever taught how to walk.

3. The discussion of walking serves the primary function of:

(A) Contrasting a biological function of the body with a cultural one.
(B) Suggesting that not all bodily functions are equal.
(C) Emphasizing that biological factors have dominance over cultural ones.
(D) Playing devil's advocate with the suggestion that walking and talking are similar.

4. Which of the following, if proven true, would weaken the author's claim that speech is "a non-instinctive, acquired, 'cultural' function" (line 53)?

(A) The finding that humans develop language even in the remotest parts of the world
(B) The discovery of a person who grew up outside of society but refers to things using words
(C) The suggestion that even the most abstract ideas can be expressed in language
(D) Newborns make noise even before they are able to recognize the presence of people

5. It can be reasonably inferred from the passage that:

(A) Before this publication, the concept of speech as we know it was not defined in scientific terms.
(B) Arguments differentiating biological and cultural influences of language are highly contentious.
(C) Some have cited spontaneous expressions of pain as proof that language is instinctive and symbolic.
(D) The author relies heavily on empirical evidence to establish his premises.

6. When the author asserts that an involuntary expression of feeling "is part and parcel of the emotion itself" (lines 71-72), he is responding to the assumption that:

(A) The "utterance is indeed instinctive" (lines 64-65).
(B) The utterance is "indicative of the emotion itself" (lines 60-61).
(C) Language is "a merely conventional system of sound symbols" (lines 55-56).
(D) The cry of pain and the cry of joy are fundamentally different linguistic acts.

7. According to the author, why does "a definition of language, however, that is so extended as to cover every type of inference become...utterly meaningless" (lines 88-90)?

(A) One cannot infer the meaning of an utterance unless it is in his or her language.
(B) Utterances without language (like "Oh!") must be interpreted in context.
(C) Assigning meaning to every linguistic utterance is too subjective to be feasible.
(D) Language has no inherent meaning.

8. The primary purpose of this passage is to:

(A) Theorize about the primacy of nurture over nature.
(B) Speculate about the origins of language.
(C) Contrast the physical and cultural dimensions of speech.
(D) Challenge a common perception that many people have about language.

9. The author's discussion in the last paragraph of what is "overheard" serves the primary function of:

(A) Disproving that utterances have any intrinsic meaning without someone interpreting them.
(B) Exploring the characteristics of sound in the natural world.
(C) Arguing that sounds convey as much meaning as utterances.
(D) Suggesting that speech symbols always express messages while sounds do not.

10. All of the following are concessions that the author makes except:

    (A) Utterances brought about through pain or joy are instinctive.
    (B) In a certain sense, the individual is predestined to talk.
    (C) One can learn how to walk in a new environment.
    (D) The involuntary cry of "oh!" is a true speech symbol.

Read this passage carefully and then answer the questions that follow.

Social Science: This passage discusses an invention with widespread social impact.

The ancestor of the monetary system is, of course, the barter system. A farmer could exchange his produce for the fish obtained by a fisherman or the cloth produced by a weaver. However, dickering over the relative value of different things tends to be time-consuming and troublesome, and so societies tended to converge towards a common medium of exchange.

The medium that gained widespread acceptance was precious metals such as gold and silver, which were eventually converted into coinage. Coins are said to have been invented by the Lydians, a people of Asia Minor, sometime after 640 BC. The Greeks, the Romans, the Byzantines, and others established and spread various coin currencies over the ensuing centuries. By the time of the Renaissance, European states were producing new coins of their own. Coins are still with us, though they are now little more than tokens made of non-precious metals.

In a particularly imaginative rethinking of coins, the American science-fiction writer Larry Niven once proposed that coins be made out of radioactive waste, which would solve the nuclear waste disposal problem, ensure that money circulated rapidly, and lend a new meaning to the expression "money burning a hole in your pocket."

Niven was of course joking, but when the first paper money was introduced in China a millennium ago, many must have thought it was just as great a joke. Who would rest their fortunes in mere pieces of paper? Kublai Khan, the Mongol emperor who ruled China in the 13th century, emphasized that it wasn't a joke when he decreed that those who refused to accept paper money would be executed. He also confiscated all gold and silver, even that which was carried in by foreign visitors. This was the purpose of Chinese paper money: to ensure total state control over precious metals.

The story of paper money in Europe is far less totalitarian. According to tradition, the first European to introduce paper money was a Swedish banker named Johan Palmstruch, whose Stockholm Banco began to issue the stuff in 1661. The offering went well enough at first, but success led to the bank's overextension. Palmstruch, like any good modern banker, called to the government for financial help. Unlike a modern banker, he was taken to trial for mismanagement and sentenced to death.

Despite the unhappy ending to Palmstruch's scheme, the idea was one whose time had come, and paper money was adopted by other European countries.

The Americans showed an interest in paper money even before independence. Many colonies enthusiastically printed their own currencies in the mid-18th century. As it turned out, they were too enthusiastic, and in 1764 the British Crown banned further issues of colonial banknotes. This was no doubt prudent, but it was also done in a high-handed fashion. In any case, the issue of money was one of the thousand little cuts that drove the Americans to revolt against Britain. The colonies declared themselves as independent states and printed money on their own again, as did the Continental Congress. They all proved just as undisciplined as they had been before. This is why the Constitution reserved the right to print money for the Federal government, though currency wasn't issued until 1797; even then, the issue of currency did not include paper money.

Many people resisted the notion of a currency that was not backed by precious metals, reasoning that paper currency was inherently worthless. But the problem with paper currencies was not that they were inadequately backed by precious metals; instead, the problem was that governments were too often reliant on simply printing more money rather than creating more wealth. It is relatively easy to print more banknotes, but not so easy to increase the overall wealth of a nation, and so if twice the number of banknotes is printed given the same amount of wealth, the value of each banknote is cut in half. The most famous example of this was the Weimar Republic that ran post-World War I Germany, where inflation took place by a factor of trillions.

Money, as the saying goes, "is worth what everyone thinks it's worth." The real concern is discipline in the printing of money. If too much money is printed, it becomes devaluated. If too little is printed, it stifles commerce. The actual amount of money printed is a tricky issue, especially in modern times since now maybe about 10% or less of all the money in prosperous countries is in the form of physical coins or banknotes, the rest existing only in the form of ledger entries in electronic accounting books. Not only are banknotes no longer backed by gold; the bulk of money isn't even backed by banknotes. If bankers and governments have proven irresponsible with the printing of money before, what new atrocities might they think of in an era of "virtual" money?

11. The primary purpose of this passage is to:

    (A) Discuss the development of an economic necessity and its potential flaws.
    (B) Entertain with a series of anecdotes then pose a probing question to the reader.
    (C) Suggest that the lack of wealth can have widespread effects.
    (D) Argue that the progression of an economic tool is not entirely positive.

12. The main function of the third paragraph in relation to the passage as a whole is most likely to:

    (A) Introduce a seemingly silly concept that would eventually prove viable in another context.
    (B) Provide an analogue to help the reader understand the original strangeness of paper currency.
    (C) Create a narrative bridge between otherwise neutral historical facts.
    (D) Introduce through humor the major concerns of modern currency.

13. It can be inferred from lines 28-39 that the Chinese people's major problem with paper currency was:

    (A) They had trouble believing that paper could hold value like precious metals.
    (B) The totalitarian nature with which the king implemented the measure.
    (C) They did not understand how serious the change would be.
    (D) Their attachment to the gold and silver that they had accumulated.

14. According to the passage, the difference between European and Chinese development of paper currency was:

    (A) One was mandated by the state while the other arose privately.
    (B) One was meant to increase public funds while the other was meant to increase private funds.
    (C) One was implemented gradually while the other was implemented all at once.
    (D) One ended well while the other ended tragically.

15. The author suggests that paper currency during colonial and revolutionary times in America was all of the following EXCEPT:

    (A) One of the motives for independence from Britain.
    (B) A matter of pride for the colonies.
    (C) Highly inconsistent.
    (D) Eventually discarded as inefficient.

16. The author of the passage would most likely agree with which of the following statements?

    (A) The printing of money is an inherently flawed idea.
    (B) Governments and bankers have an obligation to exercise responsibility regarding money.
    (C) Considering the plausibility of inflation due to the overprinting of money, governments should stop printing money.
    (D) Theft and mismanagement of money will probably result from our dependence on the internet.

17. When the author asserts that "‘money is worth what everyone thinks it's worth’," (lines 89-90), he or she most likely means:

    (A) The strength of currency is its widespread recognition.
    (B) The economic power of a nation depends on how it is perceived by other nations.
    (C) The value of currency is universally accepted and therefore universally valid.
    (D) The value of currency depends on how nations create and use it in the real marketplace.

18. According to the passage, the nature of coins today is fundamentally different from their original nature in that:

    (A) They hold no inherent value.
    (B) Their importance is mostly symbolic because paper currency is more widely used.
    (C) The precious metals they are made of is less valuable.
    (D) Their use is more universal.

19. The last paragraph differs from the first paragraph in that in the last paragraph the author:

(A) Uses and expands on popular opinion.
(B) Uses more statistics to support his arguments.
(C) Introduces a problem and leaves it unresolved.
(D) Incorporates more technical language.

20. The author's style in the passage can best be described as:

(A) Facetious but knowledgeable.
(B) Flippant but sympathetic.
(C) Conversational but methodical.
(D) Entertaining but helpful.

 Version 2.0

Read this passage carefully and then answer the questions that follow.

Social Science: This passage is adapted from *The Problem of Ohio Mounds* by Cyrus Thomas, which was originally published at the end of the eighteenth century.

The historical evidence is, as we have seen, conclusive that some of the tribes of Native Americans were mound builders. As the country was inhabited only by Native Americans at the time of its discovery, and as we have no evidence of its having ever been occupied by any other people, every fact indicating a similarity between the arts, customs, and social life of the mound-builders and those of the Native Americans is an evidence of the shared identity of the two peoples. The greater the number of these resemblances, the greater the probability of the correctness of the theory, as long as we find nothing irreconcilable with it.

One of the first circumstances which strikes the mind of the archaeologist who carefully studies these works as being very significant is the entire absence of any evidence in them of architectural knowledge and skill approaching that exhibited by the ruins of Mexico and Central America, or even equaling that exhibited by the Pueblo people.

It is true that truncated pyramidal mounds of large size and somewhat regular proportions are found in certain sections, and that some of these have ramps or roadways leading up to them. Yet when compared with the pyramids of Mexico and Yucatan the differences in the manifestations of architectural skill are so great as to furnish no grounds whatever for attributing the two classes of works to the same people. The facts that the works of the one people consist chiefly of wrought and sculptured stone, and that such materials are wholly unknown to the other, forbid the idea of any relationship between the two.

Though hundreds of groups of mounds marking the sites of ancient villages are to be seen scattered over the Mississippi Valley and Gulf States yet nowhere can there be found an ancient house. This had previously led archaeologists to believe that these mounds were created by a people that lived a roving, restless life that would not justify the time and trouble necessary to erect such permanent structures. However, the last inference is irreconcilable with the magnitude and extent of many groups of these remains. It is therefore irresistible to infer that the houses of the mound-builders were constructed of perishable materials; consequently that the builders were not sufficiently advanced in art to use stone or brick in building.

One chief objection to the Native American origin of these works is, as already stated, that their builders must have been sedentary, and as remains of neither stone nor brick structures are found which could have been used for this purpose, we must assume that their dwellings were constructed of perishable material, such as was supplied in abundance by the forest region in which they dwelt. It is therefore apparent that in this respect at least the dwellings of mound-builders were similar to those of Native Americans.

The mortuary customs of the mound-builders, as gleaned from an examination of their burial mounds, ancient cemeteries, and other depositories of their dead, present so many striking resemblances to those of the Native Americans when first encountered by the whites, as to leave little room for doubt regarding their identity.

"The commonest mode of burial among North American Natives," we are informed by Dr. H. C. Yarrow, "has been that of interment in the ground, and this has taken place in a number of ways." The different ways he mentions are, in pits, graves, or holes in the ground; in stone graves or cists; in mounds; beneath or in cabins, wigwams, houses or lodges, and in caves.

The most common method of burial among the mound-builders was by inhumation also, and all the different ways mentioned by Dr. Yarrow as practiced by the Native Americans were in vogue among the former. The chief value of this fact in this connection is that it forms one item of evidence against the theory held by some antiquarians that the mound-builders were Mexicans, as the usual mode of disposing of the dead by the latter was cremation.

Finally, the pottery of the mound-builders has often been referred to as proof of a higher culture status, and of an advance in art beyond that reached by the Native Americans. The vase with a bird figure found in an Ohio mound is presented in most works on American archaeology as an evidence of the advanced stage of the ceramic art among the mound-builders; but Dr. Rau, who examined the vase, says:

"Having seen the best specimens of 'mound' pottery, I do not hesitate to assert that the clay vessels fabricated by the Native Americans of the modern-day Midwest were in every respect equal to those exhumed from the mounds of the Mississippi Valley."

The statement so often made that the mound pottery, especially that of Ohio, far excels that of the Native Americans is not justified by the facts.

21. The primary purpose of the passage is to:

(A) Describe the arts, customs, and social life the ancient mound-builders.
(B) Compare and contrast North American mound-builders with the builders of ancient Mexican pyramids.
(C) Refute the claim that the pottery of the mound-builders is superior to that of native North American peoples.
(D) Put forth a theory about the identity of the mound-builders.

22. According to the passage, why was it previously believed that the mound-builders were nomadic?

(A) Their dwellings were made of perishable materials.
(B) Hundreds of mounds were found in the Mississippi Valley and Gulf States.
(C) No remains of their dwellings have been found.
(D) It was assumed that they did not have the architectural skill to build permanent homes.

23. Based on the information in paragraph 3, it can be reasonably inferred that:

(A) The mound-builders and the builders of Mexican and Yucatan pyramids never had contact.
(B) Most mounds are pyramidal in shape and regular in proportion.
(C) The architecture of the mounds does not contain sculptured stone.
(D) The mound-builders' work is less intricate than but equal in value to the pyramids of Mexico.

24. The phrase "magnitude and extent" (line 43) refers to:

(A) The size and established nature of the mound-builders' settlements.
(B) The size and complexity of the mounds.
(C) The importance and degree of the mounds.
(D) The importance and established nature of the mound-builder's settlements.

25. In line 78, "in vogue" most nearly means:

(A) Common.
(B) Modern.
(C) Fashionable.
(D) Traditional.

26. According to the passage, the primary purpose for including information about burial methods is to:

(A) To compare the burial methods of the mound-builders to those of native North Americans.
(B) To link a practice of ancient peoples to more understandable customs of today.
(C) To allow a noted archaeologist to be quoted in favor of the author's thesis.
(D) To refute the theory that ancient Mexican people built the mounds.

27. The author's tone can best be described as:

(A) Cautious skepticism.
(B) Confidently argumentative.
(C) Scholarly ambivalence.
(D) Detached disagreement.

28. The primary purpose for the author including the quote by Dr. Rau is to:

(A) Extol the quality of native North American pottery.
(B) Corroborate the idea that the vase with the bird figure is advanced ceramic art.
(C) Present a point of view that differs from his own.
(D) Give credibility to his own assertion that mound pottery is equal in quality to native North American pottery.

29. Which of the following would the author likely agree with?

I. Generally, the North American mounds and the pyramids of Mexico are architecturally similar.
II. The dwellings of the mound-builders were similar to those of native North Americans.
III. The quality of the clay vessels of native North Americans exceeds that of the mound-builders.

(A) I only
(B) II only
(C) I and III only
(D) I, II, and III

30. The passage suggests which of the following?

    (A) It was once thought that the mound-builders were an advanced civilization superior to native North Americans.
    (B) The lack of certain building materials limited the architectural complexity of the mounds.
    (C) The superior pottery of the mound-builders exemplifies their advanced nature.
    (D) There are more archaeologists who agree with the author's thesis than those that disagree.

Read this passage carefully and then answer the questions that follow.

Social Science: This passage is adapted from Plato's *Republic.*

The relation of good men to their governments is so peculiar, that in order to defend them I must take an illustration from the world of fiction. Conceive the captain of a ship, taller by a head and shoulders than any of the crew, yet a little deaf, a little blind, and rather ignorant of the seaman's art. The sailors want to steer, although they know nothing of the art; and they have a theory that it cannot be learned. If the helm is refused them, they drug the captain's wine, bind him hand and foot, and take possession of the ship. He who joins in the mutiny is termed a good pilot and what not; they have no conception that the true pilot must observe the winds and the stars, and must be their master, whether they like it or not;—such a one would be called by them fool, prater, star-gazer. This is my parable; which I will beg you to interpret for me to those gentlemen who ask why the philosopher has such an evil name, and to explain to them that not he, but those who will not use him, are to blame for his uselessness.

The philosopher should not beg of mankind to be put in authority over them. The wise man should not seek the rich, as the proverb bids; but, every man, whether rich or poor, must knock at the door of the physician when he has need of him. Now the pilot is the philosopher—he whom in the parable they call star-gazer, and the mutinous sailors are the mob of politicians by whom he is rendered useless. Not that these are the worst enemies of philosophy, who is far more dishonored by her own professing sons when they are corrupted by the world.

Need I recall the original image of the philosopher? Did we not say of him just now, that he loved truth and hated falsehood, and that he could not rest in the multiplicity of phenomena, but was led by a sympathy in his own nature to the contemplation of the absolute? All the virtues as well as truth, who is the leader of them, took up their abode in his soul. But as you were observing, if we turn aside to view the reality, we see that the persons who were thus described are a small and useless class. The uselessness of philosophers is explained by the circumstance that mankind will not use them. The world in all ages has been divided between contempt and fear of those who employ the power of ideas and know no other weapons.

The many will probably remain incredulous, for they have never seen the natural unity of ideas, but only artificial juxtapositions; not free and generous thoughts, but tricks of controversy and quips of law;—a perfect man ruling in a perfect state, even a single one they have not known. And we foresaw that there was no chance of perfection either in states or individuals until a necessity was laid upon philosophers—those whom we called the useless class—of holding office; or until the sons of kings were inspired with a true love of philosophy. Whether in the infinity of past time there has been, or is in some distant land, or ever will be hereafter, an ideal such as we have described, we stoutly maintain that there has been, is, and will be such a state whenever the Muse of philosophy rules.

Will you say that the world is of another mind? O, my friend, do not revile the world! They will soon change their opinion if they are gently entreated, and are taught the true nature of the philosopher. Who can hate a man who loves him? Or be jealous of one who has no jealousy? Consider, again, that the many hate not the true but the false philosophers—the pretenders who force their way in without invitation, and are always speaking of persons and not of principles, which is unlike the spirit of philosophy. For the true philosopher despises earthly strife; his eye is fixed on the eternal order in accordance with which he moulds himself into the Divine image (and not himself only, but other men), and is the creator of the virtues private as well as public. When mankind sees that the happiness of states is only to be found in that image, will they be angry with us for attempting to delineate it?

31. In the parable of the ship captain (paragraphs 1-2), the mutinous sailors do not understand that:

(A) The captain's physical characteristics make him better equipped to steer the ship.
(B) The captain is the master of the winds and the stars.
(C) The seaman's art can, in fact, be learned.
(D) A ship must be navigated by the stars, which is the proper way to steer.

32. As it is used in line 38, the word *absolute* most nearly means:

(A) Not to be doubted or questioned.
(B) Perfect.
(C) Positive.
(D) Final.

33. According to the passage, all of the following are characteristics of the philosopher EXCEPT:

(A) He loves truth and hates falsehood.
(B) He despises earthly strife.
(C) He looks past earthly phenomena and is drawn to the natural unity of ideas.
(D) He uses controversy and law.

34. Why are people unlikely to trust "those who employ the power of ideas and know no other weapons" (lines 46-48)?

(A) Most people have not had an experience with truth.
(B) People have been deceived by philosophers before.
(C) Most people naturally distrust politicians.
(D) People feel safer with a leader who uses force.

35. According to the passage, why are philosophers a "useless class" (line 43)?

(A) Their vision of a perfect state will likely not be realized.
(B) People often do not understand the value of the philosopher.
(C) Mankind has never seen a perfect philosopher.
(D) The philosopher is not in the business of politics.

36. When the author says "O, my friend, do not revile the world!" (line 66), we can infer that the author:

(A) Is speaking to a close group of friends.
(B) Perceives jealousy in those that disagree with him.
(C) Believes in the world's ability to change for the better.
(D) Is afraid that someone will overhear their conversation.

37. According to the passage, which of the following would be an example of a false philosopher?

(A) "The mob of politicians" (lines 28-29)
(B) "A small and useless class" (lines 42-43)
(C) "Her own professing sons when they are corrupted by the world" (lines 31-32)
(D) "He moulds himself into the Divine image" (lines 77-78)

38. The rhetorical questions in lines 69-70 serve primarily to:

(A) Get the reader to consider a new way of thinking.
(B) Describe the true nature of the philosopher.
(C) Suggest strategies for philosophers to change the world's opinion.
(D) Illustrate the speaker's attitude toward his listeners.

39. According to the author, which of the following illustrate ideals that are in conflict?

I. virtue vs. truth
II. rich vs. poor
III. unity of ideas vs. artificial juxtapositions

(A) I only
(B) III only
(C) I and III only
(D) I, II, and III

40. The primary purpose of this passage is to:

(A) Assert that philosophers would make good rulers.
(B) Discuss the obstacles inherent in the creation of a perfect state.
(C) Describe the relationship between good men and their governments.
(D) Describe the characteristics of philosophers.

Read this passage carefully and then answer the questions that follow.

Social Science: The following passage is adapted from Machiavelli's *The Prince.*

Considering the difficulties which men have had to hold to a newly acquired state, some might wonder how, seeing that Alexander the Great became the master of Asia in a few years, and died whilst it was scarcely settled (whence it might appear reasonable that the whole empire would have rebelled), nevertheless his successors maintained themselves, and had to meet no other difficulty than that which arose among themselves from their own ambitions.

I answer that the principalities of which one has record are found to be governed in two different ways; either by a prince, with a body of servants, who assist him to govern the kingdom as ministers by his favor and permission; or by a prince and barons, who hold that dignity by antiquity of blood and not by the grace of the prince. Such barons have states and their own subjects, who recognize them as lords and hold them in natural affection. Those states that are governed by a prince and his servants hold their prince in more consideration, because in all the country there is no one who is recognized as superior to him, and if they yield obedience to another they do it as to a minister and official, and they do not bear him any particular affection.

The examples of these two governments in our time are the Turk and the King of France. The entire monarchy of the Turk is governed by one lord, the others are his servants; and, dividing his kingdom into sanjaks, he sends there different administrators, and shifts and changes them as he chooses. But the King of France is placed in the midst of an ancient body of lords, acknowledged by their own subjects, and beloved by them; they have their own prerogatives, nor can the king take these away except at his peril. Therefore, he who considers both of these states will recognize great difficulties in seizing the state of the Turk, but, once it is conquered, great ease in holding it.

The causes of the difficulties in seizing the kingdom of the Turk are that the usurper cannot be called in by the princes of the kingdom, nor can he hope to be assisted in his designs by the revolt of those whom the lord has around him. His ministers, being all slaves and bondmen, can only be corrupted with great difficulty, and one can expect little advantage from them when they have been corrupted, as they cannot carry the people with them, for the reasons assigned. Hence, he who attacks the Turk must bear in mind that he will find him united, and he will have to rely more on his own strength than on the revolt of others; but, if once the Turk has been conquered, and routed in the field in such a way that he cannot replace his armies, there is nothing to fear but the family of this prince, and, this being exterminated, there remains no one to fear, the others having no credit with the people; and as the conqueror did not rely on them before his victory, so he ought not to fear them after it.

The contrary happens in kingdoms governed like that of France, because one can easily enter there by gaining over some baron of the kingdom, for one always finds malcontents and such as desire a change. Such men, for the reasons given, can open the way into the state and render the victory easy; but if you wish to hold it afterwards, you meet with infinite difficulties, both from those who have assisted you and from those you have crushed. Nor is it enough for you to have exterminated the family of the prince, because the lords that remain make themselves the heads of fresh movements against you, and as you are unable either to satisfy or exterminate them, that state is lost whenever time brings the opportunity.

Now if you will consider what was the nature of the government of Darius, you will find it similar to the kingdom of the Turk, and therefore it was only necessary for Alexander, first to overthrow him in the field, and then to take the country from him. After which victory, Darius being killed, the state remained secure to Alexander, for the above reasons. And if his successors had been united they would have enjoyed it securely and at their ease, for there were no tumults raised in the kingdom except those they provoked themselves.

41. According to the passage, the kingdom of Alexander the Great would have remained secure if:

(A) Alexander the Great had not died prematurely.
(B) There had not been barons in the kingdom who desired change.
(C) The family of Darius had been exterminated.
(D) Alexander the Great's successors did not succumb to in-fighting.

42. The author asserts that taking a kingdom like France is facilitated by:

(A) The slaves and bondmen who desire change.
(B) The number of barons who are beloved by their own subjects.
(C) The possibility that barons would support the conqueror.
(D) The baron's subjects who would rather have their lord in power.

43. As it is used in line 36, the word *prerogatives* means:

(A) Rights or privileges.
(B) People who live under rule.
(C) Decisions.
(D) Motivations.

44. The primary difficulty in acquiring such a state as that of the Turk is:

(A) The unity of the prince and his ministers.
(B) The unity of the Turkish people.
(C) The cumbersome size of the empire.
(D) The affection that the people hold toward their prince.

45. According to the context of the second paragraph, the author mentions that the barons "hold that dignity by the antiquity of blood" (line 16) primarily to suggest that:

(A) The barons are unworthy of their status in the kingdom.
(B) Barons' positions are precarious because they are not bestowed by the king.
(C) The barons will eventually consider their own states more important than the kingdom.
(D) The barons hold no inherent allegiance to the king.

46. When the author reminds the reader that the slaves and bondmen "cannot carry the people with them, for the reasons assigned," (lines 49-50), he is referring to the fact that:

(A) They "can only be corrupted with great difficulty" (line 47).
(B) The lord of the country "shifts and changes them as he chooses" (line 32-33).
(C) The people "do not bear [them] any particular affection" (line 25-26).
(D) The prince keeps them "by his favor and permission" (line 15).

47. It can reasonably be inferred that the primary function of the first sentence (lines 1-10) in relation to the rest of the passage is to:

(A) Introduce a particular case study which will be elucidated using examples in the passage.
(B) Emphasize the distinctiveness of one conqueror's achievement in relation to other cases.
(C) Point out the most common downfall of otherwise ideal conquests.
(D) Suggest the speed at which a conquest can be established and destroyed.

48. According to the passage, one conquering a state like that of the Turk has "no one to fear" if they do the following:

I. Exterminate the family of the monarchy
II. Rely on no other government insider
III. Win the affection of the people

(A) I only
(B) I and II only
(C) II and III only
(D) I, II, and III

49. The author suggests that barons are a problem when attempting to keep a state like France because of all of the following EXCEPT:

(A) The conqueror cannot exterminate all the barons.
(B) If they helped the conqueror, they might expect something in return.
(C) Their power comes from their subjects, not from the king.
(D) Disgruntled barons will perpetually lead rebellions against the conqueror.

50. The passage can best be described as:

(A) A dispassionate thesis.
(B) A calculated strategy.
(C) A cruel scheme.
(D) A regretful retrospection.

rP16: ADVANCED NATURAL SCIENCE PASSAGES

TOPIC OVERVIEW

In Lesson 6, you became familiar with question types for Natural Science passages and learned to differentiate between Idea/ Explanation, Point/Counterpoint, and Other passages. In this lesson, you'll learn how to tackle some of the more difficult aspects of Natural Science passages, including questions without line references and especially dense material.

QUESTIONS WITHOUT LINE REFERENCES

One of the more difficult types of questions for Natural Science passages is the detail question that lacks any line references to contextualize it. Typically, detail questions are fairly straightforward: You know exactly what you are looking for, and you find it fairly easily within the passage.

These questions can get sticky in passages with lots of new and perhaps difficult information. The detail might be hard to locate within the passage, and you risk spending too much time reading and re-reading the passage to locate the detail at hand.

Your strategy for dealing with these questions begins before you even read them: while you're actively reading. Make plenty of notes tracking the information in the passage, circling key words like **unique nouns** that suggest the topic of the paragraph or section. You stand a good chance of locating the topic of a detail question down the road.

Once you have made your notes and read the question at hand, scan the passage for the detail you need. Keep your eyes open for key phrases from the question that will indicate the information you're looking for. But even when you find the key phrase, read around it to make sure you've found the exact detail you're looking for.

Your strategy for dealing with detail questions without line references is to:

1. Read actively and circle *unique nouns* and *key phrases* in the passage.
2. Scan for key phrases from within the question to locate the detail within the passage.
3. Choose the answer choice that matches the detail in the passage the closest.

ESPECIALLY DENSE MATERIAL

There's no getting around it: You may find some of the passages you read difficult, boring, and especially hard to get through. However, it's important not to write a passage off as "simply too hard" and abandon the material in favor of making a guessing game out of its questions. No matter how dense the material, you can always make some headway that will improve your performance.

If you find a passage particularly difficult, be sure to start with the broadest questions. You may have a difficult time with the finer details of a topic, but you can probably determine the **main idea** of nearly anything.

As always, active reading should be the foundation of your work. As you are actively reading, skip over sentences you just can't work out and come back to them only if they come up in one of the questions.

Try to get a broad sense of the point of each paragraph and make a short note in the margin. This will help you track the progression of ideas within the passage.

For passages giving you an especially hard time, focus more on the particular questions and let them guide your foray into the passage. You want to increase your chance of fully understanding the material you're being questioned on. Begin with broad questions and questions including line references. Save the "detail without line reference" questions for last, and make your best guess if you cannot find the detail itself.

Read this passage carefully and then answer the questions that follow.

Natural Science: This passage describes the inspirations and career of a particular scientist.

Ernst Haeckel studied medicine at Würzburg with Rudolf Virchow, who taught him the importance of cell theory, and at Berlin with Johannes Müller, who remained his inspiration and ideal of a teacher. His main cultural influences were Alexander von Humboldt, and, like all educated Germans, J.W. Goethe. Haeckel never wanted to be a physician but aimed for a synthesis of his interest in zoology with his artistic ability and sensibility. The decisive event of his career was the patronage and friendship he received from the anatomist and morphologist Carl Gegenbaur. This led to an appointment at the University of Jena, where he stayed all his life, and a scientific journey to southern Italy where he studied marine invertebrate zoology, in particular radiolarians, which first suggested to him a close connection between the scientific study of nature and its inner beauty.

On his return to Jena in 1860, Haeckel read the German translation of Charles Darwin's *Origin of Species*. He was thoroughly won over by the book to the extent that he became the most outspoken supporter and propagandist of an evolutionary view, one which combined Lamarckian and Darwinian elements with the morphological interpretation of the aesthetic aspects of nature – thus fulfilling Goethe's and Humboldt's ideal of the unity of culture.

In 1866 Haeckel published his major theoretical work, *Die GenerelleMorphologie der Organismen* (The General Morphology of Organisms). It was, however, a difficult book and seldom read. In response he went on to publish his lectures on evolution in *NatuerlicheSchpfungsgeschichte* (The History of Creation) which, on the other hand, in its many editions from 1868 onwards, was a great success.

Haeckel's view of evolution can be summarized as follows: at no point did God create anything, whether inorganic or organic. All is originated through an incessant progressive process leading from the simplest to the most complex – organic matter originating from inorganic matter through spontaneous generation – a process called Entwicklungsgeschichte, the "history of development". In this process lower living forms start from a simple cell and follow a long evolutionary path leading to higher forms. The process of life, in its increasing intricacy, can be represented best in the branching forms of the tree and Haeckel, an excellent artist, drew many beautiful such trees. In them we find explained what he believes to be the fundamental law of natural evolution, the Biogenetic Law, that is "Ontogeny recapitulates phylogeny". Every living form travels in its embryological development (ontogeny) through stages which resemble – recapitulate, in fact – the stages through which the group to which that animal belongs itself went through in the course of its evolution (phylogeny). The gaps in the geological record of evolutionary process can be filled by hypothetical passages, and thus embryology and its foundation, cell theory, solves the evolutionary problems left unsolved by paleontology. The highest forms are nothing but lower forms which in their history have grown to their higher position in the tree of life – a new version of Lamarck's transformism. A worm follows an evolutionary path which takes it to higher and higher forms – man being of course the highest in its most elevated aspect, educated man. Indeed, we may conclude that a German professor is nothing but a progressed worm! Natural selection is seen by Haeckel as applicable not so much to individuals but mainly to groups, the Phyla – a word introduced by Haeckel himself (one of the many new words he invented, although only a few, such as "ecology", have survived).

This scheme can be applied to any part of the living world, whether fungi, plant, animal or, by consequence, to the highest pinnacle of evolution, man. In Haeckel's thought, man is basically an evolved ape and, looking further back, an evolved worm. The main character which distinguishes man from apes is language and to fill the gaps between speechless apes and speaking man Haeckel hypothesized a link which he called "Pithecanthropus alalus", that is "speechless apeman". He had been interested in languages since the days of his friendship with Jena philologist August Schleicher, supporter of an evolutionary interpretation of languages, and was aware of the studies performed by his cousin Wilhelm Bleek in South Africa on the language spoken by the Bushmen which Bleek suggested represented the nearest approximation to the original language of humankind. Haeckel used Bleek's studies to claim that there was a hierarchy of languages corresponding to the hierarchy of races which spoke them. He claimed that this hierarchy of languages showed that the "lower" human races were closer to apes than to the "higher" races – the highest being the educated man descended from the ancient Greeks. Culture was for Haeckel a much stronger method of studying humans than the physical anthropology propounded by his former teacher Virchow.

1. The passage suggests that Haeckel's first commercial attempt was unsuccessful because of its:

(A) Inaccessibility.
(B) Subject matter.
(C) Controversial nature.
(D) Theoretical failings.

2. According to the passage, gaps in evolutionary timelines can best be explained by:

(A) The Phyla classification.
(B) A discourse about religion.
(C) Cell theory.
(D) Paleontology.

3. The reader can reasonable infer that Johannes Müller was:

(A) A rival of Carl Gegenbaur.
(B) A professor of cell biology.
(C) A disciple of Rudolf Virchow.
(D) A biological theorist.

4. The passage compares a worm to a professor (lines 72-73) in order to:

(A) Show the differences between species.
(B) Show the inherent frailty of humans.
(C) Show the complete tree of life.
(D) Show the power of language to compel evolution.

5. According to the passage, Haeckel believed that natural selection is best applied:

(A) To humans.
(B) To the Phyla.
(C) To individuals.
(D) To evolutionary trees.

6. According to the passage, which of the following is NOT listed as one of Haeckel's contributions to the scientific community?

(A) A theory about the unity of science and religion
(B) A theory about the confluence of society and nature
(C) Talks about evolution
(D) Part of the lexicon

7. The word *synthesis* (line 8) most nearly means:

(A) Emulsion.
(B) Deduction.
(C) Separation.
(D) Confluence.

8. According to the passage, Haeckel believed that which of the following was most responsible for human development?

(A) An inherent, inner beauty
(B) Language
(C) Primal instinct
(D) Natural selection

9. The passage suggests that Haeckel believed that human development:

(A) Is directly traceable to a common ancestor.
(B) Originated near South Africa.
(C) Occurred within the last 3,000 years.
(D) Developed simultaneously at various points in the world.

10. The passage suggests that Haeckel believed that humans developed from all of the following EXCEPT:

(A) Apes.
(B) Worms.
(C) Monkeys.
(D) Single-cell organisms.

Read this passage carefully and then answer the questions that follow.

Natural Science: This passage discusses the features of a variety of mineral.

The earliest known rocks are largely igneous. Sedimentary rocks are formed from the breaking down of igneous rocks, and the origin of rocks therefore starts with the formation of igneous rocks. Igneous rocks are formed by the cooling of molten rock material. The ultimate source of this molten material does not here concern us. It may come from deep within the earth or from comparatively few miles down. It may include preexisting rock of any kind which has been locally fused within the earth. Wherever and however formed, its tendency is to travel upward toward the surface. It may stop far below the surface and cool slowly, forming coarsely crystallized rocks of the granite and gabbro types. Igneous rocks so formed are called plutonic intrusive rocks. Or the molten mass may come well toward the surface and crystallize more rapidly into rocks of less coarse, and often porphyritic, textures. Such intrusive rocks are porphyries and diabases, among others. Or the molten mass may actually overflow at the surface or be thrown out from volcanoes with explosive force. It then cools quickly and forms finely crystalline rocks of the rhyolite and basalt types. These are called effusives or extrusives, or lavas or volcanics, to distinguish them from intrusives formed below the surface. The intrusive masses may take various forms, called stocks, batholiths, laccoliths, sills, sheets and dikes, definitions and illustrations of which are given in any geological textbook. The effusives or volcanics at the surface take the form of sheets, flows, tuffs, or agglomerates.

Some of the igneous rocks are themselves "mineral" products, as for instance building stones and road materials. Certain basic intrusive igneous rocks contain titaniferousmagnetites or iron ores as original constituents. Others carry diamonds as original constituents. Certain special varieties of igneous rocks, known as pegmatites, carry coarsely crystallized mica and feldspar of commercial value, as well as a considerable variety of precious gems and other commercial minerals. Pegmatites are closely related to igneous after-effects, discussed under the next heading. As a whole, the mineral products formed directly in igneous rocks constitute a much less important class than mineral products formed in other ways, as described below.

The later stages in the formation of igneous rocks are frequently accompanied by the expulsion of hot waters and gases which carry with them mineral substances. These become deposited in openings in adjacent rocks, or replace them, or are deposited in previously hardened portions of the parent igneous mass itself. They form "contact-metamorphic" and certain vein deposits. Pegmatites, referred to above, are in a broad sense in this class of "igneous after-effects," in that they are late developments in igneous intrusions and often grade into veins clearly formed by aqueous or gaseous solutions. Among the valuable minerals of the igneous after-effect class are ores of gold, silver, copper, iron, antimony, mercury, zinc, lead, and others. While mineral products of much value have this origin, most of them have needed enrichment by weathering to give them the value they now have.

No sooner do igneous rocks appear at or near the earth's surface, either by extrusion or as a result of removal by erosion of the overlying cover, than they are attacked vigorously by the gases and waters of the atmosphere and hydrosphere as well as by various organisms,—with maximum effect at the surface, but with notable effects extending as far down as these agents penetrate. The effectiveness of these agents is also governed by the climatic and topographic conditions. Under conditions of extreme cold or extreme aridity, weathering takes the form mainly of mechanical disintegration, and chemical change is less conspicuous. Under ordinary conditions, however, processes of chemical decomposition are very apparent. The result is definitely known. The rocks become softened, loose, and incoherent. Voids and openings appear. The volume tends to increase, if all end products are taken into account. The original minerals, largely feldspar, ferro-magnesian minerals, and quartz, become changed to clay, mixed with quartz or sand, calcite or dolomite, and iron oxide, together with residual particles of the original feldspars and ferro-magnesian minerals which have only partly decomposed. In terms of elements or chemical composition, water, oxygen, and carbon dioxide, all common constituents of the atmosphere and hydrosphere, have been added; and certain substances such as soda, potassa, lime, magnesia, and silica have in part been carried away by circulating waters, to be redeposited elsewhere as sediments, vein fillings, and cements.

11. The passage's assertion in lines 6-9 suggests that:

(A) The type of materials that form igneous rocks varies.
(B) The origin of the igneous rocks is unknown.
(C) The passage will center on surface rocks.
(D) Molten lava forms into unpredictable shapes.

12. "Flows" and "tuffs" (line 32) are examples of:

    (A) Igneous rocks that are not yet formed.
    (B) Igneous rocks that form underground.
    (C) Metamorphic and sedimentary rocks that were once igneous.
    (D) Igneous rocks that form on the surface.

13. The passage mentions that igneous rocks can be valuable because:

    (A) They sometimes carry valuable materials.
    (B) They are markers for more valuable rocks nearby.
    (C) They sometimes arrive in crystallized forms.
    (D) They often carry hot water and gasses.

14. The passage suggests that "igneous after-effects" (line 44) are made valuable due to:

    (A) Attachment to gasses and hot water.
    (B) The mineral value contained within the rocks.
    (C) Their contact with organisms.
    (D) Exposure to the surrounding rocks.

15. In context, the word *enrichment* (line 66) most nearly means:

    (A) Polish.
    (B) Supplement.
    (C) Intensity.
    (D) Adornment.

16. The passage suggests that extreme weather conditions:

    (A) Mask chemical changes.
    (B) Slow the effects of erosion.
    (C) Prevent igneous rocks from rising to the surface.
    (D) Change the composition of mineral deposits.

17. The passage says that chemical changes in igneous rocks cause all of the following EXCEPT:

    (A) Infusion of elements present in the environment.
    (B) Pockets devoid of rock.
    (C) Hardening of the rock.
    (D) Softening of the rock.

18. The author states that igneous rocks are older than sedimentary rocks because:

    (A) The material used to form sedimentary rocks is less stable than that which forms igneous rocks.
    (B) Sedimentary rocks are formed from igneous rocks.
    (C) Carbon dating proves that igneous rocks are older.
    (D) Sedimentary rocks are formed on the surface, while igneous rocks are not.

19. Unlike mineral products formed inside igneous rocks, contact metamorphic rocks:

    (A) Never arrive at the surface.
    (B) Often spawn veins of valuable minerals.
    (C) Are more vulnerable to erosion.
    (D) Retain their shapes indefinitely.

20. The passage's primary purpose is to:

    (A) Suggest an alternative.
    (B) Argue a point.
    (C) Inform about a phenomenon.
    (D) Clarify a misconception.

Read this passage carefully and then answer the questions that follow.

Natural Science: This passage discusses an important movement in biology and techniques that have aided its advancement.

With only a few exceptions, every cell of the body contains a full set of chromosomes and identical genes. Only a fraction of these genes are turned on, however, and it is the subset that is "expressed" that confers unique properties to each cell type. "Gene expression" is the term used to describe the transcription of the information contained within the DNA, the repository of genetic information, into messenger RNA (mRNA) molecules that are then translated into the proteins that perform most of the critical functions of cells. Scientists study the kinds and amounts of mRNA produced by a cell to learn which genes are expressed, which in turn provides insights into how the cell responds to its changing needs. Gene expression is a highly complex and tightly regulated process that allows a cell to respond dynamically both to environmental stimuli and to its own changing needs. This mechanism acts as both an "on/off" switch to control which genes are expressed in a cell as well as a "volume control" that increases or decreases the level of expression of particular genes as necessary.

Two recent complementary advances, one in knowledge and one in technology, are greatly facilitating the study of gene expression and the discovery of the roles played by specific genes in the development of disease. As a result of the Human Genome Project, there has been an explosion in the amount of information available about the DNA sequence of the human genome. Consequently, researchers have identified a large number of novel genes within these previously unknown sequences. The challenge currently facing scientists is to find a way to organize and catalog this vast amount of information into a usable form. Only after the functions of the new genes are discovered will the full impact of the Human Genome Project be realized.

The second advance may facilitate the identification and classification of this DNA sequence information and the assignment of functions to these new genes: the emergence of DNA microarray technology. A microarray works by exploiting the ability of a given mRNA molecule to bind specifically to, or hybridize to, the DNA template from which it originated. By using an array containing many DNA samples, scientists can determine, in a single experiment, the expression levels of hundreds or thousands of genes within a cell by measuring the amount of mRNA bound to each site on the array. With the aid of a computer, the amount of mRNA bound to the spots on the microarray is precisely measured, generating a profile of gene expression in the cell.

Microarrays are a significant advance both because they may contain a very large number of genes and because of their small size. Microarrays are therefore useful when one wants to survey a large number of genes quickly or when the sample to be studied is small. Microarrays may be used to assay gene expression within a single sample or to compare gene expression in two different cell types or tissue samples, such as in healthy and diseased tissue. Because a microarray can be used to examine the expression of hundreds or thousands of genes at once, it promises to revolutionize the way scientists examine gene expression. This technology is still considered to be in its infancy; therefore, many initial studies using microarrays have represented simple surveys of gene expression profiles in a variety of cell types. Nevertheless, these studies represent an important and necessary first step in our understanding and cataloging of the human genome.

As more information accumulates, scientists will be able to use microarrays to ask increasingly complex questions and perform more intricate experiments. With new advances, researchers will be able to infer probable functions of new genes based on similarities in expression patterns with those of known genes. Ultimately, these studies promise to expand the size of existing gene families, reveal new patterns of coordinated gene expression across gene families, and uncover entirely new categories of genes. Furthermore, because the product of any one gene usually interacts with those of many others, our understanding of how these genes coordinate will become clearer through such analyses, and precise knowledge of these inter-relationships will emerge. The use of microarrays may also speed the identification of genes involved in the development of various diseases by enabling scientists to examine a much larger number of genes. This technology will also aid the examination of the integration of gene expression and function at the cellular level, revealing how multiple gene products work together to produce physical and chemical responses to both static and changing cellular needs.

21. According to the first paragraph, the expression of most genes is:

(A) Dormant.
(B) Obvious.
(C) Corrosive.
(D) Tangential.

22. The passage suggests that the expression of genes is dependent upon all of the following EXCEPT:

(A) Genetics.
(B) Motivation.
(C) Requirements.
(D) Environment.

23. According to the passage, the Human Genome Project has:

(A) Eliminated millions of false genes.
(B) Completed research on gene expression.
(C) Proven ineffective in determining gene sequence.
(D) Sparked new research.

24. The tone of the last paragraph is:

(A) Soporific.
(B) Wariness.
(C) Excitement.
(D) Pessimism.

25. According to the passage, microarrays are important because they:

(A) Measure a level of cell expression.
(B) Indicate the type of mRNA used.
(C) Bind to DNA templates.
(D) Paint a complete picture of the human genome.

26. According to the passage, microarrays can:

(A) Regenerate living tissue from damaged tissue.
(B) Measure the sum total of cell expression in a subject.
(C) Coordinates gene families into a cohesive data set.
(D) Measure the expression output of individual or collective samples.

27. Which of the following is NOT a quality of microarrays?

(A) Their small size
(B) Their ability to alter cell construction
(C) Their ability to analyze cell expression
(D) Their ability to measure large or small samples

28. As used in the passage, the word *complementary* (line 24) most nearly means:

(A) Praiseworthy.
(B) Supplementary.
(C) Favorable.
(D) Iniquitous.

29. The passage suggests that gene expression is important for:

(A) Understanding all ways in which organisms respond to stimuli.
(B) Understanding the function of genes.
(C) Realizing the potential of gene therapy.
(D) Engineer exciting, new variants of species.

30. The passage suggests that genes are responsible for:

(A) Developing disease.
(B) Maintaining equilibrium in the body.
(C) The ability to learn new tasks.
(D) Destroying viruses as they enter the body.

Read this passage carefully and then answer the questions that follow.

Natural Science: This passage discusses an important issue in medicine.

Adverse Drug Reaction. These three simple words convey little of the horror of a severe negative reaction to a prescribed drug. But such negative reactions can nonetheless occur. A 1998 study of hospitalized patients published in the Journal of the American Medical Association reported that in 1994, adverse drug reactions accounted for more than 2.2 million serious cases and over 100,000 deaths, making adverse drug reactions (ADRs) one of the leading causes of hospitalization and death in the United States. Currently, there is no simple way to determine whether people will respond well, badly, or not at all to a medication; therefore, pharmaceutical companies are limited to developing drugs using a "one size fits all" system. This system allows for the development of drugs to which the "average" patient will respond. But, as the statistics above show, one size does NOT fit all, sometimes with devastating results. What is needed is a way to solve the problem of ADRs before they happen. The solution is in sight though, and it is called pharmacogenomics.

The way a person responds to a drug (this includes both positive and negative reactions) is a complex trait that is influenced by many different genes. Without knowing all of the genes involved in drug response, scientists have found it difficult to develop genetic tests that could predict a person's response to a particular drug. Once scientists discovered that people's genes show small variations (or changes) in their nucleotide (DNA base) content, all of that changed—genetic testing for predicting drug response is now possible. Pharmacogenomics is a science that examines the inherited variations in genes that dictate drug response and explores the ways these variations can be used to predict whether a patient will have a good response to a drug, a bad response to a drug, or no response at all.

Right now, there is a race to catalog as many of the genetic variations found within the human genome as possible. These variations, or SNPs (pronounced "snips"), as they are commonly called, can be used as a diagnostic tool to predict a person's drug response. For SNPs to be used in this way, a person's DNA must be examined (sequenced) for the presence of specific SNPs. The problem is, however, that traditional gene sequencing technology is very slow and expensive and has therefore impeded the widespread use of SNPs as a diagnostic tool. DNA microarrays (or DNA chips) are an evolving technology that should make it possible for doctors to examine their patients for the presence of specific SNPs quickly and affordably. A single microarray can now be used to screen 100,000 SNPs found in a patient's genome in a matter of hours. As DNA microarray technology is developed further, SNP screening in the doctor's office to determine a patient's response to a drug, prior to drug prescription, will be commonplace.

SNP screenings will benefit drug development and testing because pharmaceutical companies could exclude from clinical trials those people whose pharmacogenomic screening would show that the drug being tested would be harmful or ineffective for them. Excluding these people will increase the chance that a drug will show itself useful to a particular population group and will thus increase the chance that the same drug will make it into the marketplace. Pre-screening clinical trial subjects should also allow the clinical trials to be smaller, faster, and therefore less expensive; therefore, the consumer could benefit in reduced drug costs. Finally, the ability to assess an individual's reaction to a drug before it is prescribed will increase a physician's confidence in prescribing the drug and the patient's confidence in taking the drug, which in turn should encourage the development of new drugs tested in a like manner.

Right now, in doctors' offices all over the world, patients are given medications that either don't work or have bad side effects. Often, a patient must return to their doctor over and over again until the doctor can find a drug that is right for them. Pharmacogenomics offers a very appealing alternative. Imagine a day when you go into your doctor's office and, after a simple and rapid test of your DNA, your doctor changes her/his mind about a drug considered for you because your genetic test indicates that you could suffer a severe negative reaction to the medication. However, upon further examination of your test results, your doctor finds that you would benefit greatly from a new drug on the market, and that there would be little likelihood that you would react negatively to it. A day like this will be coming to your doctor's office soon, brought to you by pharmacogenomics.

31. The most likely audience for this passage is:

(A) Medical researchers.
(B) Pharmaceutical companies.
(C) Primary care doctors.
(D) General medical consumers.

32. The passage suggests that a major factor in determining the effect of a drug is:

    (A) Diet.
    (B) Inherited genes.
    (C) Blood pressure.
    (D) Body mass index.

33. The passage states that pharmaceutical companies have had to cultivate a "one size fits all" (line 16) because:

    (A) They could not afford to tailor drugs to specific patients.
    (B) They did not pay attention to pharmacogenomical research.
    (C) They could not identify specific genetic traits.
    (D) Adverse drug reactions are a rare occurrence.

34. The passage states that the major advantage of using DNA microarrays is:

    (A) Lack of side effects.
    (B) Simplicity.
    (C) Accuracy.
    (D) Efficiency.

35. The passage suggests that SNP screenings will benefit pharmaceutical companies by:

    (A) Allowing each drug to be customized.
    (B) Showing that clinical trials are essential.
    (C) Reducing the cost of clinical trials.
    (D) Eliminating the need for clinical trials.

36. As used in line 51, *impeded* most nearly means:

    (A) Embarrassed.
    (B) Manacled.
    (C) Hampered.
    (D) Encouraged.

37. Which of the following, if true, would most undermine the promise of pharmacogenomics?

    (A) The cost of testing will remain prohibitive for the next five years.
    (B) New diseases will demand more extensive testing.
    (C) SNP screenings give false readings in a large number of cases.
    (D) Pharmaceutical companies want to break from the "one size fits all" model.

38. Which of the following is NOT listed as a benefit of pharmacogenomics?

    (A) increasing access to gene therapy
    (B) helping doctors to make informed decisions
    (C) reducing negative side effects to medicines
    (D) reducing visits to medical offices

39. The passage suggests that which of the following traits of SNPs are useful for pharmacogenomics?

    (A) health
    (B) size
    (C) quantity
    (D) order

40. Which word best describes pharmacogenomics as an approach to medicine?

    (A) flawed
    (B) aggressive
    (C) passive
    (D) preventative

Read this passage carefully and then answer the questions that follow.

Natural Science: This passage discusses the challenges faced by researchers in a particular area of science.

Interstellar flight is a common theme in science-fiction stories, but in reality the obstacles to such expeditions are enormous. An alternative approach to interstellar exploration is to survey the sky for transmissions from a civilization on a distant planet, but such a "Search for Extra-Terrestrial Intelligence (SETI)" effort is faced with obstacles as well.

Visiting another civilization on a distant world would be fascinating, but at present such a trip is beyond our capabilities. However, it is perfectly within our capabilities to develop a communications system using a powerful transmitter and a sensitive receiver, and using it to search the sky for alien worlds whose citizens have a similar inclination.

SETI is still no trivial task. Our Galaxy is 100,000 light-years across and contains more than 200 billion stars. Searching the entire sky for some faraway and faint signal is an exhausting exercise. Some simplifying assumptions are useful to reduce the size of the task:

One is to assume that the vast majority of life-forms in our Galaxy are based on carbon chemistries, as are all life-forms on Earth. While it is possible that life could be based around atoms other than carbon, carbon is well known for the unusually wide variety of molecules that can be formed around it.

The presence of liquid water is also a useful assumption, since it is a common molecule and provides an excellent environment for the formation of complicated carbon-based molecules that could eventually lead to the emergence of life.

We must also theorize exactly what to search for. Because radio transmissions can travel intact for vast distances, scientists have chosen to search for this particular form of evidence of extraterrestrial life. Whether other life forms would actually use anything we might recognize as a radio transmission is, of course, debatable; however, this is the form of communication that scientists believe we are most likely to be able to detect.

A fourth assumption is to focus on Sun-like stars. Very big stars have relatively short lifetimes, meaning that intelligent life would not likely have time to evolve on planets orbiting them. Very small stars provide so little heat and warmth that the only planets in very close orbits around them would be iceballs, and in such close orbits these planets would be tidally "locked" to the star, with one side of the planet perpetually baked and the other perpetually frozen.

About 10% of the stars in our Galaxy are Sun-like, and there are about a thousand such stars within 100 light-years of our Sun. These stars would be useful primary targets for interstellar listening. However, we only know of one planet where life exists, our own. There is no way to know if any of the simplifying assumptions are correct, and so as a second priority the entire sky must be searched.

Searching the entire sky is difficult enough. To find a radio transmission from an alien civilization, we also have to search through most of the useful radio spectrum, since there is no way to know what frequencies aliens might be using. Trying to transmit a powerful signal over a wide range of wavelengths is impractical, and so it is likely that such a signal would be transmitted on a relatively narrow band. This means that a wide range of frequencies must be searched at every spatial coordinate of the sky.

There is also the problem of knowing what to listen for, since we have no idea how a signal sent by aliens might be modulated, and how the data transmitted by it encoded. Narrow-bandwidth signals that are stronger than background noise and constant in intensity are obviously interesting, and if they have a regular and complex pulse pattern are likely to be artificial. However, while studies have been performed on how to send a signal that could be easily decoded, there is no way to know if the assumptions of those studies are valid, and deciphering the information from an alien signal could be very difficult.

There is yet another problem in listening for interstellar radio signals. Cosmic and receiver noise sources impose a threshold to power of signals that we can detect. For us to detect an alien civilization 100 light-years away that is broadcasting "omnidirectionally" -- in all directions -- the aliens would have to be using a transmitter power equivalent to several thousand times the entire current power-generating capacity of the entire Earth. It is much more effective in terms of communication to generate a narrow-beam signal whose "effective radiated power" is very high along the path of the beam, but negligible everywhere else. This makes the transmitter power perfectly reasonable, but the problem then becomes one of having the good luck to be in the path of the beam.

41. According to the passage, the objective of SETI is to:

    (A) Discover extraterrestrial life.
    (B) Build more advanced instruments to explore distant worlds.
    (C) Research planets that would be suitable for humans to colonize.
    (D) Understand more about the composition of distant planets.

42. The passage states that SETI makes assumptions in order to:

    (A) Increase the funding for its mission.
    (B) Be more precise in its search.
    (C) Discover more interesting findings.
    (D) Reduce the scope of its search.

43. The passage suggests that life forms are most likely:

    (A) Capable of interstellar travel.
    (B) Carbon-based.
    (C) Capable of surviving with minimal external heat.
    (D) Adapted to varied gravities.

44. The primary purpose of the passage is to:

    (A) Postulate about the composition of life.
    (B) Describe what makes SETI so compelling.
    (C) Denote the difficulties in searching for extraterrestrial life.
    (D) Suggest the high probability of extraterrestrial life existing.

45. The passage suggests that scientists use "radio transmission(s)" (line 64) because:

    (A) They are easier to decode than other transmissions.
    (B) They can contain a much greater amount of information.
    (C) They can travel intact for great distances.
    (D) They are inexpensive to generate.

46. As used in the passage, the word *spectrum* (line 66) most nearly means:

    (A) Color.
    (B) Range.
    (C) Technology.
    (D) Restriction.

47. Which of the following, if true, would invalidate some of SETI's methodology?

    (A) The ability of scientists to transmit radio messages on multiple frequencies at the same time
    (B) A revelation about the number of large stars in the galaxy
    (C) The presence of strong radio waves coming from a specific star cluster
    (D) The discovery of silicon-based life forms on earth

48. Which of the following is not listed as a potential problem of SETI?

    (A) The inability to visit distant star systems
    (B) Assumption about radio signals that could be invalid
    (C) The inability to comprehend all radio signals
    (D) The amount of information that must be processed

49. The passage suggests that in order to transmit radio signals omnidirectionally, humanity would have to:

    (A) Use arrays on Earth to amplify transmission power.
    (B) Harness power external to the Earth.
    (C) Transmit signals from outside the Earth's orbit.
    (D) Coordinate all of humanity's transmission capabilities.

50. The passage suggests that radio signals that pulse irregularly are:

    (A) Artificial.
    (B) Natural.
    (C) Distant.
    (D) Local.

rP17: TONE

TOPIC OVERVIEW

You have already learned that your goal is to read actively in order to create a map of a passage and that this map will allow you quickly to find the facts that you need to answer questions correctly.

This lesson will show you how attention to tone, or the author's attitude toward the subject, will help you to make a map of the passage.

CREATING A TONE MAP

Tone deals with the author's feelings toward the subject. Because we cannot see or hear the author while reading, we have to infer the tone from the author's words rather than his or her facial expressions or voice.

An author's choice of words will convey a lot about his or her attitude toward the subject. Certain words contain an emotional charge or underlying meaning that will convey the author's tone. For example, if the author refers to "woeful poverty" rather than "difficult living conditions," one can infer that he or she has strong feelings about that topic.

You can keep track of whether the tone of a portion of the passage is positive or negative by placing a plus (+) or minus (-) sign beside it while you are actively reading the passage. You can show how strongly positive or negative a paragraph is by using more or fewer pluses or minuses. If a portion is mixed in tone, use a mixture of pluses and minuses.

In addition to having a positive or negative tone, a portion of passage may have an *ironic* tone. A piece of writing is ironic if the author means something other than the face value of the words. If, for example, the author writes "The announcement of budget cuts was music to the teachers' ears," you can imagine that he or she is being ironic in order to prove a point (in this case, that the teachers were in fact displeased about the budget cuts).

Whenever you come across a hint like this, write an "I" in the margin and try to think of the real meaning of the ironic portion as you write your summary. You will need to draw a conclusion based on what you know about the author and the passage, but you may be required to stretch farther than you would for a standard conclusion question.

READING THE TONE MAP

The balance of pluses and minuses in your margins can tell you how subjective or objective the writing is. Subjective writing favors one view of an issue, while objective writing tends to deal with both the positive and negative aspects of a topic.

In the margins of a passage written in an objective style, you should see moderate numbers of both pluses and minuses. If a passage is overwhelmingly positive or negative, it is almost certainly written in a more subjective style. A more balanced passage is probably objective, but will be subjective if the author uses highly personal or emotional language. If the tone is very strong, you will probably make more marks in the margins. If there are a very small number of plus and minus marks, the passage is probably either neutral or objective in tone.

When answering questions that deal with one of the portions of the passage marked with an "I" (for "ironic"), be sure to pay special attention to any notes that you have made about the deeper meaning of the portion. If the entire passage was written in an ironic tone, you will probably see many "I"s in the margins.

In summary, attention to tone will help you to create a map of a passage and to understand that map.

As you actively read:
1. Decide if the tone is positive or negative; mark with + or -.
2. Mark ironic portions with "I".

After reading the entire passage:
1. Decide whether the passage is objective (balanced pluses and minuses) or subjective (unbalanced or has highly personal/emotional language).
2. Decide whether the tone is positive, negative, or mixed/neutral and how strong the tone is.
3. Pay special attention to ironic portions when answering questions.

This aspect of your map will come in handy when answering questions involving the author's *tone*, *attitude*, or *perspective*.

Read this passage carefully and then answer the questions that follow.

Prose Fiction: *The following passage was adapted from* *The Cross-Cut* *by Courtney Ryley Cooper.*

It was over. The rambling house, with its rickety, old-fashioned furniture—and its memories—was now deserted, except for Robert Fairchild, and he was deserted within it, wandering from room to room, staring at familiar objects with the unfamiliar gaze of one whose vision suddenly has been warned by the visitation of death and the sense of loneliness that it brings.

Loneliness, rather than grief, for it had been Robert Fairchild's promise that he would not suffer in heart for one who had longed to go into a peace for which he had waited, seemingly in vain. Year after year, Thornton Fairchild had sat in the big armchair by the windows, watching the days grow old and fade into night, studying sunset after sunset, voicing the vain hope that the gloaming might bring the twilight of his own existence,—a silent man except for this, rarely speaking of the past, never giving to the son who worked for him, cared for him, worshiped him, the slightest inkling of what might have happened in the dim days of the long ago to transform him into a beaten thing, longing for the final surcease. And when the end came, it found him in readiness, waiting in the big armchair by the windows. Even now, a book lay on the frayed carpeting of the old room, where it had fallen from relaxing fingers. Robert Fairchild picked it up, and with a sigh restored it to the grim, fumed oak case. His days of petty sacrifices that his father might while away the weary hours with reading were over.

Memories! They were all about him, in the grate with its blackened coals, the old-fashioned pictures on the walls, the almost gloomy rooms, the big chair by the window, and yet they told him nothing except that a white-haired, patient, lovable old man was gone,—a man whom he was wont to call "father." And in that going, the slow procedure of an unnatural existence had snapped for Robert Fairchild. As he roamed about in his loneliness, he wondered what he would do now, where he could go; to whom he could talk.

He had worked since sixteen, and since sixteen there had been few times when he had not come home regularly each night, to wait upon the white-haired man in the big chair, to discern his wants instinctively, and to sit with him, often in silence, until the old onyx clock on the mantel had clanged eleven; it had been the same program, day, week, month and year. And now Robert Fairchild was as a person lost. The ordinary pleasures of youth had never been his; he could not turn to them with any sort of grace. The years of servitude to a beloved master had inculcated within him the feeling of self-impelled sacrifice; he had forgotten all thought of personal pleasures for their sake alone. The big chair by the window was vacant, and it created a void which Robert Fairchild could neither combat nor overcome.

What had been the past? Why the silence? Why the patient, yet impatient wait for death? The son did not know. In all his memories was only one faint picture, painted years before in babyhood: the return of his father from some place, he knew not where, a long conference with his mother behind closed doors, while he, in childlike curiosity, waited without, seeking in vain to catch some explanation. Then a sad-faced woman who cried at night when the house was still, who faded and who died. That was all. The picture carried no explanation.

And now Robert Fairchild stood on the threshold of something he almost feared to learn. Once, on a black, stormy night, they had sat together, father and son before the fire, silent for hours. Then the hand of the white-haired man had reached outward and rested for a moment on the young man's knee.

"I wrote something to you, Boy, a day or so ago," he had said. "That little illness I had prompted me to do it. I—I thought it was only fair to you. After I'm gone, look in the safe. You'll find the combination on a piece of paper hidden in a hole cut in that old European history in the bookcase. I have your promise, I know—that you'll not do it until after I'm gone."

Now Thornton Fairchild was gone. But a message had remained behind; one which his patient lips evidently had feared to utter during life. The heart of the son began to pound, slow and hard, as, with the memory of that conversation, he turned toward the bookcase and unlatched the paneled door.

1. Which of the following statements does NOT describe Robert Fairchild's reaction to his father's death:

(A) A feeling of uncertainty.
(B) An anticipation of loneliness.
(C) Fear.
(D) Grief.

2. The narrator’s use of the word “picture” in line 63 serves to illustrate:

(A) The primarily visual nature of Robert Fairchild's earliest memories.
(B) A child's version of a family event.
(C) A metaphor for an unexplained historical event.
(D) The fading quality of recollections.

3. According to the fourth paragraph, which of the following is an accurate analogy for Robert Fairchild's situation?

(A) A loyal servant without a king.
(B) A defenseless child without a protector.
(C) A seasoned employee without a job.
(D) A dependable soldier without a general.

4. Which of the following did Robert Fairchild feel towards his living father?

I. reverence
II. pity
III. impatience

(A) I only
(B) II and III only
(C) I, II, and III
(D) none

5. Robert Fairchild is hesitant to read what his father wrote because:

(A) Thornton Fairchild almost never spoke.
(B) He does not want to know something that his father could not tell him directly.
(C) He suspects that it will contain the reason why his father longed for death.
(D) Robert Fairchild is naturally fearful.

6. The narrator's use of the words "unnatural existence" (line 39) refers primarily to:

(A) Robert Fairchild's abstinence from the pleasures of youth.
(B) The unusual situation of a child taking care of a parent.
(C) The strangeness of Thornton Fairchild's daily ritual.
(D) The extraordinary patience of Robert Fairchild.

7. At the time of the events of the story, Robert Fairchild is:

(A) Just returning from his father's funeral.
(B) An old man reflecting on his father's death.
(C) Exploring the house that his late father and he shared.
(D) Thinking about selling the house that his father died in.

8. Robert Fairchild can most accurately be characterized as:

(A) Selfish and brooding.
(B) Young and devoted.
(C) Unsure and unaware.
(D) Self-denying and uncomplaining.

9. The questions in lines 60-61 (“What had been... wait for death?”) serve primarily to:

(A) Emphasize the unknown nature of life's basic qualities.
(B) Cause the reader to hypothesize about the cause of Thornton Fairchild's lifestyle.
(C) Mirror Robert Fairchild's train of thought.
(D) Separate temporally the events of the previous paragraph.

10. Robert Fairchild suggests that one of the only things that his father ever spoke about was:

(A) His longing to understand the past.
(B) His desire to die.
(C) His gratitude toward Robert's devotion.
(D) His love for his dead wife.

Read this passage carefully and then answer the questions that follow.

Humanities: *The following passage was adapted from Free Culture by Lawrence Lessig.*

In 1928, a cartoon character was born. An early Mickey Mouse made his debut in May of that year, in a silent flop called *Plane Crazy*. In November, in New York City's Colony Theater, in the first widely distributed cartoon synchronized with sound, *Steamboat Willie* brought to life the character that would become Mickey Mouse.

Synchronized sound had been introduced to film a year earlier in the movie *The Jazz Singer*. That success led Walt Disney to copy the technique and mix sound with cartoons. No one knew whether it would work or, if it did work, whether it would win an audience. But when Disney ran a test in the summer of 1928, the results were unambiguous.

"The effect on our little audience was nothing less than electric," said Disney. "They responded almost instinctively to this union of sound and motion. I thought they were kidding me. So they put me in the audience and ran the action again. It was terrible, but it was wonderful! And it was something new!" Disney's then partner, and one of animation's most extraordinary talents, Ublwerks, put it more strongly: "I had never been so thrilled in my life."

Disney had created something very new, based upon something relatively new. Synchronized sound brought life to a form of creativity that had rarely—except in Disney's hands—been anything more than filler for other films. Throughout animation's early history, it was Disney's invention that set the standard that others struggled to match. And quite often, Disney's great genius, his spark of creativity, was built upon the work of others.

This much is familiar. What you might not know is that 1928 also marks another important transition. In that year, a comic (as opposed to cartoon) genius created his last independently produced silent film. That genius was Buster Keaton. The film was *Steamboat Bill, Jr.*

Steamboat Bill, Jr. appeared before Disney's cartoon *Steamboat Willie*. The coincidence of titles is not coincidental. *Steamboat Willie* is a direct cartoon parody of *Steamboat Bill*, and both are built upon a common song as a source. It is not just from the invention of synchronized sound in *The Jazz Singer* that we get *Steamboat Willie*. It is also from Buster Keaton's invention of *Steamboat Bill, Jr.*, itself inspired by the song "Steamboat Bill," that we get *Steamboat Willie*, and then from *Steamboat Willie*, Mickey Mouse.

This "borrowing" was nothing unique, either for Disney or for the industry. Disney was always parroting the feature-length mainstream films of his day. So did many others. Early cartoons are filled with knockoffs—slight variations on winning themes; retellings of older stories. The key to success was the brilliance of the differences. With Disney, it was sound that gave his animation its spark. Disney added to the work of others before him, creating something new out of something just barely old.

Sometimes this borrowing was slight. Sometimes it was significant. Think about the fairy tales of the Brothers Grimm. If you're as oblivious as I was, you're likely to think that these tales are happy, sweet stories, appropriate for any child at bedtime. In fact, the Grimm fairy tales are, well, for us, grim. It is a rare and perhaps overly ambitious parent who would dare to read these bloody, moralistic stories to his or her child, at bedtime or anytime.

Disney took these stories and retold them in a way that carried them into a new age. He animated the stories, with both characters and light. Without removing the elements of fear and danger altogether, he made funny what was dark and injected a genuine emotion of compassion where before there was fear. And not just with the work of the Brothers Grimm. Indeed, the catalog of Disney work drawing upon the work of others is astonishing when set together: *Snow White* (1937), *Fantasia* (1940), *Pinocchio* (1940), *Dumbo* (1941), *Bambi* (1942), *PeterPan* (1953), *Mulan* (1998)—not to mention a recent example that we should perhaps quickly forget, *TreasurePlanet* (2003). In all of these cases, Disney (or Disney, Inc.) ripped creativity from the culture around him, mixed that creativity with his own extraordinary talent, and then burned that mix into the soul of his culture. Rip, mix, and burn.

This is a kind of creativity. It is a creativity that we should remember and celebrate. There are some who would say that there is no creativity except this kind. We don't need to go that far to recognize its importance. We could call this "Disney creativity," though that would be a bit misleading. It is, more precisely, "Walt Disney creativity"—a form of expression and genius that builds upon the culture around us and makes it something different.

11. As used in line 68, the word *grim* most nearly means:

(A) Tragic.
(B) Depressing.
(C) Unintelligible.
(D) Heartbreaking.

12. In line 14 when the author says "the results were unambiguous" he most likely means:

(A) The marriage of sound and motion won the audience.
(B) Disney had successfully united sound and motion.
(C) All of the audience understood the plot of the cartoon.
(D) Walt Disney and UbIwerks were thrilled with their new technique.

13. In lines 19-20, Disney's assessment of *SteamboatWillie* might best be described as:

(A) Remarkable.
(B) Overstated.
(C) Ardent.
(D) Paradoxical.

14. It may be most reasonably inferred from the passage that:

(A) The Brothers Grimm worked for Disney.
(B) The author believes that *TreasurePlanet* is one of Disney's best films.
(C) Walt Disney's partnership with UbIwerks did not last.
(D) Buster Keaton had a long, successful career.

15. From Paragraphs 5-7, all of the following may be reasonably be inferred, EXCEPT:

(A) Some elements of *Steamboat Willie* were borrowed from *Steamboat Bill, Jr.*
(B) The author believes that early cartoonists lacked imagination.
(C) *Steamboat Bill, Jr.* was likely a silent film.
(D) Many early cartoons were based on earlier works.

16. The primary purpose of Paragraph 9 is to:

(A) Show that Disney cartoons have both succeeded and failed.
(B) Offer specific examples of how Disney transformed earlier works into new creations.
(C) Present a list of Disney's adaptations of Grimm's fairytales.
(D) Prove that Disney had a sense of humor that helped him bring fun and joy to grim old fairy tales.

17. From the passage, it may be most reasonably inferred that:

(A) The author believes Disney cartoons are uniformly great.
(B) Walt Disney had great respect for the Brothers Grimm.
(C) The author values originality above all other creative qualities.
(D) Some Grimm's fairy tales are not suitable for young children.

18. The author of the passage would most likely agree with which of the following statements about "Walt Disney creativity":

I. It was invented by Walt Disney as a clever way to sell tickets to his cartoons.
II. It uses existing elements of culture to create new artistic forms.
III. Calling it "Disney creativity" would be imprecise.

(A) I only
(B) I and III only
(C) II and III only
(D) I, II, and III

19. The author most likely uses the expression "rip, mix, and burn" (line 90) to make which point?

(A) Sometimes copyright laws should be broken in the name of creativity.
(B) Old stories should be taken apart and retold in ways that reflect the new culture.
(C) The ability to rip, mix, and burn computer images from old cartoons has revolutionized modern animation.
(D) Disney's approach to cartoon-making is analogous to computer techniques in which data taken from several sources is presented in a new form.

20. Which of the following statements best describes the author's central argument?

    (A) Creative expression need not be based on original ideas.
    (B) Content creators should draw on older stories for inspiration.
    (C) Being creative is the fastest route to fame.
    (D) There is more than one type of creativity

Read this passage carefully and then answer the questions that follow.

Social Science: *This passage discusses the implications of a decision.*

Just recently our neighbor to the north, Canada, minted their last penny. In the U.S., pennies are still in common use, although a growing number of people believe that we should follow Canada's lead in discontinuing our most miniscule monetary denomination.

The movement to eliminate the U.S. penny began with Arizona Representative Jim Kolbe, who introduced the Price Rounding Act of 1989, a piece of legislation that would have ended the minting and distribution of pennies. Kolbe tried again in 2001 and 2006, but none of his anti-penny bills advanced in the House. Though Kolbe maintains that his motives in eliminating the penny are solely for the fiscal good of the nation, one must wonder why the anti-penny movement began with a single persistent legislator.

Kolbe's first piece of legislation, introduced in 1987, aimed to eliminate the paper dollar in favor of the dollar coin. It seems that Kolbe's minor obsession with U.S. currency is inspired by Arizona's copper industry. Kolbe's home state of Arizona is the nation's leading producer of copper. Copper is an ingredient in both pennies and dollar coins, but dollar coins use far more copper than pennies. From the point of view of an Arizona copper magnate, there is more money to be had in making dollar coins than pennies.

Despite Kolbe's rather transparent pork-barrel motivations, the U.S. penny debate deserves more serious attention. Aside from Arizona's potential copper sales increase, there are many reasons to consider eliminating the most annoying of American small change, the penny.

The most obvious reason to end the use of the penny is its cost of production. It costs the National mint 2.4 cents to mint a penny at an estimated loss of $200 million per year. The primary reason for these costs is the soaring price of zinc, which makes up approximately 98% of each penny. Interestingly, the zinc industry spends a great deal of money lobbying Congress in support of the penny each year.

Many argue that the cost of production of pennies could be lowered by altering the makeup of the penny to substitute a cheaper metal, such as aluminum, in place of the current zinc. Others point out that the nickel, the next largest denomination of coin, also costs more than its face value to create – roughly 11 cents per 5 cent nickel.

But even aside from the cost of production of the penny, there are several logical reasons to end use of this tiny denomination. Jeff Gore, a University of California-Berkeley graduate student, calculates that each cash transaction involving pennies takes an extra 2.5 seconds to complete. At a rate of $15 per hour for the average American, those extra seconds cost roughly $5 billion per year in lost productivity. A bill that instituted a system of rounding to the nearest nickel would all but eliminate these extra productivity costs, netting billions for the American economy.

All currency is intended to facilitate exchange, but the penny seems to have outlasted its utility in that arena. The vast majority of today's pay phones, vending machines, parking meters, and toll booths no longer accept pennies, limiting the usefulness of pennies. The prevalence of "take a penny, leave a penny" cups at cash registers across the country support this claim, suggesting that even most consumers view pennies as superfluous clutter. In fact, one could argue that the number of pennies that are simply abandoned shows that many consumers are already effectively rounding their purchases to the nearest nickel.

Some oppose the elimination of the penny out of concern for consumers, arguing that a rounding system would essentially create an extra sales tax. In fact, in a 2012 poll, 77% of those surveyed expressed concern that elimination of the penny would significantly increase costs. But economists have estimated that rounding would increase prices by an average of a mere $0.00025 per transaction, an amount so small that almost no one would feel the pinch.

Elimination of small denominations of currency is hardly unprecedented, even within the United States. Up until 1857, the U.S. circulated a half-cent coin, which was discontinued because of its miniscule buying power – that coin had a buying power equivalent to 11 cents in today's terms, far more buying power than the modern penny. The current penny debate has been poisoned by the moneyed interests that sparked the debate in the first place, but it is still an issue worth discussing, especially at a time when the United States' government is facing budget shortfalls and enforced cuts.

21. It can be inferred from the passage that the author's attitude towards lobbyists is:

(A) Impartial.
(B) Critical.
(C) Approving.
(D) Indifferent.

22. All of the following are justifications for discontinuing use of the penny EXCEPT:

(A) The cost to mint a penny is more than the penny is worth.
(B) Cash transactions take longer when pennies are used leading to lost productivity.
(C) Economists have estimated the cost to the consumer of getting rid of the penny would be so small that it is likely to go unnoticed.
(D) The zinc industry makes money from the productions of pennies.

23. According to the passage, Jim Kolbe's first piece of legislation aimed to eliminate the paper dollar in favor of a dollar coin because:

(A) Paper money is less durable than a dollar coin.
(B) Dollar coins would be for the fiscal good of the nation.
(C) Arizona would make money from the production of a dollar coin.
(D) A dollar coin would be more useful for consumers than the penny.

24. In line 6, *denomination* most closely means:

(A) Designation.
(B) Quantity.
(C) Doctrine.
(D) Subjugation.

25. According to paragraph 8, it is no longer possible to use pennies when completing a transaction at:

I. a bank
II. toll booth
III. gas station

(A) II and III only
(B) II only
(C) I and III only
(D) I, II, and III only

26. The cost of production for the penny could be lowered by:

(A) Substituting a cheaper metal for the zinc.
(B) Using only copper to make the coin.
(C) Replacing the copper with a cheaper metal.
(D) Using only zinc to make the coin.

27. The primary purpose of the passage is:

(A) To provide the history of legislation put forth by Arizona Representative Jim Kolbe.
(B) To explain how lobbying works in Congress.
(C) To describe the current penny debate in the United States.
(D) To chronicle the use of the penny coin in Canada.

28. It can be inferred the author's reference to "Kolbe's rather transparent pork-barrel motivations" (lines 29-30) that Jim Kolbe is:

(A) Looking out for the best interests of the nation.
(B) Concerned about the consumers' opinions of the penny.
(C) Trying to help the copper industry in his home state make more money.
(D) Helping the zinc industry lobby in Congress.

29. The circulation of the half-cent coin was discontinued because:

(A) It was costly to produce.
(B) It had very little buying power.
(C) Consumers refused to use it.
(D) It was replaced with the penny.

30. The passage implies that the author:

(A) Believes aluminum should be used in penny production.
(B) Advocates the elimination of the penny.
(C) Is fervently opposed to the penny.
(D) Believes that discontinuing pennies will lead to financial burden.

Read this passage carefully and then answer the questions that follow.

Social Science: *This passage describes the role of a nation in politics and history.*

The history of the Panamanian isthmus, since Spaniards first landed on its shores in 1501, is a tale of treasure, treasure seekers, and peoples exploited; of clashes among empires, nations, and cultures; of adventurers and builders; of magnificent dreams fulfilled and simple needs unmet. In the wake of Vasco Nuñez de Balboa's torturous trek from the Atlantic to the Pacific in 1513, conquistadors seeking gold in Peru and beyond crossed the seas and recrossed with their treasures bound for Spain. The indigenous peoples who survived the diseases, massacres, and enslavement of the conquest ultimately fled into the forest or across to the San Blas Islands. Indian slaves were soon replaced by Africans.

A century before the English settled Massachusetts Bay, Panama was the crossroads and marketplace of the great Spanish Empire, the third richest colony of the New World. In the seventeenth century, however, the thriving colony fell prey to buccaneers of the growing English Empire, and Panama entered a period of decline and neglect that lasted until gold was discovered in California.

The geopolitical significance of Panama has been recognized since the early 1500s, when the Spanish monarchs considered digging a canal across the isthmus. In 1879 a French company under the direction of Ferdinand de Lesseps, builder of the Suez Canal, began constructing a canal in Panama. The project fell victim to disease, faulty design, and ultimately bankruptcy and was abandoned in 1889.

By the turn of the twentieth century, the United States had become convinced that a canal should be built to link the two oceans. In addition, President Theodore Roosevelt was attracted by the separatist tendencies of Panama, then a department of Colombia. When Panama rebelled against Colombia in 1903, Roosevelt deployed United States naval vessels to discourage the Colombian forces and proudly claimed the role of midwife at the birth of the Republic of Panama.

Since its completion in 1914, the Panama Canal has been Panama's economic base, and the United States presence has been the republic's major source of frustration. The provisions of the treaty concluded in 1903 between John Hay and Philippe Bunau-Varilla (the Hay-Bunau-Varilla Treaty) granted the Canal Zone "in perpetuity" to the United States and made Panama a virtual protectorate of the United States.

Despite the negotiation of treaty amendments in 1936 and 1955, limiting the freedom of the United States to intervene in Panama's internal affairs, various problems between the two countries continued to generate resentment among Panamanians. Aside from the larger issue of jurisdiction over the zone--which split the country into two parts--Panamanians complained that they did not receive their fair share of the receipts from the canal, that Panamanian workers in the zone were discriminated against in economic and social matters, and that the large-scale presence of the United States military in the zone and in bases outside the zone cast a long shadow over national sovereignty.

After serious rioting in 1964 that indicated the intensity of nationalistic aspirations concerning the status of the canal, the United States agreed to enter into negotiations for a new treaty. Meanwhile, studies relating to the construction of a new canal were undertaken. In 1971 after a four-year interlude, negotiations were renewed. In 1977 two new treaties were signed, one providing for Panamanian assumption of control over the canal in the year 2000 and the other providing for a permanent joint guarantee of the canal's neutrality.

The focal point of consensus in Panamanian political life, cutting across both social and partisan divides, has been nationalism. Nationalistic sentiments, directed primarily against the highly visible and dominant presence of the United States, have been catered to in varying degrees by all who have held positions of leadership or have sought popular support. Public demonstrations and riots, as occurred in 1927, 1947, 1959, and 1964, have been effective in influencing policy, especially in relation to the country's stance vis-à-vis the United States. National leaders have alternately responded to and contributed to an explosive climate of public opinion. They have carefully kept popular resentment narrowly focused on the United States presence.

Until the National Guard seized control in 1968, power had been wielded almost exclusively by a small number of aristocratic families that created an oligarchy government. The middle class was constrained from challenging the system because most of its members depended on government jobs. Also, the slow pace of industrialization had limited the political role of urban labor. The lower classes lacked organization and leadership. They had been distracted from recognizing common problems by the ethnic antagonisms between those of Spanish or mestizo background and the more recent immigrants, Antillean blacks from Jamaica and other parts of the West Indies.

31. This passage can be best described as:

    (A) A persuasive essay on the necessity of better treaties between the U.S. and Panama.
    (B) A critique of the U.S. treatment of Panamanian workers.
    (C) A chronicle of the history of Panama and the Panama Canal.
    (D) The story of Vasco Nuñez de Balboa's trek from the Atlantic to the Pacific.

32. According to the second paragraph, Panama entered a period of decline and neglect because:

    (A) Gold was discovered in California.
    (B) The English settled Massachusetts Bay.
    (C) The Spanish failed to construct a canal.
    (D) Panama fell prey to buccaneers from the English Empire.

33. The French company under the direction of Ferdinand de Lesseps was unable to complete their canal project due to all of the following EXCEPT:

    (A) A lack of funding.
    (B) Nationalistic sentiments of the Panamanians.
    (C) A shortage of workers due to tropical disease.
    (D) The faulty design of the canal that they were building.

34. In lines 96, *wielded* most nearly means:

    (A) Maintained.
    (B) Exuded.
    (C) Wrested.
    (D) Applied.

35. All of the following caused the Panamanians to resent the United States EXCEPT:

    (A) The large scale presence of the United States military.
    (B) The lack of Panamanian jurisdiction over the Canal Zone.
    (C) Panamanians wanted less than their fair share of receipts from the canal.
    (D) Panamanian workers were discriminated against in economic and social matters.

36. Panama was controlled by a small number of aristocratic families before the National Guard seized control of the country in 1968 for a variety of reasons including:

    (A) The fast pace of industrialization limited the role of urban labor in politics.
    (B) Most of the middle class was dependent on private sector jobs.
    (C) The lower class was distracted by the creation of a strong relationship between the indigenous people and the new immigrants.
    (D) The lower class lacked organization and leadership.

37. It can be reasonably be inferred that the national leaders of Panama have contributed to the resentment of Panamanians towards the U.S. in order to:

    (A) Prevent the focus of the people from turning on the national leaders to fix the country's problems.
    (B) Avoid the increase of the nationalistic pride of the Panamanians.
    (C) Thwart the United States in making policy changes that might benefit Panama.
    (D) Increase the number of immigrants from Jamaica and other parts of the West Indies.

38. What does the author mean by "the geopolitical significance of Panama" (line 25)?

    (A) Panama could influence world politics because it was the third richest colony of the New World.
    (B) With a canal, Panama could place a key role in world politics because its location would provide the easiest route between the Pacific and Atlantic Oceans.
    (C) Panama could play a role in the economics of the world because its location would provide the perfect environment to grow a variety of cash crops.
    (D) Panama had the backing of the United States and Spain, which gave it greater influence in world politics.

39. What can be inferred about U. S. President Theodore Roosevelt's motivations when he showed interest in helping Panama rebel against Colombia?

    (A) There were very strong anti-American sentiments in Panama and President Roosevelt thought he could help improve the relationship by helping Panama rebel.
    (B) President Roosevelt felt very strongly that the nationalistic sentiment in Panama should be supported.
    (C) President Roosevelt wanted to assist Panama in setting up a democratic government.
    (D) As its own country, Panama would be easier for the U.S. to control; hence the U.S. would control the Panama Canal.

40. Panama has had conflict with which of the following?

    I. English Buccaneers
    II. 17th century French armies
    III. Colombia

    (A) I and II only
    (B) II and III only
    (C) I and III only
    (D) I,II, and III

Read this passage carefully and then answer the questions that follow.

Natural Science: *This passage describes a body of research related to an atmospheric phenomenon.*

Crucial to humanity's understanding of the planet is an understanding the conditions behind what became known as the Arctic ozone hole of 2011. According to NASA, a combination of extreme cold temperatures, man-made chemicals, and a stagnant atmosphere were to blame.

Even when both poles of the planet undergo ozone losses during the winter, the Arctic's ozone depletion tends to be milder and shorter-lived than the Antarctic's. This is because the three key ingredients needed for ozone-destroying chemical reactions —chlorine from man-made chlorofluorocarbons (CFCs), frigid temperatures and sunlight— are not usually present in the Arctic at the same time: the northernmost latitudes are generally not cold enough when the sun reappears in the sky in early spring. Still, in 2011, ozone concentrations in the Arctic atmosphere were about 20 percent lower than its late winter average.

The new study shows that, while chlorine in the Arctic stratosphere was the ultimate culprit of the severe ozone loss of winter of 2011, unusually cold and persistent temperatures also spurred ozone destruction. Furthermore, uncommon atmospheric conditions blocked wind-driven transport of ozone from the tropics, halting the seasonal ozone resupply until April.

"You can safely say that 2011 was very atypical: In over 30 years of satellite records, we hadn't seen any time where it was this cold for this long," said Susan E. Strahan, an atmospheric scientist at NASA.

"Arctic ozone levels were possibly the lowest ever recorded, but they were still significantly higher than the Antarctic's," Strahan said. "There was about half as much ozone loss as in the Antarctic and the ozone levels remained well above 220 Dobson units, which is the threshold for calling the ozone loss a 'hole' in the Antarctic – so the Arctic ozone loss of 2011 didn't constitute an ozone hole."

The majority of ozone depletion in the Arctic happens inside the so-called polar vortex: a region of fast-blowing circular winds that intensify in the fall and isolate the air mass within the vortex, keeping it very cold.

Recent observations from satellites and ground stations suggest that atmospheric ozone levels for March in the Arctic were approaching the lowest levels in the modern instrumental era.

Most years, atmospheric waves knock the vortex to lower latitudes in later winter, where it breaks up. In comparison, the Antarctic vortex is very stable and lasts until the middle of spring. But in 2011, an unusually quiescent atmosphere allowed the Arctic vortex to remain strong for four months, maintaining frigid temperatures even after the sun reappeared in March and promoting the chemical processes that deplete ozone.

The vortex also played another role in the record ozone low.

"Most ozone found in the Arctic is produced in the tropics and is transported to the Arctic," Strahan said. "But if you have a strong vortex, it's like locking the door -- the ozone can't get in."

To determine whether the mix of man-made chemicals and extreme cold or the unusually stagnant atmospheric conditions was primarily responsible for the low ozone levels observed, Strahan and her collaborators used an atmospheric chemistry and transport model (CTM) called the Global Modeling Initiative (GMI) CTM. The team ran two simulations: one that included the chemical reactions that occur on polar stratospheric clouds, the tiny ice particles that only form inside the vortex when it's very cold, and one without. They then compared their results to real ozone observations from NASA's Aura satellite.

The results from the first simulation reproduced the real ozone levels very closely, but the second simulation showed that, even if chlorine pollution hadn't been present, ozone levels would still have been low due to lack of transport from the tropics. Strahan's team calculated that the combination of chlorine pollution and extreme cold temperatures were responsible for two thirds of the ozone loss, while the remaining third was due to the atypical atmospheric conditions that blocked ozone resupply.

Once the vortex broke down and transport from the tropics resumed, the ozone concentrations rose quickly and reached normal levels in April 2011.

Strahan, who now wants to use the GMI model to study the behavior of the ozone layer at both poles during the past three decades, doesn't think it's likely there will be frequent large ozone losses in the Arctic in the future.

"It was meteorologically a very unusual year, and similar conditions might not happen again for 30 years," Strahan said. "Also, chlorine levels are going down in the atmosphere because we've stopped producing a lot of CFCs as a result of the Montreal Protocol. If 30 years from now we had the same meteorological conditions again, there would actually be less chlorine in the atmosphere, so the ozone depletion probably wouldn't be as severe."

41. The passage suggests that all of the following contributed to the loss of ozone in the Arctic in 2011 EXCEPT:

(A) A high concentration of CFCs in the air.
(B) Unusually cold temperatures.
(C) A vortex of air that did not permit ozone from the tropics to enter the area.
(D) The loss of ozone in the Antarctic.

42. As it is used in lines 65, the phrase "locking the door" most nearly means:

(A) Keeping something out.
(B) Keeping something in.
(C) Keeping something safe.
(D) Making up one's mind.

43. The passage suggests that the Montreal Protocol:

(A) Has sped the development of ozone holes.
(B) Has been successful in its aims.
(C) Came too late to be of help during the disastrous winter of 2011.
(D) Has successfully funded ozone research for the next 30 years.

44. The main point of the passage's last two paragraphs is that:

(A) Chlorine in the atmosphere was the main culprit for the loss of ozone in the Arctic.
(B) The Montreal Protocol guarantees that the ozone layer will be protected.
(C) It is unlikely that such severe ozone depletion in the Arctic will recur.
(D) The meteorological conditions that caused the ozone depletion tend to recur ever 30 years.

45. Strahan's outlook for the future of the presence of ozone in the Arctic can best be described as:

(A) Defeated.
(B) Grim.
(C) Optimistic.
(D) Ambivalent.

46. The passage implies that the term "Arctic ozone hole of 2011" is a misnomer because:

(A) The lack of ozone was not one great hole, but more of a series of pinholes.
(B) The hole developed in late 2010.
(C) More ozone was depleted in the Antarctic than in the Arctic.
(D) The amount of ozone in the atmosphere remained well above the threshold for being considered a "hole".

47. According to the passage, the severe loss of ozone occurred:

(A) Isolated within the fast-moving winds of the polar vortex.
(B) At the highest northern latitude.
(C) Near the equator.
(D) During late spring, when temperatures should have been much higher.

48. The author's main point is to:

(A) Highlight an occasion in which the Global Modeling Initiative was particularly useful.
(B) Reassure his or her audience that a recurrence of ozone loss is unlikely to happen.
(C) Explain the conditions that led to the Arctic ozone hole of 2011.
(D) Illuminate the dangers of CFCs.

49. The passage states that without the presence of chlorine in the atmosphere, ozone levels in the Arctic would have:

(A) Remained high.
(B) Still been lower than usual.
(C) Varied as the polar vortex formed and disintegrated.
(D) Hit at a record low.

50. Strahan and her collaborators used an atmospheric chemistry and transport model to determine:

(A) Whether or not Antarctic ozone depletion would affect conditions in the Arctic.
(B) The threshold level of chlorine necessary to affect ozone levels.
(C) Why the polar vortex did not move south as usual.
(D) How the presence of frigid temperatures affected the depletion of ozone.

c2 education
be smarter.

rP18: STRUCTURE

TOPIC OVERVIEW

This lesson will show you how an attention to the relationships between paragraphs will improve your ability to create and read your map of each passage. This skill will help you answer Literary Analysis questions and others that may ask about the organization or intention of the parts of the passage.

CREATING A STRUCTURE MAP

The structure of a passage is the author's organization technique. Every paragraph of a passage is connected to the ones before and after it through a logical relationship. This logical relationship develops the story for Narrative passages, or develops some kind of rhetorical feature (rhetoric is the art of persuasion) for passages proving or presenting a point or points.

Together, these relationships reveal a great deal about the author's overall goal and allow the reader to successfully navigate the meaning of the passage.

There are several different relationships that one paragraph can have to another. Some of the most common relationships have to do with showing the passage of time, offering support or opposition, or offering additional description.

Paragraphs have a time relationship if one paragraph tells what happens next in a narrative.

A paragraph supports another if it contains new details that reinforce and build upon an idea from another paragraph. Words and phrases like "moreover", "furthermore", and "for example" are clues that a paragraph supports another.

Opposition paragraphs contain new opinions or information that contradicts ideas presented earlier in the passage. Words and phrases like "however" and "on the other hand" often appear at the beginning of opposition paragraphs.

Description paragraphs continue the explanation of an idea or give background information about a character or setting.

Remember that these are only a sample of the most common relationships; you may find others as you read.

Ask yourself how each paragraph relates to the ones around it and include a brief note about the type of relationship as you actively read.

READING THE STRUCTURE MAP

Patterns in the relationships between paragraphs reveal the overall structure of the passage. The paragraphs in an Idea/Explanation passage will support one another or include lots of description. If many paragraphs oppose each other, you are most likely reading a Point/Counterpoint passage. If the paragraphs follow one another in order by time, you are reading a Narrative passage. (Most Prose Fiction passages are narratives.) Narrative passages often contain large amounts of description as well.

You may remember that in Idea/Explanation passages it is most important to keep track of main ideas and that in Point/Counterpoint it is important to keep track of names and viewpoints. In Narrative passages it is important to keep track of causes and effects and the relationships between people.

If a passage does not fit into one of these categories it is an Other passage. Examine the relationships between paragraphs and use your best judgment to decide how to navigate an Other passage.

Remember, while reading a passage, follow these steps as you actively read:

1. Determine the relationships between paragraphs.
2. Describe the relationships in brief notes.

After reading the passage, look for patterns in relationships between paragraphs to determine the structure of the passage:

- Idea/Explanation—Focus on main ideas.
- Point/Counterpoint—Focus on names and viewpoints.
- Narrative—Focus on cause and effect and relationships between people.
- Other—Use your best judgment.

Read this passage carefully and then answer the questions that follow.

Prose Fiction: This passage was adapted from *Murder in the Gunroom* by H. Beam Piper.

Humphrey Goode was sixty-ish, short and chunky, with a fringe of white hair around a bald crown. His brow was corrugated with wrinkles, and he peered suspiciously at Rand through a pair of thick-lensed, black-ribboned glasses. His wide mouth curved downward at the corners in an expression that was probably intended to be stern and succeeded only in being pompous.

"Mr. Rand," he began accusingly, "when your secretary called to make this appointment, she informed me that you had been hired by Mrs. Gladys Fleming."

"That's correct. Mrs. Fleming wants me to look after some interests of hers, and as you're executor of her late husband's estate, I thought I ought to talk to you, first of all."

Goode's eyes narrowed behind the thick glasses.

"Mr. Rand, if you're investigating the death of Lane Fleming, you're wasting your time and Mrs. Fleming's money," he lectured. "There is nothing whatever for you to find out that is not already public knowledge. Mr. Fleming was accidentally killed by the discharge of an old revolver he was cleaning. I don't know what foolish feminine impulse led Mrs. Fleming to employ you, but you'll do nobody any good in this matter, and you may do a great deal of harm."

"Did my secretary tell you I was making an investigation?" Rand demanded incredulously. "She doesn't usually make mistakes of that sort."

The wrinkles moved up Goode's brow like a battalion advancing in platoon front. He looked even more narrowly at Rand, his suspicion compounded with bewilderment.

"Why should I investigate the death of Lane Fleming?" Rand continued. "As far as I know, Mrs. Fleming is satisfied that it was an accident. She never expressed any other belief to me. Do you think it was anything else?"

"Why, of course not!" Goode exclaimed. "That's just what I was telling you. I—" He took a fresh start. "There have been rumors—utterly without foundation, of course—that Mr. Fleming committed suicide. They are, I may say, nothing but malicious fabrications, circulated for the purpose of undermining public confidence in Premix Foods, Incorporated. I had thought that perhaps Mrs. Fleming might have heard them, and decided, on her own responsibility, to bring you in to scotch them; I was afraid that such a step might, by giving these rumors fresh currency, defeat its intended purpose."

"Oh, nothing of the sort!" Rand told him. "I'm not in the least interested in how Mr. Fleming was killed, and the question is simply not involved in what Mrs. Fleming wants me to do."

He stopped there. Goode was looking at him sideways, sucking in one corner of his mouth and pushing out the other. Rand began to suspect that Goode might be an egotistical windbag. Such men could be dangerous, were usually quite unscrupulous, and were almost always unpleasant to deal with.

"Then why," the lawyer demanded, "did Mrs. Fleming employ you?"

"Well, as you know," Rand began, "the Fleming pistol-collection, now the joint property of Mrs. Fleming and her two stepdaughters, is an extremely valuable asset. Mr. Fleming spent the better part of his life gathering it. It's one of the largest and most famous collections of its kind in the country."

"Well?" Goode was completely out of his depth by now. "Surely Mrs. Fleming doesn't think...?"

"Mrs. Fleming thinks that expert advice is urgently needed in disposing of that collection," Rand replied, carefully picking his words to fit what he estimated to be Goode's probable semantic reactions. "She has the utmost confidence in your ability and integrity, as an attorney; however, she realized that you could hardly describe yourself as an antique-arms expert. It happens that I am an expert in antique firearms, particularly pistols. Furthermore, not being a dealer, or connected with any museum, I have no mercenary motive for undervaluing the collection. That's all there is to it; Mrs. Fleming has retained me as a firearms-expert, in connection with the collection."

Goode was looking at Rand as though the latter had just torn off a mask, revealing another and entirely different set of features underneath. He was still a bit resentful; people had no right to confuse him by jumping about from one category to another, like that. "Now understand, I'm not trying to be offensive, but it seems a little unusual for a private detective also to be an authority on antique firearms."

"Mr. Fleming was an authority on antique firearms, and he was a manufacturer of foodstuffs," Rand parried, carefully staying inside Goode's Aristotelian system of categories and verbal identifications. "My own business does not occupy all my time, any more than his did, and I doubt if an interest in the history and development of deadly weapons is any more incongruous in a criminologist than in an industrialist."

1. Humphrey Goode's stated concern with Rand's investigation is:

   (A) Its origin in the feminine anxiety of Mrs. Fleming.
   (B) Its potentially negative impact on Mr. Fleming's business.
   (C) That a reopening of the investigation could include Goode as a suspect.
   (D) That a reopening of the investigation will harm the Flemings' public name.

2. Which of the following does NOT describe one of Humphrey Goode's reactions during the conversation?

   (A) Suspicion and distrust
   (B) Utter confusion
   (C) Slight resentment
   (D) Righteous anger

3. As it is used in line 52, the word *currency* means:

   (A) Significance.
   (B) Money.
   (C) Income.
   (D) Contemporaneousness.

4. Which of the following is an accurate description of the passage?

   (A) An arms dealer is hired to represent the interests of a recently widowed woman.
   (B) A private detective disarms the suspicions of an attorney while investigating a murder.
   (C) Two men engage in a conversation veiled with secrecy and distrust.
   (D) A murder suspect defends himself against the accusations of a private detective.

5. Rand's tone in the sixth paragraph can be best described as:

   (A) Exasperated disbelief.
   (B) Playful anger.
   (C) Feigned indignation.
   (D) Misplaced annoyance.

6. Rand cites all of the following as proof of his neutrality in the matter of selling Mr. Fleming's firearms EXCEPT:

   (A) His disassociation with a museum.
   (B) His status as a firearms expert.
   (C) That he does not sell arms.
   (D) His oath as a private detective.

7. It can be reasonably inferred from the passage that Humphrey Goode's "semantic reactions" (lines 80-81) refers primarily to:

   (A) His sensitivity to the detective's choice of words.
   (B) His unwillingness to share information.
   (C) His resentment for the detective's presence.
   (D) His propensity to disagree.

8. The reference to tearing off a mask in line 92 serves primarily to illustrate:

   (A) The nature of Rand's disclosure of new information.
   (B) Humphrey Goode's understanding of Rand's intentions.
   (C) Rand's ability to uncover Humphrey Goode's hidden motives.
   (D) Humphrey Goode's intent to expose Rand's true purpose for his visit.

9. It can reasonably be inferred that Rand views his conversation with Humphrey Goode with a mixture of:

   (A) Disdain and amusement.
   (B) Contempt and anxiety.
   (C) Irreverence and delight.
   (D) Boredom and trepidation.

10. Rand's last statement to Humphrey Goode (lines 104-108) serves primarily to:

   (A) Engage in philosophical questioning.
   (B) Win over by appealing to authority.
   (C) Persuade with the use of logic.
   (D) Charm with wit.

Read this passage carefully and then answer the questions that follow.

Humanities: The following passage is adapted from *On Laziness* by Christopher Morley.

It is our observation that every time we get into trouble, it is due to not having been lazy enough. Unhappily, we were born with a certain fund of energy. We have been hustling about for a number of years now, and it doesn't seem to get us anything but tribulation. Henceforward we are going to make a determined effort to be more languid and demure. It is the bustling man who always gets put on committees, who is asked to solve the problems of other people and neglect his own.

We remember a saying about the meek inheriting the earth. The truly meek man is the lazy man. He is too modest to believe that any ferment and hubbub of his can ameliorate the earth or assuage the perplexities of humanity.

O. Henry said once that one should be careful to distinguish laziness from dignified repose. Alas, that was a mere quibble. Laziness is always dignified, it is always reposeful. Philosophical laziness, we mean - the kind of laziness that is based upon a carefully reasoned analysis of experience. We have no respect for those who were born lazy; it is like being born a millionaire: they cannot appreciate their bliss. It is the man who has hammered his laziness out of the stubborn material of life for whom we chant praise and alleluia.

The laziest man we know—we do not like to mention his name, as the brutal world does not yet recognize sloth at its community value—is one of the greatest poets in this country; one of the keenest satirists; one of the most rectilinear thinkers. He began life in the customary hustling way. He was always too busy to enjoy himself. He became surrounded by eager people who came to him to solve their problems.

"It's a queer thing," he said sadly. "No one ever comes to me asking for help in solving my problems." Finally the light broke upon him. He stopped answering letters, buying lunches for casual friends and visitors from out of town; he stopped lending money to old college pals and frittering his time away on all the useless minor matters that pester the good-natured. He sat down in a secluded café with his cheek against a seidel of dark beer and began to caress the universe with his intellect.

People respect laziness. If you once get a reputation for complete, immovable, and reckless indolence the world will leave you to your own thoughts, which are generally rather interesting.

Doctor Johnson, who was one of the world's great philosophers, was lazy. Only yesterday our friend the Caliph showed us an extraordinarily interesting thing. It was a little leather-bound notebook in which Boswell jotted down memoranda of his talks with the old doctor. And lo and behold, this was the very first entry in that treasured little relic:

He told me in going to Ilam from Ashbourne, 22 September, 1777, that the way the plan of his Dictionary came to be addressed to Lord Chesterfield was this: He had neglected to write it by the time appointed. Dodsley suggested a desire to have it addressed to Lord Chesterfield. Doctor Johnson laid hold of this as an excuse for delay, that it might be better done perhaps, and let Dodsley have his desire. Doctor Johnson said to his friend, Doctor Bathurst: 'Now if any good comes of my addressing to Lord Chesterfield it will be ascribed to deep policy and address, when, in fact, it was only a casual excuse for laziness.'

Thus we see that it was sheer laziness that led to the greatest triumph of Doctor Johnson's life: the noble and memorable letter to Chesterfield in 1775.

Mind your business is a good counsel; but mind your idleness also. It's a tragic thing to make a business of your mind. Save your mind to amuse yourself with. The lazy man does not stand in the way of progress. When he sees progress roaring down upon him he steps nimbly out of the way. The lazy man doesn't (in the vulgar phrase) pass the buck. He lets the buck pass him. We have always secretly envied our lazy friends. Now we are going to join them. We have burned our boats or our bridges or whatever it is that one burns on the eve of a momentous decision. Writing on this congenial topic has roused us up to quite a pitch of enthusiasm and energy.

11. Throughout the passage, the author makes repeated use of all of the following literary techniques EXCEPT:

(A) Archaic diction.
(B) Majestic plurals.
(C) Elegy.
(D) Allusion.

12. As used in line 14, the word *ameliorate* most likely means:

(A) Alleviate.
(B) Compensate.
(C) Improve.
(D) Change.

13. Based on his description in Paragraphs 3-5 of the type of lazy person he disrespects, the author would most likely have a low opinion of which of these people:

    (A) A scientist who settles on a remote desert island after concluding that the complex problem he had been trying to solve was, in fact, unsolvable.
    (B) An award-winning concert pianist who never practices because she has natural talent.
    (C) A thief who gladly goes to prison after he learns that crime doesn't pay.
    (D) A bright student who gets poor grades because instead of studying he spends his time imagining world peace.

14. The author of the passage most likely regards O. Henry's comment about laziness and dignified repose in the third paragraph as

    (A) Interesting but inadequate.
    (B) Confusing and problematic.
    (C) Humorous but inappropriate.
    (D) Vague and argumentative.

15. In Paragraph 4, the author describes the "laziest man we know" as

    I. A sharp thinker.
    II. A great writer.
    III. A victim of the world's brutality.

    (A) I only
    (B) I and II only
    (C) II and III only
    (D) I, II, and III

16. According to the passage, Doctor Johnson was all of the following EXCEPT:

    (A) The author of a dictionary.
    (B) Friends with Doctor Bathurst.
    (C) A philosopher.
    (D) A well-known physician.

17. It can be most reasonably inferred from the passage that:

    (A) The Caliph had stolen Boswell's notebook.
    (B) The author believes that people respect laziness but detest lazy people.
    (C) Lord Chesterfield was an important person in the 19th century.
    (D) The author thinks that busy people are stupid because they are over-worked.

18. In the final paragraph of the passage, the author suggests that "the lazy man":

    (A) Does not use vulgar language.
    (B) Must avoid the tragedy of being business minded.
    (C) Avoids all forms of labor that might distract him from his own amusement.
    (D) Sometimes burns boats or bridges.

19. As used in line 88, the word *congenial* most nearly means:

    (A) Pleasant.
    (B) Exhausting.
    (C) Exhilarating.
    (D) Fanatical.

20. The overall tone of the passage might best be described as:

    (A) Comedic and livid.
    (B) Comic and satirical.
    (C) Reckless and biting.
    (D) Abrasive and humorous.

Read this passage carefully and then answer the questions that follow.

Social Science: This passage discusses the role of certain types of media in American politics.

In the 1992 presidential primaries, the public perceived the campaign as a largely negative one. Candidates traded criticisms and allegations. As the campaign unfolded, would-be voters gave low marks to the news media. Frequently, critics charge that news reporting focuses on the superficial, personal characteristics of candidates and ignores the issues underlying elections. Observers of the political process also target advertising, which they say distorts positions and trivializes important issues. At the same time, it is suggested that the predominance of polling by news outlets turns elections into popularity contests and causes candidates to follow rather than lead voter opinion on contemporary issues.

Advertising, by its nature, takes positions. Commercials suggest that the advertiser's product is better than a competitor's or is important to the viewer's well being. Such a claim may or may not be true, and the question is not always so easy for the reader, viewer, or listener to evaluate. In the opinion of one political writer, however, the brainwashing powers of national political advertising have long been exaggerated by some advertising men who, after all, make their money on commission from a percentage of the purchase of television time. And he goes on to say that in the view of many media consultants, traditional television advertising is becoming even less effective in this era of channel surfing, mute buttons, and the Internet. What still matters most in a national race, candidates and operatives will tell you, is what they rather patronizingly call earned or free media-the press.

The ramifications of advertising in politics can sometimes be positive. Advertisements can help the public become aware of political candidates and issues and educate would-be voters about what is at stake in campaigns. In fact, commercials can be more instructive in that regard than debates-debates are seen to be more effective in improving candidate name recognition and knowledge of party affiliation.

As is true of other types of human relationships, first impressions can be very important as voters form their opinions about political candidates. Research on election decisions suggests that candidates' use of the media can have a strong impact upon those who make up their minds about candidates during the campaign. Such voters are more likely to be swayed by political appeals than are people who have decided whom to choose before a campaign starts. While partisan voters use the media because they are interested in politics, undecided voters refer to media sources for information about parties, candidates, and issues. Whatever its positive or negative effects, exposure to the news media does influence public awareness of elections. On the local level, for example, newspaper stories and advertisements can raise public awareness of municipal and school board elections, to the extent that voter turnout increases as a result.

Furthermore, men and women react differently to the media analysis that generally follows political debates. A study during the 1988 vice-presidential debates showed that females took less extreme views of candidates after viewing post-debate analysis. By contrast, such analysis had little effect on the extremity of views expressed by politically involved males. During the 1988 presidential campaign, the "gender gap," a perception that men and women perceived the leading candidates differently, was much discussed. George Bush's campaign planners were able to battle the gap through the way in which the candidate was portrayed in advertising. In the 1996 and 2000 presidential campaigns, the candidates were vying for the votes of the elusive "soccer moms"-those young suburban women, characterized as thoughtful, careful, and hard to convince.

Like gender, race plays a role in how people view social issues and even how people respond to questions about such issues. Various studies have indicated that a member of one race will answer questions from an interviewer of another race in such a way as to avoid alienating the interviewer. It can be argued that even when an interviewer and interviewee are of the same race, survey results should be scrutinized carefully when the interviewer's questions concern a candidate of a different race. What remains to be explored is whether race should be treated as an uncontrolled variable in political surveys involving at least one white and one African American candidate.

The most important question in a presidential election year is whether there will be too much media coverage of the national candidates. The danger is that the voters will tire of the candidates. If the candidates are constantly on television over a long period of time, they may wear out their welcome with the voters by the time the election takes place, and the fear is that many citizens may not even bother to turn out to vote.

21. The author's purpose in writing this passage is:

(A) To provide a detailed history of the use of advertising in politics.
(B) To follow the turnout of women and minority voters from 1992 to 2006.
(C) To offer various examples of how the media affects elections.
(D) To explain how the media conducts and uses polling in political elections.

22. According to the passage, observers of the political process suggest that candidates follow rather than lead voter opinion on contemporary issues because:

(A) There is a gap between men and women voters.
(B) Voters base their opinions about candidates on first impressions.
(C) There is a predominance of polling by news outlets.
(D) The candidates do not already have opinions about contemporary issues.

23. According to the passage, the positive ramifications of advertising include:

I. Commercials are less instructive in educating would-be voters about issues than debates.
II. Would-be voters are educated about what is at stake in the campaign.
III. Advertising increases candidate name recognition.

(A) I only
(B) II only
(C) I and II only
(D) I, II, and III

24. In line 79, *vying* most nearly mean:

(A) Comparing.
(B) Commanding.
(C) Bidding.
(D) Competing.

25. According to the passage, the impact of newspaper stories and advertisements on a local level is:

(A) A decrease in voter turnout.
(B) A decrease in public awareness for presidential elections.
(C) An increase in local political debates.
(D) An increase in public awareness of municipal and school board elections.

26. It can be inferred from the author's reference to the way George Bush's campaign planners were able to battle the gender gap that George Bush:

(A) Used advertising as a way to change how he was viewed by both men and women.
(B) Was generally not liked by the "soccer mom" population.
(C) Changed men's opinion of the Bush Administration.
(D) Made advertisements that were directed at thoughtful women.

27. The passage asserts all of the following about commercials EXCEPT:

(A) They suggest that the product is important to the viewer's well-being.
(B) They provide more public awareness of candidates and issues than debates.
(C) All media consultants see commercials as more effective in the current era.
(D) The claims in commercials may not be true.

28. In the last paragraph, the author warns that the danger of too much media coverage of the national candidates is:

(A) Voters may tire of the candidates.
(B) Candidates may not use commercials in the future.
(C) Voters will be confused about the major issues.
(D) Partisan voters may lose interest in politics.

29. The author's attitude towards the media coverage of national candidates is best characterized as one of:

(A) Optimism.
(B) Cautiousness.
(C) Indifference.
(D) Respect.

30. The author implies that survey results should be scrutinized if the race of the interviewer and interviewee are the same when answering questions about a candidate of a different race because:

(A) The interviewer may not want to ask the question.
(B) The interviewee may not answer the question honestly.
(C) The interviewee may be offended by the question.
(D) The interviewer may change the question to one about a candidate they like.

Read this passage carefully and then answer the questions that follow.

Natural Science: This passage describes the plans and motivations for a particular scientific experiment.

Some of the core beliefs about what causes Alzheimer's and Parkinson's, two related diseases causing degenerated mental function and dementia, may be wrong, and flying an experiment on the International Space Station could provide the best way to show it.

Scientists want to send a set of proteins to the space station where the material would be free to collect together into large, complex structures without gravity tearing them apart.

Their thought is that Alzheimer's and other diseases, including those that develop from head injuries in sports, occur not because normal proteins become corrupted, but because with aging, or after repeated concussions, changes occur in the environment within the brain that cause certain proteins to cling together in ever-larger threads that choke off brain cells, slowly depriving a person of memories and brain functions.

David Tipton, chief medical officer at the Kennedy Space Center in Florida, said current theories about the cause of Alzheimer's and similar diseases perhaps misidentify the problem.

"We believe it may be a colloidal chemical process rather than a biochemical process," Tipton said. “NASA has an extensive history of studying crystal formation and processes similar to the protein development the researchers propose. Astronauts operated crystal-growing experiments during space shuttle missions and during flights to the Russian Mir space station.

"We've been able to see almost at the atomic level how these individual protein molecules join together," said Woodard. "We can see that it is not consistent with normal biochemistry. But if we look outside the field of biochemistry and look at another field called colloidal chemistry, we actually find very similar processes, except that they aren’t usually associated with living organisms."

The research can only go so far on Earth because gravity keeps the protein structures from growing beyond a certain size in the laboratory before they collapse of their own weight.

"It appears we might have the technology and experience to answer a few questions here," Tipton said.

The scientists want to send a container holding the proteins to the International Space Station to find out if protein strands grow as the researchers expect. If their theory holds, the proteins should clump together in larger structures than are seen in Earth’s normal gravity.

"In zero-gravity, these colloidal interactions can occur much faster because gravity isn't pulling the colloid out of suspension," Tipton said. "In Alzheimer's, it takes 20, 30, 40 years. If you wait 20, 30 or 40 years, you're research isn't going to move very fast."

As the particles accumulate, they may even take on a different state in the same way that the particles which make up paint behave one way when the paint is wet, but collect together and become a solid coating as the paint dries in the air.

"It appears that perfectly normal proteins are capable of aggregating to form threads that then accumulate to choke these cells," Dan Woodard, aerospace physician and fellow researcher, said. "The mystery is why for many people these proteins can remain soluble and function normally in the brain for an entire lifetime, while in other cases the same proteins undergo aggregation."

Answering that small riddle may prove to be the fundamental element in solving the whole problem.

"Sometimes we can provide a piece of the puzzle that is vital in all the other pieces fitting together," Tipton said.

Depending on what a space-based experiment shows, the researchers say they would still be far removed from testing on actual brains.

"We're several years from working on brains," Tipton said. "We're still working to demonstrate that this theory could indeed be the cause of protein aggregation into the types of fibers that are seen in brains."

Both Tipton and Woodard are confident their theory is on the right track to detecting the cause of the brain-crippling diseases.

"In the vast majority of people who get Alzheimer's, no genetic change has been identified," Woodard said. "The proteins are in fact genetically normal, so something else must be the driving factor in causing aggregation. We believe it must have something to do with colloidal forces. We have to remember that proteins are still just ordinary chemicals and are subject to non-biological actions."

31. The passage states that researches want to grow proteins in space rather than on Earth because:

(A) Without the force of gravity affecting them, the proteins will quickly be able to grow in such a way that mimics protein growth in Alzheimer's patients.
(B) Gravity prevents the proteins from being able to stick to each other at all, so a zero-gravity laboratory is needed.
(C) If proteins are unaffected by gravity, they will be much easier to manipulate for experimentation.
(D) Patients with Alzheimer's experience brain conditions that mimic zero-gravity.

32. The passage implies that proteins in the brains of Alzheimer's patients are:

(A) Mostly impacted by biochemical processes.
(B) Not affected by the destructive force of gravity in the same way as proteins grown in a laboratory are.
(C) Genetically abnormal.
(D) Soluble.

33. In the eleventh paragraph, the author likens wet paint drying to brain proteins in order to:

(A) Suggest that waiting around for a cure for Alzheimer's is like "watching paint dry".
(B) Imply that the formation of harmful protein structures is a slow process.
(C) Illustrate the idea that the proteins in the brains of Alzheimer's patients may change states.
(D) Demonstrate that, in Alzheimer's patients, proteins begin as liquids and end as hard, brittle structures.

34. What is the "piece of the puzzle" referred to in lines 75-76?

(A) The eventual application of insights gained aboard the International Space Station to Alzheimer's patients
(B) The answer to exactly how proteins are affected by colloidal forces
(C) The long-sought-after cure for Alzheimer's and other degenerative brain diseases
(D) A new insight into the formation of harmful proteins that could provide more answers about the causes of Alzheimer's

35. According to the passage, the difference between those who do not suffer from Alzheimer's and those who do is that proteins in the Alzheimer's patients' brains:

(A) Do not remain soluble.
(B) Refuse to aggregate.
(C) Disintegrate before they perform their normal functions.
(D) Are not subject to normal gravitational forces.

36. According to the passage, researchers believe that the forces responsible for the formation of abnormal protein structures in Alzheimer's patients are:

(A) Biochemical.
(B) Gravitational.
(C) Colloidal.
(D) Genetic.

37. The author of the passage would most likely agree that:

(A) The process of growing crystals in space is rather delicate.
(B) Space travel can be useful in more than one area of research.
(C) Science is coming close to a cure for Alzheimer's.
(D) Little can be done to replicate the complex conditions of the brain in a laboratory environment.

38. As it is used in line 18, the word *choke* most nearly means:

(A) Gag.
(B) Strangle.
(C) Collapse.
(D) Swallow.

39. The author's main point is to:

(A) Emphasize the uses of space travel in various fields of science.
(B) Prove that protein cells can be joined by colloidal forces.
(C) Convey a promising development in the world of Alzheimer's research.
(D) Critique the theory put forth by Drs. Tipton and Woodard.

40. The main point of the last paragraph is to:

    (A) Summarize Tipton and Woodard's theory.
    (B) Explain the cause of Alzheimer's to the recently-diagnosed.
    (C) Contradict an earlier statement about the formation of protein structures.
    (D) Emphasize the need for a zero-gravity environment for the experiment to be successful.

Read this passage carefully and then answer the questions that follow.

Natural Science: This passage describes what is known about an astronomical entity.

The Small Magellanic Cloud (SMC) is one of the Milky Way's closest galactic neighbors. Even though it is a small, or so-called dwarf galaxy, the SMC is so bright that it is visible to the unaided eye from the Southern Hemisphere and near the equator. Many navigators, including Ferdinand Magellan who lends his name to the SMC, used it to help find their way across the oceans.

Modern astronomers are also interested in studying the SMC (and its cousin, the Large Magellanic Cloud), but for very different reasons. Because the SMC is so close and bright, it offers an opportunity to study phenomena that are difficult to examine in more distant galaxies.

New Chandra data of the SMC have provided one such discovery: the first detection of X-ray emission from young stars with masses similar to our Sun outside our Milky Way galaxy. The new Chandra observations of these low-mass stars were made of the region known as the "Wing" of the SMC.

Astronomers call all elements heavier than hydrogen and helium -- that is, with more than two protons in the atom's nucleus -- "metals." The Wing is a region known to have fewer metals compared to most areas within the Milky Way. There are also relatively lower amounts of gas, dust, and stars in the Wing compared to the Milky Way.

Taken together, these properties make the Wing an excellent location to study the life cycle of stars and the gas lying in between them. Not only are these conditions typical for dwarf irregular galaxies like the SMC, they also mimic ones that would have existed in the early Universe.

Most star formation near the tip of the Wing is occurring in a small region known as NGC 602, which contains a collection of at least three star clusters. One of them, NGC 602a, is similar in age, mass, and size to the famous Orion Nebula Cluster. Researchers have studied NGC 602a to see if young stars -- that is, those only a few million years old -- have different properties when they have low levels of metals, like the ones found in NGC 602a.

Using Chandra, astronomers discovered extended X-ray emission, from the two most densely populated regions in NGC 602a. The extended X-ray cloud likely comes from the population of young, low-mass stars in the cluster, which have previously been picked out by infrared and optical surveys, using Spitzer and Hubble respectively. This emission is not likely to be hot gas blown away by massive stars, because the low metal content of stars in NGC 602a implies that these stars should have weak winds. The failure to detect X-ray emission from the most massive star in NGC 602a supports this conclusion, because X-ray emission is an indicator of the strength of winds from massive stars. No individual low-mass stars are detected, but the overlapping emission from several thousand stars is bright enough to be observed.

The Chandra results imply that the young, metal-poor stars in NGC 602a produce X-rays in a manner similar to stars with much higher metal content found in the Orion cluster in our galaxy. Scientists speculate that if the X-ray properties of young stars are similar in different environments, then other related properties -- including the formation and evolution of disks where planets form -- are also likely to be similar.

X-ray emission traces the magnetic activity of young stars and is related to how efficiently their magnetic dynamo operates. Magnetic dynamos generate magnetic fields in stars through a process involving the star's speed of rotation, and convection, the rising and falling of hot gas in the star's interior.

The combined X-ray, optical and infrared data also revealed, for the first time outside our Galaxy, objects representative of an even younger stage of evolution of a star. These so-called "young stellar objects" have ages of a few thousand years and are still embedded in the pillar of dust and gas from which stars form, as in the famous "Pillars of Creation" of the Eagle Nebula.

41. The main point of this passage is to:

(A) Explain the source of X-ray emission in cosmic bodies.
(B) Highlight some of the interesting features of certain regions of the Small Magellanic Cloud.
(C) Determine the importance of metals in the composition of stars.
(D) Reveal new discoveries made in the science of Magellanic navigation.

42. According to the passage, the Small Magellanic Cloud is:

(A) Nearby and dim.
(B) Distant and invisible.
(C) Small but bright.
(D) Dense but dim.

43. The passage states that the Wing is especially good for studying the life cycle of stars because it:

(A) Has less gas, dust, stars, and metals than does the Milky Way.
(B) Is the closest to the Milky Way.
(C) Contains the most stars undergoing dramatic life cycle changes.
(D) Is the most visible from the International Space Station.

44. Though not explicitly stated, the passage implies that Chandra, Spitzer, and Hubble are:

(A) The three scientists most involved in studying galaxies outside the Milky Way.
(B) Instruments used for collecting data from objects in space.
(C) The names of three of the young stars being observed.
(D) Nearby nebulas whose light shines on the Small Magellanic Cloud.

45. The author of this passage would most likely agree that:

(A) Recent data collected from the NGC 602 region has revolutionized the way we think of our solar system.
(B) As a young star with a similar mass to those found in in the Small Magellanic Cloud, our sun also emits X-ray radiation.
(C) The most important function of space exploration is to find solar systems similar to our own.
(D) Young stellar objects" usually disintegrate before they form into fully-fledged stars.

46. What are the "very different reasons" referred to in line 11?

(A) Astronomical rather than metaphysical reasons
(B) Experimental rather than religious reasons
(C) Exploratory rather than aesthetic reasons
(D) Scientific rather than navigational reasons

47. Paragraph 5 implies that studying the Small Magellanic Cloud could help us to understand:

(A) What our galaxy might look like in several millions of years.
(B) The distribution of metals in our own galaxy.
(C) Conditions present in the early universe.
(D) Galaxies unlike the standard dwarf irregular galaxy.

48. Information in the passage links a star's metal content with:

(A) The strength of its winds.
(B) Its ability to be detected.
(C) Its size.
(D) Its gravitational force.

49. As it is used in line 34, the word *early* most nearly means:

(A) Too soon.
(B) Young.
(C) Eager.
(D) Prehistoric.

50. The author mentions Ferdinand Magellan in the first paragraph for all of the following reasons EXCEPT:

(A) To demonstrate the relative closeness and brightness of the Small Magellanic Cloud.
(B) To explain where the Small Magellanic Cloud got its name.
(C) To name the discoverer of the Small Magellanic Cloud.
(D) To contrast older reasons for interest in the Small Magellanic Cloud with more recent ones.

rP19: ADVANCED LITERARY ANALYSIS

TOPIC OVERVIEW

In Lesson 10, you learned some strategies for tackling literary analysis questions. In this section, you'll learn how to approach tougher questions from this same category. These types of questions involve drawing inferences from subtle material, handling tone shifts and author's versus character's tone, and dealing with multiple in-question quotations.

SUBTLE INFERENCES

You are already familiar with inference questions—questions that ask you to draw some kind of conclusion based on the information provided in the passage. This involves making an educated, logical guess about a fact not presented in the passage, but hinted at by the information given. This can be fairly straightforward (for example, if the passage states that the sky was blue, you can infer that there probably wasn't a storm at that time), but it can also be far more subtle. A passage might state that there was a "somber vase of lilies in the entryway, and several black coats on the rack". From this information, you might be asked to infer that there was a funeral or wake at the location in question. For these types of advanced inference questions, it helps to familiarize yourself with *symbolism*, or seemingly straightforward facts that are intended to represent something else. In this case, the "somber vase of lilies" symbolizes death, and the "several black coats" indicate that many people, dressed in black, are present in another room.

The ACT won't ask you to draw a conclusion so subtle that you're likely to miss it entirely, but paying attention to subtle details (and circling them while actively reading) will help you understand difficult passages.

VARIATIONS IN TONE

You already know that the tone is the author's attitude toward a topic, but it's important to remember that the author, narrator, characters, and people within a passage might have different tones toward the same subject. In a Social Science passage, two psychologists might have completely different tones toward the topic of discussion. Pay attention to quotation marks and the phrase "according to" (as in, "According to Dr. Jones, this may not be the case.") to separate the attitudes of characters or people within the text from those of the narrator or author.

IN-QUESTION QUOTATIONS

Often, a question will include a quotation (or quotations) from the passage within the question itself. This can be tricky when quotations within the question include two different speakers or tones. When a question includes quotations from the passage, be sure to:

1. Return to the passage and read the context around the quotation.
2. Mark the question with some notes about the speaker, topic, and tone for each quotation.
3. Reread the question, keeping in mind the context of each quotation.

Keeping this information in mind, you'll be able to tackle advanced literary analysis questions without a problem.

Read this passage carefully and then answer the questions that follow.

Prose Fiction

My father brought my mother from the Philippines after marrying her there. The only photo that she has is of herself on their wedding day. She is wearing an ill-fitting dress, and she looks positively unnerved. I asked my father about this once, and he said the day they married was the same day they flew out of the country. Except for that photo, there is no proof that my mother existed before marrying my father. She never talked to me about the village outside of Manila from which she was plucked, but I imagine that it was dusty and smelled of chickens and goats.

For many years, before I had use for a mirror, I thought that my hair was blonde and my eyes were blue. I grew up in a white neighborhood, so I assumed that I was like everyone else. I cried when I first realized that my face was not like my friends' faces. My mother comforted me and told me that my dark hair and olive skin were both beautiful and useful. She said that when she picked me up from pre-school, she could spot me in an instant because my black hair contrasted so thoroughly in a crowd of blonde heads. She said that I was just like her. This made me cry even more.

My father always took me to school open houses because mother got anxious in public. She spoke English but always feared she would say something slightly wrong and be laughed at or misinterpreted. There were no other Filipinos in our town, from what I could tell, so she only heard her language on the satellite channel that my father ordered from the cable company. During one school open house, in the presence of my father, my third grade teacher asked me where my mother was from. I lied and told her that she was from here. My father scowled at me.

"Ena!" He looked at the teacher and smiled. "No, her mother is from the Philippines. But Ena has never been there." Ee-nah, my father said. My teacher always pronounced my name Eh-nah.

I learned the only culture that I was exposed to, the American culture. Mother never tried to teach me her dialect of Tagalog, and since we adopted father's religion, she did not teach me any of her sacraments. When I had friends over to play, she would tell them how I did not speak her language, and that she was sure that they, at least, weren't ashamed of their parents. Even as late as high school (though I tried to avoid inviting friends over) she would hover around the house and only break her habitual silence, it seemed, to embarrass me. When I confronted her about this, she said that if I was going to be embarrassed of her, I might as well have a good reason.

I can look back and see how the intervals of our contact stretched farther and farther apart. As I grew up, my mother grew more petulant and infantile in her dealings with me. Once she cooked a traditional Filipino meal, a soup with an entire fish in it, and I almost retched at the dinner table. She said that in the Philippines my attitude would be seen as a disgrace. I spat back that it was a good thing we weren't in the Philippines. She didn't speak to me for days.

My father sometimes served as translator between us. He could interpret her moods to me like an oracle interpreting the wind. Sometimes, however, the wind was silent to interpretation. Mother would finish putting the groceries away, then stop abruptly and rearrange everything she had done. "It's not in the right place," she would say.

Other days she would stare at herself in the photo of her wedding day, as if trying to see what was behind her.

Three days before summer officially began, a truck being driven in a high speed chase collided head-on with my father's car. The police said he died instantly.

Mother sat with her back eerily straight on our living room couch, surrounded by members of our church congregation, mostly father's acquaintances. She called my father's phone every few minutes. Dad's friends whispered that she wanted to hear her husband's voice again, but I knew that dad never set up his voicemail greeting. Mother called because she thought he would answer. Eventually she would rise, panic-stricken, from her place and say she needed to go to the hospital to check on her husband. Several women from our church had to physically restrain her.

I know now that in losing my father, my mother lost the last connection that bridged her homeland and this strange place. That bridged her and me. She sometimes looked at me blankly, as if to say, "You may be of me, but you're not mine." And I can't disagree.

1. The narrator describes the photo of her mother in the first paragraph primarily to:

   (A) Illustrate a prevailing practice in the Philippines.
   (B) Reveal the extent of her mother's poverty before moving to America.
   (C) Suggest that the beginning of her mother's life in America was sudden and terrifying.
   (D) Imply that her father was unaware of her mother's true feelings that day.

2. It can be inferred from the second paragraph that the reason the narrator cries in lines 16-24 is that:

(A) She resents the idea that she looks like her mother.
(B) She senses that her mother is more than physically different from others.
(C) She thinks her mother is unattractive.
(D) She is ashamed of her mother.

3. According to details in the passage, the narrator differs from her mother in which of the following aspects?

I. appearance
II. religion
III. language

(A) I only
(B) I and II only
(C) II and III only
(D) I, II, and III

4. The point of view from which the passage is told is best described as that of:

(A) A woman recounting her experience of growing apart from her mother.
(B) A girl growing up and adjusting to life in the United States.
(C) A girl growing up with a mother who is having difficulty adapting to life in the United States.
(D) A woman recounting the events that led up to the death of her father.

5. Which of the following does NOT describe the narrator's mother's reaction to her husband's death?

(A) Shock
(B) Aggression
(C) Disbelief
(D) Hysteria

6. It can be inferred from the passage that the narrator views her socialization into American mainstream as:

(A) Principally her mother's failure.
(B) A somewhat conscious decision.
(C) A cruel twist of fate.
(D) An inevitable occurrence.

7. The main point of the seventh paragraph is that the narrator's mother:

(A) Is mostly incomprehensible to the narrator.
(B) Is unwilling to accept reality.
(C) Misses her homeland.
(D) Only revealed her true feelings to her husband.

8. The passage suggests that the narrator's mother only had contact with her native country through:

(A) Filipino organizations.
(B) Television.
(C) Her church.
(D) Newspapers.

9. The tone of the passage can best be described as:

(A) Resigned.
(B) Nostalgic.
(C) Self-pitying.
(D) Bitter.

10. It can be inferred that the narrator's mother studies the photograph in paragraph eight in order to:

(A) Lament her decision to come to the United States.
(B) Understand her current situation better.
(C) Relive the moment in which the picture was taken.
(D) Remember something about her life in the Philippines.

Read this passage carefully and then answer the questions that follow.

Prose Fiction: This passage was adapted from *Children of the Tenements* by Jacob A. Riis.

Yette Lubinsky was three years old when she was lost from her Essex Street home. She had gone from the tenement to the corner where her father kept a stand, to beg a penny, and nothing more was known of her. Weeks after, a neighbor identified one of Yette's little frocks as the match of one worn by a child the neighbor had seen dragged off by a rough-looking man. But though Max Lubinsky, the peddler, and Yette's mother camped on the steps of Police Headquarters early and late, anxiously questioning everyone about their lost child, no other word was heard of her. By and by it came to be an old story, and the two were looked upon as fixtures of the place.

They were poor and friendless in a strange land, the very language of which was jargon to them, as theirs was to us, and they were shouldered out. It was not inhumanity; at least, it was not meant to be. It was the way of the city, with everyone for himself; and they accepted it, uncomplaining. So they kept their vigil on the stone steps, in storm and fair weather, every night taking turns to watch all who passed. When it was a policeman with a little child, as it was many times between sunset and sunrise, the parent on the watch would run to meet them, eagerly scanning the little face, only to return, disappointed but not cast down, to the step upon which the other slept, head upon knees, waiting the summons to wake and watch.

Their mute sorrow appealed to me, then doing night duty in the newspaper office across the way, and I tried to help them in their search for the lost Yette. They accepted my help gratefully but without loud demonstration. Together we searched the police records, the hospitals, the morgue, and the long register of the river's dead. She was not there. Having made sure of this, we turned to the children's asylums. We had a description of Yette sent to each one, with the minutest particulars concerning her and her disappearance, but no word came back in response. A year passed, and we were compelled at last to give up the search. It seemed as if every means of finding out what had become of the child had been exhausted, and all alike had failed.

During the long search, I had occasion to go more than once to the Lubinskys' home. They lived up three flights. The hall was pitch-dark, and the whole building redolent of the slum; but in the stuffy little room where the peddler lived there was, in spite of it all, an atmosphere of home that set it sharply apart from the rest . One of these visits I will always remember. I had stumbled in, unthinking, upon their Sabbath-eve meal. The candles were lighted, and the children gathered about the table; at its head, the father, every trace of the timid, shrinking peddler of Mulberry Street laid aside with the week's toil, was invoking the Sabbath blessing upon his house and all it harbored. I saw him turn, with a quiver of the lip, to a vacant seat between him and the mother, and it was then that I noticed the baby's high chair, empty, but kept ever waiting for the little wanderer. I understood; and in the strength of domestic affection that burned with unquenched faith in the dark tenement after the many months of weary failure, I read the history of this strange people that in every land and in every day have conquered even the slum with the hope of home.

Yette returned, after all, and the way it happened was stranger than all the rest. Two long years had passed, and the memory of her had long since faded out of Mulberry Street, when, in the overhauling of one of the orphanages we thought we had canvassed thoroughly, the child turned up, as unaccountably as she had been lost. All that I ever learned about it was that she had been brought there, picked up by someone in the street, probably, and, after more or less inquiry that had failed to connect with the search at our end of the line, had stayed there. Not knowing her name, —she could not tell it herself – they had given her one of their own choosing; and thus disguised, she might have stayed there forever but for the fortunate chance that cast her up to the surface once more, and gave the clue to her identity at last. The frock she had worn when she was lost proved the missing link. The mate of it was still carefully laid away in the tenement. So Yette returned to fill the empty chair.

11. According to the passage, the narrator's attitude toward the Lubinskys is best described as one of:

(A) Curiosity.
(B) Disappointment.
(C) Sympathy.
(D) Disinterest.

12. Yette's parents and the narrator search for her at all of the following places EXCEPT:

(A) The hospital.
(B) The children's asylums.
(C) The newspaper office.
(D) The register of the river's dead.

13. According to lines 30-34, the narrator learned of the missing girl because:

(A) He was questioned by the parents.
(B) He spoke to a peddler who saw Yette's parents on the street corner.
(C) He was a neighbor of the Lubinskys who saw Yette taken by a rough-looking man.
(D) He was doing night duty at the newspaper office across from the Police Headquarters.

14. How does the narrator describe the Lubinskys' tenement (lines 46-52)?

I. The hall was well-lit.
II. The building smelled of the slum.
III. The Lubinskys' room was homey.

(A) I only
(B) II only
(C) I and III only
(D) II and III

15. According to the passage, how was Yette eventually identified?

(A) She remembered her name and address two years later.
(B) She was identified at an orphanage by the frock she was wearing when she was lost.
(C) She was picked up by someone on the street who recognized her and brought her to her parents.
(D) Her parents found her while they were canvassing the orphanages.

16. As he is portrayed in the passage, Max Lubinsky can be best described as

(A) Assertive, but ignorant to the ways of city life.
(B) Timid, but dedicated to his family.
(C) Poor, but determined to rise in society.
(D) Intelligent, but unable to understand the language of the city.

17. It can be inferred from the passage that the Lubinskys have:

(A) One child.
(B) Two children.
(C) More than two children.
(D) A large extended family.

18. As it is used in line 88, *mate* most nearly means:

(A) Match.
(B) Partner.
(C) Colleague.
(D) Spouse.

19. The passage indicates that Yette was not found when the narrator and her parents were originally searching for her at the orphanages because:

(A) She was given a different name as she could not remember her own.
(B) She was not at the orphanage when the narrator and her parents contacted the orphanage.
(C) She had been moved around to different orphanages, which made her hard to locate.
(D) She was wearing different clothes when she was taken to the orphanage.

20. It can inferred from the fourth paragraph that the Lubinskys' marriage is:

(A) Distant.
(B) Troubled.
(C) Affectionate.
(D) Monotonous.

Read this passage carefully and then answer the questions that follow.

Prose Fiction: The following passage was adapted from *The Colossus* by Opie Read.

When the slow years of his youth were gone and the hastening time of manhood had come, the first thing that Henry DeGolyer, looking back, could recall from a mysterious darkness into the dawn of memory was that he had awoken one night in the cold arms of his dead mother. That was in New Orleans, Louisiana. The boy's father had grandly aspired to paint the face of man upon lasting canvas, but appetite invited alcohol to mix with his art, and so upon dead walls he instead painted the trademark bull, and in front of museums he exaggerated the distortion of the human freak.

After the death of his mother, the boy was taken to the Foundlings' Home, where he was scolded by women and occasionally knocked down by a vagabond older than DeGolyer. Here he remembered to have seen his father only once. It was a Sunday when his father had come to visit, years after the gentle creature, his mother, holding her child in her arms, had died at midnight. The painter laughed and cried and begged an old woman for a drink of brandy. He went away, and after an age had seemed to pass, the matron of the place took the boy on her lap and told him that his father was dead, and then, putting him down, she casually added: "Run along, now, and be good."

The boy was then taken in by an old Italian woman. In after years he could not determine the length of time that he had lived in her wretched home, but with vivid brightness dwelled in his memory the morning when he ran away and found a free, if not an easy life, in the newsboys' lodging-house. He sold newspapers during the day, he went to a night school, and as he grew older he picked up "river items" for an afternoon newspaper. His hope was that he might become a "professional journalist," as certain young men termed themselves; and study, which in an ill-lighted room, tuned to drowsiness by the buzzing of youthful mumblers, might have been a chafing task to one who felt not the impetus of a spurring ambition, but was to him a pleasure full of thrilling promises. To him the reporter stood at the high-water mark of ambition's "freshest."

But when years had passed and he had scrambled to that place, he looked down and saw that his height was still not a dizzy one. And instead of viewing a conquered province, he saw, falling from above, the shadows of trials yet to be endured. He worked faithfully, and at one time even held the place of city editor, but a change in the management of the paper not only reduced him to the ranks, but, as the saying went, set him out onto the sidewalk. Then he wrote "specials." His work was bright, original and strong, and was reproduced throughout the country, but as he did not sign any of it, the paper alone received the credit. Year after year he lived in this unsettled way—reading in the public library, musing at his own modest fireside, catching glimpses of an important work which the future seemed to hold, and waiting for the outlines of that work to become more distinct; but the months went by and the plan of the work remained in the shadow of the coming years.

DeGolyer had now reached that time of life when a wise man begins strongly to suspect that the past is but a future stripped of its delusions. He was a man of more than ordinary appearance; indeed, people who knew him, and who believed that size grants the same advantages to all vocations, wondered why he was not more successful. He was tall and strong, and in his bearing there was an ease that, to one who recognizes not a sleeping nerve force, would have inaccurately suggested the idea of laziness. His complexion was rather dark, his eyes were black, and his hair was a dark brown. He was not handsome, but his sad face was impressive, and his smile, a mere melancholy recognition that something had been said, did not soon fade from memory.

21. According to the passage, all of the following are places Henry DeGolyer lived as a child EXCEPT:

(A) Foundlings' home.
(B) Newsboys' lodging house.
(C) A professional journalist's home.
(D) New Orleans, Louisiana.

22. Which of the following conclusions can be drawn about Henry DeGolyer?

(A) The time spent at the old Italian woman's house was unpleasant for Henry.
(B) He was inspired by the foundlings to become a journalist.
(C) His dismissal from the post of city editor was due to personal problems.
(D) Seeing the death of his mother affected young Henry strongly.

23. As it is used in line 41, *impetus* most nearly means:

(A) Importance.
(B) Stimulus.
(C) Restraint.
(D) Discouragement.

24. In line 47, what does the narrator mean by "his height was still not a dizzy one"?

    (A) Henry realized that his profession was not as elevated as he had desired.
    (B) Henry wanted to be taller than he had grown to be.
    (C) Henry noticed that the view from his office did not allow him a good view of the city.
    (D) Henry had become tired of working for the newspaper and wanted to find another job.

25. Based on his portrayal in the passage, Henry's father can best be described as:

    I. A painter.
    II. A drunkard.
    III. A journalist.
    IV. A careless father.

    (A) I and II only
    (B) II and III only
    (C) I, II, and IV
    (D) I, III, and IV

26. Which of the following can be concluded about Henry's father's career?

    (A) He was a contortionist who performed in front of museums.
    (B) His weakness for drink spoiled his original grand dreams.
    (C) It served as an inspiration for his son's eventual pursuit of a career in journalism.
    (D) Henry's father's perfectionism led to few finished paintings.

27. According to the last paragraph, Henry DeGolyer's appearance is described as:

    (A) Grotesque.
    (B) Ordinary.
    (C) Handsome.
    (D) Memorable.

28. The narrator of this passage could be most reasonably described as:

    (A) Henry DeGolyer.
    (B) A close friend of DeGolyer.
    (C) A professional journalist.
    (D) A vengeful co-worker.

29. According to the third paragraph, what happened to Henry DeGolyer while he was living in the foundlings' home?

    (A) Henry was beloved by all of the women.
    (B) The matron told Henry his father was dead.
    (C) Henry occasionally beat up boys that were older than him.
    (D) Henry was visited by his mother only once.

30. Henry DeGolyer's "specials" (lines 54) can most accurately be described as:

    (A) Controversial.
    (B) Monotonous.
    (C) Unpopular.
    (D) Outstanding.

Read this passage carefully and then answer the questions that follow.

Humanities: This passage describes a historical movement in painting.

"Nothing is good nowadays. Back in the old days, things were done right." How many times have you heard this sentiment expressed? Each generation looks back on its past with rose-colored glasses, decrying the present and glorifying the past. Artists are no different; especially during the rise of modern art, many traditionalists declared that art's only glory lay only in its history, not in its future. Even as far back as 1848, disgust with current the artistic trends of the time caused some young artists to declare that in fact, the last 300 years of art had been poisoned by one man, Raphael. These artists – seven in all total, but influencing many more – came to be known as the Pre-Raphaelite Brotherhood or PRB. And while their coalition was only together for seven years, they left made a lasting impact on European art.

In 1840s London, painters studied under certain schools, the greatest of which was the Royal Academy of Art. This academy had produced many of the greatest artists of the last few decades, and any painter worth his salt – and who had enough money to afford the tuition – studied there. However, the curriculum of the school was somewhat conservative; painters were taught to paint the same way, that is, in the style of the Renaissance master Raphael. As noted 19th century art critic John Ruskin said:

"We begin by telling the youth of fifteen or sixteen that Nature is full of faults, and that he is to improve her; but that Raphael is perfection, and that the more he copies Raphael the better; that after much copying of Raphael, he is to try what he can do himself in a Raphaelesque, but yet original manner: that is to say, he is to try to do something very clever, all out of his own head, but yet this clever something is to be properly subjected to Raphaelesque rules, is to have a principal light occupying one seventh of its space, and a principal shadow occupying one third of the same; that no two people's heads in the picture are to be turned the same way, and that all the personages represented are to have ideal beauty of the highest order..."

A group of young students at the Academy resented this fixation on Raphael's style, arguing that the primitive style of art before Raphael's ascendancy was superior to works inspired by the Renaissance painter. Dante Gabriel Rossetti, John Everett Millais, and William Holman Hunt are the three men primarily associated with this small rebellion. After a meeting in 1848, they enumerated four core principles of the brotherhood they had formed: first, to have genuine ideas to express; second, to study nature attentively, so as to know how to express those ideas; third, to sympathize with what is direct and serious and heartfelt in previous art, to the exclusion of what is conventional and self-parodying and learned by rote; finally, and most indispensible of all, to produce thoroughly good pictures and statues.

These mission statements led the members of the brotherhood to adopt a variety of focuses. For example, they often painted scenes from the Bible or Shakespeare, topics they saw as deserving of their talent. They also wanted to focus on realism in their paintings, as opposed to what they saw as the artificiality of the traditional style. These conflicting focuses led to some controversy when, for example, John Everett Millais exhibited his painting "Christ in the House of His Parents." Many onlookers were morally outraged to see Jesus and his family in a dusty hovel, with his mother Mary looking like a common farmwoman. The Pre-Raphaelites argued that they were striving to depict their subjects realistically, rather than in the too-pretty idealized style of the Raphaelites.

How does one recognize a pre-Raphaelite painting? Due to the Brotherhood's focus on realism, many of the paintings are incredibly detailed, down to the dirt on the floors and the sweat on a person's collar. The colors on Pre-Raphaelite paintings are bright and vivid compared to other paintings of the time period; they painted on bright white canvas, which gave this desired effect. And if none of those details at has clued you in, many artists of the Pre-Raphaelite Brotherhood incorporated the initials "PRB" somewhere in their paintings.

The Pre-Raphaelite Brotherhood dissolved in 1855; its members went in different directions with their art. Millais and Hunt continued to create works of art that were almost photorealistic in their detail, while Rossetti began to focus more and more on the mystical and religious elements of his art work. Though the movement had lasted only seven years, it had a lasting impact.

31. The primary purpose of the first paragraph is to:

(A) Examine the dissatisfaction that each generation feels with the present.
(B) Offer an aphoristic introduction to a topic.
(C) Attack Raphael for his role in poisoning the art of the early 1800s.
(D) Describe why seven famous artists took the name Pre-Raphaelite Brotherhood.

32. From the passage, it may be most reasonably inferred that in 1840s London:

    (A) The majority of students studied at the Royal Academy of Art.
    (B) The pre-Raphaelite movement gained more popularity after the group had disbanded.
    (C) The pre-Raphaelites expressed a desire to move away from art that relied too heavily on Shakespeare and the Bible.
    (D) Raphaelesque painters only painted religious scenes.

33. John Ruskin's quote contains all of the following, EXCEPT:

    (A) Sarcasm.
    (B) A complaint about a teaching method.
    (C) Skepticism.
    (D) A criticism of Raphael.

34. As used in line 37, the phrase "subjected to" most likely means:

    (A) Contrasted with.
    (B) Exposed to.
    (C) Subordinated to.
    (D) Compared to.

35. According to the passage, it may be inferred that the members of the PRB held which of the following beliefs about Raphaelesque art:

    I. It lacked directness.
    II. It was conventional and self-parodying.
    III. It was too focused on nature.

    (A) I only
    (B) I and II only
    (C) II and III only
    (D) I, II, and III

36. In line 22, the phrase "worth his salt" most nearly means an artist who is:

    (A) Deserving of one's pay.
    (B) Gaining a significant following.
    (C) Worthy of accolade.
    (D) Publicly promoting their artwork.

37. In the fifth paragraph, the author contrasts the PRB's effort to "depict their subjects realistically" with the Raphaelite's tendency to :

    (A) Accept the unrealistic demands of the Royal Academy of Art.
    (B) To criticize realistic portrayals of Jesus and his family.
    (C) Create art that idealized its subjects.
    (D) Use dark colors and grim images.

38. Based on the passage, it may be inferred that the PRB dissolved because:

    (A) The members of the brotherhood wanted to pursue divergent artistic interests.
    (B) Millais, Hunt, and Rossetti graduated from art school.
    (C) After 7 years, the PRB was no longer on the cutting edge of art.
    (D) Millais quit the brotherhood after he was criticized for "Christ in the House of His Parents".

39. The tone of the passage may best be described as one of:

    (A) Unadorned antipathy.
    (B) Artistic fervor.
    (C) Probing interest.
    (D) Heightened concern.

40. Based on the passage, the author is likely to agree with which of the following conclusions:

    (A) It is an artist's duty to dismantle established styles of art.
    (B) Artists must sometimes challenge the status quo.
    (C) Works of art still reflect notions created by the PRB.
    (D) Artists should strive to create realistic works of art.

Read this passage carefully and then answer the questions that follow.

Social Science: This passage analyzes a historical phenomenon.

South Korea is home to nearly thirty thousand American troops, the result of a military and political alliance that spans six decades. Yet despite the level of support and cooperation that the U.S. and South Korea have long enjoyed, the South Korean beef protests of 2008 highlighted cracks in this foreign relationship.

Many Americans were surprised by the vehement protests that took place in South Korea in 2008 following South Korean President Lee Myung-Bok's decision to reopen the South Korean market to U.S. beef imports. South Korea had banned imports of U.S. beef in 2003 following an incident of BSE, also known as Mad Cow Disease.

On April 27, 2008, just days after President Lee visited U.S. President George W. Bush at Camp David, the South Korean broadcast network MBC aired the first in a multi-episode series titled "Is American Beef Really Safe from Mad Cow Disease?" The program included numerous instances of factual misrepresentations and was clearly intended to suggest that American beef was unsafe for consumption. Despite (or because of) the propagandist nature of the program, it helped to spark violent protests against the decision to allow U.S. beef imports.

But why would thousands of South Koreans engage in violent protest against beef? Would the reaction have been the same if the beef came from someplace else? Or was there more at play than hamburgers and steaks?

While many protestors were legitimately concerned with the safety of U.S. beef products (spurred on, no doubt, by the MBC program's spurious claims that Koreans are genetically susceptible to Mad Cow Disease), other protestors were more concerned with the economic impact of U.S. beef imports. Being a mountainous country, South Korea isn't exactly the ideal environment for a thriving cattle industry. As a result, Korean beef is incredibly expensive, costing more than twice that of imported U.S. beef. Thus many Koreans, particularly those affiliated in any way with the Korean beef industry, had a vested interest in preventing the importation of U.S. beef. But given the relatively miniscule size of Korea's beef industry, even the economic impact of lifting the ban on U.S. beef imports is insufficient to explain protests of this magnitude.

No, the real issue at stake was not beef, but nationalism.

The decision to lift the ban on U.S. beef products was part of a broader deal for the Korea-U.S. Free Trade Agreement (KORUS FTA), a treaty that would establish trade between the two countries for years to come. Despite South Korea's lengthy relationship with the U.S., tensions remain, especially among those Koreans who feel that the U.S. has been too overbearing.

South Koreans have a long list of past grievances. After all, Korea has been a small fish in a big pond throughout much of its history. This strategically located peninsula was subject to the manipulation of Chinese emperors who demanded tributes, occupied by Japanese rulers who forbade the Korean language, and then divided by the Cold War rivalries of the U.S., Russia, and China. It's no wonder if South Korean citizens might be a bit sensitive to overbearing super powers.

Viewed through this lens, one can see how South Koreans might have seen Lee's concessions over U.S. beef imports as kowtowing to U.S. interests. This was, after all, one of Lee's first important foreign relations decisions as President, and from the point of view of many South Korean citizens, he folded under the slightest pressure.

The disdain that many South Koreans held for President Lee became evident in one of their most popular rallying cries: "Lee Myung-bak is Lee Wan-yong!" Lee Wan-yong is the South Korean version of Benedict Arnold. As a royal court minister at the turn of the last century, Lee Wan-yong helped Imperial Japan annex Korea, resulting in decades of oppression.

To call President Lee a traitor for making trade concessions to the U.S. may suggest that South Korean protesters viewed the U.S. as an enemy as well, but in most respects, South Korean citizens view the U.S. favorably. In fact, polls suggest that South Koreans view the U.S. the most favorably of all countries in the world. Thus it would seem that the protestors' animosity was not directed at the U.S. at all, but solely at President Lee.

The problem was not that President Lee made concessions to the U.S.; the problem was that President Lee did not appear to defend South Korea's rights vehemently enough. The nationalist pride of many South Korean citizens demands that South Korean leaders put on a strong face to the world, and Lee's willingness to fold on beef imports was an insult to that pride.

President Lee eventually apologized to his countrymen, saying that he should have paid more attention to their health concerns. But by the time Lee apologized, the protests were no longer about beef – if they ever were in the first place.

41. The primary purpose of this passage is:

(A) To explain all of the diplomatic strategies used by President Lee when dealing with foreign countries.
(B) To provide a comprehensive history of the occupation of South Korea by Japan.
(C) To examine the various reasons that might have led to the South Korean beef protests of 2008.
(D) To compare the quality of South Korean beef to U.S. beef.

42. Why did South Korea ban U.S. beef imports in 2003?

(A) U.S. beef imports were very expensive.
(B) There was an incident of Mad Cow Disease contamination in U.S. beef.
(C) A South Korean television series misrepresented the safety of U.S. beef.
(D) South Korean citizens protested the sale of U.S. beef in South Korea.

43. South Koreans might be sensitive to overbearing countries for all of the following reasons EXCEPT:

(A) Chinese emperors demanded tributes from Korea.
(B) South Korean was forced to join the Soviet Union.
(C) Japanese rulers occupied Korea.
(D) Cold War rivalries divided the country.

44. As it is used in line 35, *spurious* most nearly means:

(A) Unfair.
(B) Unlawful.
(C) Erroneous.
(D) Valid.

45. According to the passage, South Korean beef is expensive because:

(A) South Korea is not an ideal location to raise cattle due the mountainous nature of the country.
(B) The quality of South Korean beef is superior to any other beef.
(C) South Korea dedicates more land to cultivating rice than raising cattle.
(D) South Korean farmers charge more for the beef they sell.

46. Some of the motivations that the author mentions for the protests include:

I. Safety concerns about U.S. beef.
II. Nationalism.
III. The impacts on South Korea's beef production.

(A) I and III only
(B) II only
(C) I and II only
(D) I, II, and III

47. The author's attitude toward the South Korean broadcast network, MBC, is best characterized as:

(A) Objective.
(B) Distrustful.
(C) Bitterness.
(D) Mocking.

48. As described in lines 77-84, it can be inferred that the South Koreans view Lee Wan-yong as:

(A) A national hero.
(B) A fair and just leader.
(C) An apathetic government official.
(D) A despised traitor.

49. As he is portrayed in this passage, President Lee is most likely viewed by South Koreans as:

(A) Unconcerned.
(B) Respected.
(C) Oblivious.
(D) Considerate.

50. What best describes the expectations of the South Koreans towards their leaders?

(A) They demand their leaders to show an indifference of the needs of other countries.
(B) They prefer their leaders to be popular around the world.
(C) They expect their leaders make deals with other countries to keep the peace.
(D) They want their leaders to show strong national pride.

rP20: STRATEGY REVIEW

TOPIC OVERVIEW

Now that you've learned the strategies you'll need to excel on the ACT Reading Test, you're ready to apply what you've learned to the test itself. Reviewing these strategies and putting them into practice will ensure that you maximize your new knowledge and, with it, your score.

ACTIVE READING STRATEGY REVIEW

As you are actively reading, your main goals are:

1) breaking up the passages into portions
2) underlining key facts
3) summarizing each portion or paragraph.

In addition, remember to:

- **Track the author's tone and attitude**. Remember to use +'s and –'s to track the speaker's attitude (positive or negative) toward the subject.
- **Track differing opinions** in the margins as you read.
- If you notice an obvious feature of **structure or rhetoric**, such as one paragraph providing an example of an idea brought up in another, make note.
- **Give yourself as many hints as you can** during your first read-through. This will save you time and effort later on.

ELIMINATION STRATEGY REVIEW

Remember that incorrect answer choices are usually wrong for predictable reasons. The most common types of wrong answers are as follows:

- **No Evidence**: the fact or statement given cannot be supported exclusively by information in the passage.
- **Proven Wrong**: the fact or statement given is mentioned somewhere in the passage, but is proven wrong by surrounding evidence.
- **Too General**: the fact or statement given makes a broad statement that may contain some aspect of the correct answer, but generalize too much.
- **Too Specific**: the fact or statement given may contain some aspect of the correct answer, but provides more detail than the question is asking for.
- **Wrong Section**: the fact or statement given is technically true according to the passage, but does not actually answer the question asked.

If a question falls into one of these categories, you can eliminate it. Select your answer from the options that remain, and choose the one that best answers the question.

While there are a variety of types of questions, most of the wrong answers will fall into one of these categories. Thus, familiarizing yourself with the common wrong answers will help you on the most kinds of questions.

Read this passage carefully and then answer the questions that follow.

Prose Fiction

My father hired a taxi to take us to Masaya, which was north of the town we were staying in. He said it was famous for Nicaraguan artisan crafts, and that you could buy a sturdy hammock for almost nothing at all. On the way, the taxi driver asked me something I couldn't understand, so my father replied for me. They both laughed.

I did not appreciate the joke at my expense, so I asked him what he had said.

"I said, 'Yes, of course he speaks Spanish, can't you tell?'"

Masaya's streets were cobbled, and the concrete houses were colorfully painted. Zipping up and down the streets were small, cube-shaped but roundly beveled red vehicles that looked like they could be escape pods from a space ship. Intergalactic shipwreck survivors looking for a hospitable planet. Dad explained that they were motorcycles converted into enclosed taxis, and that they were great on gas and convenient for short trips.

We stopped briefly at a scenic lookout from which we could survey the small lake that took its name from the historic town that surrounded it. Or maybe the town took its name from the lake. I heard the clanging of small bells that seemed to get closer, and I looked over to see a man toiling to push what looked like a large cooler on wheels up the hill that lead to the lookout. Ice cream, my dad informed me, and walked to meet the man. He wore no uniform, which I found dicey.

Dad and the man exchanged words briefly and then cash, and then he offered our taxi driver a popsicle before returning to me. Grown men eating popsicles together seemed odd to me, but then again, I hadn't seen a woman in Masaya yet. Maybe Masaya had no women.

"Are you sure this is safe to eat?" I asked.

"Look at it," he answered. "It's wrapped in plastic with a cartoon Eskimo printed on it. You think someone made this in their home?"

We leaned over the railing and took in the view of the expansive lake. Across the lake the city continued, and I heard faint cheers from a bright blue stadium in the distance. My father explained to me that the stadium was named after Roberto Clemente. My father was a boy when the earthquake of 1972 leveled Managua, the capital and the largest city in the country. It was reported that the Somoza government siphoned international relief aid to build mansions for senators and members of the National Guard, while the rest of the population improvised shacks and shanties. This prompted baseball player Roberto Clemente to fly to Nicaragua personally to deliver supplies, but his plane crashed en route. My father said that Clemente symbolized the country's tragic destiny. Not even the blameless good will of an outsider could endure the curse of the Nicaraguan people.

"But tragedy makes for great poets," he concluded. He was finishing his popsicle when I realized mine had mostly melted onto the pavement. He frowned at me, maybe thinking that I had done it on purpose.

When Dad asked the taxi driver to take us to the market, the taxi driver explained that there were two: the old market and the new. On the way to the old market, my father explained that the new market was for foreigners, that the prices would be dubiously high. The old market would be more fun to haggle in.

There was a hazy order to the open air market -- fruits and vegetables here, pirated CDs and DVDs mostly over there, everything plastic near the back, and even further back the butchers, which is where that smell probably originated. Here and there a booth with an uncategorizable service or specialty punctuated the "order," underscoring the nebulous nature of the market. I looked up to see streaks of sun filtering through the corrugated tin roofs and tarp.

As we walked I looked down to see that the gutters covered by planks or grills were choked with grime, scraps of food, and unknown debris. I wondered if the new market had air conditioning.

My father found the area where women were selling hammocks. At once, four women motioned him to come to their booths. He feigned interest in one hammock in the booth of a younger woman and casually asked the price. At the woman's answer, he sucked in air through his teeth, which I took to be the universal signal for "expensive." The woman looked at me, said something, and to my surprise, kissed the air in my direction. I didn't need a translator for that one. I was stunned by the sexual advance for a second and flattered the next, but my father chuckled and explained, "Son, that's how we point to things here. With our mouths." He puckered his lips in my direction.

The woman glanced briefly at me before continuing her sales pitch. I felt myself blush bright red at my misunderstanding of "our" custom.

1. The point of view from which the passage is told is best described as that of:

   (A) A man reflecting on the customs of a foreign country.
   (B) A young man returning to his home country after a long absence.
   (C) A man accompanying his father on his final vacation before dying.
   (D) A young man experiencing the native country of one of his parents.

2. The passage establishes all of the following about the narrator EXCEPT:

   (A) He does not speak Spanish.
   (B) He is a child.
   (C) He is not familiar with the modes of transportation of the country.
   (D) He is worried about cleanliness.

3. The use of quotation marks around the word *our* (line 102) serves to emphasize:

   (A) The uncertainty with which the narrator identifies with the country of his father.
   (B) The confusion the narrator feels toward his father's explanation.
   (C) The narrator's rejection of the custom.
   (D) A rejection of the link between the narrator and his father.

4. Which of the following statements best describes the function of the fourth paragraph?

   (A) It serves as a transition between two physical spaces.
   (B) It introduces a clever pragmatism that will be followed by other examples.
   (C) It is a jumping off point for a series of internal interpretations.
   (D) It is a first impression that emphasizes the unfamiliarity of the narrator's surroundings.

5. According to the passage, when the narrator neglects to eat his ice cream, his father feels:

   (A) Annoyed that his son has become so wasteful.
   (B) Dismayed that his son has squandered his money.
   (C) Displeased at the implication that his son didn't want to eat it.
   (D) Upset that his son wasn't listening.

6. The narrator depicts the market using all of the following descriptions EXCEPT:

   (A) Malodorous.
   (B) Dirty.
   (C) Expensive.
   (D) Crudely built.

7. The main point of the ninth paragraph is to:

   (A) Relate a historical event in Nicaraguan history.
   (B) Connect the prevalence of a national pastime to a historical tragedy.
   (C) Explain the origin of a national landmark.
   (D) Interpret a historical event in terms of a national characteristic.

8. The narrator can most accurately be characterized as:

   (A) An unwitting tourist.
   (B) A self-conscious visitor.
   (C) A suspicious foreigner.
   (D) A condescending outsider.

9. The incident at the market serves primarily to:

   (A) Suggest that the narrator will eventually learn how to interpret social cues.
   (B) Emphasize the narrator's discomfort with Nicaraguan people.
   (C) Underscore the narrator's unfamiliarity with Nicaraguan cultural norms.
   (D) Hint at the narrator's budding sexuality.

10. It can be inferred from the passage that the narrator's father wishes to visit Masaya for all of the following reasons EXCEPT:

   (A) To introduce his son to a Nicaraguan woman.
   (B) To show his son authentic Nicaraguan culture.
   (C) To buy a hammock.
   (D) To spend time with his son.

Read this passage carefully and then answer the questions that follow.

Humanities: This passage has been adapted from Max O'Rell's *Woman and Artist*, originally published in 1900.

Of all the rustic neighbourhoods bordering on London city, there is none prettier, fresher, and more verdant than St. John's Wood. It is the refuge of workers in search of light, air, and tranquility. Painters, sculptors, writers, journalists, actors, and musicians—in fact, the majority of the highest intellectual Bohemia—inhabit these semi-rural acres. Among the leafy haunts of St. John's Wood, numberless masterpieces have been produced by writers and artists whose fame has rung through the world. It is there, in short, that chiefly congregates the artistic intelligence of London.

No. 50 Elm Avenue, St. John's Wood, did not attract the gaze of the passer-by. Walled around and almost hidden by large trees, the house, which could be seen through the iron gates, was a modest, unpretentious, two-storied structure. The house was furnished with great taste; everything spoke of that comfort which the English value before luxury. A thousand and one little details told of an artistic woman's hand reigning supreme in the little domain, and one left the house feeling that these people are happy and evidently well-off; there may be artists who vegetate, but Philip Grantham is not one of them. The garden was admirably kept, the lawn smooth and soft as a Turkey carpet to the foot; and when the sun filtered through the trees to the grass, you could imagine yourself in the depths of the country, instead of near the centre of a great city.

The studio was a favourite room of the Granthams. Loving care had been expended upon it, and the result was a worker's paradise that invited to lofty labours and cozy conversation. Dora Grantham was her husband's comrade in art, and all the leisure that was hers, after seeing well to her household, was spent at Philip's side. The studio was more than comfortable—it was even luxurious, with its beautiful Renaissance mantelpiece of carved oak, its rich oriental rugs and curtains and hanging eastern lamps. All these gave an atmosphere of restful, dreamy ease to the place; and the fresh flowers that in all seasons filled the rare porcelain vases struck a note of gaiety among the somberness of the old oak furniture. A thousand curios from all the ends of the earth had been accumulated in this beloved apartment, and here, too, stood Dora's Pleyel piano and Philip's bookcase of precious volumes on art, all richly bound. A huge screen, blithe with eastern embroideries, hid the door that opened into the road; and in this veritable nest, nothing reminded of a hustling and bustling world outside. In summer, through the open door that led into the garden, one got a delicious vista of green foliage and turf.

In the centre of the studio stood two easels of almost equal size, and when I have told you that at these two easels, placed side by side, quite near each other, worked Philip and Dora, you will rightly understand that this studio had not been so fitted up to serve as a mere workshop, but that all its details had been suggested by the love of two kindred artistic spirits, who adored each other and passed most of their time there in loving rivalry and mutual encouragement.

At the time when this story begins, Philip was thirty-six and Dora twenty-seven. They had been six years married, and possessed a lovely little girl of five, so full of dainty grace and childish fascination, that when Philip was showing a new picture to a friend, and watching out of the corner of his eye to see if his work was being admired, as often as not the friend would say, "Ah, yes! that is a fine creation, a beautiful picture; but there," indicating the lovely child, "is your chef-d'œuvre—nothing can match her." And as in Philip's nature the parent outweighed the painter, he would proudly smile and reply, "You are right."

Philip and Dora had begun their married life in the most modest fashion, but fortune had smiled on them. Each year the painter had become better known and valued, and his pictures more sought after. Every succeeding year had deepened the sincere and strong love of these two lovers and friends, who led a calm, sweet existence, and trod, side by side, a flowered path, under a cloudless sky, with hope, glad labour, honour, and security as companions on the road.

11. The primary purpose of the first paragraph is to:

 (A) Introduce the main idea of the passage.
 (B) Give a general description of a neighborhood before zeroing in on the focus of the passage.
 (C) Describe the types of places where intellectual Bohemians congregate.
 (D) Give a detailed description of the best neighborhood bordering London.

12. Based on information in the passage, artists would most likely be attracted to which of the following environments?

(A) A central city park with children running around and playing
(B) A quiet, solitary room with a desk
(C) A peaceful plant-filled garden
(D) A beach at sunset with the sound of waves in the background

13. Each of the following is a trait given by the author to describe the Granthams' house EXCEPT:

(A) Unpretentious.
(B) Furnished with great taste.
(C) Large and easily noticeable.
(D) Comfortable.

14. The primary function of the third paragraph is to:

(A) Examine the gaudiness of the Granthams' interior design.
(B) Give an example of a typical rustic English home.
(C) Convey the personalities of the Granthams by describing their room.
(D) Describe how the studio was a room that promoted an ideal artistic environment.

15. In the passage, the word "somberness" (line 45) most nearly means:

(A) Melancholy.
(B) Abrasiveness.
(C) Darkness.
(D) Mournfulness.

16. The use of the phrase "chef-d'œuvre" in line 75 of the passage can most closely be described to mean:

(A) Creation.
(B) Beautiful picture.
(C) Lovely child.
(D) Masterpiece.

17. It can be inferred from the author's reference to "two easels of almost equal size" and "placed side by side" (lines 56-57) that:

(A) The studio was arranged and decorated in such a way that fostered creativity.
(B) Philip and Dora's marriage was characterized by mutual affection.
(C) Philip considered Dora an equal artistically.
(D) Philip and Dora spent the most time in the centre of the studio.

18. The passage indicates that:

I. Philip became better known as an artist every year.
II. Philip and Dora were known as vegetating artists.
III. Philip came from a wealthy family.

(A) I only
(B) I and III only
(C) II and III only
(D) I, II, and III

19. Based on the passage, the author is likely to agree on which of the following comparisons between urban and rustic neighborhoods?

(A) Urban neighborhoods are exciting whereas rustic neighborhoods are dull.
(B) Urban neighborhoods are loud whereas rustic neighborhoods are silent.
(C) Urban neighborhoods are hustling whereas rustic neighborhoods are calming.
(D) Urban neighborhoods are crowded whereas rustic neighborhoods are empty.

20. The tone of the passage can best be described as:

(A) Warm admiration.
(B) Zealous praise.
(C) Ardent exoneration.
(D) Poignant conviction.

Read this passage carefully and then answer the questions that follow.

Social Science: This passage has been adapted from *Geronimo's Story of His Life*, originally published in 1906.

My grandfather, Maco, had been the chief of the Nedni Apaches. I never saw him, but my father often told me of the great size, strength, and sagacity of this old warrior. Their principal wars had been with the Mexicans. They had some wars with other tribes of Indians also, but were seldom at peace for any great length of time with the Mexican towns.

Maco died when my father was but a young warrior, and Mangus-Colorado became chief of the Bedonkohe Apaches. When I was but a small boy my father died, after having been ailing for some time. When he passed away, carefully the watchers closed his eyes, then they arrayed him in his best clothes, painted his face afresh, wrapped a rich blanket around him, saddled his favorite horse, bore his arms in front of him, and led his horse behind, repeating in wailing tones his deeds of valor as they carried his body to a cave in the mountain. Then they slew his horses, and we gave away all of his other property, as was customary in our tribe. The custom of the Apaches is not to keep any of the property of the deceased. The unwritten tribal laws forbid it, because we think that otherwise the children or other relatives of one who had much property might be glad when their father or relatives die. After his body was deposited in the cave, his arms beside him, his grave was concealed by piles of stone. Wrapped in splendor, he lies in seclusion, and the winds in the pines sing a low requiem over the dead warrior.

After my father's death, I assumed the responsibility of looking after my mother. She never married again, although according to the customs of our tribe, she might have done so immediately after his demise. Usually, however, the widow who has children remains single after her husband's death for two or three years, but the widow without children marries again immediately. After a warrior's death, his widow returns to her people and may be given away or sold by her father or brothers. My mother chose to live with me, and she never desired to marry again. We lived near our old home and I supported her.

In 1846, being seventeen years of age, I was admitted to the council of the warriors. Then I was very content, for I could go wherever I wanted and do whatever I pleased. I had not been under the control of any individual, but the customs of our tribe prohibited me from sharing the glories of the warpath until the council admitted me. When opportunity offered, after this, I could go on the warpath with my tribe. This would be glorious. I hoped soon to serve my people in battle. I had long desired to fight with our warriors.

Perhaps the greatest joy to me was that now I could marry the fair Alope, daughter of No-po-so. She was a slender, delicate girl, but we had been lovers for a long time. So, as soon as the council granted me these privileges I went to pay a visit to her father concerning our marriage. Perhaps our love was of no interest to him; perhaps he wanted to keep Alope with him, for she was a dutiful daughter; at any rate, he asked many ponies for her. I made no reply, but in a few days appeared before his wigwam with the herd of ponies and took with me Alope. This was all the marriage ceremony necessary in our tribe.

Not far from my mother's tepee, I had made for us a new residence. The tepee was made of buffalo hides, and in it were many bear robes, lion hides, and other trophies of the chase, as well as my spears, bows, and arrows. Alope had made many little decorations of beads and drawn work on buckskin, which she placed in our tepee. She also sketched various pictures on the walls of our home. She was a good wife, but she was never physically powerful. We followed the traditions of our fathers and were happy. Three children came to us--children that played, loitered, and worked as I had done.

21. The passage can best be described as:

(A) A description of the burial traditions of the Nedni Apaches.
(B) The legend of Geronimo's grandfather, Maco.
(C) The autobiography of Geronimo.
(D) A parable about the benefits of marriage.

22. What can be inferred by No-po-so's asking Geronimo for many ponies to marry Alope?

(A) No-po-so was in need of a lot of ponies and he knew Geronimo had the ponies he needed.
(B) No-po-so asked for many ponies because Geronimo's father had stolen ponies from No-po-so many years before.
(C) No-po-so was trying to make it easier for Geronimo to marry Alope by asking for ponies, which were easy to acquire.
(D) No-po-so asked for a high price for Alope to discourage Geronimo from marrying her.

23. As it is used in line 4, *sagacity* most nearly means:

(A) Perspicacity.
(B) Naivety.
(C) Indiscretion.
(D) Aspersion.

24. The watchers did all of the following to Geronimo's father before he was taken to the cave for burial EXCEPT:

(A) Painted his face afresh.
(B) Wrapped him in a rich blanket.
(C) Closed his eyes.
(D) Bore his arms beside him.

25. According to the last paragraph, Alope adorned the tepee with:

I. Little decorations of beads
II. Painted work on skunk fur
III. Various sketched works on the walls of the home

(A) I only
(B) II only
(C) I and III only
(D) I, II, and III

26. According to the fourth paragraph, what was Geronimo allowed to do once he was admitted to the council of the warriors?

(A) He was no longer under the control of anyone else.
(B) He could go on the warpath with his tribe.
(C) He was allowed to marry his mother off to another man.
(D) He was permitted to assume to role of chief in the tribe.

27. In the passage, how does Geronimo describe Alope as a wife?

(A) Slender, but cruel
(B) Fair, but greedy
(C) Strong, but homely
(D) Good, but delicate

28. Geronimo's feelings about war could be described as:

(A) Dutiful.
(B) Fearful.
(C) Acquisitive.
(D) Insolent.

29. Geronimo's father's attitude toward his father, Maco, can be best characterized as one of:

(A) Disappointment.
(B) Adoration.
(C) Apathy.
(D) Ignorance.

30. According to the second paragraph, why do the Apache tribal laws forbid keeping the property of the dead?

(A) The Apache believe the dead need their property in the afterlife.
(B) The Apache believe that the children of the deceased will become lazy if they receive the property.
(C) The Apache do not want the family of the deceased to be pleased when a family member dies.
(D) The Apache want the widow to remarry, so they do not allow her to keep the property.

Read this passage carefully and then answer the questions that follow.

Social Science: This passage describes a phenomenon in American government.

As America approaches its 58th presidential election in 2016, we take it for granted that the candidate who wins that election -- no matter how partisan or contested it might be -- will become the 45th President of the United States following a peaceful transfer of power in a familiar ceremony. Indeed, this sense of inevitability is clear evidence of the strength of constitutional democracy in the United States. Aside from the election of 1860, which led to the Civil War, for two centuries America has met the test that a country is an established democracy when it consistently makes peaceful changes of government via free elections.

But this democratic tradition had to be earned. In 1800, American democracy faced one of its most serious challenges when Republican Thomas Jefferson defeated Federalist President John Adams. World history reveals that in all too many cases, political leaders defeated at the ballot have not honored the voice of the people. But America followed a different course. The Federalists handed over the reins of power to their hated rivals, setting a precedent that has guided American politics ever since.

The founding generation earnestly hoped that political parties would not arise in the United States. Parties were feared as dangerous institutions that represented a corrupting self-interest. But in the end, two parties, the Federalists and Republicans, emerged almost in spite of themselves. Though unanticipated by the Constitution, the United States became the first nation to establish truly popular parties.

Parties began to form during Washington's first presidential term. The Federalists coalesced in support of Treasury Secretary Alexander Hamilton's economic programs, and the Republicans rallied in opposition under James Madison and Thomas Jefferson.

Political parties continued to develop in the early 1790s, but as long as Washington remained in office a true party system could not emerge. While Washington sided with the Federalists, he was an enormously popular leader who appeared to be above the dirty business of partisan politics, and no one dared to challenge him at the ballot.

All that changed when Washington announced his retirement in 1796. The still primitive national parties now offered competing candidates. Republicans stood united behind a reluctant Jefferson, while the more factious Federalists offered two candidates, Vice President John Adams and Thomas Pinckney. In a close election, Adams carried the vote, but enough Federalist electors refused to vote for Pinckney that Jefferson received the second highest vote count, making him the Vice President under the existing terms of the Constitution.

During the presidency of John Adams, parties became more important than ever. As war fever gripped the young Republic in 1798, the Federalists, claiming national security, pounced on their domestic opposition by passing the notorious Alien and Sedition Acts. These measures, which among other things prohibited criticism of the government by the press, proved to be one of the great blunders in American political history. The people had rallied behind the administration against France, but now the Republicans were able to cast the Federalists as would-be tyrants quashing civil liberties. Meanwhile, Jefferson and Madison influenced Kentucky and Virginia to pass resolutions denouncing the Acts and asserting the right of the states to oppose or nullify unconstitutional laws of the federal government.

As the election of 1800 approached, the nation was in crisis. Jefferson was again the Republican standard bearer. The Federalists were again divided, with Hamilton leading an unsuccessful attempt to dump John Adams. The election was held over the course of May to December 1800, and involved the citizenry only indirectly. In most states, the legislature chose the electors, and much behind-the-scenes wrangling took place.

The Republicans emerged victorious, but then the unexpected happened. Under the Constitution at that time, each elector was to vote for two candidates without specifying who was to be president or vice president. By mistake Jefferson received the same number of votes as his running mate Aaron Burr, deadlocking the Electoral College. The election went to the House of Representatives, where each state had one vote. Burr refused to step aside, and the election was deadlocked for almost a week. By the 36th ballot Jefferson was elected. In 1804 the Twelfth Amendment corrected this problem by requiring electors to vote separately for president and vice president.

Thomas Jefferson became the third president in a peaceful transfer of power. In his inaugural address of March 4, 1801, he made a gesture of conciliation to his defeated rivals that set the tone for future party politics in America. The campaign had been bitter, he noted, but now the country must unite. Though the parties disagreed about much, what they shared was more important.

31. What is the main point of this passage?

(A) To show how the United States' political system has changed since its infancy
(B) To portray the battles between political parties in current presidential elections
(C) To show the events leading up to the election of 1800
(D) The offer a narrative of Thomas Jefferson's presidency

32. According to the passage, American history has been evidence of the strength of a constitutional democracy because:

(A) Citizens are free to vote for whichever presidential candidate they see fit and do so without fear of violence.
(B) The government utilizes a system of bipartisanship.
(C) With only one exception, power has been transferred amongst presidential candidates peacefully.
(D) Most people find their beliefs represented in one of the two presidential candidates.

33. In line 4, *contested* most nearly means:

(A) Challenged.
(B) Disputed.
(C) Biased.
(D) Troublesome.

34. The United States was the first nation to establish:

(A) Truly popular parties.
(B) Elections.
(C) Civil liberties.
(D) Ballots.

35. The author's attitude toward the election of 1800 is best characterized as one of:

(A) Homage.
(B) Admiration.
(C) Indifference.
(D) Objectivity.

36. According to the passage, all of the following were supported by the Federalist party in the elections of 1796 or 1800 EXCEPT:

(A) John Adams.
(B) Thomas Pinckney.
(C) Alexander Hamilton.
(D) Thomas Jefferson.

37. According to the fourth and fifth paragraphs, a true political party system did not form during Washington's presidency because:

(A) Political parties with well-defined ideologies had not been formed yet.
(B) Washington was profoundly respected by Federalists and Republicans alike.
(C) The founding generation considered political parties to be corrupt and dangerous.
(D) Political parties did not begin to form until a series of foreign crises caused Americans to choose sides on the proper way to deal with them.

38. In line 35, *coalesced* most nearly means:

(A) Joined.
(B) Adhered.
(C) Severed.
(D) Intermingled.

39. The author's reference to what the parties "shared" in the final line of the passage most likely means:

(A) Both parties did not want elections to become too bitter and competitive.
(B) Both parties no longer wanted to live under the rule of a monarchy.
(C) Both parties decided to require electors to vote for president and vice president separately.
(D) Both parties had a desire for the country to remain peaceful and united.

40. Jefferson and Madison influenced Kentucky and Virginia to pass resolutions asserting the right of states to oppose or nullify unconstitutional laws of the federal government as a result of:

(A) The first amendment.
(B) The Constitution.
(C) The Electoral College.
(D) Alien and Sedition Acts.

Read this passage carefully and then answer the questions that follow.

Natural Science: This passage describes the research and discoveries of a group of atmospheric scientists.

In April 2008, atmospheric scientists set up camp in Zhangye, a region between China's Taklimakan and Gobi deserts. They sorted and prepared cargo that included two mobile laboratories housed in trailers and an array of upward-looking instruments for measuring airborne dust particles. Then, the team waited for either of the two neighboring deserts to send clouds of dust blowing over camp.

The wait paid off. By early May, a heavy dust episode darkened the skies over camp as scientists and instruments looked on.

The mineral properties of the aerosol particles and the wavelength distribution of incident light combine to determine whether a dust particle reflects radiation and cools the local atmosphere, absorbs radiation and warms the local atmosphere, or both. While scientists have a good handle on dust's primary effect of reflecting and cooling at the visible wavelengths, the smaller influence of absorbing and warming at the longer infrared wavelengths has remained more of an uncertainty – and most climate models either underestimate it or do not include it at all.

When the field work concluded, atmospheric scientist Richard Hansell and colleagues combined data collected from the ground-based sensors with computer models to quantify the interaction of visible and infrared light energy.

The analysis showed that over half of dust's cooling effect is compensated for by its warming effect. The finding could clarify scientists' understanding of how dust influences moisture fluctuations in the atmosphere and surface temperatures around the planet.

The magnitude of aerosols' (including dusts') influence on climate is not well understood. That's where ground-based work can help. The team's interest was not in the global coverage of the dust – events frequently observed by satellites – but rather in the individual flecks of dust and their physical and chemical properties.

"Looking at dust from space, the spatial extent is awesome," Hansell said. "You can see large dust clouds that get stirred up and transported globally. But I'm looking from the ground-based perspective, collecting a very large volume of data to analyze dust and to look at how it interacts with radiation, in my case with infrared – the longer wavelengths."

Sunlight is composed primarily of energy at the shorter visible wavelengths known as shortwave. When shortwave radiation arrives to Earth's atmosphere and encounters dust particles, some of the energy is reflected back to space. Cooling results because Earth's surface doesn't receive as much radiation had the dust not been there; an effect that's relatively straightforward to observe.

The challenge stems from the much weaker signal of the longwave radiation – the invisible radiation emitted by the earth, atmosphere, clouds and anything else with a temperature. Dust can absorb this type of radiation and thus contribute to warming. But the process depends on the particles' size, composition, optical properties, and how those parameters affect the transfer of energy between the particles and the atmosphere.

Compared to small-sized aerosols such as smoke, larger particles including dust are more efficient at absorbing longwave radiation. In addition to size, dust particle composition also matters. Minerals such as silicates and clays are better than others at absorbing longwave radiation.

To determine the warming influence of dust, Hansell and colleagues measured dust size and composition. At the same time, the team in Zhangye used an interferometer to describe changes in the spectral intensity of the longwave radiation.

Combining the measured parameters in a computer model, the researchers calculated the longwave energy at Earth's surface with and without dust aerosols present to determine the Direct Aerosol Radiative Effect (DARE), a parameter that describes how aerosols modulate the energetics of the atmosphere.

The team found that dust's radiative impact, and hence its warming influence, conservatively ranges from 2.3 to 20 watts per square meter of radiation at the surface in Zhangye. Collectively, dust's longwave warming effect counters more than half of dust's shortwave cooling effect.

"The influence of dust on longwave radiation is a lot bigger than we expected," Hansell said.

The magnitude of that influence, however, can vary from one location to another. "Compared to our previous study of Saharan dust measured at Sal Island Cape Verde, the longwave effects of dust at Zhangye were found to be about a factor of two larger, owing to differences in the dust absorptive properties and proximity to the desert sources, he said.

Still, with dust holding on to more heat than previously thought, scientists can begin to reassess dust's role in changes observed near Earth's surface, such as air temperature and the moisture budget. For example, dust's warming effect on the atmosphere could be an underestimated factor driving evaporation, and atmospheric convection and stability.

41. According to the passage, the excursion to Zhangye was most concerned with:

(A) Dust particles' capacity to absorb infrared light and warm the surrounding air.
(B) Dust particles' primary effect of reflecting visible light and cooling the surrounding air.
(C) Recording dust episodes near the Gobi desert and tracking their impacts on global temperature.
(D) Tracking the movement of dust clouds via satellite technology.

42. The passage states that most climate models:

(A) Emphasize the presence of visible light.
(B) Overestimate the effects of small-size aerosols.
(C) Underestimate or fail to include the potential warming effects of dust.
(D) Are especially effective at accounting for human error.

43. It can be inferred that Hansell's use of the word *awesome* in line 44 is meant to describe:

(A) His feeling of excitement at the possible sights that may exist somewhere else in space.
(B) His feeling of whimsy at the myriad of sights to see in space.
(C) His feeling of wonder at the massive scale of the dust clouds.
(D) His feeling of dread at the overwhelming scale of the sight.

44. According to the passage, whether or not a dust particle will absorb long-wave radiation depends on the particle's:

(A) Size and composition.
(B) Density and location.
(C) Speed and makeup.
(D) Origin and speed.

45. The passage states that the computer simulations run after the dust storm concluded that the warming effect of dust particles in Zhangye:

(A) Could not be determined from the given data.
(B) Were stronger than their cooling effect.
(C) Were negligible.
(D) Offset half of their cooling effect.

46. The main point of the final paragraph is that:

(A) Now is the time for scientists to begin building more accurate climate models.
(B) The warming effect of dust particles may help explain other aspects of the global climate.
(C) Dust is a much greater contributor to global warming than previously thought.
(D) The results of the Zhangye experiment can be directly extrapolated to the planet at large.

47. The passage suggests that the results of experiments on Sahara dust found at Sal Island Cape Verde prove that:

(A) dust located closer to its origin reflects more heat than dust that has traveled a great distance.
(B) dust located closer to its origin absorbs more heat than dust that has traveled a greater distance.
(C) dust located closer to its origin is unable either to reflect or absorb heat.
(D) not all dust around the globe absorbs and reflects the same amount of heat.

48. According to the passage, dust with a higher radiative impact would:

(A) Suggest that the dust was made up of a combination of small- and large-sized particles.
(B) Suggest that the dust was made up mostly of large-sized particles.
(C) Warm the atmosphere.
(D) Cool the atmosphere.

49. The passage states that the shortwave radiation reflected by dust comes mostly from:

(A) The sun.
(B) The earth, atmosphere, and clouds.
(C) The deserts where dust clouds originate.
(D) Man-made energy sources.

50. The quote given in lines 91-92best serves to:

(A) Underscore the need for more experiments in the Zhangye region.
(B) Sum up the results of the Zhangye experiment.
(C) Raise questions about the direction of particle science.
(D) Highlight the changing nature of scientific "fact".

Made in the USA
Middletown, DE
23 December 2015